Flash™ 5 Cartoons and Games

f/x & Design

Bill Turner

James Robertson

Richard Bazley

CORIOLIS™

President, CEO
Keith Weiskamp

Publisher
Steve Sayre

Acquisitions Editor
Beth Kohler

Development Editor
Catherine E. Oliver

Product Marketing Manager
Patricia Davenport

Project Editor
Greg Balas

Technical Reviewer
Harry Henderson

Production Coordinator
Meg E. Turecek

Cover Designer
Jody Winkler

Layout Designer
April E. Nielsen

CD-ROM Developer
Chris Nusbaum

Flash™ 5 Cartoons and Games f/x and Design

Limits of Liability and Disclaimer of Warranty

The author and publisher of this book have used their best efforts in preparing the book and the programs contained in it. These efforts include the development, research, and testing of the theories and programs to determine their effectiveness. The author and publisher make no warranty of any kind, expressed or implied, with regard to these programs or the documentation contained in this book.

The author and publisher shall not be liable in the event of incidental or consequential damages in connection with, or arising out of, the furnishing, performance, or use of the programs, associated instructions, and/or claims of productivity gains.

Trademarks

Trademarked names appear throughout this book. Rather than list the names and entities that own the trademarks or insert a trademark symbol with each mention of the trademarked name, the publisher states that it is using the names for editorial purposes only and to the benefit of the trademark owner, with no intention of infringing upon that trademark.

The Coriolis Group, LLC
14455 N. Hayden Road
Suite 220
Scottsdale, Arizona 85260

(480)483-0192
FAX (480)483-0193
www.coriolis.com

Library of Congress Cataloging-In-Publication Data
Turner, Bill.
Flash™ 5 cartoons and games f/x and design / by Bill Turner, James Robertson, Richard Bazley
p. cm
ISBN 1-57610-958-5
1. Computer games--Programming. 2. Computer animation. 3. Flash (Computer file). I. Robertson, James. II. Bazley, Richard. III. Title.
QA76.76.C672 T87 2001
006.6'96--dc21 00-069423
CIP

Printed in the United States of America
10 9 8 7 6 5 4 3 2 1

A Note from Coriolis

Thank you for choosing this book from The Coriolis Group. Our graphics team strives to meet the needs of creative professionals such as yourself with our three distinctive series: *Visual Insight*, *f/x and Design*, and *In Depth*. We'd love to hear how we're doing in our quest to provide you with information on the latest and most innovative technologies in graphic design, 3D animation, and Web design. Do our books teach you what you want to know? Are the examples illustrative enough? Are there other topics you'd like to see us address?

Please contact us at the address below with your thoughts on this or any of our other books. Should you have any technical questions or concerns about this book, you can contact the Coriolis support team at **techsupport@coriolis.com**; be sure to include this book's title and ISBN, as well as your name, email address, or phone number.

Thank you for your interest in Coriolis books. We look forward to hearing from you.

Coriolis Creative Professionals Press
The Coriolis Group
14455 N. Hayden Road, Suite 220
Scottsdale, AZ 85260

Email: **cpp@coriolis.com**

Phone: (480) 483-0192
Toll free: (800) 410-0192

Visit our Web site at ***creative.coriolis.com*** *to find the latest information about our current and upcoming graphics books.*

Other Titles for the Creative Professional

Dreamweaver™ 4 Visual Insight
By Greg Holden, Scott Wills

Paint Shop Pro™ 6 Visual Insight
By Ramona Pruitt and Joshua Pruitt

Flash™ 5 f/x and Design
By Bill Sanders

Flash™ ActionScript f/x and Design
By Bill Sanders

Dreamweaver™ 4 f/x and Design
By Laurie Ulrich

Illustrator® 9 f/x and Design
By Sherry London

GoLive™ 5 f/x and Design
By Richard Schrand

Adobe InDesign™ f/x and Design
By Elaine Betts

Photoshop® 6 In Depth
By David Xenakis

QuarkXpress™ 4 In Depth
By William Harrel and Elaine Betts

To my wife, Julia, who puts up with my ranting
about the world more than anyone should.
To my children, Trent and Majenta, who laugh when I rant,
and for being the best kids a father could ever ask for.
To my wonderful mother, for always knowing just the right art supply
to get me for Christmases and Birthdays.
To my brothers, Roy and Jim, for not telling on me when we were kids.
—Bill Turner

❧

First of all, I'd like to thank my parents who have always encouraged me in everything that I've done, and I'd like to dedicate this book to Kirsten, who's love and support has helped me enormously.
—James Robertson

❧

For Ann, Matthew, and Jonathan.
—Richard Bazley

❧

About the Authors

Bill Turner, is a self-taught artist. At age 15, he sold his first cartoons to an underground college radio station to create the station's T-shirt logos. His still cartoon work has appeared in various national magazines and in editorial pages of newspapers. Bill remembers first going online back when AOL was known as Q-link, with a 300-baud modem on a Commodore 64—painful. His first Macintosh entered the picture in 1990, providing the tools to apply his talents to the animated cartoon, where he's created animations in both 2D and 3D for commercial broadcast. His commercial still illustrations, mixing photo realistic 3D and surrealistic PhotoShop techniques, have appeared in *The Wall Street Journal*, *Playboy*, *Penthouse*, trade magazines, and corporate brochures too numerous to count. Upon discovering Flash (then FutureSplash), he knew this was the ticket to realizing his dream. A cartoonist at heart, he created one of the first interactive animated cartoon Web sites, *Dubes*, in early 1996, which made its way to Macromedia's Cutting Edge Gallery. *Dubes* was also featured in a chapter on Shockwave in the book *HTML Publishing for Netscape* (Netscape Press, 1997), long before the Flash phenomenon had taken hold. Bill also worked as contributing author and technical editor for the *Flash 4 Bible* by Jon Warren Lentz and Robert Reinhardt (IDG Books, 2000). In that book, he covered the techniques on making broadcast quality cartoon productions totally in Flash for high-end video delivery. He created the show *Weber*, about a web-footed, snorkel wearing, human-ruffling pelican, at odds with those who'd doom him into extinction. His Flash Web work can be found at **Shockwave.com**, **CampChaos.com**, **iFilm.com**, and others. He is also collaborating with master Flash programmer and co-author James Robertson, in the creation of mind-boggling Internet games. The home of turnertoons productions, inc. may be found at **turnertoons.com**.

James Robertson grew up at a time when the home-computer revolution was just beginning, and he has always been involved in writing programs that push the boundaries, and redefine the limits of the current computer systems. At an early age, he had software published on computer magazine cover-disks, which led to various freelance jobs with publishers and software distributors. This also led to a career where he traveled to numerous countries around the world as a technician, acting as a consultant to numerous multinational companies and educational establishments. His job included conducting training sessions, and teaching clients about the latest technical advances in Internet technology, as well as numerous presentations and demonstrations at some of the Europe's largest Internet exhibitions. During this time, James never left the world of software programming, and over the years, he has mastered numerous programming languages on a whole range of computer systems. James has now worked in the Internet arena for the last six years, and has an unparalleled knowledge of both the hardware and software that are used on the World Wide Web. He has been hand-coding HTML sites for many years, and has also mastered various Web programming languages, such as JavaScript, VBScript, Java, and ASP. James' philosophy has always been, "that nothing is impossible." So, when he first came across Macromedia Flash v3, he instantly realized the power of the product, and that he would now be able to offer his Web clients the sites that THEY wanted. When Flash v4 was released, with an in-built scripting language, James was able to produce some new effects that nobody had thought were possible. He wrote a "Real3D" engine in Flash, which rotated 3D objects in real-time; this was quickly followed by his first game *Pong*, which was a tribute to the first true video game. He has followed this with more effects and games, including the first Isometric 3D game to be written in Flash. His programming talents were recognized recently, when he was awarded his second Shockwave Site of the Day award for his infuriating *Crates 2* puzzle game. James resides in a quiet part of England, on the edge of the Ashdown Forest.

Richard Bazley showed an interest in animation from a very early age. Richard went on to achieve his childhood ambition to work at Disney, not only as an Animator, but as a Lead Animator on Disney's *Hercules* (Amphitryon and Alcmene), working with the famed British political cartoonist, Gerald Scarfe, on some of the designs. He got his first job in animation on the Disney blockbuster *Who Framed Roger Rabbit?* and got to work with Oscar™-winning Animation Director, Richard Williams, the artist whose work originally inspired him to get into the business. For the past decade, Richard has worked as a Supervising Animator at three of the major animation studios: Sullivan Bluth Studios, Walt Disney Feature Animation, and Warner Bros. He is most well known in the industry for his work on the critically acclaimed, *The Iron Giant*, supervising three of its sequences. He has also contributed to *Pocahontas* (John Smith), *Osmosis Jones* (Drix), and many more classic animated films. He has a broad and knowledgeable grounding in the arts having received a B.A.(hons.) in Graphic Design. Early in his career, he was an Art Director for two of the top advertising agencies in London, and created many ads for Richard Branson's Virgin Atlantic, including press and radio. His other advertising work has appeared in all major British newspapers, as well as magazines such as *Vogue* and *Tatler*. Online you can find many interviews about his work on films, as well as in articles in the British papers. He recently (in 2000) produced and directed an animated short entitled, *The Journal of Edwin Carp*, which features the voice talents of Hugh Laurie. The short has been featured in the magazines: *Televisual* (including the cover), *New Media Creative, Computer Arts*, and *Digit Magazine*. It was executed in the Flash computer program, and the film is also featured in *The Flash 5 Bible* (Lentz/Reinhardt), in which Bazley was a contributor.

Acknowledgments

Books seldom fly from thin air onto the pages. They need a bit of help. I was fortunate to have a group of highly skilled professionals to lend a hand in the writing of this book. Without the following people, we would have never been able to have the pleasure of sharing our knowledge with you.

First off, I want to extend a huge thanks to Jon Warren Lentz, co-author of the *Flash 5 Bible*, and founder of **www.Flash-Guru.com**, for helping to convince The Coriolis Group that this book was worth publishing, and for being a generous soul with his insights, help, and friendship. Thanks Jon!

A huge thanks to my co-authors, James Robertson and Richard Bazley. James, in my opinion, is one of the best Flash programmers out there in the game world today. His skills run much deeper than simply scripting Flash. On more than one occasion, his puzzle creating talents have caused me more hair loss (via extraction) than I'd like to admit. The Flash knowledge he shares with us in this book is top notch. It's an honor indeed to be his associate. Richard Bazley's animation work has entertained millions. Whenever I watch *The Iron Giant* and see Richard's scenes, I become inspired. Richard has been behind many animated films of note, and it's been my pleasure to have his insight included in this book. I would also like to thank contributor and Web server technical guru, Corey Johnson, of CNIweb.net. Corey's help on this book and other Web server matters is much appreciated.

I would like to thank the people at The Coriolis Group: Acquisitions Editor Beth Kohler for taking on our idea of making a Flash book that is a bit different from other computer graphics books. Her professionalism and attention to detail (even while becoming a mother for the first time) was deeply appreciated. Project Editor Greg Balas, a true man of his word. If he says something will be there, it will. I'm amazed at his ability to juggle a million chainsaws at once. In addition, I would like to thank Meg Turecek, Production Coordinator, April Nielsen, Layout Designer, Jody Winkler, Cover Designer, and Patti Davenport, Product Marketing Manager. In addition, Development Editor, Catherine Oliver, was an enormous help in taking the thoughts of artists and programmers and making sense of it all for us. I hope we weren't too scatterbrained. Enormous thanks also to Technical Reviewer, Harry Henderson, who could be relied on to catch the boo-boos, and to make great suggestions. His attention to technical detail helped immensely. Also, thanks to copyeditor, Sharon Hamm, her microscope on the English language is focused indeed. I don't know where this book would be without her. Finally, thanks to Melissa Reynolds Brittain for proofreading, and Emily Glossbrenner for indexing the book.

Last, but certainly not least, I would like to thank all the people who've influenced my life via friendship. Too many people to list, but a few stand out: Pat Culbertson, my lifelong friend, for always beating me at any video game, but never gloating. Jim Cheal, whose friendship, camaraderie, and support is fortunate for me indeed. Jim also ran the Web servers where my first Flash cartoon work appeared a million years ago (Internet time, actually 1996), thereby giving this book it's start. Finally, thank you Mr. Crabbe wherever you are!

—*Bill Turner*

Contents at a Glance

Table of Contents

Foreword

The pedigree of these three authors is indisputable. **Bill Turner**, creator of both the *Weber* cartoon/game series and *The Murkys*, is widely regarded as a Flash pioneer. **Richard Bazley** is a veteran animator who has contributed to some of the finest feature-length, studio projects of the past decade. Richard's first solo project, *The Journal of Edwin Carp*, was made possible by the unique features of Flash. One of the finest artists working with ActionScript, **James Robertson**, is the coder behind the *Walter Adventure Game*, which may be the most ambitious Flash game ever released.

If you are new to Flash, this book will definitely get you started with using Flash to create cartoons and games. If you are already familiar with Flash, this book will take you to another level of expertise. It delivers a wealth of information about cartoons and character animation. It shows you how to plan and create a cartoon show, and then shows you how to use those same cartoon elements in concert with advanced scripting and programming to develop interactive games (for distribution as freestanding applications, or on CD-ROM and the Internet).

The greatest strength of this book is that it teaches readers the general techniques involved in cartoons, character animation, and games, rather than giving them the limited ability to create only a specific example. In this regard, *Flash 5 Cartoons and Games f/x & Design*, rises above nearly all other Flash books. Most Flash books are just too narrow and specific: "Press this button, open that dialog, click here, do this, do that, equals Flash." While some readers find this manner of presentation useful for getting started, it has a severe limitation: The reader learns only how to do that specific task. In contrast, *Flash 5 Cartoons and Games f/x & Design* prepares you to adapt the techniques, and to use them in your own work without getting lost. Furthermore, because the focus is on the creative problem solving, rather than on the technology used, the techniques explained in this book will still be applicable for many years. For example, in the programming sections, the code has been made as simple as possible, so that it may be applicable to other programming languages like Flash 4, Java, C++, even Flash 6. Similarly, the authors deliver the theory and logic of the art of animation in such a way, that this book is of enduring value, even to a cartoonist who chooses to work with more traditional techniques of paper and pencil. Finally, with regard to examples: The gaming source code and animation examples that are included on the CD-ROM are worth the price of the book alone.

So, if you are standing in the bookstore isle, examining the many books now available to teach you Flash, let me summarize my view of this book: *Flash 5 Cartoons and Games f/x & Design* is one of the few Flash books that every Flash artist—both neophyte and guru—really *should* have.

—Jon Warren Lentz, *Flash Bible* co-author, and founder of **www.Flash-Guru.com**.

Introduction

Flash has the tools to create a revolution in animated cartoons. There's no doubting this fact. Flash cartoons are having a pervasive impact all over the Internet. What you may not know is that these very same Flash creations will be having an impact on television, and even film in the near future, if not already. The application is quickly becoming the heart of the independent animator's new studio. What once took armies of artists, and extraordinary amounts of equipment and financing, can now be done by one person, on a single personal computer. Gone are the days of sending thousands of cels out to be inked and colored. The benefits are that independent creators can now realize their vision with just an idea, talent, a relatively inexpensive computer, and the tenacity to do it.

The game creation aspect of Flash will quickly be following (and maybe surpassing) this revolution in cartooning. It is not a stretch to believe that games created in Flash will soon occupy many hours of time spent on the Internet. It's in this space, that art and technology meet at their best. Games with clever designs and captivating high quality graphics and animation are a certain hit. Playstation 2 and Dreamcast can rest easy for now, but for how long? Because of the ever-increasing functionality of scripting in Flash, and because of creators who push Flash to its limits with new ways of thinking, we'll bet that Playstation 2 and Dreamcast won't be able to rest easy for too long.

What this Book Covers

We aim to make the learning experience fun. After all, cartoons are fun. It seemed ridiculous to us to make this book like a reference manual. There are plenty of great sources for learning the basics of Flash. However, this means that you'll need a rather well rounded experience with the program itself, as we will not be explaining every tool and function in the usual way. Indeed, sometimes it's best to view the tools in a very *unusual* way.

If you're a pro at drawing cartoons, make yourself at home, and dig in. If you're not a professional cartoonist, one of the really nice things about the art form is its accessibility. Practically everyone can doodle, and indeed, sometimes these doodles are the highest form of the art of cartooning. Spontaneity is very desirable, and something that Flash accommodates quite well. The aim is to bring your skills into motion, and to give you the insight needed to create your own animated masterpiece from start to finish, be it for the Internet, or broadcast quality videotape.

To achieve this, we try to cover everything you'll need to consider in creating a cartoon show. We start out with some tips on writing humor and storyboarding, and then move into the development of cartoon characters. Certainly, a good cartoon needs sound, and we supply a good starting point for your exploration in the sound chapter. Background scenery and camera moves are also discussed and covered in a way we've yet to see in any other book. Then, we get to the meat of character animation itself, by using simple animated examples that teach complex motion principles. We also supply you with a rather useful mannequin system (much like the artist's wooden mannequin that's been around for years), for setting up any kind of animated human movement you could imagine without drawing a thing. Where would a cartoon be without lip-synching and facial expressions? Lip-synching and facial expressions are covered in depth in Chapter 6. Then, in Chapter 7, we discuss final output of your cartoon creation to not only the Web, but also to video and film as well.

Throughout the chapters we supply projects for you to follow along with to re-enforce the theories discussed. All projects come with complete FLA files containing all the elements needed. There are more than 75 of these Flash 5 authoring files included on the CD-ROM. Another plus is the inclusion of the entire FLA file of a full blown two-minute cartoon music video show, Weber's *Human Blues*.

The gaming section will maintain the fun cartoon feel, but by the very nature of programming, and its strict syntax, it may get a bit more serious. There's a discussion on designing games and strategy, and the rules of game play. Remember, all rules exist to be broken, and we would not be doing a good job if we did not break them as well. Of course, your job will be to take the knowledge learned here to the next level by creating your own new rules and games.

We will be dissecting an entire Trivia Game that you could grow into something completely different if so desired. The Trivia Game we have supplied (with a full authoring file), has a neat twist of using Artificial Intelligence in helping the player with the answers.

Last, but certainly not least, a massive commercial quality isometric 3D adventure game will be gutted and explained. For your inspection, we've also included the entire Flash 5 file of the game itself. This is such a complicated game, that each of the major parts have been broken into smaller FLA files, for easier comprehension, and included on the CD-ROM. We believe that it is unprecedented for any Flash book to reveal the secrets behind such an ambitious game.

Who this Book Is For

If you've read all the manuals and other wonderful reference material out there, but have wanted to take your animation storytelling, or game design and programming skills to the next level, you're in the right place. If you're a polished professional cartoonist looking to get into the Flash Internet revolution, this book will be a tremendous help in getting there. Likewise, it will be useful for the aspiring cartoonist who wants to create professional animated cartoons. This book has something for everyone. Even if you're not a cartoon artist, perhaps you're a writer wanting to know the mechanics behind the animation process; you'll find that it's all in here.

If creating Flash 5 games are your desire, but you're confined by the complexity of it all, this book can get you on the road to success. By having working examples to follow along with, the complex can become much more understandable. Once you've grasped the techniques used in the games provided here, you'll be making some really cool Flash games on your own. Now let's have some fun and make some entertainment!

Chapter 1

Getting and Planning Your Story

Before you start animating, you need to have a story, so that your cartoon grabs and holds your audience. You want viewers to be wondering, "What's going to happen next?" This chapter discusses some elements of humorous cartoon stories and gives you practice with storyboarding in Flash.

by Bill Turner and
Richard Bazley

Cartoon Humor-Writing Basics

Although cartoons can be used to tell practically any story—as witnessed in comic books (which, ironically, are seldom funny) and the graphic novel—they usually have a humorous slant. Because cartoons have been around for many years, certain rules and devices have emerged that can help guide you through the writing process. These guidelines, which we'll discuss in this section of the chapter, are meant as simple starting points, because the creation of humor is a subjective undertaking.

In this section, we'll discuss some of the guidelines and devices you can use to create humorous cartoons. We'll also briefly discuss another consideration: the role of viewer experience. That is, what's funny to some people isn't funny to others. And sometimes, something's funny only if it's funny *right away,* as in political cartoons.

The Single-Panel Cartoon: Fast Humor

One of the best ways to get started with developing humorous cartoons is to study what you find funny, and a good place to start is with print cartoons. Animation adds a wonderful dimension of life and movement to a cartoon, but studying the still-cartoon format can be very advantageous to see what makes the art form tick. This knowledge will be quite handy in storyboarding your creation as well.

The still, single-panel cartoon might be the hardest to master. After all, you have only one picture with a few words (or, if it's really great, no words) to explain setup, history, environment, character, or personality dynamics, and—oh, yeah—to be funny. Gary Larson's *The Far Side* newspaper panels and George Booth's *New Yorker* cartoons are excellent examples of mastery of the craft. In this type of cartoon (also known in the "biz" as a *gag cartoon*), if the readers take more than seven seconds to figure out what the point is, you've lost them, and the cartoon is a failure.

You should not expect viewers to work at "getting" the cartoon. If they have to work too long, you might lose them. Timing of the graphic layout is essential here. This timing is the interplay between how a viewer's eyes scan the art, and how they relate that art to the words they will read (or, in the case of animation with sound, the sounds they will hear).

Cartoon Layout: From Left to Right

Most of the Western world reads from left to right, and our minds instinctively read even graphics this way. Therefore, your cartoon should always read from left to right, keeping the surprise element to the right side. The caption, as well, will follow these rules, leaving the twist or punch line for last—preferably *the* last word. "But what does this have to do with animation?" you may ask. Even though the cartoon is in motion and will, therefore, create more distractions, the mind will still look from the left first. Even though animation presents a series of superimposed frames to show motion, the viewer's eye is still "expecting" a left-to-right progression as in reading.

You can see the validity of this rule even in late-night talk shows hosted by comedians. The guests always sit on the left side of the viewer's screen. This positioning supports the host's timing, letting him or her get in the witty comment last—and on the right side of the screen. Left to right—no doubt about it. You can break this rule (as you can any rule), but a keen understanding of its importance will help you avoid unnecessary mistakes that might cause others to misunderstand your creativity.

Humor Devices

Being funny is indeed an art. What's hilarious to one person brings a stony face to another, and possibly infuriates a third. While nothing is carved in stone about what someone will consider humorous, you can employ some basic devices that humor can build upon. When you're writing your new, short cartoon animation, you can always improvise and experiment to help define new humor devices.

The Hidden Element of Surprise (and Misfortune)

The element of surprise is probably one of the most basic and dependable sources of a chuckle. Because it catches the viewer off guard, surprise is the basis of nearly all humor. The slipping-on-a-banana-peel scenario, which has endured for years, owes its fame to this tool of humor. When the element of surprise is employed, the unsuspecting character finds himself in an unfortunate position and pays the price, as Figure 1.1 illustrates.

It was too late. Bertha's density had surpassed the floor's tensile strength.

Figure 1.1
Here, we see the element of surprise. Notice that the graphic reads from left to right, with gray adding emphasis to the hole created.

As heartless as our reaction might seem, we love to laugh at the misfortune of others, as long as their misfortune is not taken to an extreme. The challenge is where to draw this line—between acceptable and unacceptable misfortune. Cross the line, and you'll find your story wandering into the land of the tasteless—not entirely a bad thing, but sure to bring its share of infuriated viewers along with the gut-busting laughter from others.

The Weight Shift

You can sometimes find humor by shifting the weight, or tone, of a situation from the dead serious into the realm of the ridiculous, the technique used in Figure 1.2. Highlighting the unimportant in the midst of a grave encounter provides a surprise diversion that results in the viewers' release in laughter. Anyone who has appreciated Monty Python's *Flying Circus* or *The Meaning of Life* will recognize the use of this device at its finest. Political cartoons also use the weight, or tone, shift to great advantage to bring attention to the folly of elected officials.

The example in Figure 1.2 might find you thinking, "This isn't funny. It's a nuclear attack that'll annihilate innocent people." True. The humor lies more in the political reflection and the ridiculous reaction the father is having. Possibly, he has championed the nuclear arms buildup for years. Though unsaid, the attire and tinge of smugness in his expression relates nuances to explain political affiliation. The cartoon is illustrating a moment of misplaced celebration. Maybe we're laughing at the father (or humanity itself) for still not understanding the gravity of such a terrible situation. Because it attempts to persuade opinion against or for an issue, this type of humor falls

Figure 1.2
Shifting the subject from the serious to the ridiculous can cause the viewer to both chuckle and reflect.

more in the political-humor genre. In using political humor, you run the risk of alienating roughly half of your viewers. No matter where you might stand on a political issue, pleasing everyone is impossible. And that impossibility is not a bad thing. Pleasing everyone is seldom the point in successful political humor. Just be ready to take the heat for whatever you put out in this genre of humor.

The Foolhardy

We can find the device of the foolhardy in lots of humor in which the character, who is the butt of the joke, makes an absolutely ignorant statement, solidifying the character's overwhelming lack of knowledge or consideration of the situation at hand. This scenario evokes in the viewer what's known as the "I know more than you know" laugh. A classic example of this device in use is the ongoing saga of Elmer Fudd and Bugs Bunny—hunter and prey. The problem is the prey is far more clever than the hunter. Elmer believes he has Bugs cornered in his rabbit hole and gleefully shoves the shotgun in, proclaiming to have the bunny right where he wants him. Through the magic of cartoons, Bugs has the shotgun barrel bent around, as he exits through another hole under Elmer's rump. Bugs then proceeds to have a little nonchalant chat with Elmer. Elmer explains that he'll be cooking that "wascally wabbit" for dinner now, pulls the trigger, and blows his own butt into tatters. When used in a self-deprecating way, this device can bring out the secret "I've made that mistake before, too, but I'll never tell anyone I did" laugh.

The Old vs. the New

What could be funnier than watching someone caught in a time or social-status shift—the well traveled, fish-out-of-water premise? *The Beverly Hillbillies* is a perfect example of this device in use. Calling the elaborately expensive swimming pool a "cement pond" is still a hoot. Figure 1.3 illustrates the modern, meeting the cliché. On the other hand, dumping a modern character, dependent on today's luxuries, into a situation in which he has to shoot a bear with a slingshot for dinner can have its moments as well.

The Big vs. the Little

Another device involves giving insignificant items huge power and deflating larger items into trifling roles—the role switch plays on people's expectations. A classic cartoon example of this device is the elephant that shrieks in fear at the sight of a mouse. This device can also be used in conjunction with the weight-shift element, in which, for example, a feather falling from a bird demolishes a skyscraper office building.

The Universal and the Particular

Humor depends on many things. Mostly, humor depends on the viewers' life experiences. Something that might be a riot to corporate executives will have no meaning at all to high school students, because corporate executives and high-

Figure 1.3
The old cartoon cliché of the cannibals capturing the explorers and cooking them for dinner takes a twist with the injection of a computer into the equation.

school students see the world around them quite differently. We can all relate to certain things; to generate the largest audience possible for your humor, you will stick with experiences we all share. Finding the common element of experience is a wonderful goal to embrace, but the most difficult to achieve. Satire and parody work well because they're often playing off the collective knowledge in the public's mind of some media event, usually via television, music, or newspapers. The problem with this form of humorous storytelling is its short shelf life. When the story runs out of steam in the media, the humor becomes stale and unfunny.

Certainly, these devices are merely a few things you might mix together when you're writing a humorous story line. The book of humor is constantly being written and, hopefully, it will never end. When you're writing a humorous (or even dramatic) story line, always keep in mind that you're telling the story not only by the spoken words, but also—and maybe even more so—by the expressions the reader or viewer sees. The body language, the attire, and the surroundings all contribute, as a team, to help the spoken word. If a picture speaks a thousand words, an animation may not need words at all.

Adapting an Existing Story

When translating a book to animation, you are telling a story in a very different medium that has different requirements. In the written story, much depends on the reader to interpret how he or she visualizes the story. When you create your animation based on an existing story, the visualization is *your* interpretation. Your interpretation most likely won't be what the reader had in their mind while he or she was reading the story. This difference can obviously lead to disagreement between the original story and your interpretation, particularly when you're adapting a classic written work.

This type of disagreement can occur even with the animator's best intentions. For example, when Disney's *Alice in Wonderland* was first released in England, it became a classic for generations, but the English scholars were up in arms at the interpretation. Don't worry about this dilemma; you cannot please everyone. Just be true to yourself, and create something that you are satisfied with and that you hope fulfills the artistic integrity of the original, written work.

In *The Journal of Edwin Carp*, Bazley wanted to stay as true to the flavor of the book as possible. He kept the commentary dry and understated, and he complemented this commentary with comic and quirky visuals. Because the book is supposedly a diary, it lends itself nicely to an episodic format—in other words, a series of shorts that stand on their own, yet can be placed together to make a larger story work as well. Figure 1.4 shows several storyboards from the *The Journal of Edwin Carp*.

Legal Issues

If you want to create an adaptation of a book, you will have to get permission, or the rights, to create this adaptation. To obtain permission for adapting a book, start by writing to the publisher, or to The Society of Authors for help. In some cases, the publisher won't exist anymore, so you will have to find out whether the copyright to the book was bought, or whether the author or a next of kin owns the rights. This process can involve quite an extensive amount of research.

In the case of *The Journal of Edwin Carp*, for example, the author Richard Haydn was not married and did not have children or next of kin. Through research on the Internet, we learned Haydn's date of death and where he died. We also found out that he was, in fact, an actor. He was in *The Sound of Music* and a few other recognizable films. He was also the voice of the caterpillar in *Alice in Wonderland*. We then went to the Hall of Records in Orange County, California, and researched Haydn's name, but no record existed under "Haydn." As a last-ditch attempt, we looked up other spellings, and one of these correlated with his death date. We looked at the death certificate and saw the location where he died. Also listed under Occupation on the death certificate was "Actor." This death certificate definitely was for the Richard Haydn we were looking for; but, as with many actors, his stage name had a different spelling. (Quite often, actors use different names from those that they were born with, which can make the research very difficult.) From all our research, and from what we had discovered, we were then able to locate Haydn's will, find out who his beneficiaries were, and acquire permissions to adapt his original story.

Figure 1.4
Several storyboards from *The Journal of Edwin Carp.*

If you're serious about adapting an existing work, hiring an entertainment lawyer to negotiate for you will pay off in the long run. The lawyer will know what sort of arrangement to make, how long to acquire the rights for, what percentages you should receive, and what you need to share with the copyright owner. Each case will be unique and pose its own set of hurdles. Certainly, acquiring some adaptation permissions will be easier than our experience was in the above case. But our point in covering this topic in a book about animation is to point out the need to respect the copyright of others' work. If you really want to use an existing story, do get permission before you've invested a lot of time adapting it, only to find that you can't display or distribute your masterpiece. And do not be lured into thinking that just because your adaptation is on the Internet it doesn't count—it does. The Internet *is* a publicly displayed medium, therefore any content made public is considered published.

Storyboarding in Flash

A *storyboard* is a series of drawings in panel form, in sequential order, that tells the story in visual form. Underneath each frame will be written notes that usually contain dialogue and maybe some scene description. Walt Disney was first credited with creating the storyboard. Disney Studios relied so much on storyboarding that animators often didn't have a fully written script. Animation is so visual that, on occasion, a script can actually stifle the process.

Now, you will understand why we earlier discussed the single-panel cartoon. A storyboard is essentially many, single-panel cartoons that will depict the flow of the animated cartoon. For very short subjects (less than a minute), you may forgo this device, with the warning that even 30-second television commercials are, indeed, storyboarded first to sell the idea to the client. If you're doing an individual personal project and are answering to no one, you already know what you have in mind for such a short jaunt. However, when the production is larger, and more people are involved, a storyboard is absolutely necessary.

A storyboard can be as crude or as finished as you have time and money for. Some storyboards are so crude that only the people working on the project could understand them, whereas others are marvelous works of art in their own right. The main point of the storyboard is to map out what needs to be done before you spend large amounts of time doing it, and possibly wasting that time when confusion seeps in (and it will). In its most basic form, the storyboard is a sketch over time, a roughing out of the scenes to be used to tell the story. Like the previous Figure 1.4. These are good examples of the middle ground in storyboarding.

Like the single-panel cartoon we discussed earlier, which tells a complete story with one frame, the storyboard is its more vocal cousin, which connects single panels together to tell a larger story. The drawings you make for your storyboard should be the high points of the story's flow. You don't need to bog down in

> **Note:** Flash is an incredibly versatile tool that can be used for many tasks, including storyboarding. We've included pre-made blank storyboards on the CD-ROM, in both NTSC (National Television System Committee, or American TV) format (4:3 aspect ratio)—the *storyboard_4-3.fla* file, and HDTV (High Definition Television) format (16:9 aspect ratio)—the *storyboard_16-9.fla file*, for use in creating your own storyboards. Aspect ratio refers to width by height. 4:3 would equal 4 units wide by 3 units high. Example: 400 pixelsx300 pixels.

telling the intermediate actions during the storyboard stage. If you feel a detail is important enough to include in a storyboard frame, that detail is not an insignificant part of the story; maybe it should have a board of its own. (We use the term *board* to identify one single frame in the storyboard's sequence; see Figure 1.5.)

When you use Flash for storyboard creation, it's symbols and library features can save you significant time by letting you reuse pre-created art of your characters and associated elements. After you've created these libraries, you can load them into the blank storyboard file and begin placing the needed elements into the storyboard.

Storyboarding for the Nonartist in Flash

On the CD-ROM, we've supplied you with a system of mock characters, much like the traditional artist's wooden mannequin, which you can place and pose as stand-ins. These characters can be very helpful to the nonvisual artists (such as a writer), who might be working on a storyboard, and who'll then pass the characters on to the artist for completion.

We have made a short script for which you can use the *storyboardproject.fla* file elements. By going through this exercise, you will become familiar with using Flash to create your own storyboards.

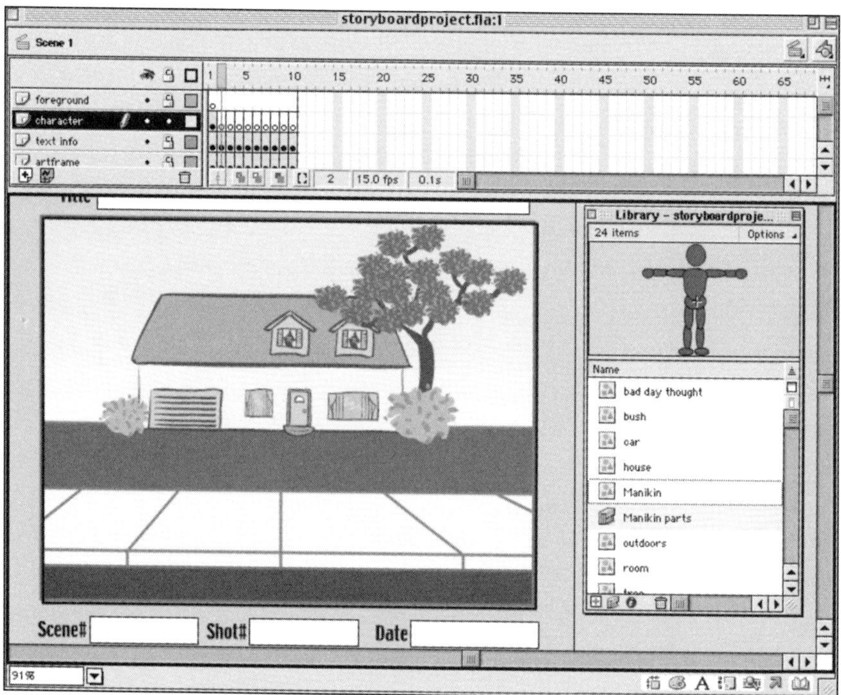

Figure 1.5
The storyboard project and library.

The Script

After a long day at the office, Mr. Mannequin arrives home with relaxation in mind. After parking the car, he discovers that the neighborhood dogs have gotten into his garbage cans and strewn the place with litter that he must now clean up.

"Man, I sure wish people would control their animals," he says after unsuspectingly sticking his hand in some rather wretched goo. He then goes on cautiously picking up the remaining renegade garbage and putting it in its proper place. "That's it! I'm buying animal-proof garbage cans ASAP!"

Mr. Mannequin then proceeds into the house, sits down, and turns on his television to catch the news; but nothing happens. It seems his television cable has been disconnected. A little more than hopping mad at this point, he flings the front door of the house open to inform the world, "Why does *everything* have to be so *difficult?* All I want is a little break after a hard day of work! Is that asking too much?"

Breaking the Script into Workable Storyboards

After opening the *storyboardproject.fla* file, you'll notice that the Library window is filled with the elements you'll need. The timeline shows that each frame in this file will be one storyboard. The layers are set up to facilitate moving the items around without disturbing the storyboard text and boundaries. To access these layers, simply unlock them.

Now that we have the short story, we need to lay it out in workable high points. The first point should be the establishing shot, or storyboard. This storyboard will show only the essential elements: the character, the car, and the neighborhood. For extra information, you could add the character thinking about the hard day he just finished.

1. Open the *storyboardproject.fla* file from the CD-ROM.
2. From the Library window, drag the symbol named **outdoors** to the layer named **background**. Arrange the symbol to fit the image boundaries in the storyboard. You can now lock this layer to prevent accidental selection or movement.
3. Now, drag the **car** symbol to the layer named **character**.
4. You can now drag the **bad day thought** symbol into place somewhere above Mr. Mannequin's head.
5. Unlock the **text info** layer, and type in the descriptions needed to explain the board. Descriptors such as scene, shot number, date, a brief explanation or script being spoken at the time, and even music score suggestions are important when you need to convey the idea to others.

Figure 1.6
The finished establishing shot of our project story.

You have just completed the establishing shot for the scene (see Figure 1.6). Easy, isn't it? Now, we'll move on to determine the next high point in the story.

The next thing to happen that is a critical part of the story and warrants a storyboard is Mr. Mannequin's discovery of garbage everywhere. We could jump right to the funny part, where he sticks his hand in garbage goo; but, then, we'd have no basis for this event to happen. Remember, humor needs a setup. We'll build this foundation next.

1. Advance to the next frame in the storyboard file, which will give you a clean slate to work with.
2. From the Library window, drag the **house corner** symbol to the **background** layer. Position the symbol to fit the image boundaries of the storyboard area. Lock the layer.
3. Now, drag the symbol **mannequin disgust** to the **character** layer. Position the mannequin to the left side (from earlier in the chapter, remember how humor should read—from left to right).
4. Drag the **garbage can over** symbol, and place it to the right of the character. This placement finishes the enforcement of the read from left to right.

Now, we have the setup complete for the punch line of this segment of our story. Next, we get to the part we've all been waiting for, hand in garbage goo. Of course, in the actual animation, you would have maybe 5 to 10 seconds of

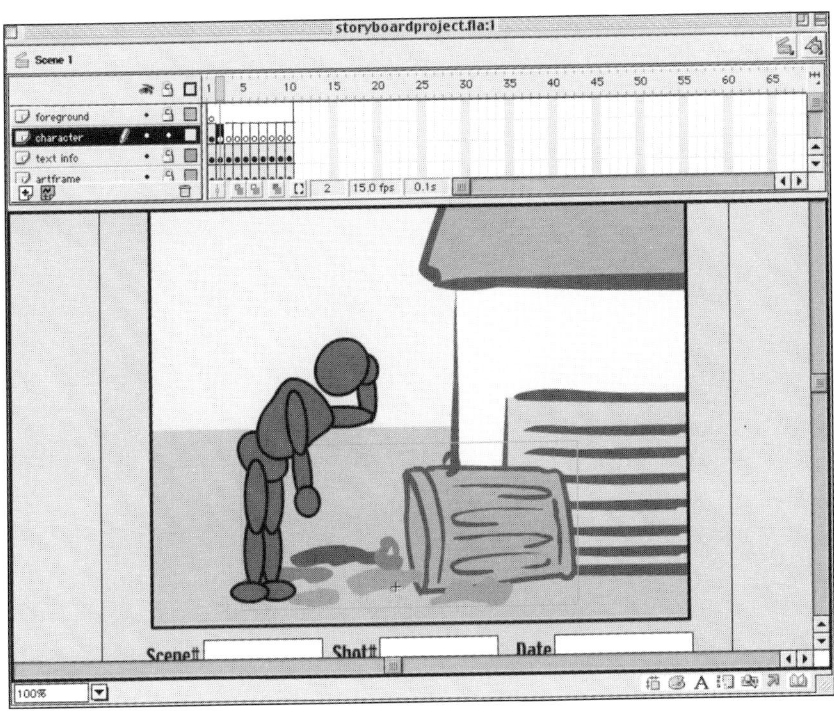

Figure 1.7
The second storyboard should look something like this, reading left to right.

the character unhappily picking up garbage, building to the punch, but the storyboard needs only the high point. If the grumbling character were saying something exceptionally important while picking up the wayward garbage, (such as considering Al Gore for the job), you could include a storyboard on that as well. For this project, though, we'll assume his comments to be standard grumbling, and go right to the punch (see Figure 1.7).

1. Advance to the next frame.
2. Drag the **hand of goo** symbol to the **character** layer.

That's it. Notice that we did not use a background or supporting imagery at all here, because we wanted to focus all attention on the character in distress. We also used a much tighter shot, which would allow for more detailed and lively expression of the character's face. During the animation of this critical part of the humor, you'd want to make notes instructing the quick cut to this scene about halfway through the line, "Man, I sure wish people would *control* their animals." Timing is very important here. Right on the beat of the word "control"—*bang*—you see the predicament of the character, which hopefully, causes laughter via a mixture of the surprise and foolhardy elements we discussed earlier.

Note: When positioning the Mannequin character, you can take the standard symbol pose (Mannequin Blank) onto the work area and break it apart (Modify>Break Apart). This action will cause the character to be separated from the original symbol and let you reposition all his limbs, torso, and so on for the pose you want.

Now that you have a grasp of what to do, we'll let you finish the rest of the storyboard. Keep in mind the need to express only high points in the story. Certainly, use as many storyboards as you need, but don't overdo it. The storyboards should be a basis for further creativity during the production (see

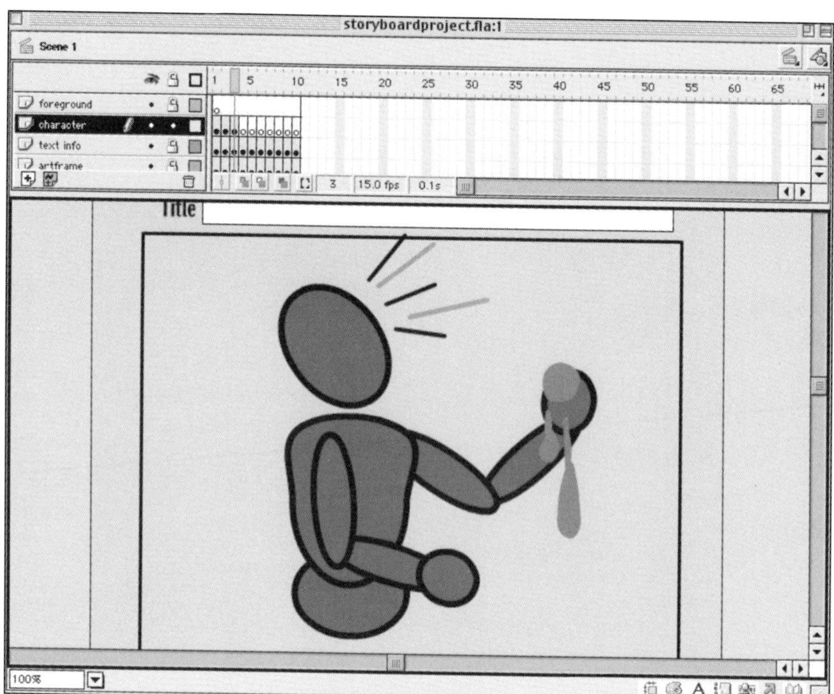

Figure 1.8
The delivered punch line.

> **Printing Frames**
>
> You can print a sequence of frames all at once using the **File|Print Margins** command on the Macintosh. In this dialog box, you can set the size and whether to print one frame or all frames. Then, do a **Print Preview** before printing so you can see what will be printed.

Figure 1.8). Overdoing the storyboards with too many explicit instructions can dampen creativity later on. Great chefs do not follow recipes to a T.

After you have all the storyboards you need, you can print each individual frame as a separate storyboard. When you have the printouts, feel free to make notes on them using the trusted analog pencil or pen. This way, everyone involved in the production can add his or her input to fine-tune the story and make the best cartoon possible.

Moving On

Next up, we'll go into a discussion of the creation and design of the characters you'll need as you create that next cartoon or game masterpiece. Even the nonartist will gather a wealth of information here—and have fun doing it.

Chapter 2

Character Development

In this chapter, we'll discuss some things you'll want to think about when you create your cartoon characters. The decisions you make when creating your characters will have ramifications throughout the animated-cartoon production process. A little forethought here can save endless hours of work during production.

By Bill Turner and Richard Bazley

Basic Design Considerations

If you're already well versed in the art of cartoon character creation, you may want to read this chapter simply to reinforce some of the devices you might already be using. If you've never created a cartoon character in your life, fear not—in the project section of this chapter, we'll be supplying you with elements to experiment with so you can practice some of the fundamentals of the craft. First, though, we'll discuss the basic elements of a cartoon character—elements such as personality, voice, and graphic style—and the kinds of decisions you'll have to make when you create your characters.

Personality: How Shapes Reflect Traits

Think of your characters as actors, and you as the director in telling a story. What's one of the first requirements of telling a story? Characters that keep the attention of the audience. To get and keep an audience, a cartoon character must have a personality and a certain something that lets the audience connect with that character—something to endear this character to the audience. So, when you create characters, one set of decisions you'll have to make concerns their personalities. What personality traits do you want your characters to have? Do you want a particular character to be happy-go-lucky, villainous, or just plain complacent? The story line you're working on will dictate these needs.

The next set of decisions involves how to *express* your characters' personality traits. How can you design your characters in ways that will help to show their personalities? What kinds of shapes typically express certain traits? If your character is a villain, soft, round shapes aren't going to help reinforce that. In fact, evil cartoon characters often use more square, pointed, or angular shapes, and nice, warm characters tend to be more rounded. It isn't a coincidence that the Seven Dwarfs are so round or Cruella DeVil (*101 Dalmatians*) is so angular.

So, when you design a character, think about which shapes will help convey the traits of that character. Also, make sure that your design fits the emotions this character is likely to express. For example, in Figure 2.1, the character on the right has been designed with an edgy nature. This character would have difficulty expressing soft emotions. Notice the contrasting details: curly hair and flowing mustache and beard, versus short, spiky hair and mustache; round nose versus angular nose; and the addition of a sharp buckle in the right-hand character's clothing.

In designing your characters, you also must take *contrast* into account. If all the characters are cute and cuddly, picking out the evil one is difficult. So, along with matching shapes to traits, you want to make sure your characters are distinct.

Voice

Although the graphic representation of your character should convey much about the personality, the actual voice with which it speaks will bring a greater part of its personality to life. Saying that voice is a critical aspect of your

Figure 2.1
Examine the differences between these two characters. The one on the left seems to have a softer, warmer personality compared to the more edgy character on the right.

character's personality and acting ability would not be an overstatement. Most cartoon creators will certainly have some idea of how their characters should speak. The main challenge lies in trying to match what you have in your mind with what can really be achieved. We'll touch on this aspect in more depth in Chapter 3, where we discuss working with sound.

Having a voice actor chosen before you design a character can help in many ways. You can study the actor's features and see whether you can get some of his or her look into the character. Sometimes, however, this approach can create too much of a caricature and might not work. Or the character may *look* nothing like the actor but, because of the way it moves, the character will *feel* very much like him or her. All these things can make your character really work. Remember, you are not creating a simple drawing; you're creating an actor who'll be performing in the story being told.

Note: On the CD-ROM, you will find some snippets of different cartoon voices. By listening to these voices, you can imagine the type of characters that could emerge.

Collective Experience: A Bridge to the Audience

It's no mistake that the world of cartoons is chock-full of ducks, bunnies, cats, dogs, and children of all proportions. The reason is simple: Everyone can relate to these beings because most everyone has had a direct relationship somewhere in life with one of them. In using these preconceived notions, or collective experience, the cartoonist starts out with a springboard from which to work. Twisting this collective experience is the absolute, main ingredient in the humor of your character. Believe it or not, that dogs can talk or that children act like seasoned adults has not always been accepted. In the animated cartoon, the absurd becomes a reality.

Building on our collective experience also lets you create complex or flawed characters that audiences will still like. For example, note that Pepé Le Pew is the bad guy whenever he shows up with stink in tow, but he somehow pulls off being the likable character in his never-ending quest for Penelope, the female cat who wants nothing whatsoever to do with him. What's happening here is that we cannot smell Pepé, so we tend to question the urgency with which he's avoided. We might also feel that Penelope should give the hopelessly romantic lover of a skunk a break. After all, he seems well mannered, and he cannot help that his biology causes flowers to wilt in his wake. We can easily relate to this because most of us have experienced wanting the unobtainable. Pepé's also cute; it's the aroma trail that's evil. So, we end up siding with the skunk. This is a fine example of the interaction or connection the character has with the audience.

Accessories

You can use accessories to help express a character's personality, or to show something about his environment, as Figure 2.2 demonstrates. This design element is crucial to Weber's character and personality; it also functions nicely for his underwater scenes and lets him basically filter out the pollution humans have brought into his environment. However, as Figure 2.3 shows, you might want to refrain from adding too many accessories to your character. Items such as a security blanket, elaborate hats, shoes with shoelaces, and ornate T-shirt designs will need to be well thought out. Keep in mind that, if you add these accessories, and your character depends on them, you'll have to draw them many times from many points of view. We are not recommending against the use of accessories; just be judicious about how you use them. However, if you had a necessary scene in which the character ridiculously over-prepared for a cookout, then this would be okay, but you wouldn't want this much stuff for everyday use.

Clothing

If you're designing a human character, you need to be cognizant of the clothing. Designing a character dependent upon elaborate clothing destines those involved to many long hours of production. A good example of such elaborate design would be to create a diva wearing a sequined dress, and to draw every single sequin (see Figure 2.4). Not only would doing one small scene take forever, but this animation would also have a hard time playing back on the average computer, as it strains to reproduce all the sequins faithfully at 15 to 24 frames per second. Of course, over-detailing also creates larger files to download. When your intended delivery vehicle is the Web, these are significant considerations. Mastering the art of *suggested detail* (see Figure 2.4 again) will take you a long way toward the goal of efficiency.

Figure 2.2
This pelican character, named Weber, constantly wears a diving mask and snorkel.

Figure 2.3
Here, we've loaded Weber down with way too many accessories. You wouldn't want the burden of drawing him repeatedly like this.

Figure 2.4
Notice the difference in the divas' dresses. The one on the left shows all the sequins, but too much detail adds more production hours and hampers playback on the average computer. The dress on the right uses just a few sparkles to suggest sequins.

Note: Use symbols to save drawing time. Fortunately, Flash 5 does ease the workload with the use of graphics symbols, saving you many tedious hours of redrawing. (We cover symbols in Chapter 5.) Still, you'll be wise to follow a philosophy of "less is more."

Color

Another important aspect of character design is the colors you will choose for your character. Use of color is an abstract area of character design, and no hard and fast rules exist. Bright, nearly full-strength, primary colors tend to say "fun" and "happy." Muddy grays, greens, and browns express quite the opposite. Unfortunately, the subject of color and human interaction is a deep subject that goes far beyond the scope of this book. Most artists already have an innate understanding of this topic. But, for those who'd like to learn more, we suggest reading Kandinsky and his theories on line and color.

Animation Considerations

So far, we've discussed what elements you will use to create a character, and how some of the choices you'll make will affect production time and playback performance. You'll have to make other, related choices about your characters that will also affect the animation process. For instance, your character's basic style—realistic or exaggerated—affects not only the character's appearance, but also its motions. A character's simplicity or complexity will also affect the animation process. And one huge factor in your animation will be your target output—film or video (which allows fuller, more detailed animation) or the Web (which places speed and size limits on the animation). We'll examine these factors next.

Choosing a Style: Realism vs. Exaggeration

Another important aspect of character design involves your character's expressions and movements—specifically, whether they'll be realistic or exaggerated.

Your character's design is important because the way it looks also determines the way you might animate it. Normally, realistic designs are animated to be believable. Many super-heroes and comic-book characters, such as Superman, and many animal characters, such as the classic *Bambi*, are good examples of the realistic form. (Even if Superman can defy the laws of gravity to some extent, his motions while doing so reflect the way a human's muscles work.)

Zany cartoon designs work better in a Tex Avery style, a broad style of animation that makes use of extremely exaggerated motions that go way beyond physical possibilities, and with little regard to real-life movement. Tex's name might not be familiar, but his legacy certainly is. He's the creative force behind Porky Pig, Daffy Duck, Bugs Bunny, and, of course, Droopy. In particular, Daffy's wild movements of reckless abandon personifies this style Tex created in the late 1930s. This style later influenced shows such as *Tom and Jerry* and *Ren and Stimpy*. All are good examples of this extreme motion in use. See Figure 2.5 for an example of realistic versus exaggerated animation styles.

Angular designs work quite well in limited animation (see "Designing for Limited Animation" later in this chapter). If you don't have to move the characters around as much, you can get quite graphic and stylized without worrying, "How the devil am I going to turn this character?" Anatomy is less of a concern when the characters are moving, not in a believable way, but in a stylized, and usually more outrageous way. Tex Avery would take stylized movements

Figure 2.5
Here, we illustrate the differences between how a realistic character and a zany character would react to an alarming situation.

to the limit without worrying about where the femur and the fibula were. He was thinking in terms of pure entertainment and storytelling. What you do in this context really depends on the effect you are going for.

Choosing Simplicity or Complexity

Worth noting is that Mickey Mouse is one of the most identifiable characters and graphic images in the world. Mickey's secret is in the simplicity of his design. Design simplicity is also extremely important for animating because, until recently, animation entailed many drawings, so the simpler the design, the faster you could animate—and, therefore, the more you could concentrate on just the performance. Flash can help you reduce the number of drawings by using symbols and loops (we will explain these devices in Chapter 5), but simplicity is still the better option unless the specifics of your project require something more complex.

You will want to design according to your project needs. If the project is a personal film, and you don't mind spending extra time on it, you could have enormously detailed characters. But do keep in mind playback performance on slower computers, and the fact that more details mean larger files to download if the Web is your target for delivery.

Some of the big studios—even those with large budgets—might do a simplification pass on the characters to eliminate what is called "line mileage" (lines drawn that may not be necessary to represent the character) so that the "cleanup artist" (the artist who draws a finished drawing over the animator's rough) can move more quickly. This simplification pass is meaningful in Flash, because fewer lines make downloading SWF (Shockwave Flash) files for your viewers faster and more efficient.

Designing for Full Animation

The high end in animation, *full animation*, usually requires that each frame of a movement is a unique drawing. Each drawing might vary ever so slightly from the previous frame to give an illusion of smooth movement. Full animation is costly and time consuming. These facts limit full animation mostly to the realm of feature films. TV, with its much shorter deadlines and economics, is hindered from using full animation.

Designing for full animation is probably not the choice you'll want to make if the Internet is your final delivery mechanism. Full animation requires many more unique frames of art and will certainly place a burden on the processor trying to play it back. However, if video or film is your destination, quality rules the day. With video output, once this output is on tape, the computer's processor is taken out of the playback equation. Eliminating the computer processor allows far more leeway in the creation process because you can do as many frames of art as you like without fear of increasing file size and hindering playback. (We will discuss outputting to video more fully in Chapter 7.)

In developing a character for full animation, you will want to create a design that lends itself to being moved around. In the early days, the very rounded construction was the norm; examples include Mickey Mouse, Tom and Jerry, and Woody Woodpecker. All these characters could be created on the basis of a few circles. The use of circles makes easier visualization of complicated moves such as a character that will turn around from a ground side view to a back 3/4 top view.

People often comment on the complexity of Disney characters. What makes those characters appear complex, however, is not the design, but the sophisticated way in which they move. This type of animation—also called *classical animation*—is usually associated with Disney. Classical animation style is more fluid, and the acting is more involved.

Note: If you design a realistic-looking character, you might have to consider the use of the Rotoscope (Chapter 5). This tool represents a much-debated technique among animators, but it's incredibly useful, as proven in many of the old classics such as "Peter Pan," where the whole film was shot in live action first.

Designing for Limited Animation

If full animation is the Rolls Royce, limited animation is the Corvette of the craft. With the limited style, creating footage *fast* is what counts. Looking good and expressing your humor or story are the goals here, with the accuracy of movement found in full animation taking a back seat.

When you're designing characters for the limited animation style, think of shows such as "The Flintstones." Here, the characters are designed so that all the parts can be separated. For example, the body can be held on one layer (one drawing) and you can just animate the arm on another layer. On yet another layer, you can do the lip sync and animate only the mouth. Of course, this means that, when you design your character, you'll want to keep in mind natural breaking points. These points should come at places such as shoulders, elbows, wrists, knees, and hips. In this respect, you design your character more along the lines of a puppet. See Figure 2.6 for an example of this design approach.

To ease the animation of such broken-joint-style characters, create each movable body part as a separate symbol. Within each symbol, be sure to align the joint's location with the center of the symbol. This alignment allows the symbol to be rotated around this center point. For example, the forearm is connected to the upper arm at the elbow; therefore, the forearm's center point should be roughly in the neighborhood of where the elbow would occur. When you've created the forearm this way, you will be able to rotate the forearm, and its axis will be the elbow area (instead of the forearm's center); this axis will cause the elbow to bend naturally, as an elbow should when it's rotated. See Figures 2.7, 2.8, 2.9, and 2.10 for examples of this process for animating the arm.

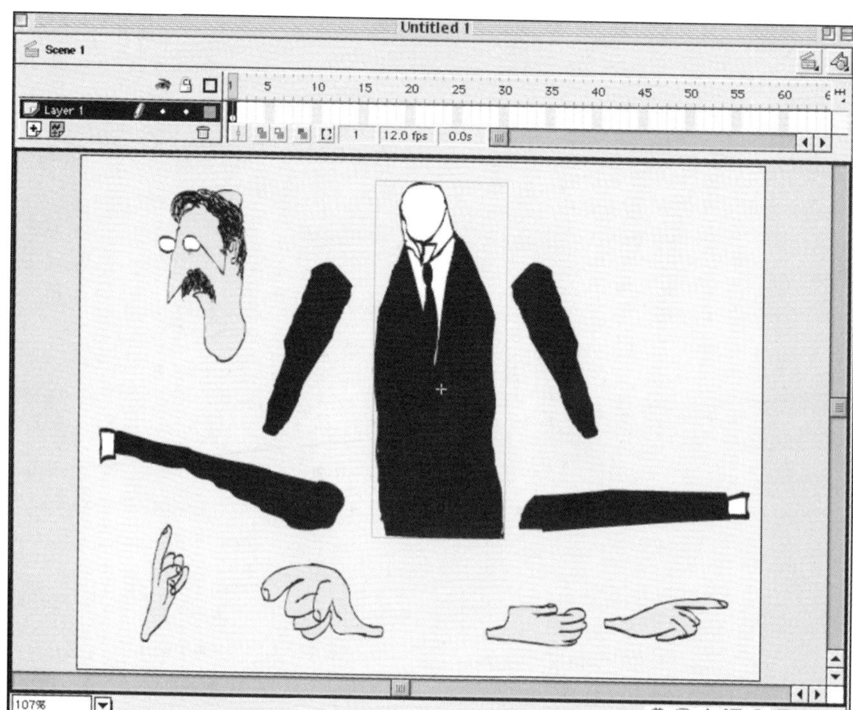

Figure 2.6
Here, we see Richard Bazley's character Edwin Carp broken into his various elements.

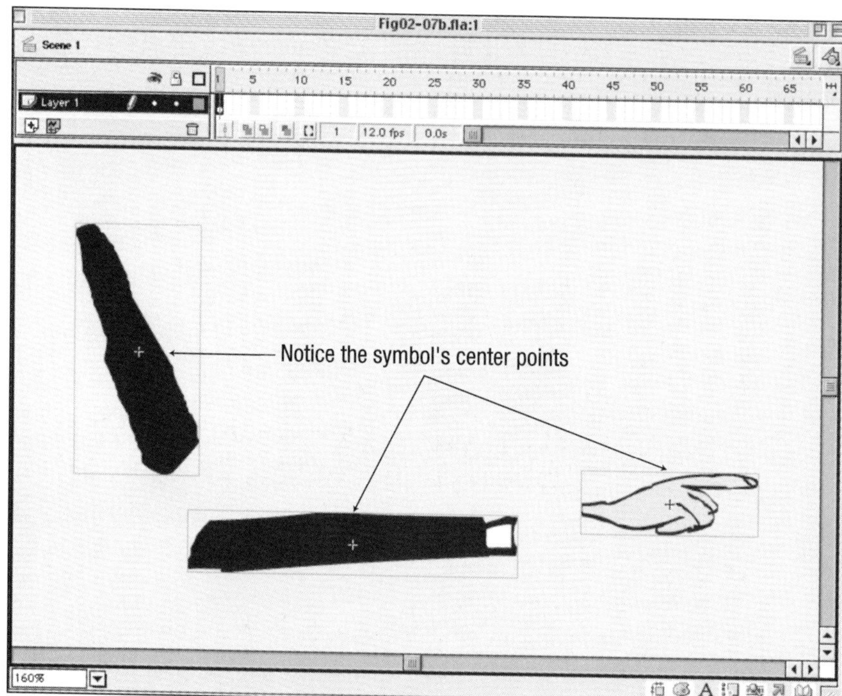

Figure 2.7
This figure shows the default method for creating new symbols. The center points are in the center of the graphics' boundaries.

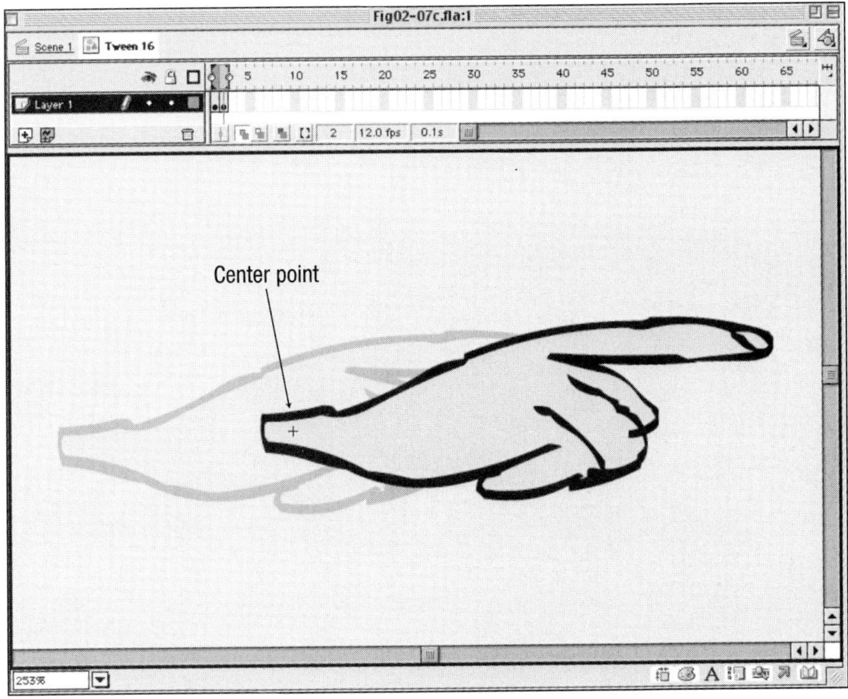

Figure 2.8

By editing the symbol itself, you can drag the graphic to place the center point at a natural joint area (here, the wrist).

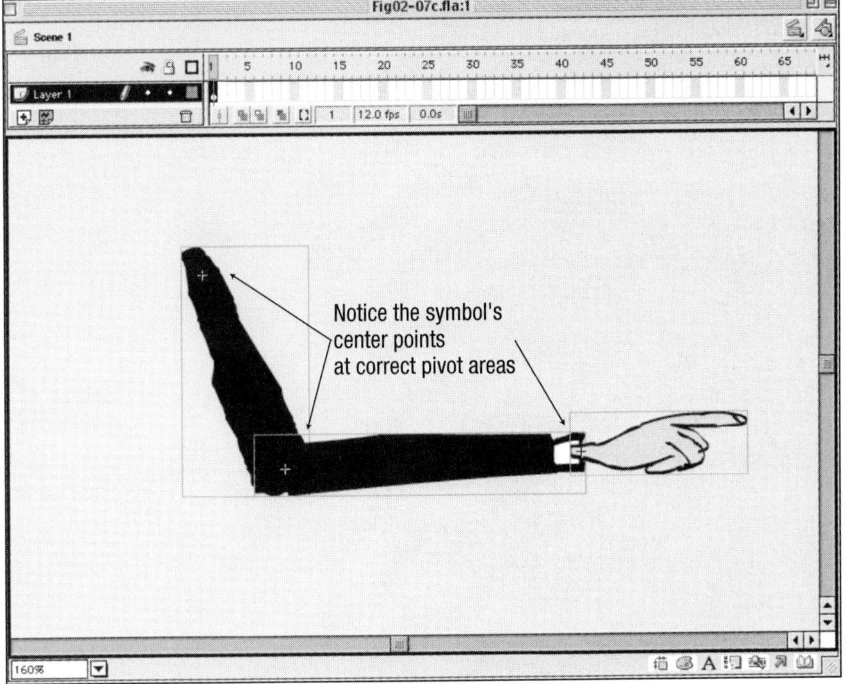

Figure 2.9

Now, when you view the arm in the main timeline, you can see the center points in a more useful position for rotating.

Figure 2.10
With all center points at joint locations, you can animate with simple rotations, assured that the position of each element relates to its base.

Sketching Characters

Sketching characters starts not with pencil and paper but, rather, on the canvas of the artist's mind. Ideas for great characters will emerge in the observation of daily life. Keeping a keen eye on everything around you with regard to characters when paper and pencil (much less, a computer) are not handy will be of immense value when you do sit down to the computer to create. Even such a mundane activity as a trip to the grocery store can be teeming with food for both the brain and the belly. This way of *seeing* is a main ingredient that separates the artist from the accountant.

Figure Study

Many approaches exist to drawing the figure—from the architectural and sometimes stylized work of Burne Hogarth, to the fluid and pictorial style of Topolski. Neither extreme is right or wrong. In fact, both ways are worth exploring in classes—it's a bit like going to a gym and stretching different muscles. The classical approach (the Renaissance style) will give you all the anatomical information you need, and the quick-sketch approach will help you push your animation to be the best it can be—hitting and exaggerating a pose, finding the right attitude and, most importantly, telling a story.

Don't worry if you're not a master of figure drawing. We have seen wonderful draftsmen who are unable to animate, and lesser draftsmen who bring characters to life. So, if you struggle at your drawing, don't sweat it; just practice. See Figure 2.11 for some examples of such practice.

Figure 2.11
Some examples of sketching studies by Richard Bazley and Bill Turner, showing different approaches to visual jotting.

Art Research

The more information you have in your head, the more equipped you are to create and bring to life an animated character. Visit art exhibitions, and study great art. And, by all means, do not overlook the obvious; your nearby TV and the Internet are loaded with fine examples of animated galleries.

Many great European illustrators, including Gustave Tengren, influenced the designs of *Snow White*. The art director Eyvind Earle was influenced by Asian and Gothic art, and his work heavily influenced later films such as *Sleeping Beauty*. Eyvind Earle's design style ran all the way from the design of the trees to the horses and the characters. In the case of *Sleeping Beauty*, the characters were angular, which made things more difficult for the animators, but they were able to come up with design solutions to make the characters work.

Ronald Searle's exploratory ink-line style has had a huge influence on animated films. Searle would use minimum pencil-line construction before he did his finished drawing. He would often make "on the spot" sketches with a fountain pen. Construction lines were left in the finished drawing, and you can sometimes see a visual record of the artist as he changed his mind and redrew a line without erasing the old line. *The Aristocats* is the most obvious example of Searle's line style translated to film.

Richard Bazley's film *The Journal of Edwin Carp* takes this a stage further, and incorporates the thicks and thins and scratchy quality of the line style. The scratchy and sometimes wobbly line has a life and freshness about it. Figure 2.12 shows a sketch from this film.

Figure 2.12
Richard Bazley's *The Journal of Edwin Carp*. Searle's style works well in Flash because you get the same sense of immediacy by using a Wacom tablet and the brush tool that you would with drawing directly with a pen in a sketchbook.

Character Sketching in Flash

Even though good old pencil and paper is hard to beat for drawing, Flash gives you tools to do some serious sketching and design work. We encourage you to doodle around in Flash as much as you can. Flash is the perfect environment for experimentation because, unlike paper, Flash lets you undo, redo, and make endless versions and variations.

When you use Flash as a sketchbook, you can think in terms of the traditional pencil-and-paper sketchbook, but with the added luxury of all the editing benefits. We believe the editing capability is the most powerful of Flash's advantages for character animation. The drawing tools in Flash work exactly as you expect them to. The pencil draws lines, the eraser erases, the paintbrush paints.

Sketching—A Visual Memory Bank

When I was at art school, teachers always emphasized the importance of a sketchbook and drawing in it whenever I could. Not until years later, when I had filled many of these sketchbooks, did I realize their importance.

Every time you sketch something, you are storing away information (as a computer does) that you can use at a later date. You are also studying life "first hand," which you can caricature later at your will.

One mistake many studios make is to try to copy a Disneyesque character style. They should realize that the original artists use their first-hand experiences, combined with a study of art and children's illustration, to arrive at their character designs. We all draw from our own life's experiences, and animators are no exception.

I once designed a character and, when my father saw it, he said, "My God, that's me!" Until then, I hadn't even noticed the resemblance. But his likeness was clear as day after he had pointed it out. As a boy, I had often caricatured my father and, obviously, something had stuck in my subconscious. This demonstrates why sketching is so important.

Simple. If you're comfortable with paper and pencil, becoming comfortable with Flash's drawing tools will not require a great leap. Their functionality is close to the traditional tools you're used to working with.

Other vector illustration applications, such as Macromedia FreeHand and Adobe Illustrator, are available, and they certainly have their place in the business of animated cartoons. But, for the character animator, Flash's set of drawing tools—besides being incredibly natural to use—give you the added benefit of instant feedback with *onion skinning* (seeing the "before" and "after" frame images, which helps to form the image you're working on). You can also work in the environment where you can immediately play back the animation after you've created it. This capability gives a great incentive to learn Flash's drawing tools. If that's not enough, remember: You'll be creating large numbers of drawings to create your animated masterpiece. Do you really want the burden of needlessly exporting and importing these character drawings? Didn't think so.

Note: A Wacom tablet is essential in drawing. We highly recommend the pressure-sensitive tablet for the obvious reason that it's much more natural than trying to draw with a mouse or trackball. Until the day comes that we have direct neural digital input via brain waves, a tablet is the best mechanism we have for expressing ourselves through the vehicle of the cartoon.

Using Layers for Sketching in Flash

One of the more useful things about Flash, aside from its natural drawing tools, is the capability to work in layers. The advantages to working in layers are that you can have a sketch layer riding underneath the ink layer, and you can protect any of these layers simply by locking them.

Let's do an exercise to get used to sketching in layers in Flash:

1. Starting out with a blank document, rename the default Layer 1 **sketch**.
2. Select the pencil tool. Set its color to **light gray**, its mode to **ink** (the squiggly line pop-up), and its line width to one point. These settings will cause the pencil tool to draw like a traditional, light-sketching pencil and produce freehand drawn lines, as Figure 2.13 shows.

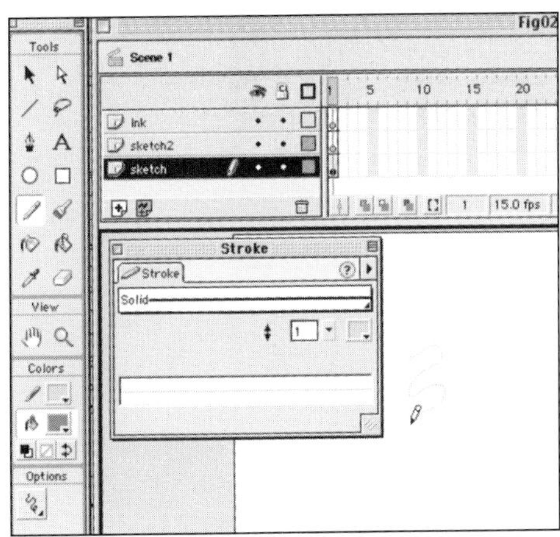

Figure 2.13
Here are the settings we'll use for this sketching exercise.

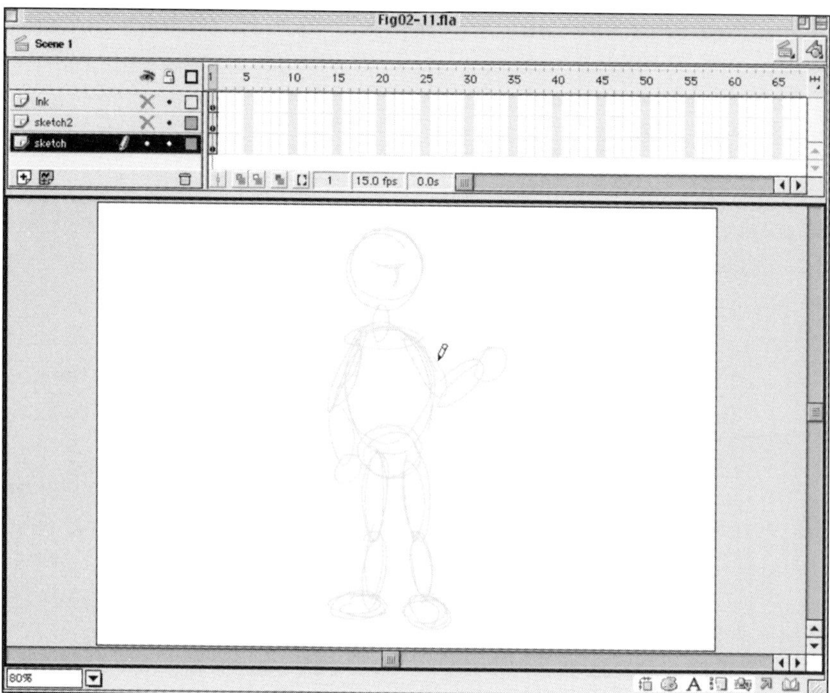

Figure 2.14
Rough out circles and ovals to approximate a character's head, arms, torso, and legs.

3. Start by roughing out circles and ovals to approximate a character's head, arms, torso, and legs, as shown in Figure 2.14. Try to be spontaneous because this will add life to the drawing.
4. Create another layer above the sketch layer, and name the second layer **sketch 2**. Set the pencil tool to a slightly darker or different gray, leaving its mode set to **ink**.
5. Begin sketching in this layer by adding detail and more form, and by using the previous sketched ovals as your guide. You should now start seeing your character emerge, as Figure 2.15 shows. When you are happy with this layer in the sketching process, you can discard the previous layer.
6. Create yet another layer above the **sketch 2** layer and name it **ink**. Set the pencil tool to **black**, leave its mode set at **ink**, and increase the line width to three points. As an option, try using the brush with pressure sensitivity turned on. This setting will give you the thick-and-thin-stroke look, but it will be more difficult to edit later on if the need arises.
7. Now, begin the final inking process. By more closely following the lines established in the sketching layer, you'll tighten the forms and create a finished character, as Figure 2.16 shows.

Figure 2.15
You should now start seeing your character emerge.

Figure 2.16
Begin the final inking process.

This method might seem like the obvious way to go about conceptualizing a character. Amazingly, some users might miss this functionality in Flash. Most vector-art programs do not allow such spontaneous drawing but, thankfully, Flash does. You can, and certainly should, simply play around with different sketchy shapes in the workspace using the layers method. By refining crude but dynamic and spontaneous forms, you'll start to realize that Flash can actually be better than paper and pencil for roughing out ideas.

PROJECT Constructing Characters

We thought it would be fun to include a project on the CD that will give you a chance to stretch your creative muscles in developing characters. Even if you're not a professional cartoonist, you should still be able to come up with some pretty neat things here. On the CD, you will find *Character Project.fla*, which is a Flash 5 authoring file that contains two distinctly different, general face shapes and a number of mouths, eyes, noses, and hairstyles. With these elements, you should be able to construct a great number of character variations (see Figure 2.17).

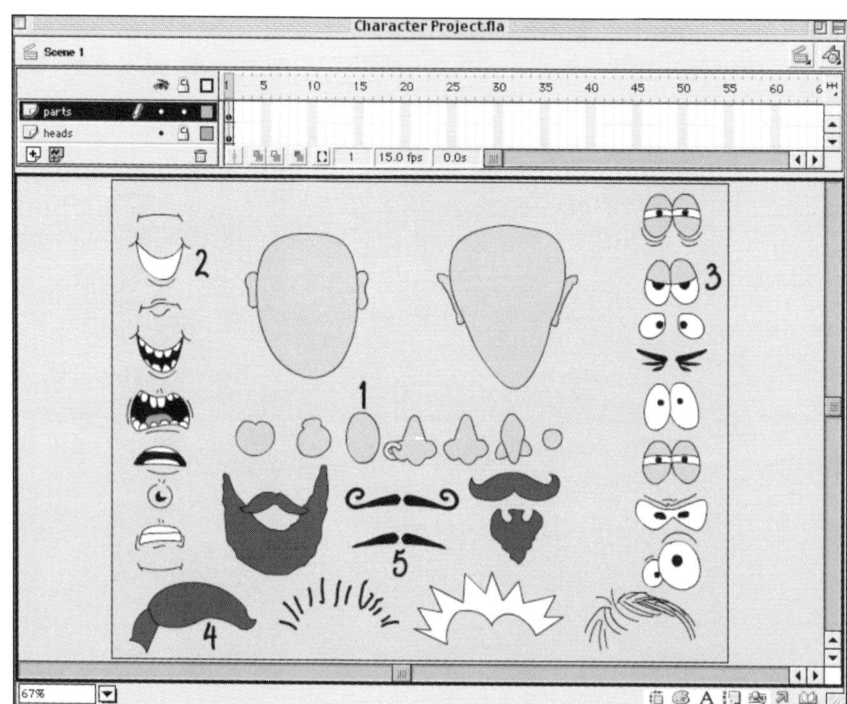

Figure 2.17
Various elements you can experiment with in developing characters.

All the various elements are grouped for easy repositioning. The base faces are grouped as well, but they lie on a layer underneath the other elements. You should lock this layer to prevent accidental movement. By altering the group's position on the layer's plane (**Modify>Arrange>Bring to Front or Send to Back**), you'll be able to pull a mustache in front of a mouth (for example see Figure 2.18).

For this project, we shall composite a rather unassuming, but likable, character who seems to have something up his sleeve. We will use the rounded head form as our base. This rounded form helps add to the likeability of the

Figure 2.18
We've arranged the elements to form a sleepy head, a retro-punk rocker, and a professor.

character (as opposed to the more triangular-shaped face, which tends to be a bit more standoffish).

1. Start by using the solid arrow tool to select the rounded nose (numbered 1) and drag it somewhere about the middle of the face. Don't worry if the nose is not positioned correctly, because you can move it later on if you want to.

2. Next, select the mouth (numbered 2), and drag it to the vicinity where the mouth usually goes. You can also resize this mouth to add emphasis to or remove emphasis from the element. You can also rotate the mouth slightly to add that bit of character.

3. Drag the eyes (numbered 3) to where eyes normally go. At this point, the eyes might be in front of the nose. You can rearrange these groups on this layer by using **Modify>Arrange>Bring to Front or Send to Back** so the nose can rest on top or in front of the eyes.

4. Now select the hair (numbered 4), and position it on the top of the head. The tops of the eyes might be obscured by the bangs of the hair. This fact alone adds a bit of cuteness to our digital chap. Bringing the eyes in front of the bangs would bring focus to the eyes and cause our friend to appear more aloof.

5. If you want, you can now add the mustache (numbered 5). This particular mustache has an air of sophistication that you might not find desirable. Sophistication tends to take away the unassuming quality that you're looking for in this character. We're having you add the mustache to illustrate just how dramatic the effect a couple of thin, black lines can have on a character's personality.

You'll notice as you go through this exercise that even the smallest of adjustments can add dramatically to the character's personality. Experiment with resizing and slightly rotating the various elements. By doing so, you should get a feel for how such adjustments influence your perception of the character at hand.

Now, you've had a chance to play in the cartoon playground. By all means, use this project file to construct as many different types of characters as you'd like. As you build your character, try to keep in mind some of the fundamentals we've discussed in this chapter. You'll find a lot of fun in this sort of experimentation. You will also come to the conclusion that small nuances can have big effects. Charles Schultz, the creator of Peanuts, based practically all of his characters on a simple head on which he changed accessories—mostly different hairstyles and clothing—to create an entire cast of characters that have endured for more than 50 years.

The subject of character concept and design can be deep indeed and could quite possibly fill a book on its own. We hope you'll take from this chapter a good foundation on which to build your own experimentation. Always keep simplicity in mind. Strangely enough, you'll find that simplicity itself can be complicated. The trick is to make simplicity look effortless. That's the appeal of cartoon art. To the average person, cartoons are approachable in the sense that people feel that they could draw them too. In reality, we know this is not the case. Mastering the art of character creation can be a lifelong endeavor that requires many years of drawing practice. Trust that, in time, after much practice, you'll find a groove and just be creating characters without having to consciously think about all the details. By then, you will have achieved a spontaneous style all your own.

Moving On

Crank up the speakers, because we'll be moving into the sonic area of cartoons and games. Without sound, your projects are...well...silent. Not bad for sleeping, but terrible when it comes to entertainment on a Flash scale.

Chapter 3

Sound

Doing a cartoon or game without sound is difficult. Sound gives a connection to the story or strategy, and is nearly as important as the graphics themselves. To overlook this powerful element of your production—or to not give it importance—is a mistake, indeed.

By Bill Turner

Taking Script to Soundtrack

You have a script with storyboards. You've created characters to act out the script. The next important step is to marry these two elements by choosing the voices and recording the voice track.

Choosing the Voice

Choosing the right voice for your characters can seem like a daunting task. You've surely heard Mel Blanc, the legendary voice behind such characters as Bugs Bunny, Porky Pig, and Daffy Duck. These characters have unmistakable voices. Bugs with his streetwise "What's up, Doc?" attitude, Porky with his painful stutter, and Daffy with his manic "whoooohooos" are icons of cartoon land. Hearing these wonderful voices makes you wonder, "How can I ever achieve this?" Well, you need to start from scratch.

The icons mentioned above didn't start out with such recognizable voices. They earned them over time. If you look back at some of the older cartoons starring Bugs Bunny, you'll find that the voice he had then is not the same as the one he's now famous for—his voice evolved through a growing and maturing process. The more that people see and hear a character, the more they will identify with the voice, no matter whether the character is voiced by professionals or amateurs (see Figure 3.1).

Figure 3.1
When Weber sings (and speaks), he does so with an amateur's voice that's been digitally manipulated. This voice matches him perfectly, but it will mature over time.

What people do notice are the quirks a voice might have. Porky can never be confused with any other character, because his stutter is clear as day, even if the words he says have trouble coming out. Following this thought will be a good idea as you develop your characters—and have some kind of quirk, accent, use of slang, or nasal, breathy, or halting aspect to the voice you use. Over time, and with maturation, the voice will fit the character it's attributed to.

If you have an endless budget, you can choose from any number of top, professional, voice actors for your production. Sometimes, you might get lucky and find top talent at a bargain. If your budget is much tighter (maybe even nonexistent), and you're a small studio, or even an individual doing a cartoon show solo, you'll need more ingenuity to come up with a good voice for your character to speak with.

Doing the voice yourself is not out of the question. Actually, this happens more than you might think. Character creators (artists, not voice pros) working in the Web and broadcast-TV realms have been known to do their own character's voice. Mike Judge, creator of *Beavis and Butthead*, did the voices, as well as the design, for his creation. After all, who would know the character better than its creator? The nice part about doing the voice yourself is that you get a chance to *be* that character—a nice little escape from the usual motions of life.

If you're apprehensive about recording your own voice, you can turn to others for help. Maybe you have a "ham" for a brother or sister, or an aunt or uncle who'd love to be a cartoon character's voice. The main thing you need to find out is whether this person can *act*. Acting is just as important in a voice as it is in live-motion film. If the relative merely reads the script, as opposed to putting feeling into it, you might need to find someone else. A good place to start is your local theatre group, or even the local, high school acting club. Getting someone who has acting skills can be a real plus, and actors from these venues might even do the job for their name in the credits—which makes the price just right. Always make sure to get signed, written permission from whomever you choose to do the voice for your character.

As the character's creator, you will know when the voice is right after you audition various sources. No rule for finding the right voice can be neatly put into writing. You'll want to look for things such as appropriate accent (you wouldn't want a New York City dweller speaking with a southern accent), speed of speech, and even how the character might mispronounce words—all these elements can have an effect on the voice you choose. Then, obviously, you'll need a female to do a female's voice. But don't let yourself become cornered by this gender association. While it's difficult (but not impossible) for a male to do a female character's voice, a female doing a male character's voice is more reasonable. In fact, a female does Bart Simpson's voice. When auditioning voices, try to close your eyes to visually ignore who's doing the voice, and imagine the character in your mind, speaking with the voice you're hearing auditioned.

Recording and Digitizing

Flash cannot actually record sound. You'll need to record or digitize the sound in another application. On the Macintosh, applications such as Peak or Deck are very good for doing the recording or digitizing. If you're using the Macintosh, you can download demos at **www.bias-inc.com**. On the PC, applications such as Sound Forge will do the trick. A PC demo is available at **www.sonicfoundry.com**. In fact, any application that can record through your computer's sound-input hardware will do in a pinch. The higher-end applications give you far more capability to manipulate the sounds once you've captured them. Things such as changing pitch and tempo (or duration) can be extremely helpful as you fine-tune your sounds, particularly on voice tracks (see Figure 3.2).

Figure 3.2
Note how large and detailed the waveform image can be—this dramatically helps the editing process.

Another helpful feature in the sound-editing application you choose is the capability to visually display the waveform for editing purposes. All the high-end applications offer this feature. But, if you're using QuickTime Player Pro, for instance, you can edit sounds, but you can't really see what your doing. You have to do all the editing by ear. That's not impossible, but being exacting in your edits is much more difficult this way.

At times, you might want to edit very small pieces of sound, such as taking out a breath after a word. For this, you'll need a professional application: An editor that lets you zoom in on the sound waveform and select small bits of sound for deletion (or other manipulation) is essential.

Multitrack editors offer you not only the capability to edit precisely, but also the capability to layer the sounds, much like you'd layer graphics in Flash. The

Voice Manipulated with Plug-Ins

An assortment of manipulated voices created with the SFX Machine plug-in is on the CD (in the Plug Samples folder); both WAV and AIF files are included. The file *normal.aif* (or .wav) is how the voice sounded before it was processed through SFX Machine. The other files—cardboardtube, metaltube, phone, and munchkin—are the results. These samples barely scratch the surface of all you can do when you're using the SFX Machine plug-in.

great thing about multitrack capabilities is the freedom you have to move around hunks of sound. This flexibility gives you the tools for tightening the timing. Having precise control over timing is especially helpful for editing voice tracks.

Many sound editors also come with a supply of built-in functions, or they have the capability to use plug-in effects from third-party applications. The usual graphic equalizer, such as the one you might have on your stereo, which shapes the tone of the sound, is a must. Other functions, such as **Normalize**, are quite useful in maintaining volume consistency and avoiding clipping. Of course, plug-ins can also add a great deal of fun when you're manipulating the digital sound. A set of plug-ins called SFX Machine is also available from **www.bias-inc.com** (see Figure 3.3). This set of plug-ins can do all sorts of fun things; such as making the voice track sound as if the character is talking on the phone, or even is stuck in a deep hole or cave. You can accomplish other cool effects with plug-ins that make the voice sound as if it's being sung by aliens or robots (see Figure 3.4).

Keep Voices Separate

Even though multitrack editors are great, when you have more than one character talking, you'll want to avoid exporting the multiple voice tracks as one track. Keeping the tracks separate is important because, once the tracks are imported into Flash, animating to discrete voice tracks is easier. Lip-synching is far easier when you can concentrate on one track at a time.

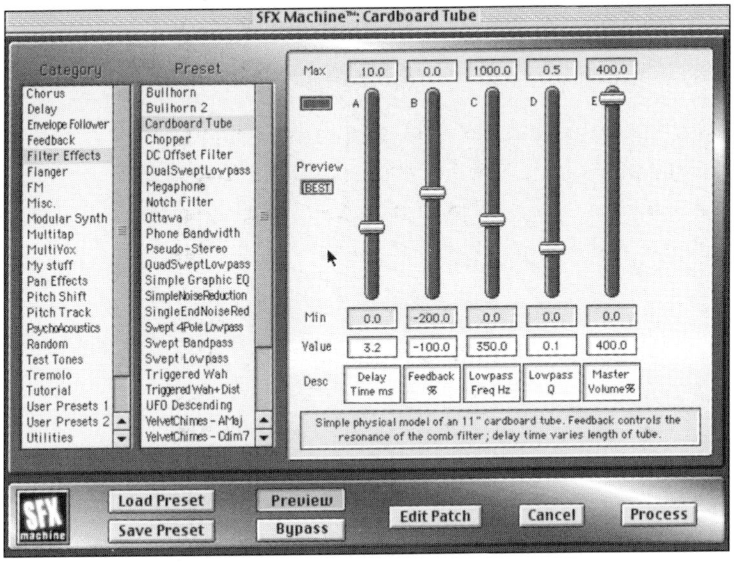

Figure 3.3
Screen shot of SFX Machine, a collection of customizable plug-ins that gives you an endless variety of fun options.

Preferably, you'll want to capture the sound directly into the computer and cut out the middleman of tape. Unfortunately, most computers are a bit noisy, with hard drives and fans spinning away. Consequently, you'll need to make sure your recording computer is in a different room than the microphones where the voice actors will be doing their thing. If this arrangement is not

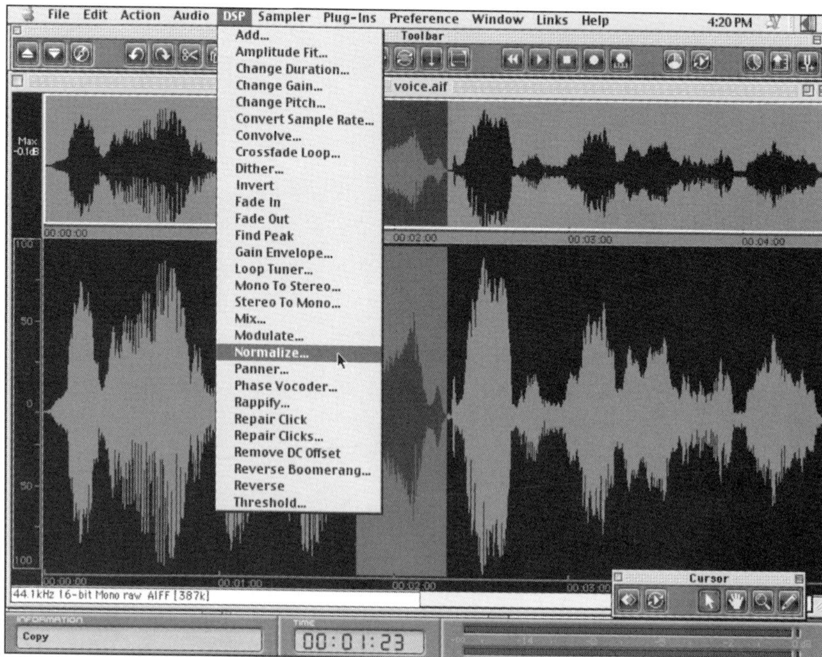

Figure 3.4
In Peak, many sound-manipulation functions are close at hand, and many others are available via plug-ins.

Note: *Clipping* refers to a sound that has gone beyond its allowed volume space. The sound has more volume than the resolution can contain. If you look at a waveform, and the section of higher volume has a flat top and bottom to it, the sound is clipped. This clipping manifests itself in a popping or crackling noise during the high-volume passage. This noise is close to the noise you'd get if you turned the volume of your stereo way up, but, in the analog world of most stereo systems, you'd get a blaring distortion instead of pops.

possible, you'll need noise-canceling microphones. Noise-canceling microphones can range in price from $30 to thousands of dollars. If you're on a tight budget, the microphones that usually come designed for voice recognition work rather well for direct voice input, and their price is usually under $50. We'll suggest that you weight the money you put aside for sound recording toward microphones. A low-quality microphone, even on a high-quality digitizer, might not allow the quality you want. Remember that your voice work will most likely be compressed in Flash using MP3, which can knock quality down considerably. If you start out with a low-quality voice track (because of insufficient microphones), the quality will only get worse with compression, not better.

If you need to record more than one voice actor at a time, look into purchasing a mixing board that will let you pipe all your microphones into one recording input on the computer. These mixers can cost from $70 to many thousands of dollars. Generally speaking, the more inputs (microphones) and control you want over the sound (equalizers, filters, and such), the more you pay. Like anything else, professional, high-end, audio equipment can be quite expensive. A good starting point in your search for quality, professional, audio equipment is B&H Photo and Video & Pro Audio. You can find these vendors at **www.bhphotovideo.com**.

You need to consider the room you do the recording in, as well. Large, cavernous rooms have too much echo, while the audio in tiny closets can sound canned. You can spend a lot of money on this aspect of recording voice tracks, sound effects with noise baffles, and other such acoustic gear. Even though such expenditures might be desirable, setting up a full-blown, professional, audio recording area in your studio might not be feasible. The next best thing is to record in a medium- (living-room) sized room, with the usual furniture and drapes to kill echoes. Also, be sure this room isn't located near an airport, railroad tracks, or high-density freeway, where the undesirable noise created will hinder your recording.

Some little things you need to be concerned with while recording a voice are the everyday sounds. Make sure to turn off the telephone and any pagers—they're sure to ring or beep at the most inopportune times. If you have a dog, or any other kind of animal that's likely to make unexpected loud noises, be sure to have it tended to elsewhere while you're recording. If the person doing the voice is seated at a table, make sure she takes off any jewelry, such as a wrist watch, that could clank unnoticed on the table's surface, or a necklace that might jangle. When you're using a chair that swivels, make sure it's well oiled so it doesn't squeak. These little sounds go largely undetected in life, but they can make an inspired voice performance useless if they intrude during the recording. Even with digital editing, removing that unwanted watchband clanking on the table, or the dog barking in the background, can be difficult. You'll want to nip these problems in the bud, before you do the recording.

Note: For the best quality, always record/digitize your audio at 16-bit, 44.1Khz, and save the file at the same rate. This combination gives you the highest quality possible when you import the file to Flash.

If all this talk about microphones, mixing boards, and soundproof rooms makes you go "Whew, that's more than I want to get into," you might want to use a local sound-recording studio to get your voices onto tape or CD. If you live in a college town, you might have a radio station with a well-equipped studio that you can rent to record your script. If you do go this route, make sure the station can burn the audio onto a standard CD. You can then import these files directly from the audio CD, using the software we discussed previously. This method saves time by bypassing the digitizing process. Save the files out of your sound editor as WAV or AIF files for importing into Flash.

Remote Recording

What do you do when the actor you want to record is thousands of miles away? Fly to that destination? Not necessarily. For the film *The Journal of Edwin Carp*, we were fortunate enough to attract the attention of top British actor Hugh Laurie to do the voice. Hugh Laurie is a film and television celebrity, and his television credits include his own TV shows with Stephen Fry in the U.K. called *A Bit of Fry and Laurie*, *The Black Adder*, and *Jeeves and Wooster*. In film, Hugh Laurie played the father in *Stuart Little*, and he was Jasper in *101 Dalmations*.

We were all set to fly to the U.K. to record Mr. Laurie when we were presented with a much cheaper and easier way, called an ISDN link. We had to book a studio in Los Angeles (The Bakery Post Production Center), and one in London (The Sound Company LTD), and these two studios connected via an ISDN link. Once the studio dialed in the other studio and got a *lock*, we were ready to record the talent. We were then able to sit anywhere within the studio space with a remote, via which, upon clicking, we could talk to the actor and give any necessary directions in real time—simple as that. This approach not only saved a plane flight, but accommodations and time, as well.

Sound Effects

Recording sound effects is an art form all its own called *Foley*. We won't pretend that we could adequately cover here something that could fill it's own book. We would, however, like to give you a hint on creating your own sound effects, and you can go from there. Otherwise, simply buying the professional effects you need from a third party is best. Let's face it: Staging a bomb going off, just so you could record the sound it makes, would be difficult. Professionals are out there who do this stuff for a living and sell it on CDs for you to use.

A really good starting point in your search for pre-recorded sound effects is The Hollywood Edge. You can find this company at **www.hollywoodedge.com**. This Web site houses an astounding number of special-effects sound collections. Of particular interest is a collection called Cartoon Trax. A five-CD set contains just about every cartoon whoop, whistle, boink, and clang you can imagine—a great asset for sonic foolishness.

Many other collections are also available that include things such as spaceships, weather (wind, thunder, etc.), cars, cars wrecking, crowds, motors, and nearly everything else that makes a noise. Having a sizable library of these sounds is a good idea, too. You never know when the need will arise, and it's nice to have them close at hand.

Recording Effects

As we mentioned earlier, while recording voice, you might want noise-canceling microphones, but these microphones can sometimes also cancel the subtle sounds that you'll want to have when you're recording sound effects. A good shotgun microphone can cover many sound-effect recording situations. A shotgun microphone is physically shaped like a shotgun barrel and has a narrow width of pick-up. Therefore, you can aim this microphone at the sound's source, which is helpful when you're recording the various objects you'll use to make sound effects. A good shotgun microphone can be a bit pricey. You can find one for as little as $75 (usually in electronics stores with the video camera equipment), with $500 to $1,000 being reasonable for a decent, professional, shotgun microphone.

Even if you have a good-sized library of sound effects, the need will arise for a sound you simply can't buy. For instance, we worked on an animation in which we needed a plastic mustard bottle to hit a tile kitchen floor—pretty straightforward: We simply recorded the actual thing happening. We set up a shotgun microphone with a long cord plugged straight into the computer's sound-in port, raided the "fridge" of mustard, and proceeded to drop the container on the floor in various ways. After we did this several times, we'd play back the sound we'd captured. We found we liked the version that included more bounces after the initial hit; it worked perfectly. This sound would have been a hard item to find in pre-recorded effects.

The kind of sounds you'll need the most are the everyday things, many of which you can create rather easily—things such as keys hitting a table, a coin dropping on the floor, and the like. Once you have a good microphone, the process is a simple matter of ingenuity, and filling the holes in your sound effects library as you need them.

Stereo Walk

Once you have your sounds, you're ready to use them in Flash. In this short project, we'll have the sound of the character's footsteps follow him across the screen. We've supplied you with all the elements you'll need for this project in the *stereosteps.fla* file (see Figure 3.5). You will need to have stereo speakers on your computer to realize the effect.

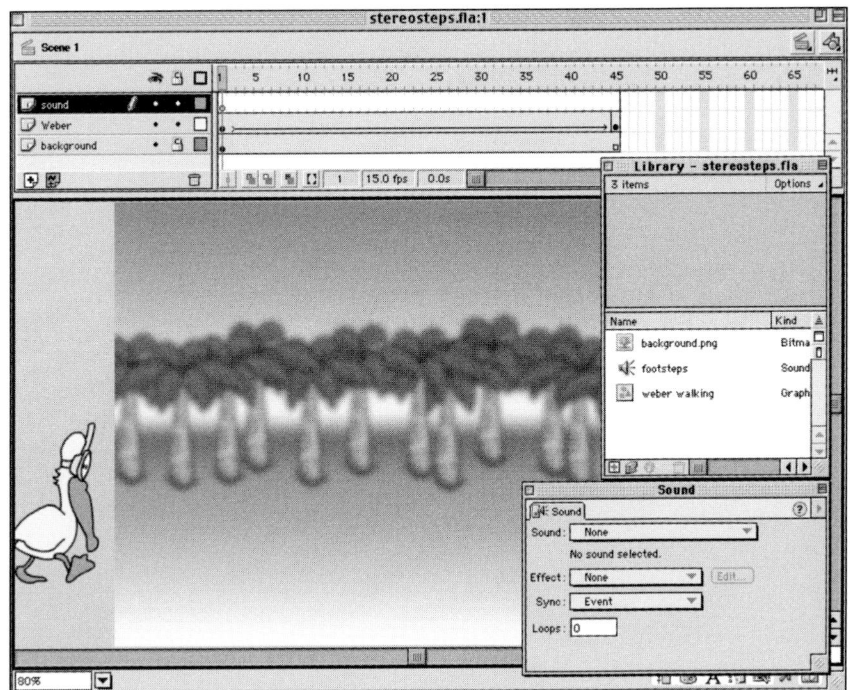

Figure 3.5
This project file will have the sound effect follow the character. The panels you'll need are shown here, as well.

1. Open the *stereosteps.fla* file and situate the window to show all layers in the Timeline.
2. Select the first frame in the **sound** layer.
3. Using the Sound panel pop-up window (it says NONE), select the footsteps sound.
4. Next to Effects, select Fade Left to Right from the pop-up window.
5. Next to Loops, type in the number **3** (see Figure 3.6).

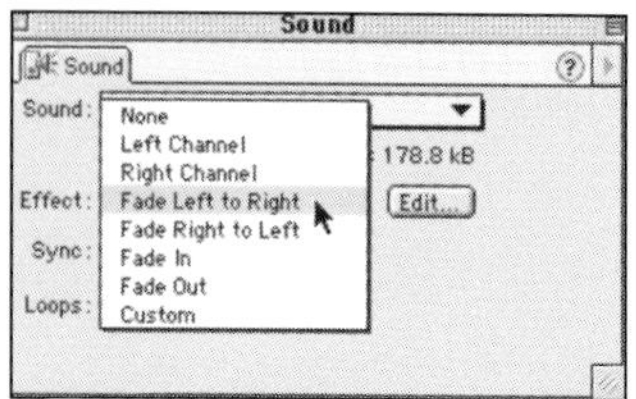

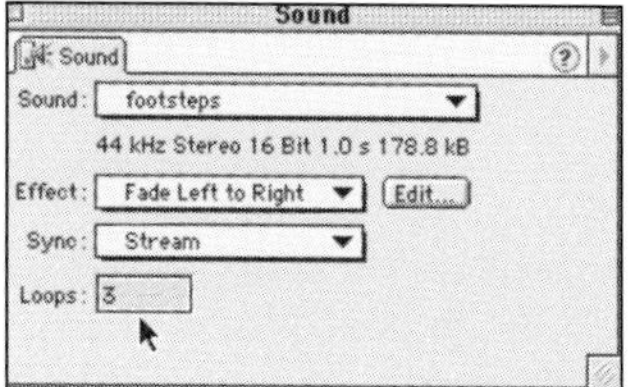

Figure 3.6
The Sound panel setup for this project.

6. Now, play back the animation. You'll notice that the effect happens, but not through the complete length of the animation. This limited play is because the automatic effect you did in Step 4 doesn't extend across the looping part of the soundtrack.

7. With the keyframe where the sound starts selected, click the Edit button in the Sound panel.

8. You'll be presented with the basic Flash sound editor (see Figure 3.7). The fade is occurring only across the first instance of the footsteps sound. Simply drag the little square where fade ends to encompass the grayed-out looping sections, as Figure 3.8 shows.

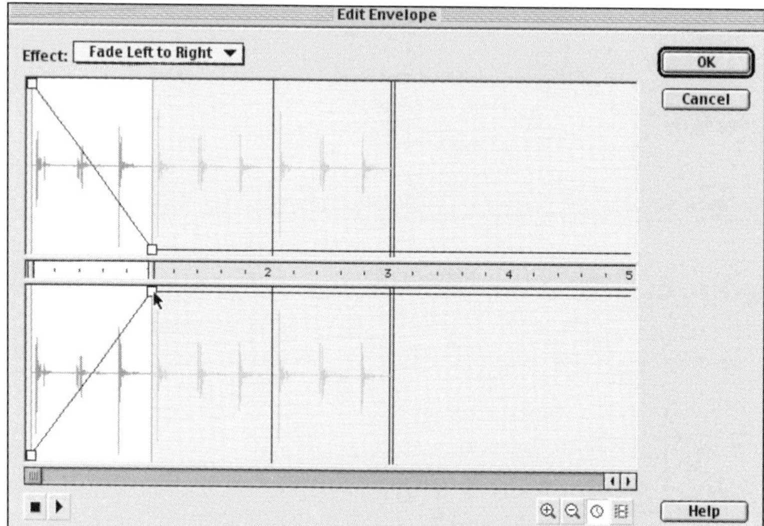

Figure 3.7
Here, we see the basic Flash sound editor showing the automatic Fade Left to Right effect.

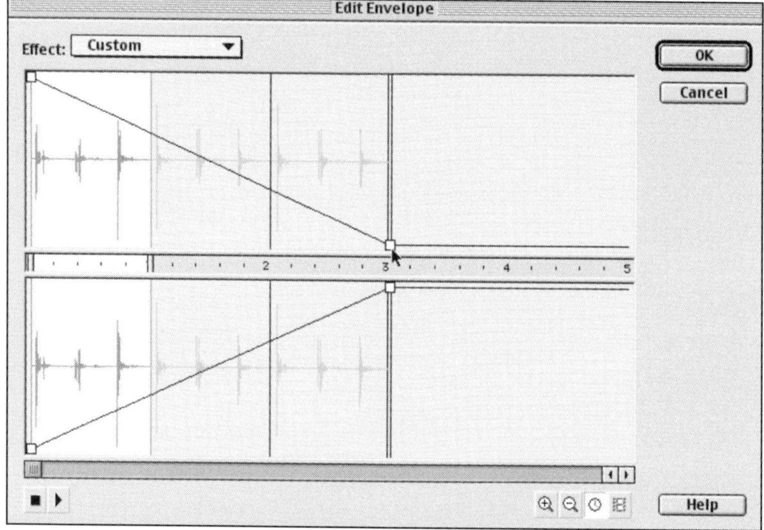

Figure 3.8
Here, the Flash sound editor is showing the fade after we've customized it across the looping sections.

9. Export the movie to SWF format. Be sure to uncheck Convert Stereo To Mono in the MP3 settings in the Publish Settings dialog box (see Figure 3.9). You should now have a character whose footsteps' sound follows him across the screen.

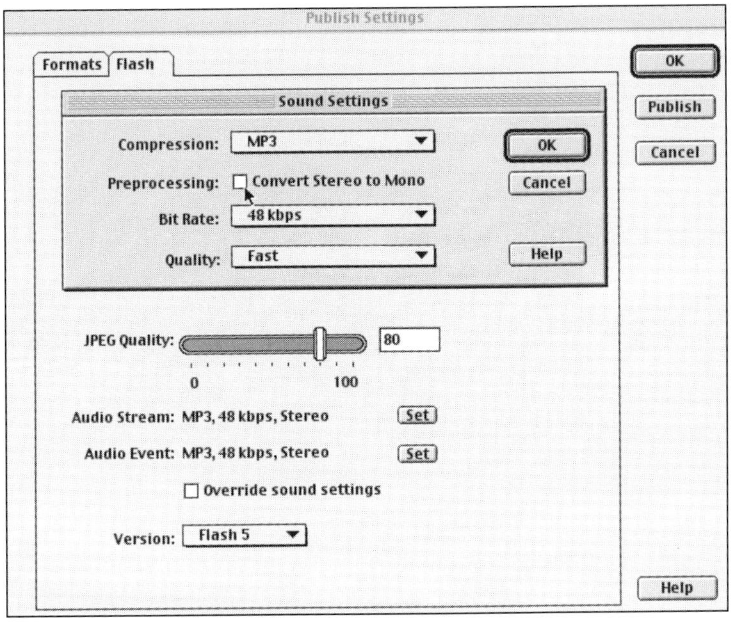

Figure 3.9
MP3 Publish settings.

Even though this project might seem rather simple, it does show some of the sound effects you *can* create in Flash. You can also use Flash to balance a character speaking on the left side of the screen to the left side of the audio, and so on. Little touches such as these can add a significant audio dimension to your cartoons and games.

Music

Music can be an important consideration in cartoon and game production. We're all somewhat aware of what music can bring to the table. What we may not know is how to get it there, legally. We will start right off with saying *never* use copyrighted music, unless you have written permission from the copyright's owner. Acquiring such permission usually means going through a labyrinth of rights issues. If you want to use that new hit tune in your cartoon or game, it will cost you plenty. If you don't properly acquire the rights, and you use the music anyway, be prepared for a letter from the artist's attorney. We said it before, but it bears repeating here: Just because something's on the Web, that doesn't make it free for the grabbing—and that goes for copyrighted MP3s as well. Think of it this way: Would you want a music group taking your animation masterpiece and using it publicly without your permission? Didn't think so.

So, where does a small studio get cool tunes? A number of companies offer what's known as royalty-free music collections. Usually, these collections won't contain any top-ten hits, but the music is professionally done, and nearly every genre you can imagine—from Hip Hop to Bach—is offered.

If royalty-free music doesn't rock your world, consider hiring a local band you like. Lots of great music goes largely unnoticed in the clubs and garages of the land. These artists will generally go for the chance of exposure in that cool, new cartoon or game you're creating. Make sure to give these artists ample credit.

Smart Sound

Smart Sound is a cross-platform, music-creation application that uses professionally mastered clips of music that you can edit and customize to taste. When you need to have a music clip that lasts only 1 minute and 32.5 seconds, simply use Smart Sound and create it yourself.

Smart Sound is a wonderful application that anyone can use. No musical background skills are needed to create compelling music beds and loops for your production. The CD includes a save-disabled demo for both Macintosh and PC that'll give you a chance to hear just how useful Smart Sound is (see Figure 3.10). (The Smart Sound demo will not let you save or export your work. We've received permission to export the material only for you to hear how well its output works with Flash.)

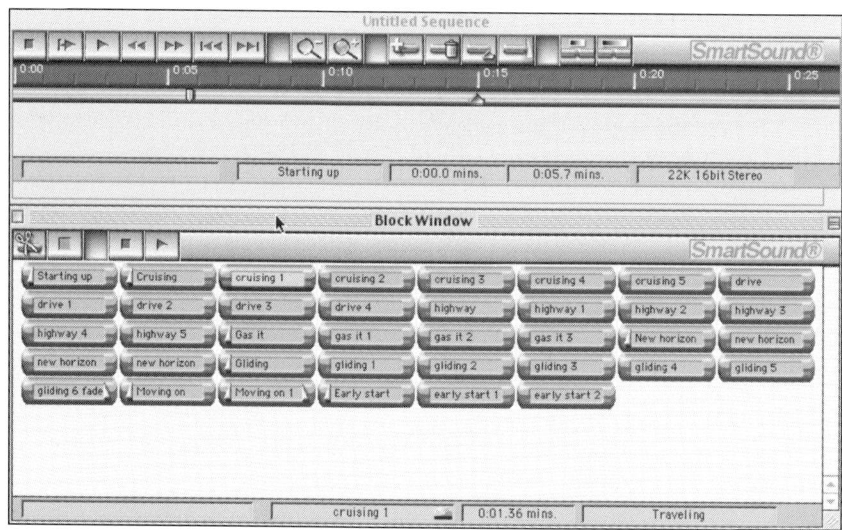

Figure 3.10
Here's a screen shot of the Smart Sound music-creation application. Notice the Block window filled with blocks of music.

You open a library (or libraries) of sounds in the Block window, as Figure 3.10 shows. You can then audition the various blocks of music by simply double-clicking them in the Block window. You'll notice, too, that each block has a short, text description that'll give you some idea for matching musical styles. Once you select a block, the time of that block's duration appears in the information bar across the bottom of the Block window. For example, if time is stated as 00:02.15, this translates to 2.15 seconds. You can also change the preferences for this readout to be in time code. So, a reading of 00:02:15 would mean 2 seconds, and 15 frames at 30 frames per second.

The Sequencer window (upper) is where you actually compose the music. This window has controls for zooming in and out, and various playback controls, such as you might have on a tape deck. Controls are also available for smoothing, quick loop, and quick end. The rulers indicate the time with a little yellow pointer that acts as the playback head, to let you know where you are in the music while it's playing. The information bar across the bottom of this window has readouts for various tool-tip-type information, the length of the work in progress, and the quality of the sound files (16-bit, 22Khz, etc.) (see Figure 3.11).

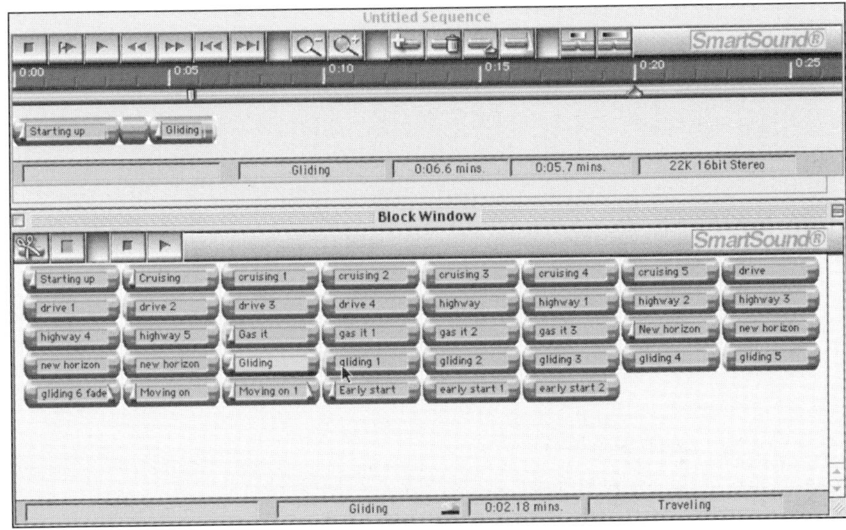

Figure 3.11
Here, you see the composing process in Smart Sound.

Using Smart Sound couldn't be any easier. You simply select a block of music from the Block window and drag the music block to where you want it in the sequencer window, as you see in Figure 3.11. Once you've dragged in a block, you'll notice little green ends light up on other blocks still in the Block window. This lighting is a hint that these sections of music will best match the last one in the Sequencer window. This feature is the greatest part of the application—you simply can't mess things up if you follow these guides. But you're a renegade. You don't want to follow the green hints. Okay, fine. When you come up against the dreaded, red lights on the ends of the music blocks (these indicate a mismatch), you can apply the smoothing function (see Figure 3.12). By using the smoothing function, Smart Sound performs a cross-dissolve between two selected blocks of music in the Sequencer window. If the music is in the same genre, beat, and so on, the smoothing will give pretty good results. Of course, if you try to squeeze a passage of classical music into the middle of a heavy-metal thrash, no amount of smoothing is going to make it right. But, then, what's crazy to one person is poetry to another. So, go ahead and experiment; you can't hurt anything.

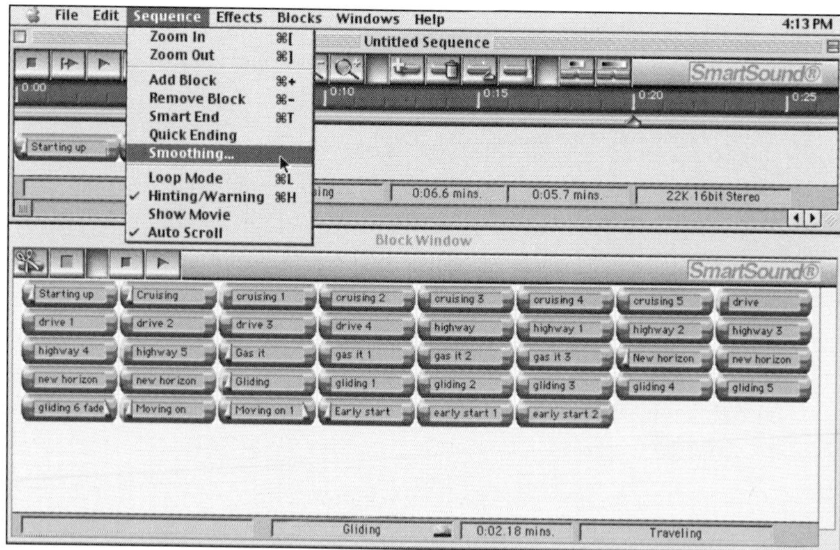

Figure 3.12
Using Smart Sound you can smooth out the transition between different musical sections.

Another really cool feature is Smart Sound's ability to create automatically seamless loops. Seamless loops are particularly useful in Flash games in which you want to keep file size small, but you have some background—or even various selections of background—music for the player to choose from. In the Sequencer window, drag the time pointer (the little, silver arrow that points toward the time ruler) to the desired length. Empty the Sequencer window of any music blocks. Click the magic Smart Loop button in the Sequencer window (the button just right of the trash can). From the available blocks open in the Block window, Smart Sound then calculates, the best it can, a seamless loop of music that fits the time space.

A set of effects filters is also available that you can apply to the music blocks. These filters do not alter the original effect in any way (you can undo the filter at any time), so you can experiment all you want. To use an effect filter, simply select the blocks you want to apply it to in the Sequencer window, and apply the filter from the Effects pull-down menu. You can do all sorts of crazy stuff, such as Glassify and Cosmic Mayhem. If you're a bit of a musician, you can import your own, homemade, musical clips into Smart Sound as well. As a matter of fact, you can import any kind of sound you want and turn it into neat little libraries of blocks for use in Smart Sound.

Although the demo comes with a limited assortment of music blocks at the lower quality of 22Khz, many collections of Smart Sound music are available on CD (higher quality, 44Khz is available in all libraries you buy). As of this writing, more than 22 CD volumes packed full of music blocks are available, and new ones are being added all the time—enough to build a library of sonic possibilities that'll keep you busy for a long, long time. The real beauty of Smart Sound lies in the capability to customize the music endlessly. Two people using the same CD of music blocks will come up with completely different music. If you need music in your Flash production, and you don't have studio musicians on hand, Smart Sound could be the answer you've been looking for.

> **Note:** The Smart Sound demo will not let you save or export your work. We've received permission to export one for you to hear how well its output works with Flash. Of course, if you buy the application, you can export all you want.

PROJECT Music Loop in Flash

As we explained earlier, we've created an automatically generated Smart loop of music. We've also supplied the loop as a WAV and AIF file in the project folder. And we've also used the previous stereo-steps project and extended its time to accommodate the looping music.

1. Open the file named *musicloop.fla* supplied on the CD.
2. Import the *SmartSoundmaximumaction.aif* file (or the *SmartSoundmaximumaction.wav* file if you're using a PC).
3. Select the first frame in the layer named **music**.
4. Using the Sound panel, choose the file you just imported from the sound pop-up window.
5. Set the Synch to Streaming.
6. Set Loop to **2**. Of course, if the animation were of a longer duration, you could set this value accordingly higher.
7. Publish, or export, the movie as usual.

Even though this is a small project, we hope that you'll take from it the fact that background music is a great thing, but the large SWF files music can make are not. By using Smart Sound, or any application that can create seamless loops of music, you can give your audience a richer experience, without an arduous download time. Notice, too, that the footsteps stereo sound effect is repeated over and over. Repeating a sound takes little to no more file size than the original sequence requires before you duplicate (repeat) it.

Sound is a complicated and deep subject—it's a profession all its own. We hope you get from this chapter an appreciation for using good sound in your Flash cartoon or game. We've barely scratched the surface on the subject. Many magazines, books, and Web sites are devoted to sound. If you'd like to pursue this subject further, here are some links for you: Film Sound Design, located at **http://filmsound.studienet.org**, has a wealth of links and a glossary of terminology. You can find anything you'd want to know about sound theory here. In addition, **www.campanellaacoustics.com/faq.htm** contains more information about sound than most people will ever need—the real nuts and bolts of the science of sound.

Moving On

Now that you have the script, characters, voices, and sound effects, you're ready to give them a place to live. We'll look into backgrounds, foregrounds, and camera moves next.

Chapter 4

Background Scenery

At this point, you have story, characters, and sound. Now, the characters need a place to live and play. This chapter addresses considerations for creating backgrounds for your animations and games.

By Bill Turner and
Richard Bazley

What Goes into Creating a Background?

After you've developed your story and your characters, you need a background for them—a place for your characters to inhabit and your story to play out. This much is obvious, perhaps—but your background can be more than a scenic backdrop. When used properly, the background can be significant in the telling of your story. The background can set the mood and atmosphere for a cartoon, it can help convey emotion, it can quickly convey information, and it can help draw viewers' attention to what's important in a scene.

In this chapter, we'll examine ways to do these things. Then, we'll look at some ways to plan for character movement: You can use various camera techniques, and you can use layers to produce the illusion of depth as a character moves in a scene. Let's start by looking at some of the choices you'll need to make and some of the conventions or devices at your disposal.

Design Considerations

Like characters, backgrounds present many design choices. The decisions you make will give the overall feel to your cartoon or game. Backgrounds can run the gamut, from actual photography and ultra-realistic painting, to simple childlike scribbling. But you should always design backgrounds to support the story or theme of your project.

What sorts of things do you need to consider when you're creating your background scenery? Many of the same things you had to consider when you created your characters (see Chapter 2); for instance:

- *What kind of style do you want to use: realism or exaggeration? Simplicity or complexity?* What style matches the style you've developed for your characters? How much movement will there be within or between background scenes? What is your target output, and are you designing for full animation or for limited animation? Answering these questions will help you determine the *level of detail* you'll want.
- *What kinds of collective experience, or common knowledge, can you draw on?*
- *What kind of mood do you want to convey, and how can you use color and lighting to do so?*

Choosing a Style

Most likely, you'll want the visual style of your background to match the visual style of your characters. (Unless you intended to create a jarring effect, you wouldn't, say, place stick figures within photo-realistic backgrounds.) In

The Aristocats, for example, the scratchy-line style followed through from the characters to the backgrounds. In fact, the backgrounds were a composite of a line drawing photocopied onto cels with a painted underlay. Sometimes, these layers would be slightly offset so the painting did not exactly match up to the line work, and this offset created an effective style.

Another style of background art contains what's known as "pools of light." In this style, you bathe the character in light by designing the background in such a way that the character stands out, keeping the busy elements away from the area in which the character will perform. This style lets the audience locate the character easily and ensures that the audience is paying attention to the character, not to the background.

Disney's *Bambi* movie is an example of a style that gives the illusion of detail. The movie has enough detail to suggest a realistic setting, but not so much that it's mistaken for photography. The background painters *suggested* foliage and trees, as opposed to painting every leaf and twig. In fact, the painters were so masterful at this style that, if you observe the backgrounds (which seem incredibly detailed) firsthand, you'll find that they're surprisingly loose. The painters could suggest detail without painting it all in.

Style Examples from the Authors

As many different styles exist as artists painting or drawing them. In Figure 4.1, we see Bazley's approach to the background. His approach creates backgrounds with a lively and energetic collection of loose lines. The objects simply take on the solid, single color of the background. When attention to a certain object is needed, he colors that object differently, while the rest of the objects remain in the overall background color.

Figure 4.1
A scene from *Edwin Carp*. Notice that only the opening to the attic departs from the background coloring.

Turner, on the other end of the design spectrum, approaches the background with a highly airbrushed look, as you can see in Figure 4.2. To achieve the airbrushed look, you will need to leave Flash and use a bitmap (or raster art) editor, such as Photoshop, and import your art into Flash. Vector art doesn't lend itself well to this sort of airbrushed background.

Figure 4.2
The surfing scene from the *Weber Human Blues* cartoon (included on the CD) is animated with a series of airbrushed paintings created in Photoshop.

Using a Change in Style to Convey Strong Emotion

You can use a radical change in background style to emphasize a scene's emotion—for example, by jumping from a realistic backdrop to an abstract one. In Figures 4.3 and Figure 4.4, you find a character bumbling and reaching for a retort to a challenge. The background (along with the camera angle) changes from one of reality to one of abstract confusion. This change helps to drive home what's going on in the character's mind as he reaches desperately for a thought.

Choosing a Level of Detail

A background for an animated cartoon can be very different from a painting you'd hang on a wall. If people are looking at a painting on the wall, they have as much time as they want to enjoy the detail and craftsmanship. With animated cartoons, though, a background might be on the screen for only a few seconds. So, before you spend weeks on a background, ask yourself, is it worth doing an elaborate painting for the short amount of screen time the shot has? Most of the time, the audience will be focused on looking at the characters. We're not saying background is inconsequential—it does matter—we just want you to consider when to use lots of detail and when to scale back. Let's start with when to scale back.

Figure 4.3
Here, Weber the pelican issues a challenge to the character seated on the dock.

Figure 4.4
Cut to the bumbling retort. The character (Mr. Murky) reaches painfully for what to say. Mr. Murky's character is one of a babbling fool. This background of confusion helps to convey that personality.

Focusing on Characters by Using Less Detail

After you have firmly established the location (we'll get to that shortly), you can use less detailed versions of your environments when characters are performing during a cartoon. Scaling back on detail helps viewers focus on the characters' performance, rather than on buildings or other background elements.

You might even use a *focus pull* to bring further attention to the characters. *Focus pull* is the technique of leading viewers to focus on the object you want them to look at. You do this by adjusting all other distant and close-up objects so that they're out of focus, thus bringing attention to the object (or character) that is in focus. If you're familiar with photography, you'll recognize this technique as that of using a large f-stop and thereby producing a short depth of field.

If your character needs extreme focus, a solid (no art) background might be helpful, such as in Figure 4.5, where a character from *Edwin Carp* shrieks in fear. The background cannot misguide your attention because all eyes are on the character. You want your backgrounds to connect with the characters to enable them to perform. You don't want the backgrounds to overwhelm the characters.

Figure 4.5
Edwin Carp's mother, as she is horrified at the coming action. Because the background is simply a solid color, it offers no distractions, and the character receives the viewer's full attention.

Using Detail to Establish Location

When you're using a background for the establishing shot (with no characters in view yet), you'll want the background to be more detailed. For example, let's say you'd like to establish a large city, such as New York or London, as the setting for your story. You'd then want a rather nice, recognizable rendition of the Statue of Liberty, the Empire State building, or Big Ben. Beyond adding to the detail of a scene, these commonly known landmarks will help the viewers instantly realize where they are.

Using the background to convey information, such as location, can go a long way in explaining things, which saves lots of dialog time. Imagine your character on a solid color background, explaining that he's in the midst of a busy city street—this would take some doing and would still be less than convincing.

Using Common Knowledge to Convey Information

As we just mentioned, one of the ways you get the most out of the detail you add is to take advantage of commonly known objects, landmarks, or landscapes to convey information quickly. For instance, pelicans often live in the tropics, always near water. In the Weber cartoon, we use a simple dock that will usually have a spectacular sunset going on behind it (see Figure 4.6). These types of colorful sky views (as you can seen in the third figure that appears in the "Color Studio" section of the book) are associated with the tropics. Even if you've never been there, you've probably seen postcards, movies, and other media forms that use a wonderfully delicious sky when they show the tropics. Making use of this preconceived notion in the viewers' minds makes it easy to convince them, in a glance, where they are.

Figure 4.6
The Weber character in the serene dock setting with a sunset.

Consider the dock you see in Figure 4.6. Many people have seen a dock made of wooden planks. If we were to make the dock a solid slab of concrete (as some docks actually are), it would lose the appeal and instant recognition. A slab of concrete is much easier to draw, but it doesn't have the effect we want. The reason we bring up such a comparison is to show that if you feel you're cheating by drawing something simple, as opposed to what's right for a scene, you probably are. By cheating here, you'd miss that important instant communication necessary to help move the story forward. (Certainly, if the dock were to zip by in an instant on screen with little importance to the story, you'd be allowed to scrimp by with whatever works as the blur of a dock.)

Using Detail When It's Central to the Story

Another time to use detail in your backgrounds is when those backgrounds are central to your story. Let's look at our dock example again. We took time to make the dock scene appealing because its use is central to Weber's story. Docks on the water are generally serene places where people go to reflect on life and relax. Pelicans like to hang out on docks, too. This setting makes for the perfect meeting spot, where human ideas meet with Weber's commentary on the human condition.

Of course, you may not be creating a cartoon about docks and pelicans, as we have been. But the ingredients, though different, should follow the same philosophy—use the necessary detail to depict something essential to the story or the characters. For instance, the cartoon strip, *Andy Capp*, nearly always took place at a bar. This environment lent itself well to the grown-up humor that the strip is famous for. If we weren't at the bar with Andy, we were viewing him in the next-best place: sleeping on the couch. This scene paved the way for his wife to complain about his uselessness.

Using the environment as a device solidifies the basis for story and humor in the viewer's mind. Using the environment in a reoccurring and interweaving way with the story will make telling that story easier. You will have established a theme.

Conveying Mood with Color

Do not underestimate the power of color. Color can stir emotions. If you sit in a room painted blue, you will feel tranquil. Blue is generally perceived as cooling and calming to the nerves, and it tends to put one in a peaceful state of mind. Red will have a very different effect. Red's most obvious association is with blood. Red screams. Red warns and grabs serious attention. Yellow and gold, maize and daffodil—all have a sunshine quality that is bright and cheerful, and that can make you feel happy and energized. Each color has its own associations, and you might be making certain color choices intuitively without having analyzed why.

Most artists have an instinctive eye for the use of color. If you want help, however, you can use certain tools, such as a color wheel, which you can purchase from an art store. The color wheel will indicate which colors are complementary to each other. For example, blue-violet is complementary to yellow-orange. In the "Color Studio" section of this book, many examples of color are at play. In the "Color Studio" section there is a frame from *Edwin Carp*, where the attic is blue-violet, and the room below glows with a complementary yellow. Many people have complimented the nice background in this figure; some of them are probably enjoying the relationship of colors, perhaps without knowing exactly why.

Conveying Mood with Lighting

An obvious application of lighting is to designate day or night. We're all familiar with the cartoon scenes where all that's visible are several glowing sets of eyeballs on a solid black background. No doubt about it, it's *dark*. This technique is a useful and easy-to-animate device that's been around for years. The ease with which we can animate this type of scene is the reason it sticks around—it's particularly useful when your characters are shut inside a box, a cave, or a closet, as in Figure 4.7.

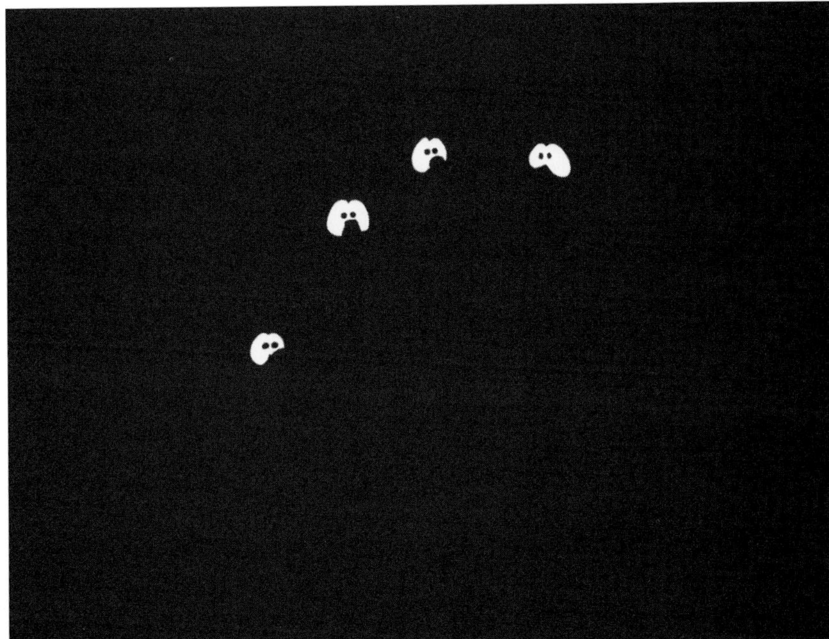

Figure 4.7
A much-used gimmick in cartooning...yep, it's really dark out.

But when there's light (which is most of the time), you'll need to think about what kind of light you want. Enter the subject of mood. On those occasions where it's needed, special lighting adds a great deal to the drama, depth, and even humor of the situation. But how on earth do you draw light? Answer: with shadows.

Creating Shadows

Without shadows, there's no such thing as light, and without light, no such thing as shadows. Light gives objects depth, but we do not *see* light—we see only the values it creates. When you see light rays, such as the ones that beam through a window in a smoky room, you're really seeing billions (quadrillions?) of tiny particles of substance (smoke) graduating from a fully lit, high value of that substance's color to an obscured, unlit, low value. The light rays will always have a soft edge. The *chaos*, or *fall-off*, from the light ray as it bounces around the particles causes the soft-edged look.

Luckily, you can easily add shadows when you're creating backgrounds in Flash. You can add the shadowy part of the scene with a layer, on which you can paint with black, set to various levels of transparency. Wherever you paint, the level of black influences the value of the colors beneath it. By adjusting the percentage of transparency in your brush color, you achieve a darker or lighter shadow cast underneath.

PROJECT Shadow Creation Exercise

1. Open the file named *shadows.fla*, supplied on the CD. This is the same file we used to create Figures 4.7 through 4.9, but this file lacks the **shadows**, which you'll be creating next.
2. Create a new layer just above the **background** layer. If the new layer is not where you want it in the stack, simply drag on the layer name, and place the layer where you want it.
3. Make a keyframe on Frame 3. Your **shadows** will start here. You might want to hide the lighting layer (which is mostly just black), because it will interfere with being able to see the painting you'll do next.
4. Select the brush tool and an appropriate size of tip.
5. Create a color swatch of black with "alpha" ("transparency") set to 40 percent. This setting creates a paint that will really just lower the value of the colors on the layer beneath it. Set the brush to this color if it's not already set that way.
6. Go about the task of painting roughly the shapes of the character casting the shadows. Keep in mind the direction of the light source—shadows move away from light sources.
7. You can now reveal the **lighting** layer you hid earlier, and you should have something similar to Figure 4.9 when the playback head is on Frame 5.

Note: When you're painting in Flash with a transparent color on the lowest level (nongrouped objects), the transparent color will simply replace the color you are painting on. This setting will not give you the shadow effect you're after. If you paint within a group, or on a layer above the image you want to shadow, your painting *will* affect the group or image, as a shadow should.

As a matter of economy, animated cartoon characters rarely have shadows on them. Painting the characters (many, many times) with that level of detail is simply too time-consuming. But the backgrounds are a different story since they generally only need to be drawn once. Keep in mind that the surface the character walks on is part of the background and is a sure lighting cue. So the background is an important consideration when you need to express a lighting mood.

Using Lighting for Humor or Storytelling

Let's go back to our group stuck in blackness (see Figure 4.7). Out of necessity, one of the characters lights a match, as you see in Figure 4.8. The environment shifts

Figure 4.8

One of the characters illuminates the darkness by lighting a match. The characters do not change, but a different mood emerges.

from one of total darkness to that of minimal light. The characters will now cast shadows on their environment, cueing the audience to that environment.

Figure 4.8 shows part of the environment—but not all of it. To see the rest, look at Figure 4.9. Now, you can see the whole environment and the full extent of the characters' problem: Too bad they are inside a shed filled with gasoline containers. We've used this particular twist in Figure 4.9 to expose the capability to use humor and drama via the background. Remember our discussion (in

Figure 4.9

The characters, still unchanged, now reveal their full predicament. Notice the shadows cast away from them because the match is the point source of light.

Chapter 1) about using the element of surprise. We're using that element here, but with the background (not the characters) being the key ingredient.

Of course, this example is a rather dramatic use of lighting to tell the story. Other uses, although subtler, are not insignificant, and should be well thought out, to put together a cohesive flow. Lighting effects—from bright afternoon sunshine, in which shadows are distinct and hard edged, to a dreary overcast day, in which shadows are soft and nearly nonexistent—can be of great use in setting the mood.

Understanding light will give you the tools to create moods. Painters, sculptors, and photographers have known and used the play of light and shadow for years. Why shouldn't cartoon animators? Sure, effective use of light takes more time, but for certain scenes, it will make a huge difference.

Planning for Movement: Camera Techniques

Note: The Internet Movie Database Web site is a great resource for learning about various terms the movie and animation industry use. This site has a detailed glossary, which you can find at **www.us.imdb.com/Glossary/**.

When you're designing a background for a particular shot in your cartoon, you should first consider whether the character might be moving around in this environment. If so, you'll want to create a background that's larger (possibly much larger) than the actual view the camera will have. In Flash, the area designated as the "stage," or work area, we will refer to here as the *camera's view*. Why? Because calling the stage a "camera view" elicits a different mindset—a camera can move, but a stage does not.

Actually, the camera view in Flash cannot really move, but all the art within it can. By using *motion tweening*, and by compartmentalizing your scene—which can animate within itself—via graphic symbols, you can pan, dolly, and zoom in and out at will.

A few basic definitions are in order before we continue. Briefly, a *zoom* is probably the most common camera move. To *zoom in* is to use the camera lens to move the view closer to the target object, magnifying the view of the object while the camera remains stationary; to *zoom out* is to use the lens to move the view further away from the target object, reducing the view of the object while the camera remains stationary. These actions are much like those you've made with any video camcorder. A *pan* is a move in which the view moves in a vertical, horizontal, and even diagonal manner through the camera's view. A *dolly* is cousin to the pan, with the difference being that, with a dolly, the camera's view follows an object or character as the background pans behind (or in front) of it. The camera itself is actually moving in a dolly, whereas, in a pan, the camera generally remains stationary at a particular location, with the lens doing the vertical, horizontal, or diagonal movement. In a *dolly in and out*, the camera actually moves in or out among the objects themselves, as opposed to a zoom, in which the camera remains stationary, and the lens magnifies or reduces.

Zooming

Zooming in Flash is a rather simple process. By using a larger-than-viewable art base or animated symbol, and motion-tweening it with scaling up (for zoom in) or scaling down (zoom out), you can create a rather effective illusion of zooming. Keep in mind that, while zooming, you should use the "Ease In" and "Ease Out" functions inside the Frame panel. The Ease function shows up after you set a keyframe to "Motion Tween" in the Frame panel. A slider lets you add easing in or out by sliding it (down for easing in, up for easing out) to the percentage you want. The higher the percentage, the more pronounced the effect. Easing out of a zoom eliminates that jarring stop at the end of the zoom (see Figure 4.10). Easing in to a zoom causes the beginning of the zoom to be more fluid.

Figure 4.10
Here, we see the first frame of zooming out in the hillbilly limousine scene of the *Human Blues* cartoon included on the CD *weberblues.swf*. The shot clearly shows viewers that the driver is busy reading and chatting on a cell phone while he's driving.

Because you can apply the Easing option only to the frame that initiates the tween, you will need to insert an intermediate keyframe. Obtaining fine control over easing can be a bit tricky. One way to do so—not only for zooming, but also for any other move that uses tweening keyframes—is to first set up your beginning and ending frames for motion tweening. Then, at about the halfway point in the tween, insert another keyframe. Now, apply the **ease in** on the first key and the **ease out** on the second (inserted) key. This combination will cause the first frame to start out moving slowly (ease in) and attain full speed by the time it reaches the middle keyframe. This middle key will inform the object to slow down just before it reaches the final destination key. Putting easing on the final destination key does nothing (see Figure 4.11).

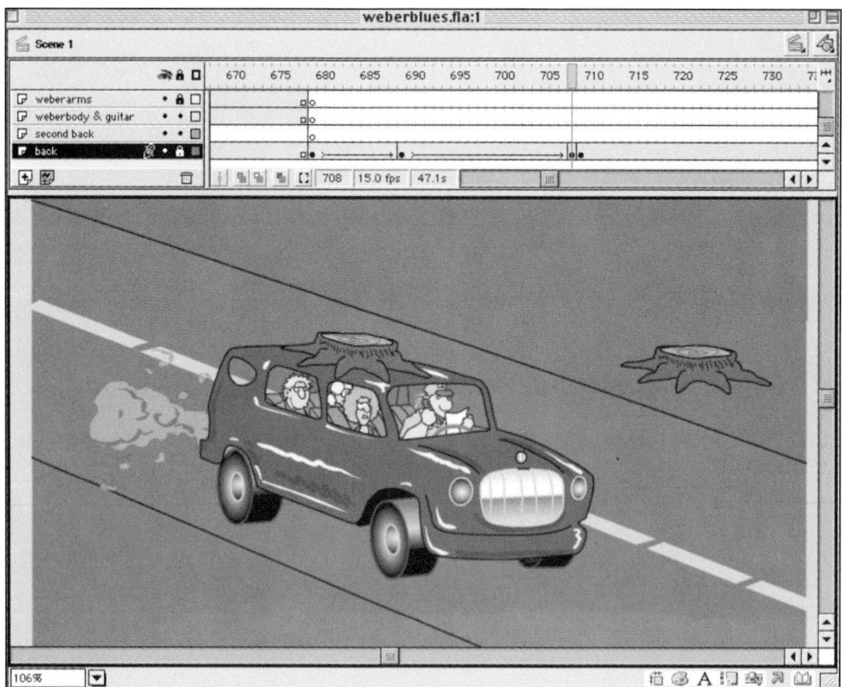

Figure 4.11
Here, we see the final, zoomed-out view of the same scene you see in Figure 4.10. As this zoom out occurs, a diagonal dolly becomes evident.

Zooming Out with Easing

1. Open the file named *zoom.fla,* included on the CD. This is the same graphic we used to create Figures 4.10 and 4.11.
2. You need only one layer (the animation is a large, self-contained symbol of other animations). Create a span of 50 frames by selecting frame 50 and hitting F5.
3. Select the keyframe on Frame 1 (the only keyframe at this point). Set this frame to "Motion Tween" via the Frame panel pop-up. The default is to scale (has "X" in its box).
4. Drag the playback head to the last frame (50), and insert a new keyframe (F6).
5. While you're at this keyframe (50), select the symbol on the art area and apply scale to 70 percent via the Transform panel, making sure you've checked the Constrain box ("Constrain" forces the object to scale equally in both width and height). You also might have to move the symbol to center the truck in the visible camera area. Setting the View>|Work Area to unchecked and View|Magnify|Show Frame is helpful. These settings prevent viewing any art that is outside the view area.
6. Drag the playback head, or hit **Enter** to play the zoom.

7. Insert a new keyframe at Frame 25.
8. Now, we'll add the easing in and out. Select the key on Frame 1. In the Frame panel, click on the pop-up slider next to the word "Easing" and slide the slider down (ease in) to 100 percent.
9. Select the key on Frame 25 and repeat Step 8 but, this time, slide the "Easing" control up (ease out) to 100 percent.
10. Playback the animation. You might want to export an SWF (Shockwave Flash) file at this time, because this Timeline might not play smoothly on slower machines in the authoring environment.

In case you get lost anywhere in this project, the finished project is provided on the CD-ROM, file name *zoom2.fla*.

Variations on the above technique exist. If you want, you can apply two intermediate keys in the tween. Ease in on the first key, and leave the second key alone. Ease out on the third key. Leave the last, destination key alone. This combination will have the effect of easing into full speed between the first two keys, maintaining constant speed between the second and third keys, but easing out between the third and final destination keys.

Panning

The term *panning* in Flash is really not used in the purist sense of the term. As we defined earlier, in a pan, the camera remains stationary but the lens scans the landscape. In a real camera, this movement would introduce a certain distortion that, although not impossible, would be extremely difficult to recreate accurately in Flash. So, for our use in Flash, we will use the pan exclusively when the entire contents of the graphic traverse the view horizontally, vertically, or diagonally.

Making the background larger than the camera's view will allow the camera to pan in various directions. If a character is to fall from a plane, you want a vertical layout to the background. If characters are running for their life from the bad guy, and panning will be across a larger stretch of real estate, the view can be what you see in Figure 4.12. Here, a horizontal layout works best.

If a diagonal move is necessary, you should work in a square layout. Because of Flash's limitations for graphics in a square layout, a diagonal pan will need to be short. Reserving diagonal moves for a dolly is generally best. We'll get to these moves next.

Using a Dolly

In a dolly shot, you are moving the camera itself in a variety of motions. Think of a dolly as if the camera (or viewer) is riding on a car, plane, boat, or even a spaceship. In movie making, a dolly move is made with an actual

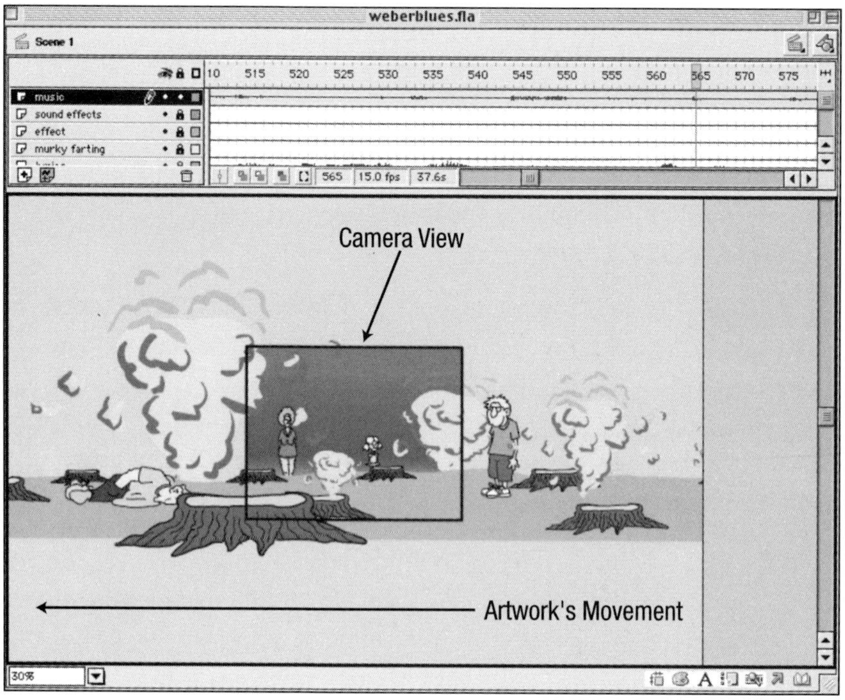

Figure 4.12
A large pan (horizontal movement) across the animation.

dolly, which can be as simple as a camera on a short track pulled along by people, or as complex as elaborate, gyro-stabilized cameras on low-flying airplanes—and beyond. Money and imagination are the only limits.

Luckily, in Flash, we won't need all that mechanical ingenuity to perform a dolly. In Flash, using a dolly is a simple matter of deciding the view you need and creating the necessary graphics to convey the illusion of movement through the scene.

Tweening Various Objects to Convey the Illusion of Movement

In Figure 4.13, we show an overall view that reveals what's happening to get this shot. This move is actually quite easy to do—and very useful. The background (water) itself is stationary, as is the animated looping symbol of Weber swimming and bubbles flowing from his snorkel. The schools of fish are also nested symbols. By *nested*, we mean that one fish is animated and is then placed inside another symbol five or six times, and then that group of symbols is used as a single entity in the scene. The nested fish are tweened to move to the left at a casual pace. This process makes the fish appear to be swimming slower than Weber, because he is stationary in the view.

What really sells this movement is the slightly transparent sand and seaweed in the far background. We made this part of the background transparent, to let it take on the coloring of the water layer that is actually behind it. But the trick makes the sand and seaweed appear as though the water is in front and all around it. The sand and seaweed symbol is tweened to the left at a slower

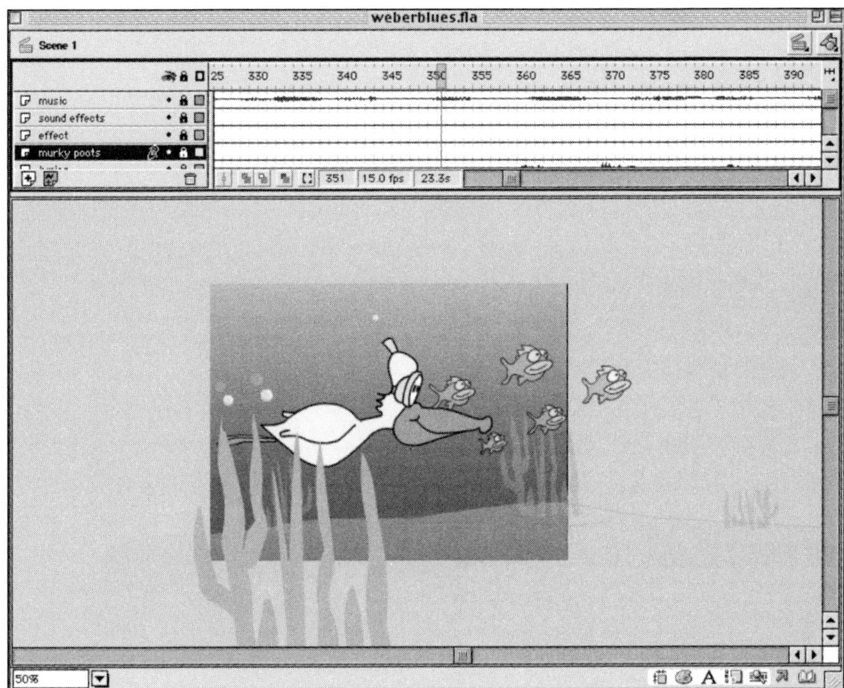

Figure 4.13
Here, we have an underwater scene in which Weber gleefully eats the fish as he swims faster than they do, with the camera following the action.

pace than the fish school is tweened. This combination produces the illusion that the fish school is moving faster, and therefore, swimming.

An added touch, to give the illusion of depth, is the large symbol of seaweed (alone in the extreme foreground) that moves in front of Weber as he swims. This seaweed symbol is also tweened to the left, but at a much faster rate than anything else in the scene—based on the principle that the closer something is to you, the faster it appears to move in relation to things that are farther away. Also, we applied no transparency to this symbol, further enforcing the illusion that it is closer. Very little water lies between you and the symbol to obscure and influence the symbol's coloring.

Using Layers to Produce the Illusion of Depth and Movement

The use of multiple layers lets you move, or weave, your character in and out of scenery elements. In the previous section, we talked about an underwater scene in which we used a dolly. The scenery elements consisted of water in the far background (or underneath layer) sand, and seaweed in a layer just above the water, and a seaweed element in the extreme foreground.

This setup not only allowed the character to move in front of some elements and behind others, but also allowed us to give the elements themselves independent movement. This technique can give an illusion of both depth in movement and visual depth.

If the flow of your animation requires that the character moves in and out of other elements in the scene, thinking about these things when you're designing the scenery itself is very important. When you're working in Flash, successful movement can be as simple as making certain that you separate the elements you want to move from the plane of artwork that lies underneath them. Ideally, any scenery element a character will weave in and out of should remain on its own layer, so you can tween that element independently of other elements in the scene.

This approach can, however, produce a timeline with many, many layers, which can become quite confusing at times. So, when you create these layers, be sure to name them something you can understand. Also, you might want to add comments (or labels) to the frames themselves in the Timeline, to help you keep track of which layer something might temporarily exist on.

Designing a scene with clearly separated elements will give you more freedom to move your character where you like. With this setup, you can use a system of layer-hopping, in which the element or character bounces from one layer to the next, changing the ordering of elements in the scene. Figures 4.14 and 4.15, in which the Weber character hops off the dock and into the water, are examples of this system.

Figure 4.14
Weber is on the dock and about to jump. Notice the active layer he's on.

When he hops into the air, Weber is on a layer in front of the dock. While he's suspended in the air above the dock, Weber is moved to a new layer below the dock layer. When he falls to meet the water, he is now behind the dock and appears to be going into the water.

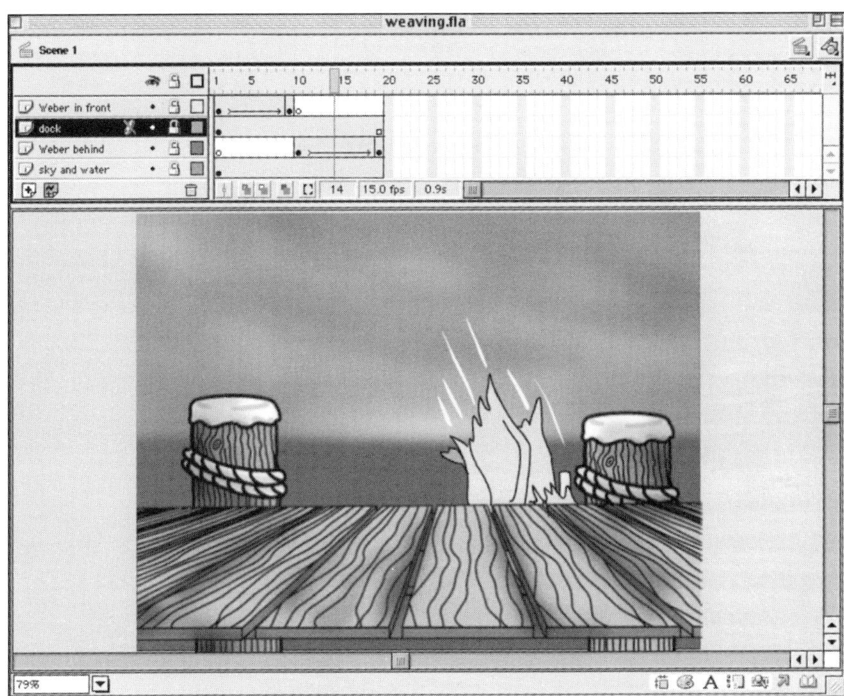

Figure 4.15
Weber is behind the dock and about to enter the water. Again, notice the layer the character is on.

Absolutely endless uses arise for this technique, as you may imagine. Situations such as the character hiding behind trees in a forest—but, of course, walking in front of others—dictates the use of weaving. Thinking of these things while you are designing your scenery is absolutely critical. If the above example had the dock and the water/sky graphic as one layer, doing this move would be nearly impossible. Even if the current scene doesn't call for weaving, a later one might. Because you probably don't want to waste time redoing the scenery, create it with weaving in mind as a matter of habit, to give yourself maximum flexibility.

Using Photoshop to Create Scenery

You do not need to create all background in Flash. A great alternative is to use a bitmap editor, such as Photoshop. Photoshop offers the power of manipulating photographs for use in Flash, and it also has some pretty handy tools that Flash simply does not have—the airbrush leaps to mind. Also, the seemingly endless supply of special effects plug-ins for "going really wild" are there, ready for use.

Many fine books are available on the subject of Photoshop. In this discussion, we intend to show you the possibilities that exist for creating backgrounds and scenery using some of the Photoshop tools. We will assume you have a comfortable, working knowledge of Photoshop. (After all, Photoshop is the most-used bitmap editor in the professional graphics world.)

Beware of File Sizes When You Use Bitmaps in Flash Projects

When you use bitmaps in your Flash projects, you must be aware that the bitmaps can make the file sizes much larger. If your work is for video and film output, file size is of little concern; for Web distribution, large files can be more serious. Bitmaps increase file size dramatically, so use them sparingly in your Web-bound projects, or your viewer will be waiting quite a while as your cartoon or game downloads. Also, whenever possible, stay away from grainy or "noisy" images, because they do not compress as efficiently as smoother art does. (But, if you have to have such images—and people will wait a little longer for something entertaining over something boring—go for it, and use the best art you can. And the best art usually means bitmaps.)

Certainly, with an application with such power and breadth as Photoshop to create stunning imagery, you have no boundaries. Whatever you can imagine (and, possibly, some things you can't) is an everyday occurrence in this application. We will leave that sort of experimentation to you. We want to show how you can seriously enhance the look of your Flash cartoons and games with Photoshop.

As of this writing, Photoshop 6 is not as widespread as Photoshop 5; so, for the purpose of the next project, Photoshop 5 will do just fine.

PROJECT Creating a Background with Focus Pull in Photoshop

We'll create scenery here that has what's known as *focus pull*. As we mentioned earlier, focus pull is similar to the photographic technique of using a short depth of field—the only thing in focus is the object or character you want the viewer to concentrate on; everything else is out of focus.

Finding the Files You Need

On the CD, you'll find the *palmtree.ai* and *project.psd* files. Finally, the project will all come together in the *focus.fla* file, in which we'll converge everything and have the Weber character walk through our scenery with all attention on him.

Working in Photoshop

To start this project, launch the Photoshop application if you have it. (If you don't have Photoshop, read through the project steps to see what's being done. Then, you can pick up with Step 15, which opens a Flash file into which the completed Photoshop file has been imported.)

1. Open the *project.psd* file. You should see an image like that in Figure 4.16. The image has a basic blurred background that represents the horizon, and a single palm tree on a layer of its own.
2. Use the **File|Place** command to locate and place the *palmtree.ai* file. This file will appear as a preview inside the work file, with bounding boxes to let you resize the graphic at will. Make this tree a good bit smaller than the original tree.

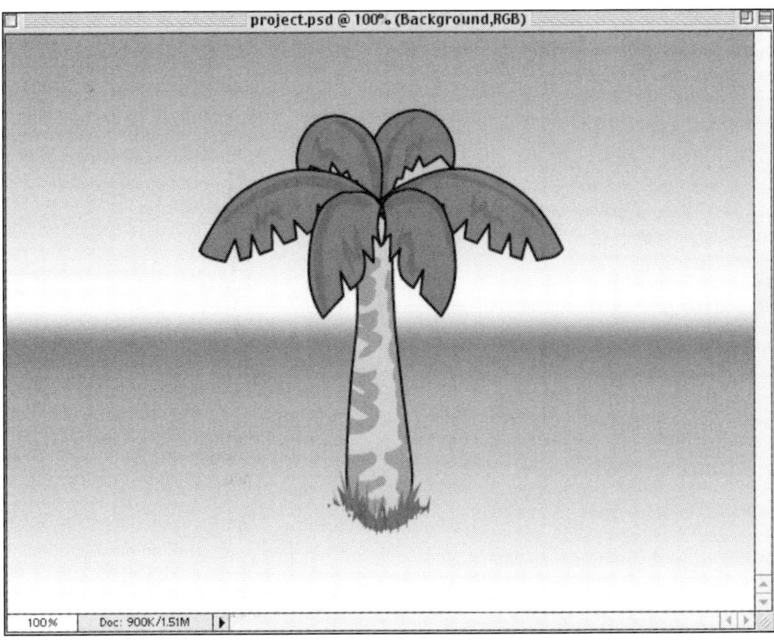

Figure 4.16
The start of our project opened in Photoshop.

3. Using the same function as in Step 2 (the **File|Place** command), repeat this placement of the palm tree but, this time, make a tree quite a bit larger than the original tree (see Figure 4.17).

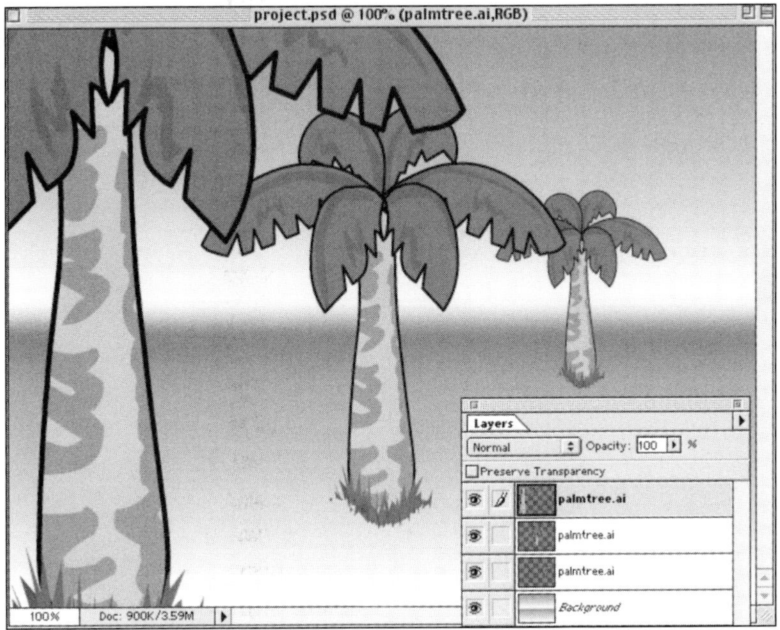

Figure 4.17
The three sizes of palm trees.

4. Now that you have the three, basic-sized trees, you can duplicate these layers to populate the jungle. You should now have something roughly like what you see in Figure 4.18. Simply put another of the larger, foreground trees on each side of the scene (you don't want your scenery to obscure the middle ground).

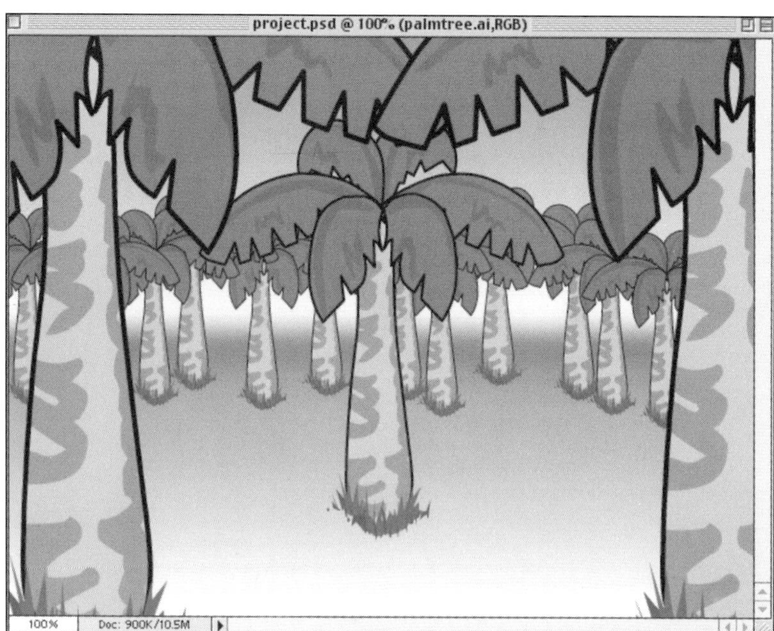

Figure 4.18
The jungle populated with trees.

Note: By placing the trees, particularly the large one, directly from the Illustrator file, you maintain the smooth resolution of the original art, no matter how much you enlarge it.

5. Now, you have a file with many layers that contain palm trees. All you need are three layers of trees, so merge all the smaller trees into one layer. Merge the two largest trees into one layer. Leave the lone, middle tree on its original layer by itself. A good time to save the file is after you've merged the layers.
6. With the trees separated into three layers, you'll apply the blurring you need to get the effect you're after. On the trees farthest away, apply the Gaussian blur filter with a setting of 3 to that layer. Do the same for the trees closest (the large ones), but at a Gaussian blur setting of 5.
7. Save the file. This file will be your master, with layers intact.
8. By control-clicking (on the Mac) or right-clicking (on the PC) on the icons in the Layer menu, you can select Layer Transparency of that layer. This selection is made into the alpha channel by choosing **Select|Save Selection**.
9. Delete the remaining layers (even the background layer), leaving only the layer for which you've created an alpha channel. *Do not save the master layered file.* Instead, choose **File|Save A Copy**, and choose PNG as the format. Be sure that the Exclude Alpha Channel option is *unchecked.* Name the file *foretrees.png*, and save the file (see Figure 4.19).
10. Revert to your original Photoshop layer file.

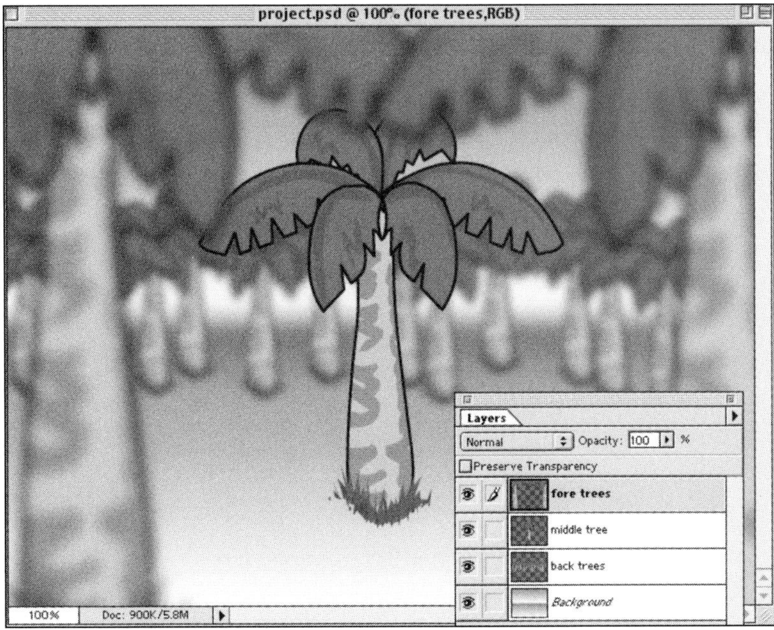

Figure 4.19
The result of the Gaussian blur filter applied to the individual layers. You'll see the effect starting to take shape.

11. Repeat Steps 8 and 9, only this time, use the lone, middle tree layer as the source for the alpha channel and the remaining layer. Name the file *middletree.png*.
12. Revert to your original Photoshop layer file.
13. Delete the foreground trees and the middle tree layer. These deletions leave you with the back trees and the horizon/grass background layer.
14. Save a copy of this file (no need for alpha here) as *background.png*.
15. Open the *focus.fla* file in Flash. Here, we've already imported the resulting files from Photoshop and issued them to the proper layers. What you'll see is nearly identical to what you had in Photoshop. Only now, you can animate a character in the focused area. Weaving characters among the layers lets the characters move around the middle tree with ease (see Figure 4.20).

Note: Mac users may want to export the file out of Photoshop as a 32-bit *Pict* file. Make sure you save the file as uncompressed (compressing *Pict* files automatically deletes the alpha channel—something you don't want to do).

As you can see from this simple project, the possibilities are endless for creating scenery in Photoshop. We hope that this project sparks your imagination. Remember to be thoughtful of file size if the Internet is your destination. But, with broadband Internet access fast approaching the mainstream, we hope these concerns will soon become a moot point in what you can do on the Net. When that happens, you'll be ready.

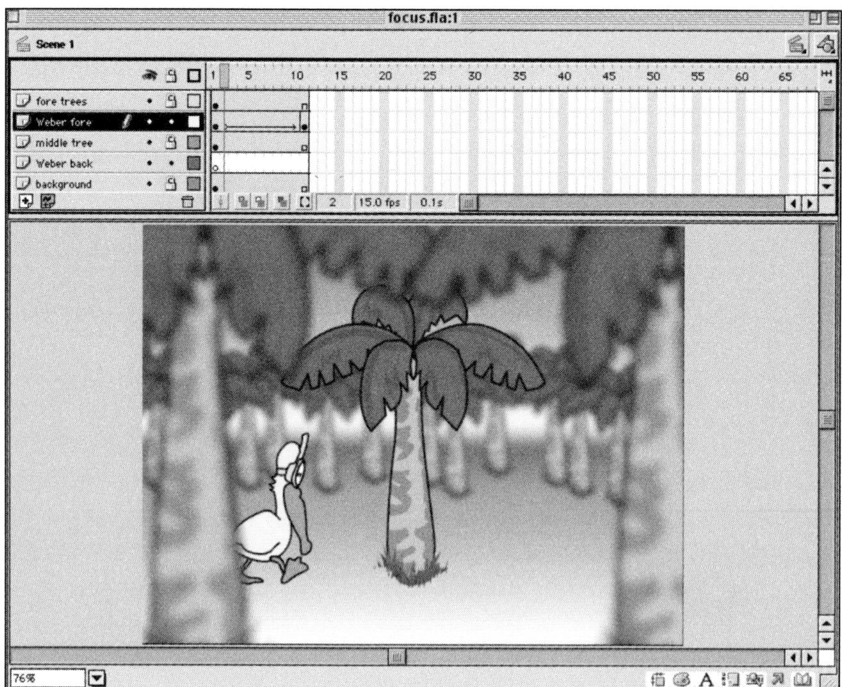

Figure 4.20
The finished project scenery, ready for animation in Flash.

Moving On

Next, we'll get into the meat of it all: character animation. Hold on to your hat, because this is where the rubber meets the road: bringing your characters to life with walking, running, jumping, and a head shaking good time. Sharpen up that Wacom stylus...you'll need it.

Chapter 5

Character Animation

Character animation is the art of motion. Generally, character animation refers to human and animal cartoon characters, but it can apply to objects as well. In either case, the art of character animation is to bring life via motion to the subject at hand.

By Bill Turner
and Richard Bazley

Defining Character Animation

Asking this question might seem strange, but with the emergence of technology in recent years, we need to categorize various forms of animation. So...what *is* character animation?

One type of animation is motion graphics, which is usually used as a way to move graphics around the screen. One place you'll commonly see motion graphics is in the *bumper* (the beginning sequence) of a news program, where the logo comes rolling in with various other information and glitz. The beginning of ABC News Nightline, and CNN news segments are good examples of this form of animation.

Another type of animation is simulation animation, much like you'd see in a NASA space animation, in which the animators are trying to portray a certain technical process, or show something that can't be filmed, such as a craft orbiting Mars, for example. You might also see these sorts of simulation animations in court reenactments.

The common factor in these forms of animation is their mechanical style. Cartoons, on the other hand, are very organic and mostly nonmechanical. Cartoons are near-pure character animation because they mostly involve an attempt to render living things in a living way.

But this is not to say that the motion-graphics and simulation forms of animation cannot have character. They certainly can, and they are far more effective when they do instill a bit of character. To help illustrate this explanation, we've provided a file called *ball.fla* (see Figure 5.1) on the CD. This simple animation will show the mechanical, in contrast to the organic, with a simple ball. This example is the essence of character animation applied to nothing more than a round circle. Notice the ball on the left is very stiff and lifeless, while the one on the right bounces with exuberance and life. The ball on the right seems to be made of a pliable substance, much like skin and muscles, to give it an "alive" appearance.

So, we can conclude that character animation not only is an attempt to animate living things, but it also adds life to nonliving objects. Character animation is an organic approach, as opposed to a mechanical one. It's also the animation form with the most flexibility and, therefore, involves a never-ending learning process.

Frame Rates

Before we get into animated motion techniques, one of the base considerations in creating motion is how much resolution you have to work with. This is not a question of printing resolution, measured in *dpi* (dots per inch), or screen resolution, measured in *pixels*, but rather a question of time resolution—the *frame rate,* measured in *fps* (frames per second). The first thing you should

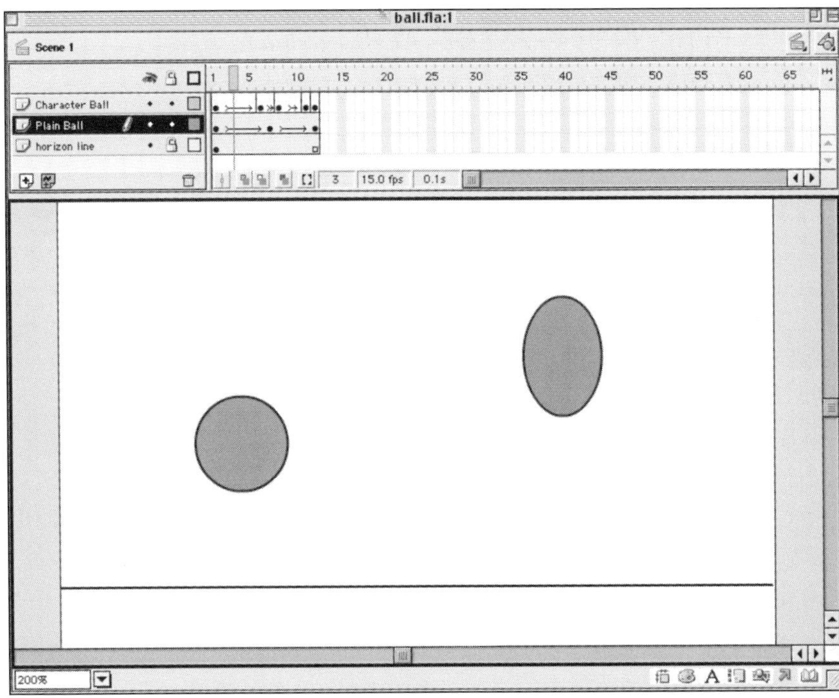

Figure 5.1
Even a simple circle can reveal character in its animated motion.

consider before commencing to animate is the frame rate, which is the number of times per second that an image is updated. The standard frame rate in film is 24fps; in NTSC (American) television, the rate is 30fps; in PAL (the television standard used in most European countries), the rate is 25fps. These rates mean that a new image will appear every 1/24th, or 1/30th, or 1/25th of a second. On the Web using Flash, the frame rate (no half frames allowed) can be whatever you want it to be. Look at Figures 5.2 and 5.3. Both circles will travel the same distance and at the same speed; the difference is that the higher frame rate will seem smoother, not faster.

Keep in mind that the average human eye has difficulty realizing a difference of any resolution above 24fps. We realize that many video game creators claim that their game animations play at 60fps, 90fps, and even 120fps. That's fine for advertising purposes—bigger numbers seem better, but in animation reality, they're useless. The TV displaying that Sony PlayStation2 game still runs at only 30fps. Even if the monitor could produce such high frame rates, the viewer's mind (via persistence of vision) simply cannot comprehend these high rates. So, why use them in your animation? The higher the frame rate, the more work you have to do.

Note: High-speed cameras used for slow motion might seem like a contradiction, but they're not. When footage is exposed at 48fps but played back at 24fps, the result is high-quality, slow motion with less blurring. If footage is shot at 24fps and played back at 12fps, the quality of slow motion is not as good.

With the exception of special technical uses, most of which concern high-speed movie cameras used for ultra-slow motion, all the films you've seen in theaters run at 24fps, and they look just fine. Actually, in many animated films, cartoon sequences being shot *on the twos* (meaning a new image for every two frames of film) are really resolved at 12fps. Again, these cartoons look just fine.

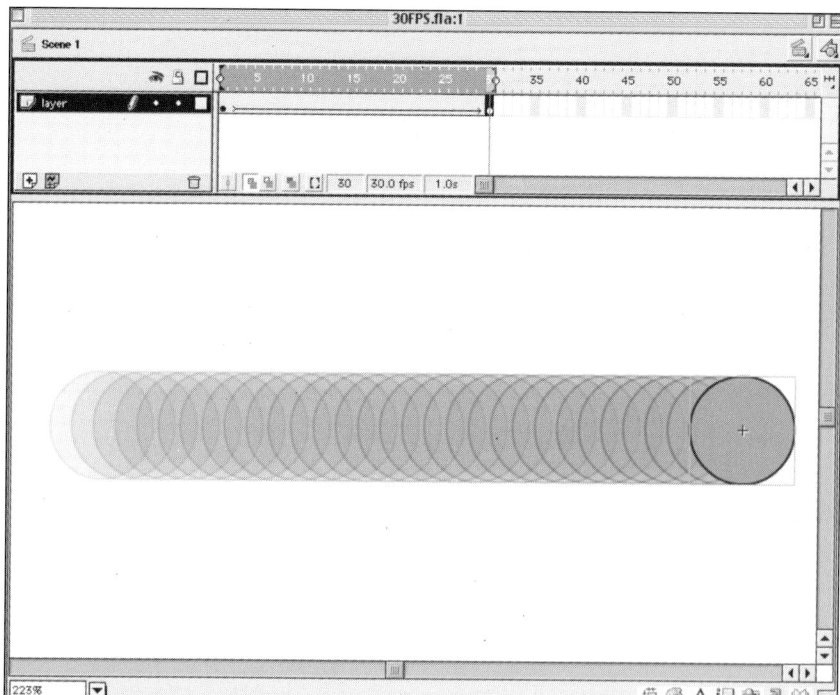

Figure 5.2
Note how many images are needed to animate the circle with the time resolution at 30fps.

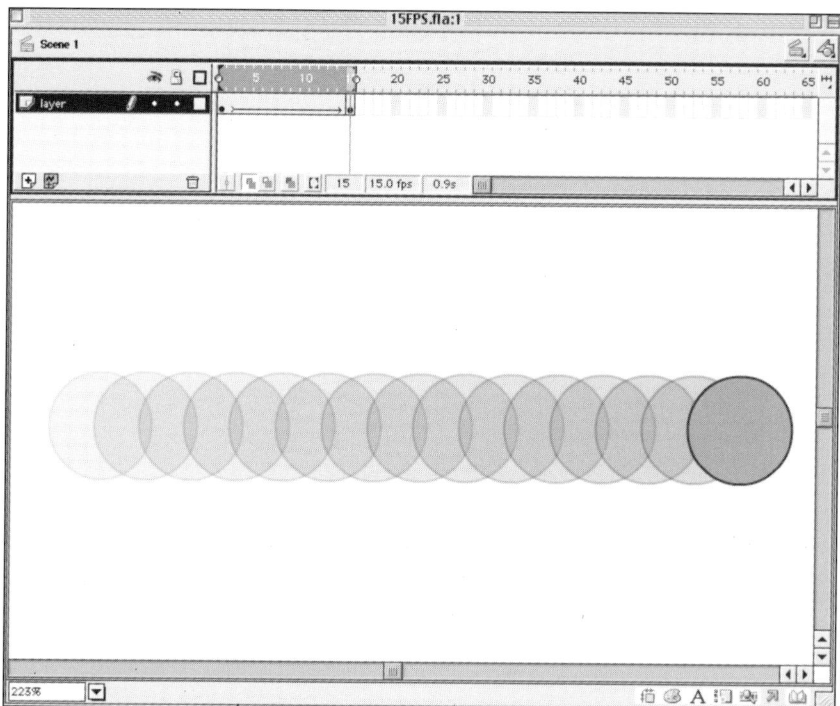

Figure 5.3
The same distance is covered in the same time, but this clip uses fewer images at 15fps.

Persistence of Vision

Persistence of vision is the phenomenon that allows animation and motion film to work. It is said that as images enter the eye, they "persist" ever so slightly. You can see this happen if you look at a light source, such as a camera's flash, which seems to stay visible after the fact. So, the theory goes, when the images are flashed quickly enough, they tend to bleed together, giving the illusion of movement. There are those who dispute this theory. If you'd like to hear the other side of this story, you can find it at **www.grand-illusions.com/percept.htm**.

You need a compromise between smoothness of motion (high frame rate), the amount of work you want to perform (how many frames per second you want to draw), and the time you have to perform the action. Generally, in Flash cartoons for Web distribution, this goal also means considering the average playback computer's processing power. Few computers in homes today can handle smoothly playing complicated, full-screen, vector graphics and sound at 30fps. Another concern with high frame rates and Web delivery can be the larger file sizes the animation makes because of the need for more art.

When you're animating for video output, you need not worry about viewers' playback computers, because tape decks will be doing the playing at 30fps, regardless. The issue here becomes finding a frame rate that video likes. Video's 30fps playback is standard, and the tape will always play at this rate, but that still represents more frames than you'll want to draw (notice that this rate is higher than the 24fps standard used in film). A good compromise is 15fps, because that rate is evenly divided into 30. Using 15fps, in essence, is "shooting on the twos" for video.

We've found that, for the most flexibility, 15fps is a pleasing middle ground for both Web and video output. After all, you might make a really cool Web cartoon and want to go out to video later on, without having to redo the entire thing at a different frame rate. This is an important consideration. Currently, Flash cannot scale time. This means that if you were to do a frame-by-frame animation at 24fps, and you changed the movie's frame rate to 15fps or 30fps (via the Movie Properties in Flash), your animation would *not* be correct anymore. The sound would be totally out of whack with the images, and making it right again would be difficult.

Techniques for Conveying Motion

Animation is all about *motion*. Animating motion can be quite an intricate practice, and it can take many years to master. What we hope to do here is to give you a good footing, using explanations and examples. Because of motion's very nature, explaining it without referring to actual animations of the different motions discussed can be difficult. Consequently, this chapter will depend heavily on your viewing the examples as we explain in the text what's going on. So, fire up your computer, and mount the CD-ROM, so you can follow along with the samples we've supplied.

Note: You can create many of the motion effects we discuss in this chapter with Flash's Scale, Rotate, and Skew commands (in the Transform panel).

We will be using simple graphics as we explain these motion concepts—they're a much more comfortable way to wrap your brain around what can be very complicated motions.

Speed Blurring

Speed blurring is used frequently in animated cartoons to convey a feeling of speed that might be faster than what the animation can physically show due to frame rate limitations. Frankly, even if the frame rate can handle the speed needed, using the following techniques makes for a much more interesting animation, as Figure 5.4 shows. The CD-ROM includes an example named *speed.swf* in the Edwin Carp Samples folder.

Figure 5.4
Here, is a scene from *The Journal of Edwin Carp*, in which a character has whooshed by, causing the boy's banana to fall out of its skin.

Sometimes, you need to express motion at a rate faster than the frame rate will allow. If you need something to move so quickly that the object will be on screen for only two or three frames (at 15fps), the object might appear to blink instead of move. The example file named *speedblur1.fla* is set up to have the shape in three frames traversing the screen. While you play the animation, you'll notice that it moves quickly, but it does have that blinking aspect, as well. You can do a couple things to help enhance the illusion of high-speed movement.

Ghosting

When you want to convey speed, one way—though not very organic or character like—is to have the shape leave a ghosted image in its wake. The *speedblur2.fla* file shows this technique (see Figure 5.5). What's done here is a simple matter of creating a new layer and using the same symbol, but trailing the new object behind the movement of the original object and lowering it's the new object's

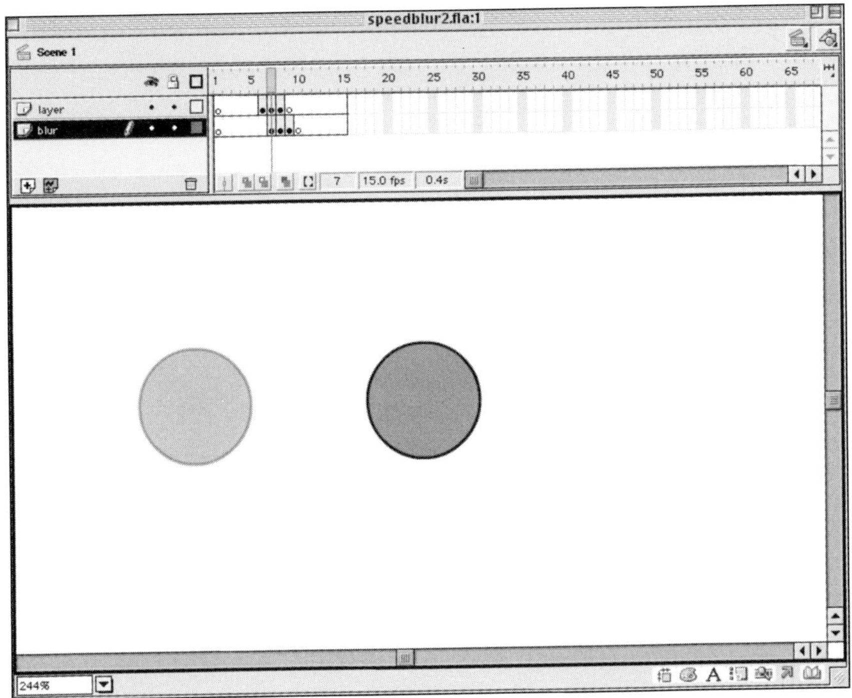

Figure 5.5
The somewhat mechanical ghosting method is one way to express speed.

opacity. This technique tends to make the object seem less blinking, but its mechanical quality is undesirable.

Tilts and Blur Lines

We're sure you've seen the cartoons in which the character blasts off screen with the speed of a rocket. What helps this effect is the use of *blur lines* following in the wake of the character's or object's movement. These blur lines are easily added with the brush or pencil tool in Flash. Open and view the *speedblur3.fla* file. Now, we're talking *speed*. Not only did we add the blur lines, but we also skewed the shape to tilt it forward, adding to the illusion of speed (see Figure 5.6). Another nice touch is to have some kind of turbulence in the wake of the speeding object. In this case, we included a few frames—after the object had left the screen—for the blur lines to play out and poof into debris. This effect is much like what happens if a large truck passes you by, leaving dust kicked up in its wake (see Figure 5.7).

Weight and Substance

To achieve a certain type of believability, the animator will need to understand and convey some of the principles that govern us all, such as "What goes up, must come down"—in other words, *weight and substance*. However, on other occasions, we might break these rules for comic effect. For example, when the coyote in Chuck Jones's *Roadrunner* cartoon runs off a cliff, he keeps on running in mid-air. He looks down and realizes that he has run off the cliff, and *then* he falls, with humorous results.

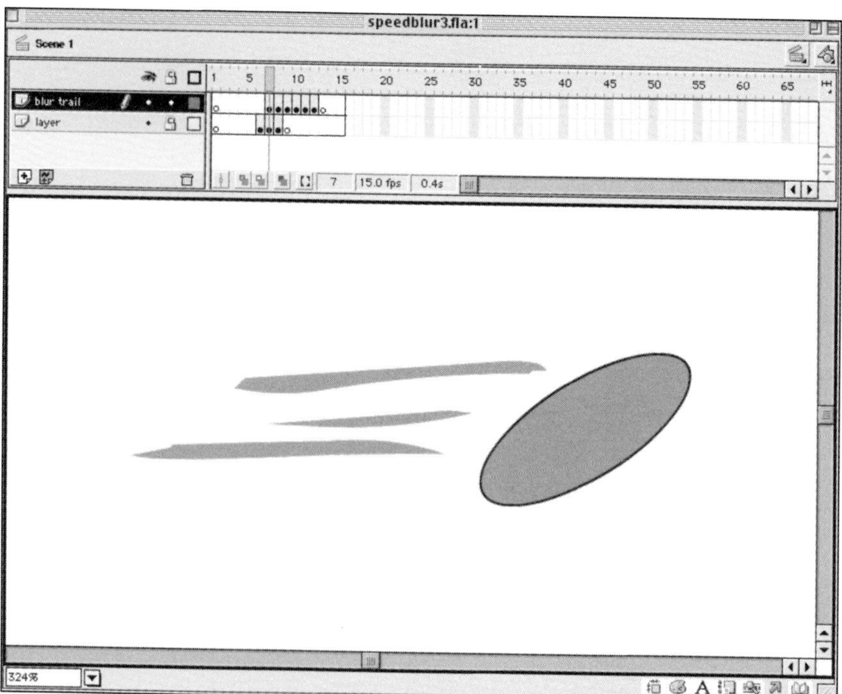

Figure 5.6
Now, our shape is cooking. Note the blur lines and the tilting forward.

Figure 5.7
You must consider weight to make your animation believable. See this image in motion in the CD-ROM file *weight.swf*.

Weight and substance have quite a lot to do with motion. If you were to drop both a feather and a steel ball from a tall building, which object would land first? These items would fall in dramatically different ways. The steel ball would make a beeline to the ground, while the feather would sway back and forth, possibly following a swirling spiral and sweeping in arbitrary directions, depending on the breeze at the time. How objects move in terms of weight and motion includes endless variations. While we don't expect anyone to know them all, giving these physical attributes their due makes sense when you're animating characters.

Without getting terribly scientific about the subject (that would go against the principle of a cartoon's fun quotient), the matter of weight is really a matter of gravity. How gravity affects an object, and how that object reacts with another object's movement, is what we're after when we animate cool characters. *Surface tension*, the rigidity or flexibility of the object being animated, also plays a keen role in animation because it gives clues to the object's substance (see Figures 5.8 and 5.9). Think of the cartoon cliché in which an anvil falls (weight and gravity) onto the head of the unsuspecting character, smashing him into the ground with such force as to leave a cutout in the ground perfectly silhouetting the character (surface tension and substance). Oh, *now* it seems like more fun.

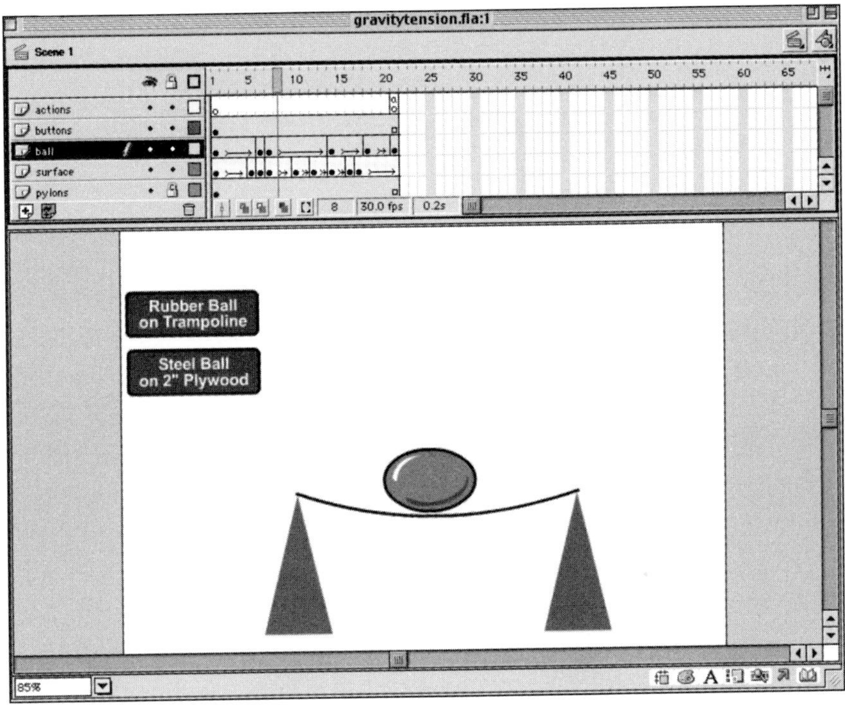

Figure 5.8
The rubber ball is on a trampoline.

Open and play the example file named *weightsubstance.swf* (you can also examine the FLA file named *weightsubstance.fla*), clicking the buttons to switch between the two examples. The goal of this example is not to be scientifically perfect (remember, we don't really like that stuff), but to show completely different materials and weights interacting with each other. The shapes we used are virtually the same in both parts of the example; the *movement* of these shapes makes you believe they are made of differing substances.

So far, we've only discussed objects in this look at weight and substance. So, what about characters? The same physical principles we apply to objects, we can and should apply to characters—and to their movements, as well. Think

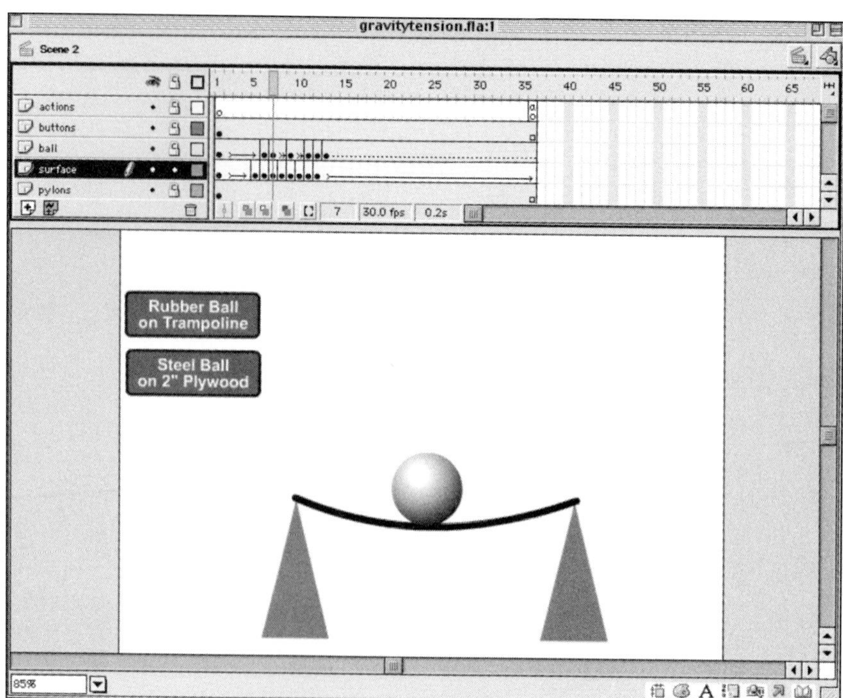

Figure 5.9
The steel ball is on thick plywood.

about the Popeye cartoons, particularly the black-and-white ones from the 1930s and '40s. Olive Oyl, in the clutches of Bluto, is tied around a tree like a rubber band, her arms and legs in knots, crying out for Popeye's help. Popeye, having just had the tar "whooped" out of him, slacks across the screen like an old, used rag, gravity getting the best of him, as his arms drag helplessly behind him. We all know that a can of spinach had better be close at hand. Luckily, there's one now—how convenient. After downing the magic leaf, Popeye turns into the Rock of Gibraltar. Now, his movements are made of steel, as he confidently rushes to Olive's defense. With a single punch, Bluto is knocked into orbiting the earth 26 times; weight and substance, used and defied. Oh yeah, Olive gets untied from the tree (see Figure 5.10).

Opposing Actions

When you use *opposing actions*, a set of motions that oppose each other, you raise your animation to a higher level. These movements take place in life all the time, and most people never realize it. But if you were to remove these motions from life, everyone would take notice immediately. The lack of opposing actions can make an animation seem stiff and lifeless. As an animator, your job is to find and study the things others take for granted (see Figure 5.10).

So what are these mysterious motions? We'll need to take a little trip back to our new friend, the circle, to find out. Only, this time, the circle will have a co-star, the rectangle, joined by the imaginary connector, the muscle. See Figure 5.11, and then open and play the CD-ROM file named *opposing.swf* to see the motion (the FLA authoring file titled *opposing.fla* is also included for you to investigate).

Figure 5.10

Edwin Carp is tossing off pieces of paper. See this in motion in the CD-ROM file named *opposingactions.swf*.

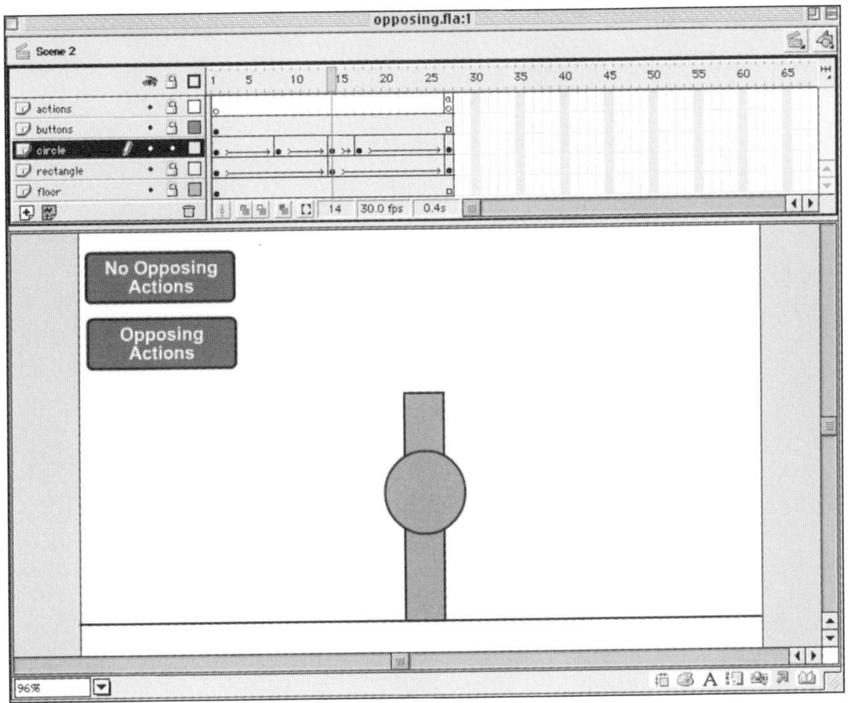

Figure 5.11

Here, is an example of opposing actions. Open the *opposing.swf* file to see the motion.

In the first part of the example, you see the circle roughly centered on the rectangle and following its motion exactly. This positioning makes the circle seem nailed on. Unless you have a specific reason, you want to avoid things that seem nailed on. Nailed on is stiff and lifeless and lacks opposing actions—the effect is simply a unit that consists of a circle and a rectangle bouncing up and down.

The second part, though, seems to jump to life. Here, opposing actions have been applied. The movement of the rectangle is not changed from the first part. But the interaction of the circle against the rectangle has changed dramatically. Our old friends gravity, weight, and substance came for a visit. Because of its weight, the circle's movement cannot be stopped by the abrupt bounce of the rigid rectangle against the floor. The circle continues downward until the elasticity of the imaginary muscle connecting the two shapes reaches its limit. This connector then slings the circle upward, shortly after the rectangle has begun its ascent. The circle now has more momentum in the upward direction than the rectangle does, but the circle reaches its apex at a later moment. Because there's not an abrupt halt at the rectangle's apex, the connector allows the circle to relax somewhat. The circle eventually catches back up to its place in the center of the rectangle.

What this discussion means for character animation is substantial indeed. Most living things are connected together by bone, tendons, elastic muscles, and skin. We are not nailed together, thank goodness. The example above makes a great deal of sense if you were to imagine the rectangle as our bone structure, and imagine the circle as the flesh connected by the muscles. The addition of opposing actions certainly removes any resemblance to machine-like movement. This is what we stated earlier about people taking serious notice—if these movements ceased, we'd all be moving like robots.

In Figure 5.12 and the animation on the CD-ROM (the *opposingactions2.swf* file), we have a scene filled with many opposing actions. As the frightened

Figure 5.12
Here's a scene with oodles of subtle, opposing actions taking place. See the *opposingactions2.swf* file.

lady runs toward you, practically everything is in motion. Her head bobs, opposed to shoulders, and her hands bob, opposed to her feet hitting the floor (even though we can't see her feet). The opposing motion goes even as far as the uvula in her throat. Even the flapping of her trailing shawl reflects the movement of her body.

When animating, you should always be thoughtful of these details. While employing this type of motion might be obvious when you're animating a child bouncing on a pogo stick, you might not so easily see its use in nearly all character movement. Opposing actions can be extremely subtle in many things people and animals do, but they're there. The more you add them in your animations, the better the animations will be.

Anticipation

Anticipation is unique to animated cartoons. This form of motion is more of a mental exercise than a motion technique. Anticipation comes into play in animation in the exaggeration of the visual to reflect the mental. Drag racing is a realty-based example in which visible anticipation takes place. In drag racing, two extremely powerful cars start from a dead stop and race a quarter of a mile ahead in a straight line to see who can cross the finish line first. It is a race of brute force and power. The start of the race is absolutely crucial. The driver's reaction time to hit the accelerator is measured in very small increments of time, and that reaction time can be the difference between winning and losing. Therefore, a huge amount of anticipation is going on here; you can almost taste it. As the signals to start the race commence (a series of lights count down to green), the cars' engines are revved. The cars tremble with the power they're about to release. Then...bang...they blast into the race.

From this example, you can imagine where the anticipation manifests itself visually. The cars, shaking and vibrating with power waiting to be released, visually depict the anticipation. When you use this effect in your animation, you are adding a visual cue that something is about to happen.

Let's go back to our circle example in the speed-blurring section. In that section, we were simply trying to visually depict speed. Here, we have added the beginning anticipation as well. Figure 5.13 and the animation on the CD-ROM (the file named *anticipation.fla*) show the motion of anticipation.

Notice that the circle starts off in its natural, circular form on the first frame. At this moment, the circle is obviously at rest. In the next few frames, the circle rears back somewhat slowly and gets a bit taller. Here, we are trying to impart the feeling that the circle is pumping up with energy. Once the circle reaches its peak, it holds that position momentarily. This hold is where maximum anticipation takes place. The next frames show the circle in its tilt-forward posture, as it begins to speed off.

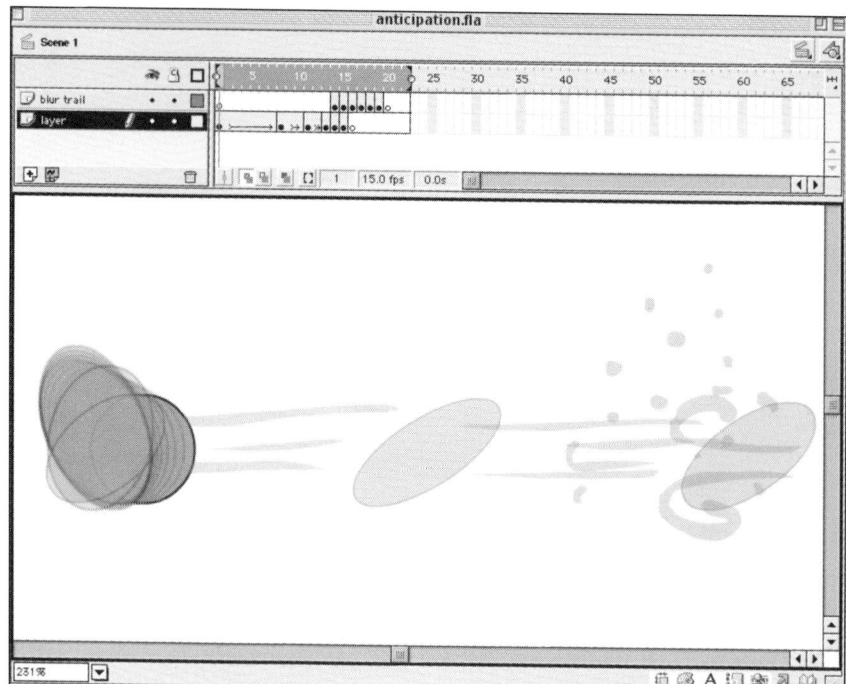

Figure 5.13
This shot, with onion-skinning of all frames turned on, shows the frames piling up, in anticipation of the coming move.

Anticipation of a motion generally is expressed with the character moving and shifting weight in the opposite direction from that in which the movement will proceed. Think of a baseball player, at bat, who rears back just before swinging at the ball. Using this kind of pre-move movement in your animations will make the sequence much more exciting as you build up to the move.

Overshooting

Overshooting is the opposite of anticipation. Whereas anticipation builds up to a movement, overshooting occurs when the motion goes beyond the desired limit. Let's go back to our baseball batter's example. If you're a fan of the game, you're sure to know that the game can sometimes be decided on an overshooting motion. It's the bottom of the ninth, the bases are loaded, the count is three balls and two strikes, and it's your team's last chance to win. In the rules of the game, the overshot action is known as a *check swing*. The batter initiates the swing, but then thinks better of it, and tries to correct the swing and stop the bat's momentum before he completes the swing. Sometimes, the batter isn't successful, and the umpire calls a strike instead of a ball.

The best way to understand this character-motion technique is to look at Figure 5.14 and open the animation file named *overshoot.swf* on the CD-ROM; this file shows an example of overshooting. (The authoring file, *overshoot.fla*, is also included for you to investigate.)

Our speeding circle has finally gotten somewhere. The problem is, a dangerous cliff has interrupted the circle's freewheeling scamper. The circle must come

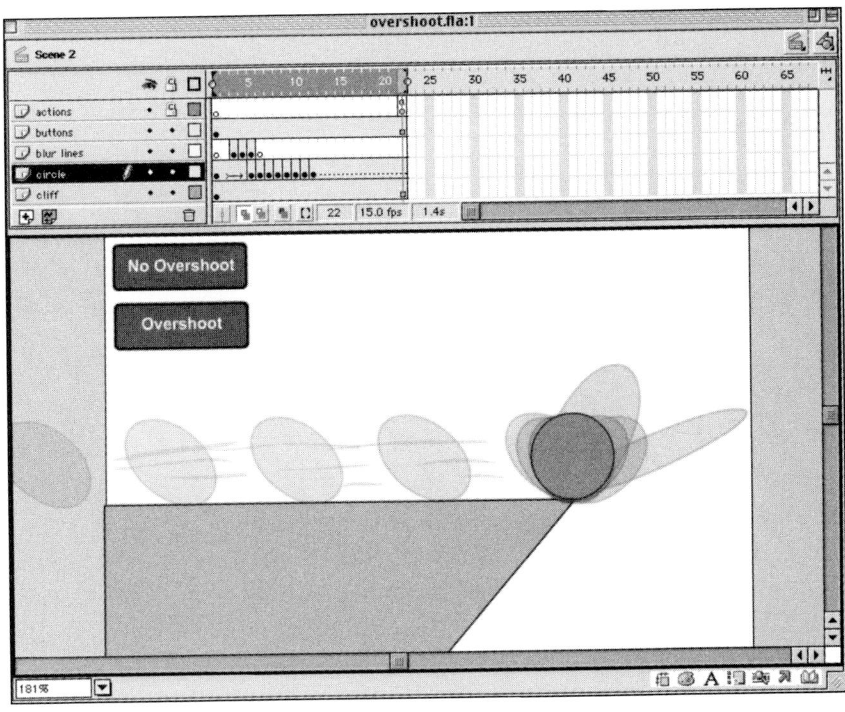

Figure 5.14
Here, we have the overshoot sequence with onion-skinning, to show all frames used.

to an abrupt halt or meet its peril. While you're viewing the example animation, and switching between versions, you'll see that the No Overshoot version does the job but is very mechanical. The circle does indeed stop in time, but it seems to do so with indifference to the danger that confronts it.

Now, click to the Overshoot version. In this version of the animation, the circle also stops in plenty of time, but it does so with a passion that seems to respect the danger confronting it. The fact that the circle enters the picture with a slanted-back posture gives the impression that it's braking, and this posture helps you understand the circle's intent to stop. Once it reaches the edge of the cliff, the circle stretches forward, leaning out over the abyss. This action creates a moment of uncertainty that adds excitement to the sequence. The circle then recoils in a rubbery way, ending up in its standard, circle shape again. All is safe.

You can use the overshooting technique in many ways. If you view the *surfing.swf* file, you can see in action how the surfer completely leaves the wave in his ride. This overshoot adds excitement, even though it is different from the fear of falling over the cliff, as in our circle example (see Figure 5.15).

Another great example of overshooting happens in the classic *Roadrunner* cartoons. Wile E. Coyote is just about to catch the roadrunner in a high-speed chase. As the coyote is about to sink his eating utensils into the bird, the bird turns his head, blows a trademark raspberry at the coyote, and turns on the turbo blast. The roadrunner now runs so fast that, as he makes a turn, he actually picks up the ribbon of road asphalt, pulling it from the ground, and stretching it with the force of his turn.

Figure 5.15
Here, we see a sequence of a surfer overshooting the wave.

Squash and Stretch

Squash and stretch is a much-used form of motion in cartoons. This technique, too, is generally used in exaggerated expression of movement. It's also used in conjunction with weight and substance, because it gives the character or object a pliable appearance.

On the CD-ROM, the file named *squashweber.swf* shows this motion technique in use (see Figure 5.16). Birds generally land a bit more gracefully than this. You might think Weber has had one too many fish to eat before this bouncy, Jell-O-like landing. The use of squash and stretch adds a much more fun and humorous movement to the sequence. Now, open the *squash.fla* file on the CD-ROM (see Figure 5.17), so we can examine what's going on in a squash-and-stretch move.

Here, we have two identical circles bouncing in a loop. The bounces take the same amount of time to complete. The circle on the left never changes shape, which makes it appear rigid and unlikely to actually bounce. It simply bounces and is boring. The circle on the right, however, seems energetic, almost gleeful, in its bounce. This circle has character.

This character is achieved by taking into account the volume of the circle, and having the circle not only scale down in the vertical direction, but also scale slightly out in the horizontal direction as it hits the solid floor. If you smash a soft rubber ball with your hand against a table, you'll find that the ball both compresses in the vertical direction of the force being applied and also tries to

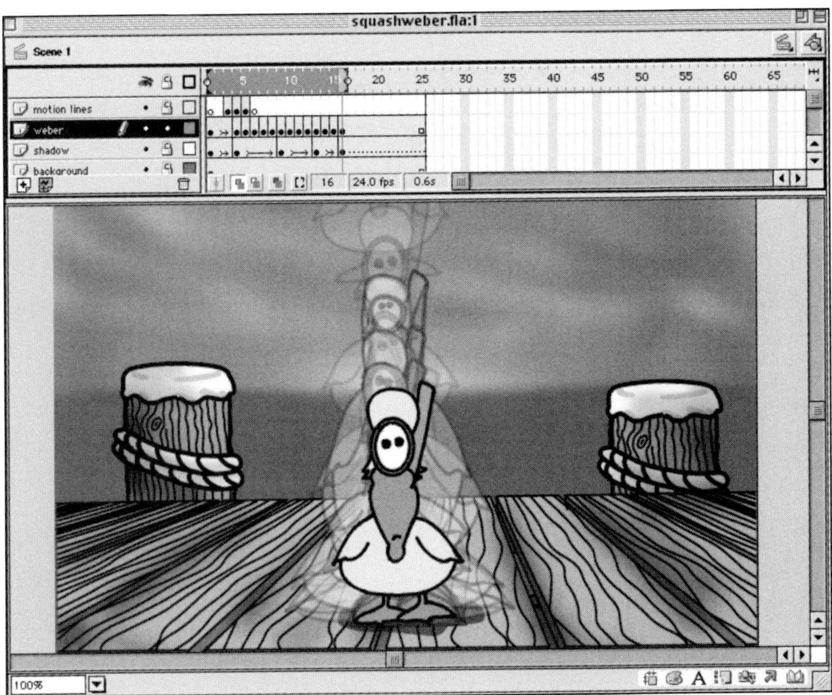

Figure 5.16
Here's an example of the squash-and-stretch technique with onion-skinning on, to reveal the prior frames. See the *squashweber.swf* file.

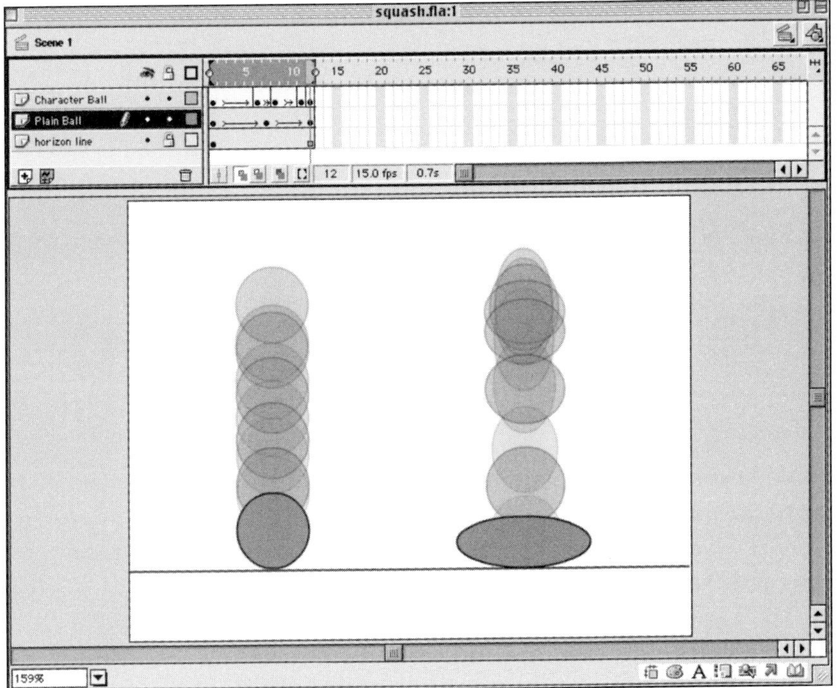

Figure 5.17
Here's the squash-and-stretch technique with onion-skinning turned on, to reveal all frames.

escape the force horizontally. The volume of the ball is simply redistributed. This principle is important to know, because if you were to simply scale an object vertically, without letting the volume escape horizontally, the squash and stretch would not be as convincing.

When the circle leaves the ground, notice that its volume recoils to a shape somewhat opposite of its shape when it hits the floor. This shape shows the energy released from the previous compression against the floor. This distortion of the shape gives the circle the enthusiastic feel. Once the circle reaches the apex of the ascent, it begins to relax back to its normal shape.

You can use squash and stretch in many situations in a cartoon animation. It's quite a fun movement to add to all sorts of situations—not just the obvious bouncing on the ground, but also things such as a head being hit by an anvil, an old jalopy of a car stuttering down the road, or even a character being stopped short by a tree.

PROJECT Animating Motion

In this project, we'll take some of the points we made about motion and put them into action. To keep things simple, we'll continue with our little friend, the circle. Certainly, you can apply all the examples and theories we've discussed so far to more complicated characters and animations.

We have supplied you with the scenes and elements that you need (see Figure 5.18). We have separated these moves into scenes (using the Flash Scene function) for clarity in discussion; you would generally not jump this quickly from scene to scene in a linear animation. We have also included various sound effects, so you can see the value they have in convincing the viewer of the motions depicted.

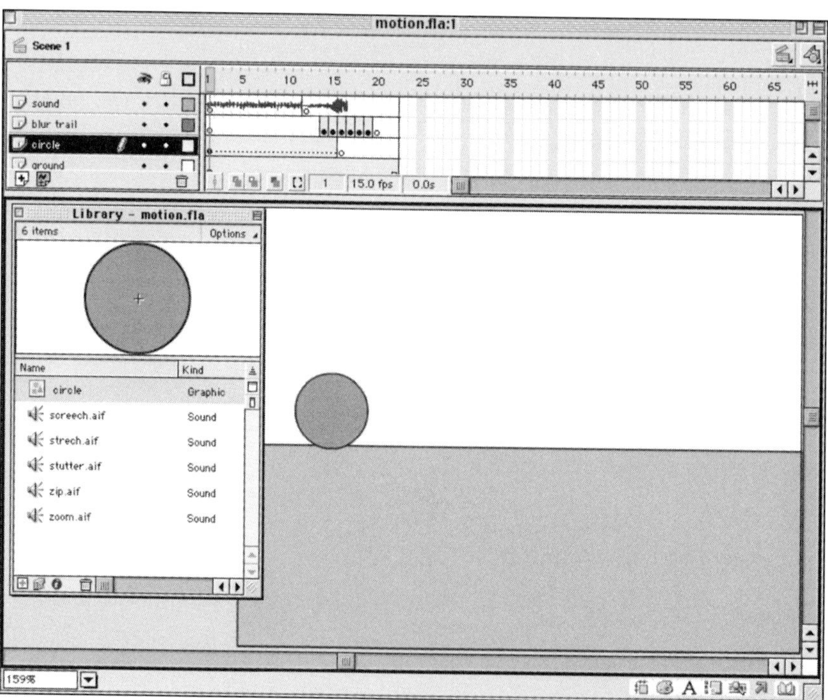

Figure 5.18
Here are the elements included in the motion project.

1. In the folder named Project Motion, open the file named *motion.fla*.
2. Go to Scene 1, and lock all layers except for the **circle** layer. We will be dealing only with the **circle** layer. You'll notice that the first frame in the **circle** layer already has Motion Tweening applied, with 69% Easing Out applied, as well.
3. Advance to Frame 8, and insert a keyframe (press F6).
4. Select the **circle** symbol on the stage. In the Transform panel, set the Scale (with Constrain unchecked) to 100% and 136%. Set the Skew to -15° and 0° (see Figure 5.19).
5. Advance to Frame 11, and insert a keyframe (F6).
6. Select the **circle** symbol on the stage. In the Transform panel, set the Scale to 100% and 154%. Set the Skew to -14° and 0°.
7. Advance to Frame 12. Insert a keyframe (F6), and turn off Motion Tweening for this frame. Leave the Scale and Skew settings alone. This combination makes the circle hold the previous posture for this frame and adds the hesitation.
8. Advance to Frame 13, and insert a keyframe (F6). Select the **circle** symbol on the stage. In the Transform panel, set the Scale to 100% and 113%. Set the Skew to 28° and 0°.
9. Advance to Frame 14, and insert a keyframe (F6). Select the **circle** symbol on the stage. In the Transform panel, set the Scale to 100% and 140%. Set the Skew to 44° and 0°. In the Info panel, set X to 122 and Y to 90.
10. Advance to Frame 15, and insert a keyframe (F6). Select the **circle** symbol on the stage. Set the Scale to 100% and 126%. Set the Skew to 38° and 0°. Set X to 252 and Y to 90.
11. Advance to Frame 16, and insert a *blank* keyframe (F7). This action eliminates the circle from the stage, and finishes the first scene of the animation. You've just completed the anticipation motion. You can play it back now if you want to see the results.
12. Go to Scene 2 via the Scene panel. Lock all the layers except for the **circle** layer.
13. Advance to Frame 6, and insert a keyframe (F6). Drag the **circle** symbol onto the stage. Set the Scale to 100% and 113%. Set the Skew to 28° and 0°. Set X to 6 and Y to 90.

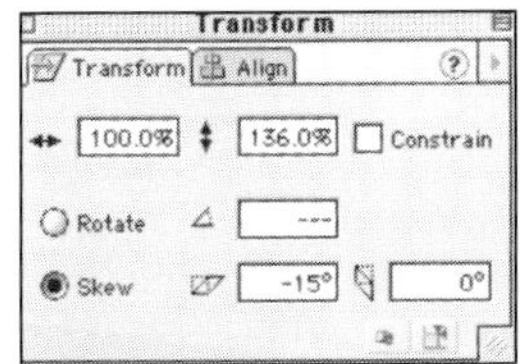

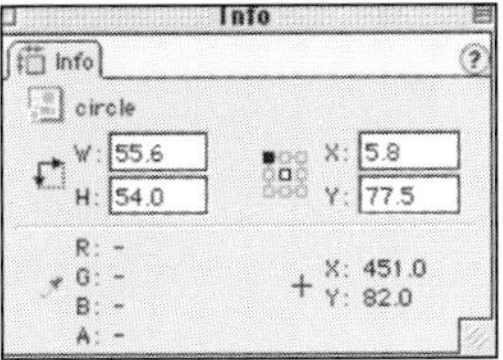

Figure 5.19

These panels are the Transform and Info panels we'll be using frequently in this project.

14. Advance to Frame 7, and insert a keyframe (F6). Select the **circle** symbol on the stage. Set the Scale to 100% and 140%. Set the Skew to 45° and 0°. Set X to 122 and Y to 90.

15. Advance to Frame 8, and insert a keyframe (F6). Select the **circle** symbol on the stage. Set the Scale to 100% and 126%. Set the Skew to 38° and 0°. Set X to 252 and Y to 90.

16. Advance to Frame 9, and insert a *blank* keyframe (F7). This action eliminates the circle from the stage, and finishes the second scene of the animation. You've just completed the speed-blur motion. You can play the scene back now if you want to see the results.

17. Go to Scene 3 via the Scene panel. Lock all the layers except for the **circle** layer. Notice that the first frame in the **circle** layer already has Motion Tween applied.

18. Advance to Frame 5, and insert a keyframe (F6). Select the **circle** symbol on the stage. Using the Transform panel, set the Scale to 100% and 110%. Set the Skew to -24° and 0°. In the Info panel, set X to 190 and Y to 90.

19. Advance to Frame 6, insert a keyframe (F6), and turn off Motion Tweening. Select the **circle** symbol on the stage. Set the Scale to 100% and 170%. Set the Skew to 20° and 0°. Set X to 208 and Y to 65.

20. Advance to Frame 7, and insert a keyframe (F6). Select the circle symbol on the stage. Using the Transform panel, set the scale to 100% and 230%. Set the Skew to 64° and 0°. In the Info panel, set X to 208 and Y to 87.

21. Advance to Frame 8, and insert a keyframe (F6). Select the circle symbol on the stage. Using the Transform panel, set the scale to 100% and 107%. Set the Skew to 20° and 0°. In the Info panel, set X to 218 and Y to 90.

22. Advance to Frame 9, and insert a keyframe (F6). Select the circle symbol on the stage. Using the Transform panel, set the scale to 100% and 106%. Set the Skew to -20° and 0°. In the Info panel, set X to 198 and Y to 90.

23. Advance to Frame 10, and insert a keyframe (F6). Select the circle symbol on the stage. Using the Transform panel, set the scale to 100% and 105%. Set the Skew to 19° and 0°. In the Info panel, set X to 210 and Y to 90.

24. Advance to Frame 11, and insert a keyframe (F6). Select the circle symbol on the stage and, using the Transform panel, set the scale to 100% and 102%. Set the Skew to -10° and 0°. In the Info panel, set X to 206 and Y to 90.

25. Advance to Frame 12, and insert a keyframe (F6). Select the circle symbol on the stage and, using the Transform panel, set the scale to 100% and 100%. Set the Skew to 0° and 0°. In the Info panel, set X to 211 and Y to 88.

26. This series of steps completes the overshoot motion section and completes the animation. You can now export to SWF to see the animation play in its entirety. Notice how the sounds reinforce the motion. If you become stuck anywhere in this project, you can find the completed version in the file named *motion2.fla*, and in the playback file named *motion2.swf*.

You've just turned a rather boring circle into a lively character animation. Certainly, you'll want to draw more than just circles when you're animating your cartoon. The point of this project is to show how little (and not-so-little) distortions add a great deal of fun, and possibly even personality, to your animations. We are not saying that simple skewing and scaling of drawings adds this, but when you think of these distortions *while you're drawing* your characters, you'll be creating very entertaining motion, and that's what cartoon motion is all about.

Human Movements

Human movement can be incredibly complex. You can spend many years studying these movements. For an animator, creating human movement is an ongoing learning experience. Observing how people (and animals) move is keenly important. You should always keep your eyes peeled, with a mind to analyzing just what's going on in a given movement. Then, as a cartoon animator, exaggerating at the right place, at the right time, can make the difference between a decent move and a splendid one (see Figure 5.20).

Figure 5.20
This scene from Edwin Carp uses a broken-joint technique for the human movement.

Even though we're using the term *human movements*, what we're really talking about is bi-ped moves, or movements of anything that walks upright on its two hind limbs. This category could include a rabbit, dog, or cat—such as Bugs, Droopy, and Sylvester—because most cartoon characters walk upright, even if the real creature does not.

We've set up some graphics similar to the circle examples we used earlier. These examples are mannequin-type devices that'll make understanding the motions easier. Think of the graphic as a skeleton over which you can drape your cartoon-character drawing. We think you'll find these pre-built mannequin movements quite helpful, long after you've gone through this book and its examples and projects. By using the mannequin movements supplied, and making your own custom sequences with them, you'll be able to test out moves quickly, without doing any drawing at all (see Figure 5.21).

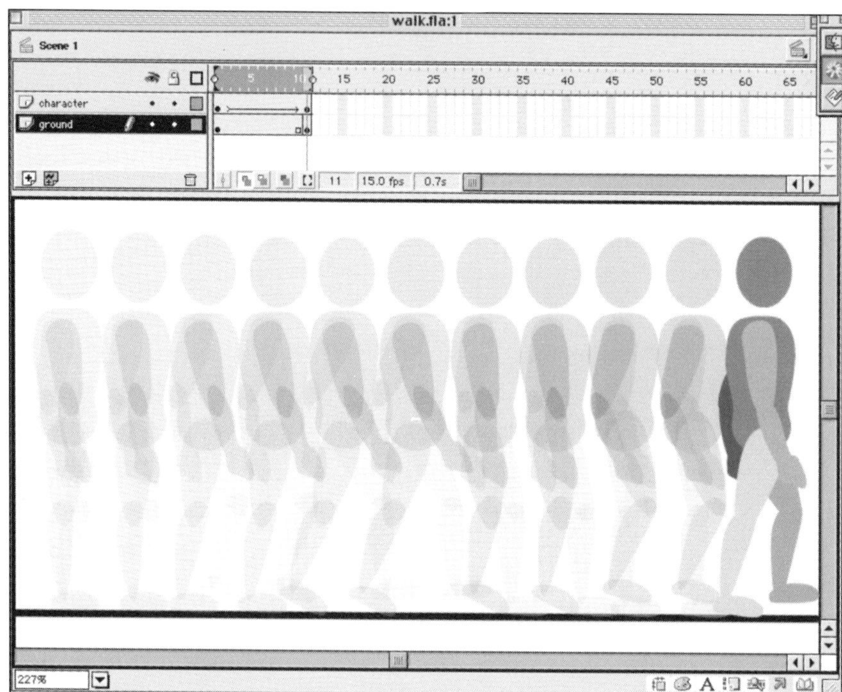

Figure 5.21
This sequence of frames (via onion skin) depicts a walk cycle.

Walking

The most used of human movements is *walking*. We walk all over the place and, sooner or later, your characters will need to do so, as well. The tricky part is that there are as many different types of walks as there are shapes of clouds. We can think of walking as a language all its own. Everyone has a unique walk and, even with the same person, various walks emerge, depending on his or her mood. Walking style can say a lot about a character. While we cannot cover every nuance that we can observe in a character's walk, we can look into some basic things a walk can say.

Normal Walk

There's really no such thing as a "normal" or standard walk. For the sake of discussion, we'll consider a normal walk to be one that really says little about the character, except that it's a way to get from one place to another (see Figure 5.22).

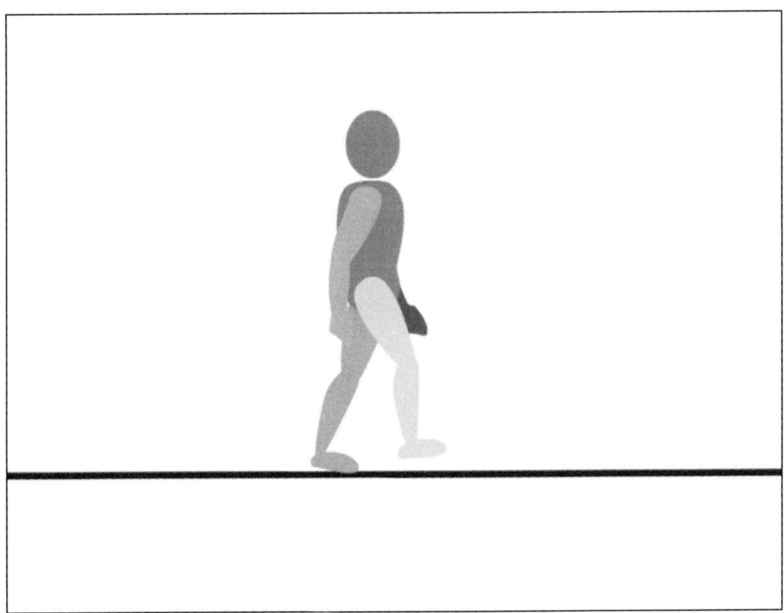

Figure 5.22
The mannequin is walking normally.

In the file named *walk.fla* (inside the Walk Examples folder), we've set up a sequence using the mannequin device for a normal walk. Open that file and play it now, making sure that looping playback is on (that is, **Control|Loop Playback** is checked). Notice that there's no real emphasis here. The character is simply walking. One important detail is the frame rate, which is 15fps. This mannequin is set up as a symbol in which that character takes one complete step. By double-clicking the symbol, you can open its timeline to observe the frames used. We considered a step to be the following: The right foot leaves the ground, moves forward, moves to the back, and stops just before its original position. Stopping the right foot just before its originating position allows the loop to be seamless. When the loop jumps back to Frame 1, the animation flows from the last frame in the loop. This cycle occupies 12 frames, which makes the entire cycle last a bit less than a second, and it is animated on the twos (every other frame).

While you're observing the movement of the legs, you might find it a bit confusing. This is why we've constructed the mannequins so that the vital parts reside on their own discrete layers. You can hide any part you want by clicking the eyeball icon of that layer (doing this puts an X through the icon). By hiding all the layers except for the one you want to view, you can isolate that movement, making it easier to understand.

Notice that the isolated leg moves in an understandable manner now. The thigh part not only rotates at the hip point, but also moves up and down, which suggests a swaying of the hips, even though we do not actually animate the hip section of the mannequin. In a walk, the hips must move, because simply bending the knee will not give the foot enough clearance over the ground. Because legs don't shrink while they're walking, the clearance needs to come from somewhere, and the hips are where we find this space. For simplification, the mannequin device has solid feet—that is, they do not bend. Real feet bend at the base of the toes while one is walking, and this effect would be more desirable when you're getting to that level of detail in your character's drawing.

Another important consideration is the arms. The arms need to move, even if only slightly, to keep balance with the movement of the legs. Generally speaking, the more the legs move, the more the arms move. You can also isolate these parts to study the swaying arm movement.

Now, isolate everything but the torso and the head layers. Notice that the torso doesn't just sit still during the walk. If it did, the walk would seem stiff and unusual. The torso has a bouncy, to-and-fro movement, in a roughly circular manner. The torso bounces in direct response to the feet meeting the ground. The head moves, too, but more smoothly, because the neck (not drawn in our examples, but imagined) acts as a shock absorber.

Proud Walk

The *proud walk* adds more language to the walk than the normal walk does. The proud walk has a bit of a march to it, giving the impression of pride. This walk is based on the normal walk, with some differences to posture. We've included the proud walk to make the point that small differences can make the walk say different things. Open the *proudwalk.fla* file, and play it as usual (see Figure 5.23).

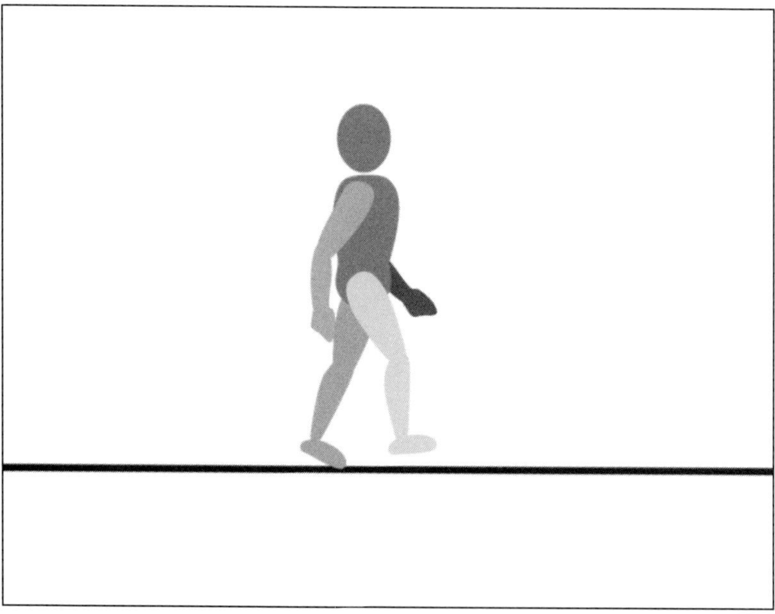

Figure 5.23
The mannequin is walking proudly.

Notice that the legs in this sequence move in roughly the same way as in the normal walk. The stride is maintained, but the posture is different. The torso tilts slightly more forward and thrusts deliberately upward with the step. This posture suggests that the chest is being held up in pride. The head has no back-and-forth movement; it moves only up and down. This limited range suggests a certain attention and straightforwardness, much like a military person would have when marching.

The arms in this sequence are where the action has changed a lot from the normal walk. The arms cover much more distance in their swing, without adding more rotation about the shoulders. The arms move in a much more determined manner, suggesting certainty of mission. This difference keeps the emphasis on the chest and completes the language of the walk.

Lazy Walk

Now here's a nice contrast in walks: the lazy, slacker walk. Open the *lazywalk.fla* file, and view it as usual. Oddly enough, this walk, too, is based on the preceding walks, yet it is totally different (see Figure 5.24).

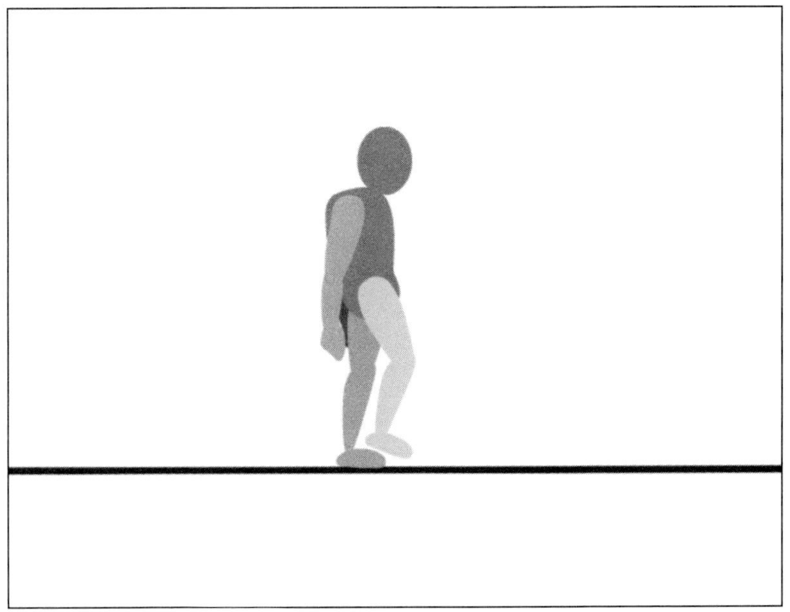

Figure 5.24
The mannequin is walking lazily.

Again, the leg movement here is roughly the same as for the normal walk. The torso, however, has changed posture dramatically. By rotating and moving back the torso, and reducing its bounce, we've given the character a completely lazy, even doofy, posture. The head is cocked forward and dropped down a bit to convey a lack of motivation. We have given the arms a different position on the shoulders, pinning them further back than normal, and letting them dangle. This dangling of the arms imparts the feeling that the character either doesn't want, or hasn't the energy, to control them.

Tired Walk

Now, we switch gears completely—a downshift, if you will. The day's been really long, and your character is beat, really beat. It's time for the *tired walk*. Open the *tiredwalk.fla* file, and view it as usual (see Figure 5.25).

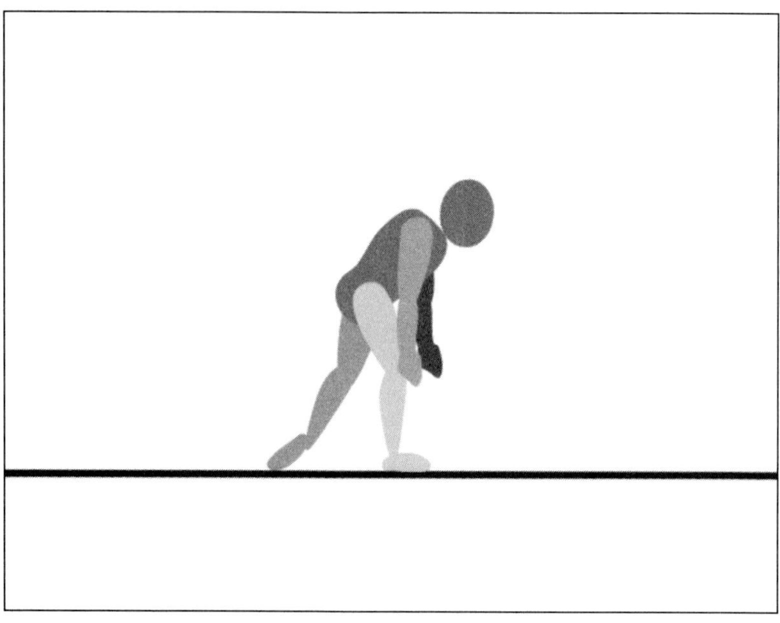

Figure 5.25
The mannequin is walking tiredly.

This walk is completely different from the previous ones. The exaggeration of posture is most evident here. The torso is tilted radically forward (done by rotating the torso clockwise). Notice, too, that the bounce is replaced with a sluggish, up-and-down movement. The head still bobs, but with much less enthusiasm, and it is mostly following the torso's lead. We've made slight use of opposing actions (remember those?) in the head's relation to the torso's movement.

The legs, too, have a totally different movement. The right leg has a stiffening, locked-knee pause as it moves to the back, sluggishly propelling the character forward. The right leg must do this to support the left leg, which barely has enough oomph to drag the foot forward.

The arms have taken a cue from the lazy walk, with the difference being that they dangle, with less motion. All these postures and motions contribute to a really tired walk.

Funky Walk

Now it's time for a little fun in our contemplation of walks. Open the *funkywalk.fla* file, and view it as usual. Whoa—*nobody* walks like that! Precisely. That's why it's called cartooning. Let your imagination go wild (see Figure 5.26).

Figure 5.26
The mannequin is doing a funky walk.

In this fun walk, we sort of went nuts with a marching-type leg movement and wildly gyrating arms. We have no idea what this character is trying to prove. Is it an offering to the sun gods? A new hip-hop dance move? What we do know is the attention we need to give to balance. Even though you can get away with being off balance for short moments, you should always try to make sure that weight is distributed in a convincing manner. Sure, cartoons can be fun and absurd, and sometimes defy the laws of gravity. But, if you constantly defy these laws, the absurd becomes standard. And then, when the time comes to break the rules, you will have no rules set up to break.

Running

Okay, we're cheating a bit. *Running* is not walking, but generally, it's the same thing, with more extension of the limbs at a quicker pace. Open the *run.fla* file, and view it as usual (see Figure 5.27).

On most of the other examples, we've animated on the twos (every other frame) at 15fps. In this example, we need a faster movement, so we have animated on the ones, in which every frame has a new image. We've also reduced, by roughly half, the number of frames in the loop. This reduction affects the amount of time the loop takes and helps achieve the faster motion we need for a running sequence.

Isolate the right leg so that it's the only one visible, and play the animation. Of course, the animation moves very quickly, as it should. We want to point out here the number of frames we used for the three phases of its movement. In the first phase, we dedicate Frames 1 through 3 to the motion of bringing the

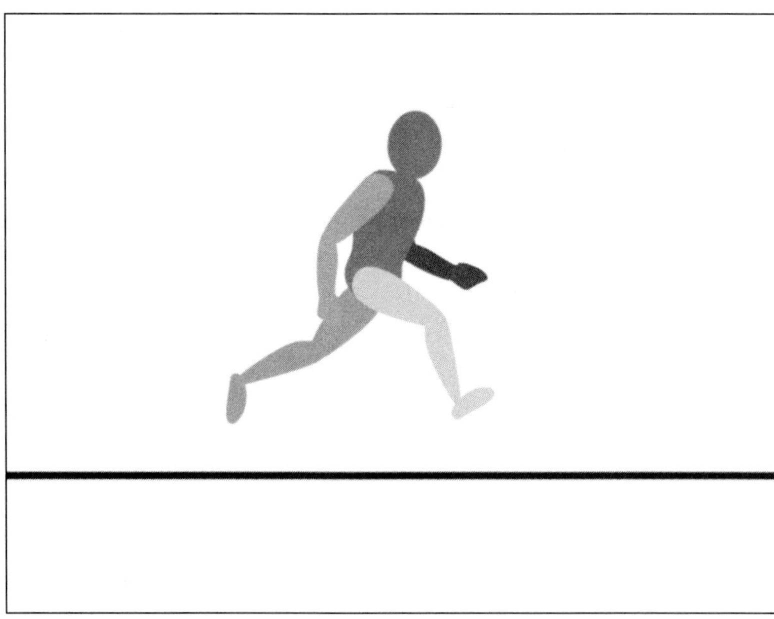

Figure 5.27
In this example, the mannequin is running.

leg forward. Notice that Frame 1 starts out with the foot off the ground. This is important, because this first frame is the one the loop will go back to after the last frame. Frames 4 and 5 make the foot meet the ground and propel the runner forward. In Frame 6, the leg leaves the ground after the push. Because only one frame is used for this phase, the leg appears to move very quickly, but then, as the animation re-enters the first phases of the loop, it moves a bit slower because it takes more frames to cover the same amount of motion. In a subtle way, when the leg prepares to push against the ground, we are using the anticipation motion we discussed earlier.

Isolate one of the arms, and you'll notice that the same anticipation is happening there, too. But the arm is reacting to the opposite of the leg's motion—opposing actions are being applied.

The Art of Fiddling

So far, we've been discussing the art of motion. So, what do you do when your character is just standing (or sitting) there? If your character needs to wait for something and simply turns to stone, you can become bored really quickly. Something needs to be going on...anything. If you take a look at people, you will quickly realize that no one sits or stands perfectly still. And if someone suddenly did, that instant would make for a good *Twilight Zone* episode. People are constantly moving, and so should your characters (see Figure 5.28).

Use of a little fiddling or fidgeting (or what have you) adds a much more interesting aspect to your animation. Open and view the *fiddling.fla* file (in the Other Examples folder). Both characters are waiting for a bus. One character

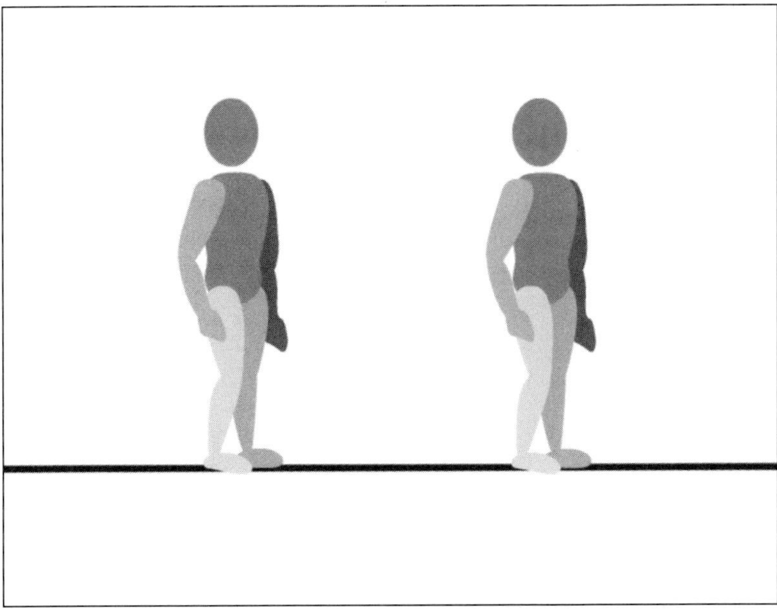

Figure 5.28
Two identical characters are waiting for a bus.

is stone still, easy to animate, and quite boring. The other, however, is checking his watch, shifting his weight, taking a deep breath, and scratching his head. Which one better conveys someone waiting?

You can use fiddling, or what some animators call "business," in many ways. Even though fiddling adds a bit more work, it pays off in a much more entertaining show. Fiddling also offers a way to inject humor into the cartoon. Whenever your script calls for a pause, try ad libbing with fiddling.

PROJECT Choreographing Moves to Music

It's time, once again, to dig in and get our mouse dirty. We've been going on about various walks and other human moves; now, it's time to try out some of them. We'll choreograph some pre-built moves using our now-familiar mannequin device. We'll be using a short music track (courtesy of the good folks at SmartSound) that we used in Chapter 3. We hope you'll get a feel from this project for using symbols of animated loops.

We have created all the animated loops for you using the mannequin (see Figure 5.29). These moves probably won't win any awards for dance—that'd be nice, but it's not our aim here. If you'd like, after you complete the project, you can go into the symbols themselves and re-animate them until your heart's content. In fact, we encourage you to do so. You'll find them very easy to work with.

In the previous project, we used the Transform and Info panels. For this project, we'll be using the Transform, Info, and Instance panels frequently (see Figure 5.30), so you might want to arrange your layout as we have done in Figure 5.29. We'll use the Transform panel to enter Scale, Skew, and Rotate

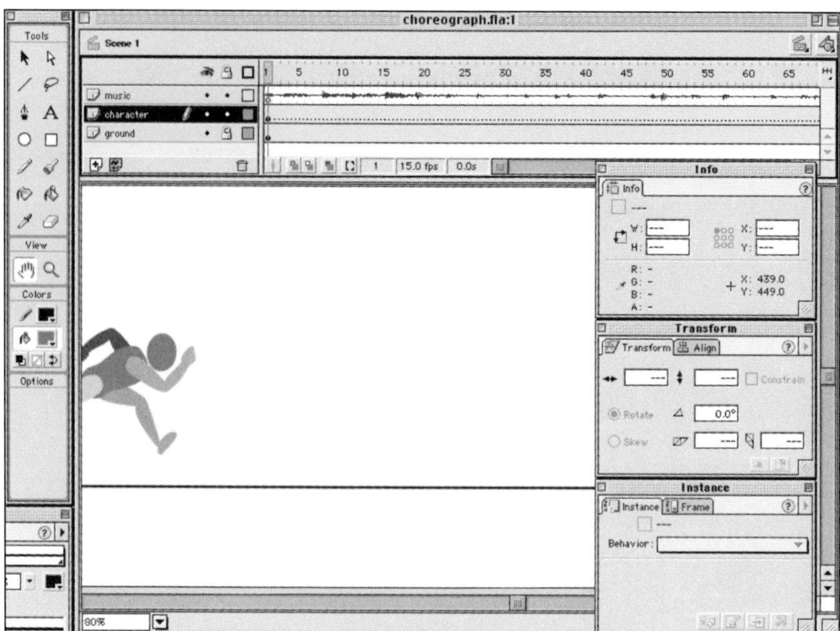

Figure 5.29
Here's everything you need for the choreography project.

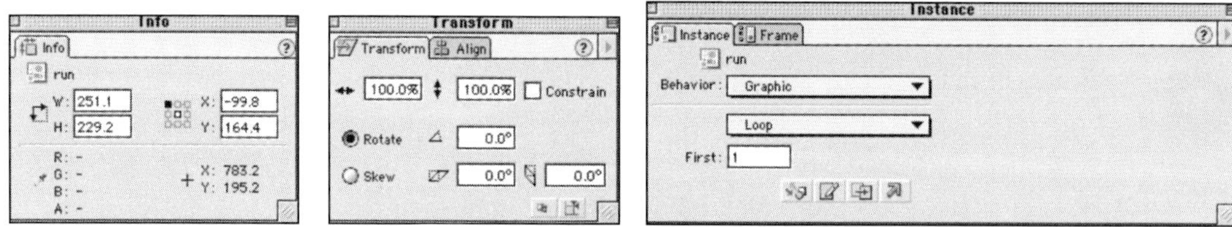

Figure 5.30
These panels are the Info, Transform, and Instance panels.

settings. We'll use the Info panel to enter X- and Y-coordinates. We'll use the Instance panel to select a symbol instance's animation option (Loop, Play Once, or Single Frame), and to specify a frame number for that option.

1. Open the file named *choreograph.fla* located inside the folder project choreograph on the CD-ROM.
2. Lock the layers named **ground** and **music** if they aren't already locked. From here on, everything will take place on the **character** layer.
3. At Frame 1, you should find the graphic symbol named **run**. (From now on, we'll shorten "graphic symbol" to just "symbol" because we'll not be using movie clips or button symbols.) The frame is set to Motion Tweening. Make sure that the Synchronize option in the Frame panel is unchecked whenever you're making motion-tweened frames. If Synchronize is checked, you will not be able to swap symbols, because the previous symbol will persist, even after you've swapped them.
4. Advance to Frame 7, and insert a keyframe (F6). In the Info panel, set X to 329 and Y to 195.

5. Advance to Frame 8, insert a keyframe, and turn off Motion Tweening. Select the run symbol on the stage and, in the Instance panel, click the Swap Symbol button. Then, choose the fiddle symbol. Back in the Instance panel, set this symbol to Single Frame, and type "2" in the first box. In the Transform panel, set the Scale to 100% and 118%. Set the Skew to 31° and 0°. In the Info panel, set X to 472 and Y to 162 (see Figure 5.31).

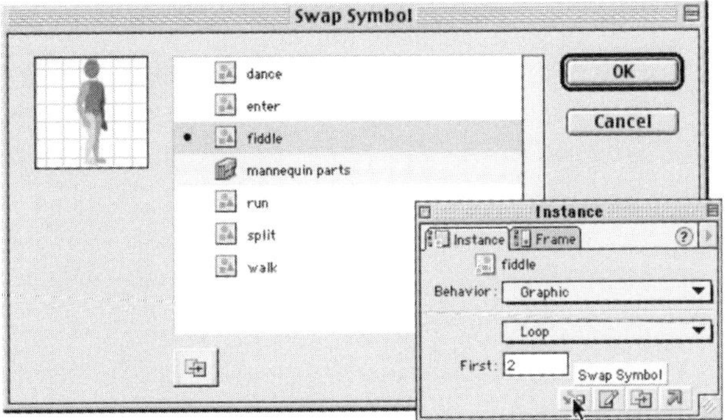

Figure 5.31
This panel is the Instance panel (in front) with the cursor on the Swap Symbol button, and the ensuing Swap Symbol dialog box for choosing the symbol you want to swap to.

6. Advance to Frame 9, and insert a keyframe. In the Instance panel, set this symbol to Single Frame, and type "3" in the First box. In the Transform panel, set the Scale to 100% and 110%. Set the Skew to -24° and 0°. In the Info panel, set X to 363 and Y to 163.

   A quick note is in order here: Flash seems to like to put arbitrary numerals after the decimal point, as in 163.4. These fractional pixels have no bearing on our project's success, so you may ignore them if they pop up. Just stick with the whole numbers we give you.

7. Advance to Frame 10, and insert a keyframe. In the Instance panel, set this symbol to Single Frame, and type "4" in the First box. In the Transform panel, set the Scale to 100% and 102%. Set the Skew to 13° and 0°. In the Info panel, set X to 473 and Y to 166.

8. Advance to Frame 11, and insert a keyframe. In the Instance panel, set this symbol to Single Frame, and type "5" in the First box. In the Transform panel, set the Scale to 100% and 100%. Set the Skew to -4° and 0°. In the Info panel, set X to 457 and Y to 165.

9. Advance to Frame 12, and insert a keyframe. In the Instance panel, set this symbol to Single Frame, and type "6" in the First box. In the Transform panel, set the Scale to 100% and 100%. Set the Skew to 3° and 0°. In the Info panel, set X to 475 and Y to 166.

10. Advance to Frame 13, and insert a keyframe. In the Instance panel, set this symbol to Single Frame, and type "7" in the First box. In the Transform panel, set the Scale to 100% and 100%. Set the Skew to 0° and 0°. In the Info panel, set X to 465 and Y to 166.

11. Now you can test the playback. You should have a character who runs in and whose feet stop on a dime, but the body has overshoot and a rubbery reaction to the abrupt halt.

12. Advance to Frame 19, and insert a keyframe. Select the fiddle symbol on the stage and, in the Instance panel, click the Swap Symbol button. Then, choose the symbol dance. Back in the Instance panel, set this symbol to Loop, and type "1" in the First box. This value will cause the symbol to loop through the animation it contains until we tell it to stop.

13. Advance to Frame 64, insert a keyframe, and turn on Motion Tweening. Select the dance symbol on the stage and, in the Instance panel, click the Swap Symbol button. Then, choose the symbol run. From the menu, choose **Modify|Transform|Flip Horizontal**. Back in the Instance panel, set this symbol to Loop, and type "5" in the First box. In the Info panel, set X to 394 and Y to 175.

14. Advance to Frame 78, and insert a keyframe. In the Info panel, set X to 152 and Y to 175.

15. Advance to Frame 79, insert a keyframe, and turn off Motion Tweening. Select the run symbol on the stage and, in the Instance panel, click the Swap Symbol button. Then, choose the symbol **dance**. Back in the Instance panel, set this symbol to Loop, and type "1" in the First box. In the Info panel, set X to 154 and Y to 148.

16. Advance to Frame 108, and insert a keyframe. Select the dance symbol. In the Instance panel, set this symbol to Single Frame, and type "30" in the First box. In the Info panel, set X to 153 and Y to 155.

17. Advance to Frame 109, and insert a keyframe. Select the dance symbol. In the Instance panel, set this symbol to Play Once, and type "25" in the First box.

18. Advance to Frame 118, and insert a keyframe. Select the dance symbol. In the Instance panel, set this symbol to Single Frame, and type "29" in the First box.

19. Advance to Frame 119, and insert a keyframe. Select the dance symbol. In the Instance panel, set this symbol to Play Once, and type "30" in the First box.

20. Advance to Frame 126, and insert a keyframe. Select the dance symbol. In the Instance panel, set this symbol to Play Once, and type "20" in the First box.

21. Advance to Frame 129, and insert a keyframe. Select the dance symbol on the stage and, in the Instance panel, click the Swap Symbol button. Then, choose the symbol split. Back in the Instance panel, set this symbol to Play Once, and type "1" in the First box.

22. Hang in there, we're almost done. Advance to Frame 148, and insert a keyframe. Select the split symbol on the stage and, in the Instance panel, click the Swap Symbol button. Then, choose the symbol enter. Back in the Instance panel, set this symbol to Loop, and type "1" in the First box.

23. Advance to Frame 152, and insert a keyframe. Select the enter symbol on the stage. In the Instance panel, set this symbol to Single Frame, and type "7" in the First box.

24. Advance to Frame 164, and insert a keyframe. Select the enter symbol on the stage. In the Instance panel, set this symbol to Single Frame, and type "8" in the First box.

25. Now, you can export to SWF and play back the project.

If you get stuck anywhere during the project, you can view the finished animation, called *choreograph2.fla*, and view the exported SWF, named *choreograph2.swf*, on the CD-ROM.

This exercise may seem like all that's done is to enter a bunch of numbers to make things happen on the stage. What we're really doing here is choreographing pre-made human motions to connect together different moves. The possibilities are endless, and limited only by how many moves (symbols) you've created. Usually when animating you will not go strictly by the numbers. That would be anti-creative. You will go by what *looks* right in motion. We had to use numbers in this project, as it's the only means of giving you the exact placement of elements so that you can see how the motions go together.

For extra credit, you can, of course, add your own moves to the mannequin by creating new symbols. But, for a really good time, if you're handy with the pencil tool, you can use the series of mannequin moves as a template to draw your character to. To do this, simply edit the symbols provided, with a new layer on top of the existing ones, and draw your character to match the mannequin underneath. Then, simply delete the layers that contain the mannequin. After you do this, you'll have your own character dancing in the main Timeline. We think you'll find the mannequin device very valuable for testing your animation of human moves. Sometimes, even professional animators become stumped trying to visualize a move. With mannequins, visualization's a snap.

Rotoscoping in Flash

Let's say you want to animate a more realistic character. Maybe you want to study real-life motion. Then, rotoscoping is for you. You're in luck, because Flash can import digital video. If you have a VCR, video camera, or other means of acquiring video into your computer, you can bring the world to you for motion study.

What Is Rotoscoping?

Rotoscoping is the art of tracing over film or video, one frame at a time in order to create an animated sequence. Depending on the level of detail you use in tracing, rotoscoping can be time consuming, but the results can be quite amazing. In days past, a section of film destined to be rotoscoped would be printed as a series of photographs, and the artist would use a light table to trace over the photographs. The resulting drawings would then be transferred back to film in the standard photographic way, via an animation stand and a special camera that exposes one frame of film at a time. This process can be very time consuming.

Computers have certainly eased the workload of rotoscoping by basically eliminating the photographic printout process, particularly if video is the subject's source. Even with film as the source, scanners are available that can digitize the individual frames for rotoscoping, and for many other digital special effects, as well. This film scanning can require fairly expensive equipment that might be out of the average, small, animation studio's reach, so we will focus on video as the source (see Figure 5.32).

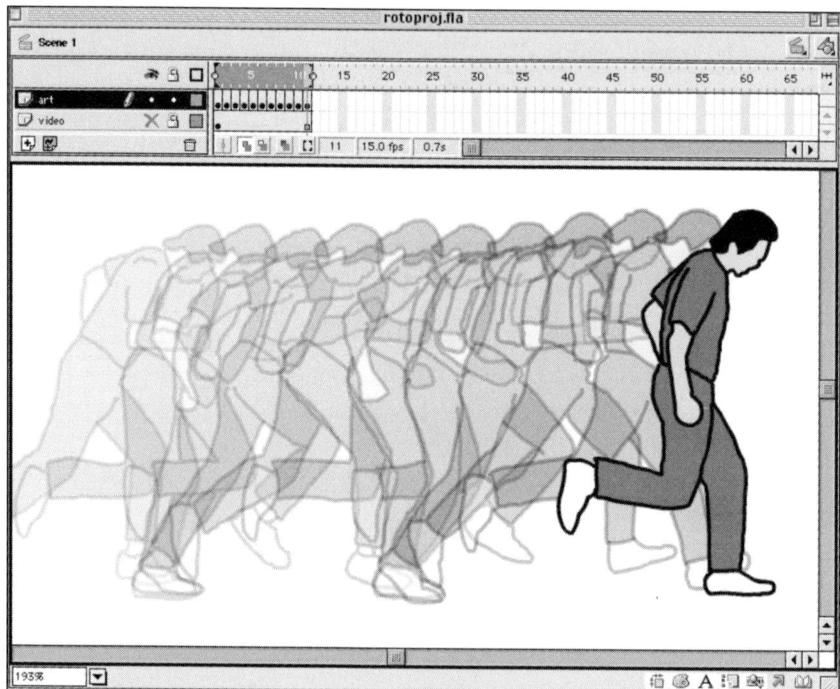

Figure 5.32
Here's a quickly rotoscoped running sequence.

A justified debate continues among animators that rotoscoping is cheating and confining, because you're basically tracing, and not originating, the art from your imagination. This might be true, but rotoscoping also is a very good learning tool for the artist new to motion study. The argument about rotoscoping being confining is especially cogent. Because you are using real life as your guide, you can easily fall into the trap of ignoring all the things we've discussed so far in this chapter. Things such as squash and stretch simply do not occur in real life, as they should in cartoons. Motion cannot be exaggerated as much in real life as it can be in cartoon animation. So, with these pitfalls in mind, we still believe rotoscoping can be useful—and even desirable—in some circumstances.

What's Needed for Rotoscoping?

For the purpose of rotoscoping in a small animation studio, you're in luck in terms of expense. You might already have all you need in equipment to do this form of animation. If you can digitize video, and you have a video camera or VCR hooked up to your computer, you're ready to go.

If you don't have such equipment, we'd suggest going with the new MiniDV format. This new video format uses a very small cassette for the video, and the image quality is high. This format also uses a fairly precise, time-code track for finding the exact frame you want in a video clip. This feature is extremely useful for editing video, as well. Even though home VCRs and video cameras have a time or footage readout, they are not very (frame) accurate. We've seen MiniDV cameras ranging in price from $800 to $1,500 for home use. A trip to your local electronics store can shed more light on prices, which are dropping as the format becomes more accepted. More professional models can range from $2,500 to $7,000 and above, depending on things such as interchangeable lenses, and so on. The professional models from Sony, JVC, Panasonic, and other manufacturers are a good bit bulkier than the home and prosumer models, and they look more like the cameras you would see TV news crews using.

Note: Prosumer is the word used to refer to the middle ground between consumer and professional electronics equipment. Mostly used in video and audio worlds.

A Firewire (or IEEE 1394, or what Sony calls iLink—they are all the same thing) interface is needed for your computer to take advantage of MiniDV's high quality. Many PCs, and nearly every Apple (excepting the lowest-end iMac) computer produced today, have this interface. Firewire is a high-speed bus that can accept more than just DV cameras and VTRs, but can also hook up a host of other peripherals. Hard drives, scanners, and a growing list of equipment can use Firewire as the interface. If your computer doesn't have Firewire you may be able to install an expansion card that will give you this capability.

Okay, you don't have any of this stuff yet, and you still want to try rotoscoping. We've anticipated this and have included a few QuickTime video clips for you to experiment with. In the folder named rotoscope, you'll find several clips, courtesy of videographer Jim Cheal (**iDVnet.com**). These are simple, short clips of walking and running, shown from a side view and head-on view (see Figure 5.33).

Figure 5.33
Here's a QuickTime video clip of a running sequence for rotoscoping.

Importing Live-Action Video into Flash

To start rotoscoping, you must first prepare the video for use in Flash. In this discussion, we'll be dealing with QuickTime video, because it's a very versatile platform for video, and it's friendly to Flash. All Macintosh computers come with QuickTime as standard, and most PCs will have the software, as well. If you do not have QuickTime, you can download it free of charge from Apple at **www.quicktime.com**. Apple also offers a Pro version for $29.95, which adds some editing functions to the QuickTime Player, but the Pro version is not necessary for using the files we've supplied for rotoscoping. As of this writing, the latest official version of QuickTime is 4.1.2.

The video files we've supplied for rotoscoping have originated from a MiniDV source and have been scaled down to 444×333 pixels. The frame rate has been lowered from 30fps to 15fps, and the video files have been saved using Component Video as the codec (*codec* is short for the compression/decompression scheme the software uses to create the video file). The video clips have no sound.

When importing video clips into Flash, you should set up the blank, Flash authoring file to match the specifications of the video. So, to match the clips supplied, make a new Flash file, and choose **Modify|Movie Properties**. In the ensuing dialog, enter a Frame Rate of "15", and for the dimensions, enter "444×333" (see Figure 5.34). If you were to use other video sources and dimensions, you would need to change these settings to match the frame rate and dimensions of the video clip you plan to import—for example, 30fps and 640×480 pixels.

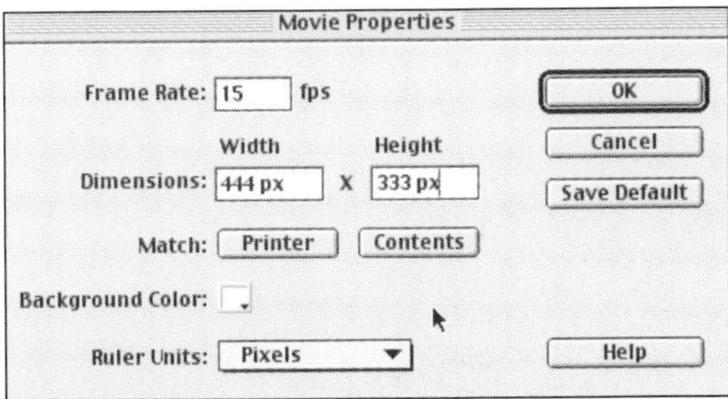

Figure 5.34
These settings are the Movie Properties settings for matching supplied video clips.

Once you have a layer set up to accept your video clip, you can then import the clip into Flash, just like you would import any other graphic, sound, or photo. One distinction, when you're importing video into Flash, is that the video itself does *not* become part of the Flash authoring file, as other still graphics, photos, and sounds do. Flash simply imports a reference or link to the video file on your drive. This difference is important if you move the Flash authoring file to another machine—you'll need to move the video clip as well, or Flash will lose track of it.

If you want the soundtrack portion (not needed for basic rotoscoping) in Flash, you will need to import it separately. Flash ignores the soundtrack of imported video clips. If you have a video-editing application such as Premiere or QuickTime Player Pro, you can extract the soundtrack, save it as an AIF or WAV file, and import it as a separate sound file in Flash. After you import both the video and the sound files, you can re-synch the video to the sound in Flash by having the two elements start on the same frame in Flash. In the Flash Sound panel, set the sound track's Sync option to Stream.

Note: When you're exporting from Flash to SWF, the imported video will not export with the animation. When you're exporting to QuickTime Video (MOV format via **File|Export Movie**), the video will export, but the sound will not, because Flash ignores video soundtracks when it imports video clips.

Now that you have the video on Frame 1, you will need to add more frames to be able to see more than just the first frame of video. If the video is long (in duration), you might need to add quite a few frames. One minute of video at 15fps would need 900 frames in Flash to enable you to see the whole clip.

Tracing Over Live-Action Video

Next, we'll step through the process of rotoscoping in Flash (see Figure 5.35). You'll need some artistic skills here, or at least good tracing skills. A Wacom or other drawing tablet is highly recommended, because drawing with a mouse or trackball can be difficult indeed.

1. Launch Flash if it's not launched already, and make a new authoring file.
2. Choose **Modify|Movie Properties**, and type in "15" for frames per second (FPS), and 444×333 for dimensions. Then, click OK.
3. Choose File|Import, and locate the supplied video clip named *runside2.mov*. You can access this file directly from this book's CD-ROM, but we recommend that you copy it to your hard drive before you import it. Save the

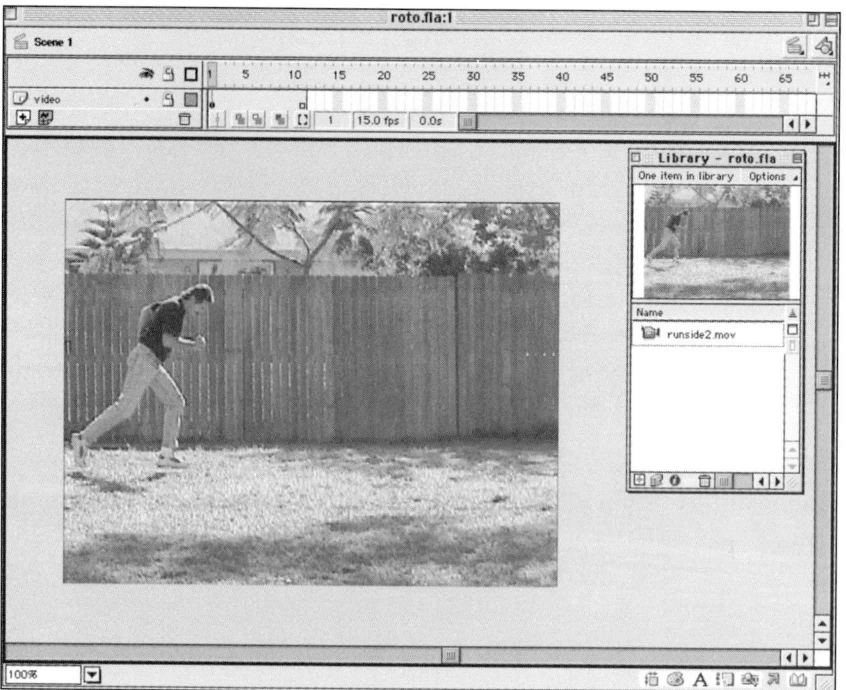

Figure 5.35
Here's the Flash environment, ready for rotoscoping.

clip in the same folder in which you will be saving this Flash project file—the clip will work faster that way.

4. You should now have the video clip with Frame 1 showing on the stage. You should rename the layer the clip resides on as **video**. Then, add a new layer, and name it **art**.
5. In the Timeline, click and drag until you've covered the area that includes Frame 11. Press F5 to insert blank frames. You should now have 11 frames in your file and be able to see the entire duration of the video clip.
6. Lock the video layer. Select the art layer and Frame 1.
7. Using the Pencil tool, you can now commence to trace over the video, using whatever level of detail you want.
8. After completing a frame, you can quickly advance and create a new, blank keyframe by pressing F7. This shortcut lets you move right along.
9. Continue until you have traced all 11 frames.
10. You can now go through with the Fill bucket, filling in the various areas of the tracing with color.
11. Hide the **video** layer by clicking its eyeball icon in the Timeline, and play back your creation. Amazing, huh?

We've included a finished version of the rotoscoped animation in the file named *roto.fla*. If you like, you can follow the same steps to rotoscope some of the other clips included on the CD-ROM.

While the results of rotoscoping can be quite fun, you can also benefit from the aspect of using it to draw your cartoon characters. By using the video as a motion guide, and drawing your character instead of tracing what's there, you will learn a lot about various motions from real life. Keep in mind that you will still need to employ the other factors we've discussed in this chapter—factors such as overshooting, squash and stretch, and opposing actions—to exaggerate the motions into cartoon land.

Moving On

Next, we'll look into the art of lip-synching. If your cartoon character plans to actually speak, you'll want to check out this chapter.

Chapter 6

Lip-Synching and Facial Expressions

With the rapid advances in technology, one would think that the lip-synching and expressions problem in character animation had been digitally resolved. Even though we've reached a level at which you can simply talk into a microphone, and the computer software types the words on your screen, we still cannot seem to automate the art of lip-synching and creating facial expressions.

By Bill Turner

Overview of Lip-Synching

Attempts have been made to automate lip-synching, but those efforts always seem to fall short of producing realistic results. The process includes too many variables, and the technology lacks the necessary "intelligence" to decide just which variable is most important to produce convincing lip movement. The human mind is very talented at deciphering these movements and, when necessary, filling in the blanks. Sure, the computer can get the mechanics right, but it stumbles dramatically on the necessary emotions to convey a thought convincingly. Computers are exceptional at recalling the most minute details of fact they've been fed, but they can't yet form an emotion or opinion from those facts. That limitation might change in the future, but for now, good, expressive lip-synching remains one of the most arduous tasks in animation—and humans have to do it.

In the first part of this chapter, we'll focus on analyzing speech and breaking that speech into digestible chunks that you can then incorporate into your character's mouth shapes and facial expressions. Once you've grasped the nature of this beast—really not as complicated as it might seem—you'll discover what's necessary, and what's not. Then you'll be better able to streamline your production process, while still convincing viewers that the voice they're hearing is coming from the animated character. We're sure that you've seen cartoons—and, particularly, overdubbed foreign films—in which the voice doesn't match the movement of the lips or the facial expressions. Mistakes such as these are extremely distracting, and they can make your characters seem less convincing.

An application tool called Magpie Pro is available to help ease this task of lip-synching. But even with Magpie Pro's help, you will at times just need to get in there and do it manually—which is why we will cover both techniques. Magpie Pro's intended use is in 3D animation applications; but, through research we've done with the program in collaboration with the program's creator, we've found a workflow that can really help in the production of Flash animated cartoons. Although setting up a project with Magpie Pro can be a bit complicated, you'll find this tool extremely useful, particularly for lip-synching long stretches of speech. We have included a demo on the CD-ROM.

Note: The animator also needs to consider the expression that the face will make to communicate a needed emotion. Although we communicate with body language and an endless number of other nuances, the place the words come from—the face—tends to take center stage. We'll discuss facial expressions later in this chapter.

Breaking Down Speech

Just like anything else, speech can be broken down into small components, which makes it easier to understand how speech is put together. The small components—or *phonemes*, as they're known—are the sounds that we string together to make up a spoken word. The animator doesn't need to understand the science behind all this, but he or she does need to understand the relationship between the sound being spoken and the mouth shape necessary to make that sound—in other words, how that sound should look on a face.

One may jump (logically) to the conclusion that a different mouth shape exists for each letter in the alphabet. That conclusion is not correct, which is good for the animator. Take a look in the mirror while you recite the alphabet. In terms of the mouth shape and position they require, the letters C, G, J, K, S, and Z are roughly identical, and the letters D, T, L, and N are also similar to each other. Of course, the O, Q, and U letters require a rounder mouth portal, but their requirements are roughly the same. The E sound tends to show both upper and lower teeth. As you recite the letters, you'll notice certain ones that really stand out from the rest. The lips must smack together on the letters B, P, M, V, W (with W, that's because you actually say the B sound), and Y (the Y requires a cross between the O and U shapes). These letters that force your lips to smack together are the very same letters that ventriloquists have a hard time perfecting as they try to hide their mouth movements while they speak.

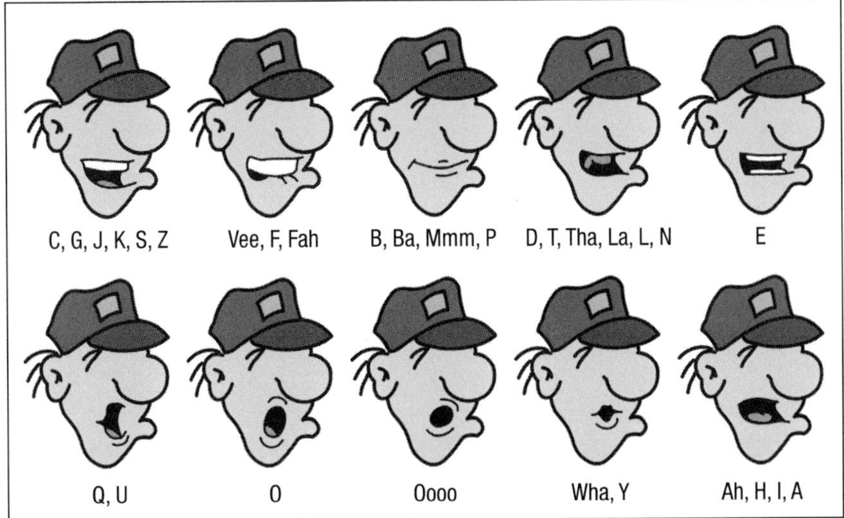

Figure 6.1
Here, we have a lip model sheet showing mouth shapes for each major phoneme for the Mr. Murky character from the Weber cartoon show. Notice that this model sheet tends toward the happy side.

Notice that the letters F and V require a slight tucking of the bottom lip under the teeth, as Figure 6.1 shows. The Fah and Vah, or Vee sounds are the real keys to convincing lip-synching. These sounds occur more than you might expect in normal speech, and they are so different from the rest of the sounds that to ignore them is synch suicide.

The lip position for a few letters is very close in lip shape to some of the other letters (particularly the A shape), with the distinguishing feature being the tongue meeting the roof of the open mouth. The tongue then relaxes to its usual position to complete the pronunciation. The T and Tha are the most-used positions that benefit from drawing tongue movement, with D, L, and N close behind. Drawing tongues may not be the most glamorous thing in the world, but tongues really help convince the viewers that the character is doing the talking.

Occasionally, adding teeth to your drawings of characters talking is also a great idea. The addition of teeth especially helps make the E sound realistic. Even though a character can express E without teeth showing, this letter occurs so often in speech that varying the character's expression can help avoid monotony or a mechanical-looking mouth.

Connecting Sounds to Make Speech

So far, we've talked about letters, but we shouldn't go by letters alone when we're talking about lip-synching. We're discussing letters because they make a good starting point for understanding speech. We all understand the alphabet. What might escape you is how these elements slur and blend together into spoken words. Analyzing speech can be quite an abstract process. The more you listen and look, the more you'll realize that we seem to be just conjuring together grunts, pops, and whooshes when we speak. Certainly, we are more sophisticated and civilized than that, aren't we? Not really. Once you put the specific language aside, you can examine the basic sounds that make up speech.

So, after you learn the mouth shapes that the letters make, and which groups of letters and sounds are similar to each other, you'll then need to learn when to *ignore* certain letters when you're doing the lip-synching for your animations. You'll want to do this because the sounds run together when we speak, so you're animating not a series of individual letters, but a series of connected sounds. Another good reason to ignore, to some extent, the individual letters when you're creating lip-synching is that doing two sentences could otherwise take forever. For example, let's say that a sentence has 118 letters and takes roughly six seconds to say out loud at a normal pace. In a 15-frames-per-second animation, you'd have only 90 places to put 118 different mouth shapes. In the unlikely event that you'd even want to do this, you couldn't. Thus, we'd rather illustrate the high points and just *suggest* the other mouth shapes—and let the viewer's mind fill in the blanks.

Causing the viewer's mind to smooth the given mouth shapes into the flowing illusion of speech is *the* goal in lip-synch animation. To achieve this goal, you must find high points in the words and synchronize the shapes (the 10 mouth shapes you see in Figure 6.1) to those high points. You'll want to exaggerate the shapes on the word or sets of words that are being spoken with emphasis or emotion. After all, cartooning is the art of exaggeration.

As we've said, most of us normally speak without much of a pause between words—we basically speak in a blur of sounds. So, examining a set of words phonetically is sometimes very helpful to find the cues needed for lip-synching.

Here's a spoken example:

"Figuring out a way to solve the world's problems ain't easy, you know."

Here's what we'd animate:

Figger eeng ot ah wa ta salv tha wurlds pro bms ait e z u no.

The second example seems quite close to what a preschool child might write, because this is how the sentence *sounds*. And a very good reason exists for our second example, too—it represents how we hear the sentence spoken. We have thrown rules of proper spelling to the wind and simplified the words. We are animating to the *sounds* of the words, not to the words as they are properly spelled. Thinking in sound, not language, makes animating much easier. Thinking in sound helps you decide when you can drop certain letters, and still provide a clear rendering of the mouth shapes the character requires to say a word. For instance, notice that we're not animating the "n" in "ain't"; we're animating just the "ait" sounds.

Let's look at the first part of this example ("Figuring out a") again: The sounds in "Figger" use the letters F, G, and R. The sounds in "eeng" use E. The sounds in "Ot" use O and T. The sounds in "Ah" use A.

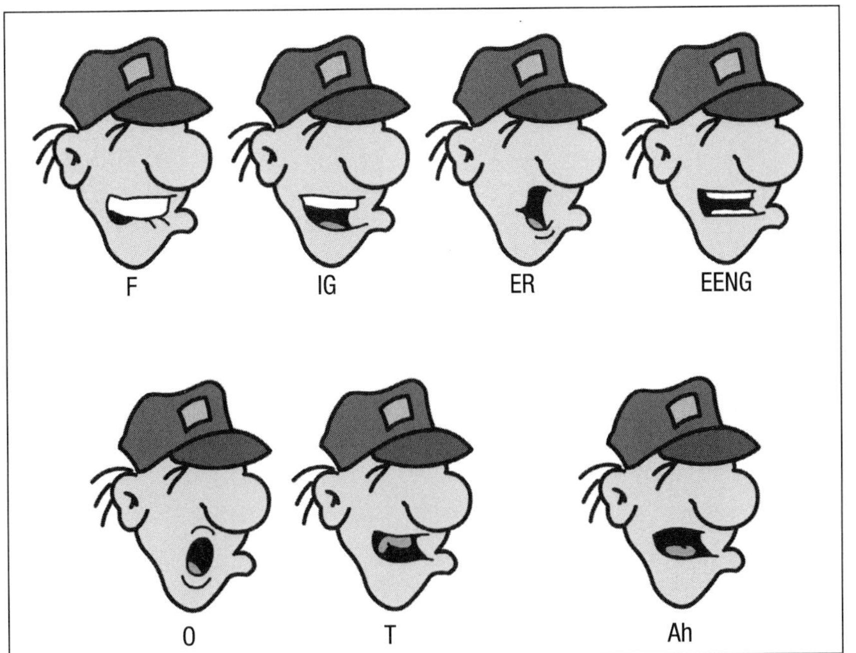

Figure 6.2
Here, we have the seven mouth shapes necessary to say "Figuring out a."

As Figure 6.2 illustrates, we'll emphasize the beginning syllable sound, leaving *hang time* (holding this mouth shape for a frame or two) before the next mouth shape appears. Depending on the speed of the speech, you'll want to include the ending sound's mouth shape. The faster the words are spoken, the more difficult it is to include the ending position. Sometimes, the beginning of the next word intrudes on the ending of the previous word. In these cases, go with the beginning mouth shape. The beginning and end of syllables are the important areas of speech, because most of us cannot comprehend the middle sections of syllables or short words.

If the speaker were to draw out a certain word, such as "world's" with "woooorlllds" (as Figure 6.3 shows), you'd want to have what we call a *transitional mouth shape*. In this case, the transitional O could hang, but scale down over the next frame or two, giving the effect of the character exhaling or shutting down the volume of that section of the word, before the animation goes to the next mouth shape.

Figure 6.3
The progression of a transitional mouth shape. Notice that the second O shape is smaller than the first O shape. This second O shape is the transition shape.

When the voice track contains words that are spoken very quickly—which is quite common in a fast-paced cartoon—you'll have a tendency to want to create a mouth shape for every single syllable. But doing so would be a mistake. Drawing every single mouth shape during a fast-paced clip of speech actually makes things more confusing and less convincing. In this situation, picking out the high points—particularly the F, P, B, and O mouth shapes—becomes very important. And use transitional mouth shapes, such as the A, E, and S, to complete the illusion.

In summary, when you're breaking down speech into components, your goal is to find the high points in a word. Breaking down the word into its syllables, determining which sounds to emphasize, and exaggerating these phonemes—or sounds that make up a word—will give you convincing lip-synchs. Overdoing the lip movements will tend to make the speech more confusing to understand—not to mention far more work. Using transitional mouth shapes helps to smooth out the movement, giving the illusion of fluidly speaking lips. Like all things in animation, simplicity is usually better. The goals here are to have convincing lip-synching (not scientifically perfect speech presentation), and to avoid having a mouth that flaps arbitrarily to the spoken words.

Charting Timing

Now that you have a good idea of what the mouths should look like for creating the illusion of speech, the next question is this: Where do you put the frames to synchronize them to the sound track? Back in the old days, BC (before computers), specialists equipped with nothing more than the vocal track transferred to film would painstakingly map out, on bar sheets (see Figure 6.4), the exact frame where each syllable occurred and it's the syllable's duration. This method actually works quite well. Unfortunately, it's time-consuming and doesn't lend itself to you changing your mind after you've made the charts.

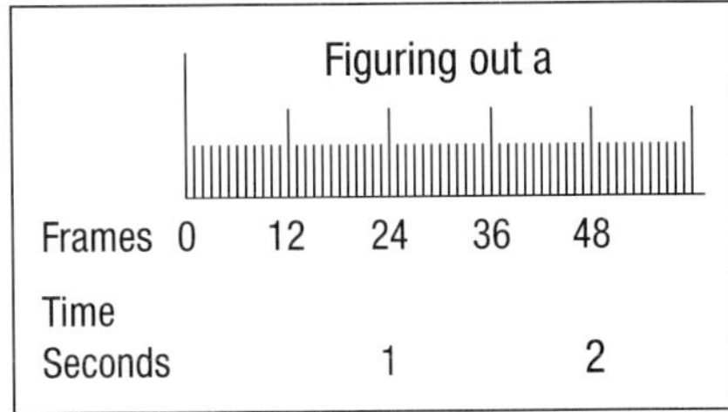

Figure 6.4
The traditional bar sheet that maps out which film frames the words fall upon.

Thank goodness for *sound waveforms* (see Figure 6.5)—and Flash's capability to scrub the sound layer in the Timeline. *Sound waveforms* are the graphic representations of the sound itself. *Scrubbing* refers to the function of dragging the playback head forward or backward across the Timeline and hearing the sound (and seeing the animation) that corresponds with the playback head's location. If you've never animated traditionally (ink, paint, paper, and film), you might not appreciate just how revolutionary this scrubbing function is. Scrubbing gives you tremendous flexibility, not only in editing, but also in determining whether your lip-synching is working before you commit it to another medium such as video or film.

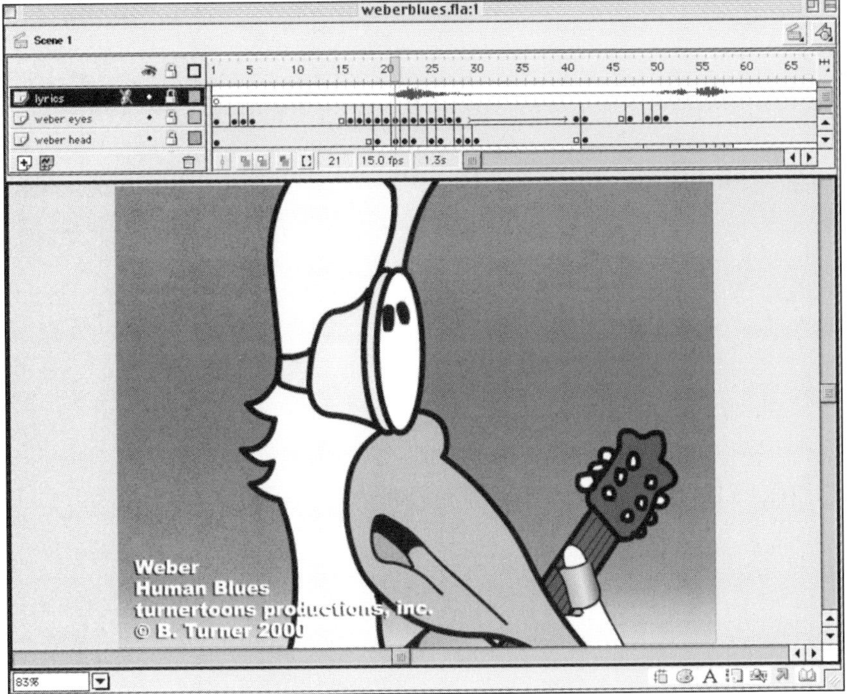

Figure 6.5
Here, we see the **lyrics** soundtrack layer, along with the **weber head** layer, where the lips reside. Notice the visible waveform and how it functions to show you where the sound is occurring in time.

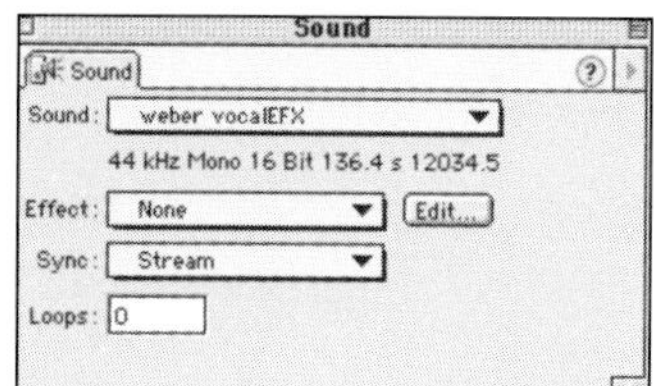

Figure 6.6
The Sync option in the Sound panel for the **lyrics** layer is set to **Stream** to facilitate scrubbing.

Currently in Flash, for any sound you want to scrub in the Timeline, you must set the Sync option to **Stream**, as Figure 6.6 shows. Setting the soundtrack to **Stream** also forces the animation to incrementally drop frames of graphics to force its synchronization with the sound playing. This forced synchronization is incredibly important when you're dealing with lip-synching. Its importance is also relevant when any graphic must absolutely synchronize with the sound that's playing.

Once you have the sound track set up in the Timeline, you can easily chart where a needed mouth shape should occur, simply by scrubbing the Timeline and listening. A good practice is to first find all the high points we spoke of earlier. Then, add the appropriate mouth shapes by using pre-created symbols, or simply drawing them as needed.

Another helpful technique for following what is being said in the sound track is to create another layer—either above, or directly below the sound layer—and use the labeling feature. Simply scrub the Timeline, find the beginning of a word, and create a keyframe in the layer you've made for labeling. Open the Frame panel and type the words being spoken, as Figure 6.7 shows. To help line up the typed words you can insert spaces where needed. This, in essence, creates a bar sheet. This technique also helps you find a certain section of speech when you're scrolling through long Timelines.

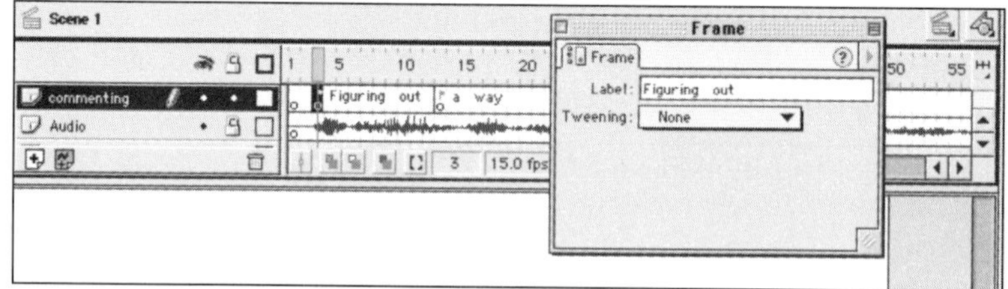

Figure 6.7
The technique of labeling speech.

Mouthless Faces

When your character is talking, face forward (looking straight ahead toward the viewer), you can save significant time by drawing the head once on its own layer, and then animating just the mouth on a layer above the head layer. Then, even if the head and face underneath need to change, you can accommodate this change on the mouth layer by adjusting your mouth drawing to fit the situation of the head, such as head movement.

PROJECT Lip-Synching a Sentence

Now that you have a good grasp of the mechanics involved in lip-synching, let's dig in and do a short animation. We'll do the lip-synching for the sentence we discussed earlier: "Figuring out a way to solve the world's problems ain't easy, you know." We have set up a file with all the necessary elements for you to implement the theories we've discussed so far. The file includes the 10 basic mouth shapes, audio track, label track with text showing where the words occur in time, and a layer with a single, mouthless face (see Figure 6.8).

1. Open the file *lipsynch.fla*, supplied on the CD-ROM.
2. Drag the playback head back and forth to get some idea of where the words occur on the Timeline (make sure your speakers are on).
3. On the **Mouth** layer, select Frame 2, and choose **Insert|Keyframe** (F6 shortcut). This is where the word "Figuring" begins.

Figure 6.8
Everything you'll need for the following project.

4. From the Library window, drag the symbol named **Vee-F-Fah** to the art area, and position it on the face.
5. Now, it's time to turn on the Onion Skin feature. Set up this feature to show the previous two frames, as Figure 6.9 shows. This arrangement will help you as you place the subsequent mouths.

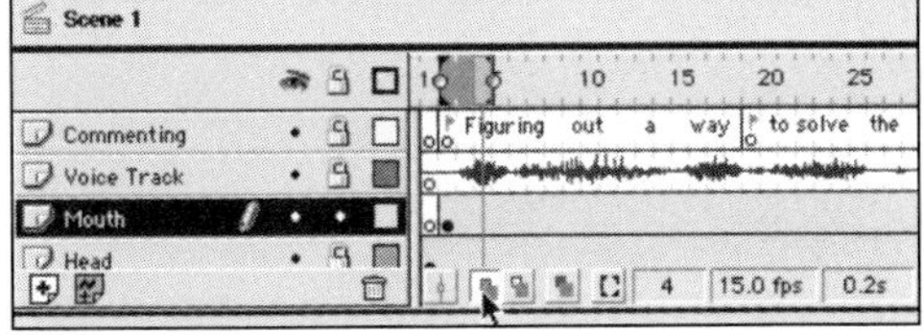

Figure 6.9
The Onion Skin setup for the lip-synching project.

6. Select Frame 4, and make a keyframe. This time use **Insert|Blank** Keyframe (or F7). Using this command inserts a new keyframe and deletes artwork on that frame simultaneously.
7. Drag the symbol **C-G-J-K-S-Z** to the face, using the ghosted onion skin image from the previous frame as a placement guide.
8. Select Frame 6, and make a new, blank keyframe, as you did in Step 6. Drag the symbol **R-Q-U**, and place it accordingly.
9. Select Frame 8, and make a new, blank keyframe. Drag the symbol **E**, and place it accordingly.

10. Select Frame 10, and make a new, blank keyframe. Drag the symbol **O**, and place it accordingly.
11. Select Frame 12, and make a new, blank keyframe. Drag the symbol **D-T-Tha-La-L-N**, and place it accordingly.
12. Select Frame 13, and make a new, blank keyframe. Drag the symbol **Ah-H-I-A**, and place it accordingly. Notice we only skipped ahead one frame, causing the previous frame to be very short. This makes the tongue appear to snap like it should in making the T sound in the word "out."
13. Select Frame 15, and make a new, blank keyframe. Drag the symbol **Wha-Y**, and place it accordingly.
14. Select Frame 17, and make a new, blank keyframe. Drag the symbol **Ah-H-I-A**, and place it accordingly.
15. Turn off Onion Skin. Drag the playback head to see the lip-synching to "Figuring out a way," or hit Enter to have the segment play back.
16. You can now proceed with the rest of the sentence ("to solve the world's problems ain't easy, you know"), using what you've learned in the above steps. If you get stuck and need a little help, you can find the finished project with all mouths in place in the *lipsynch2.fla* file on the CD-ROM. The *lipsynch2.swf* file (also on the CD-ROM) is the finished build.

Understandably, lip-synching is a tedious task, but the results can be very rewarding. Once you have a span of lip-synched animation, it's a good idea to build out (export to SWF, or to video) the file, to see it play at the proper frame rate. This trial run will reveal just how convincing the lip movements really are. The playback file will either be a joy or a disaster to watch. By viewing the file at actual speed, you might find that you have over-animated the mouth. As we mentioned earlier, over-animating can make the mouth confusing to understand. Under-animating, or not placing the emphasis on the proper syllables, will show up as a character very disengaged from the words being spoken.

Magpie Pro

Magpie Pro is a great helper application originally designed for 3D animators, to assist them in the lip-synch and expression process. Miguel Grinberg (Magpie's head developer), in conjunction with the author's request and collaboration, has now included Flash 5 support in Magpie Pro. You can find the Web site for Magpie Pro at **www.thirdwishsoftware.com**. We feel this software could be a real time-saver for animators who need to do long stretches of lip-synched animation. We have included a Save-Disabled Mac and PC demo on the CD-ROM, along with a demo file created by the author. Also included is a Flash file (*magpiepro.fla*) that demonstrates a finished animation using Magpie Pro.

While we can't completely describe the entire Magpie Pro application, we'd like to alert you to its newfound usefulness in working with Flash to create stretches of lip-synched animation that would be extremely difficult to achieve using Flash alone. You can easily accomplish results such as talking, bouncing, zooming characters using Magpie Pro and Flash 5.

Of particular interest to Flash animators is the capability to easily chart a voice soundtrack. Magpie Pro gives you a much larger, more detailed waveform to view, and finer control over scrubbing, which allows for a more precise interface to lip-synching. The application also incorporates a unique, spreadsheet style area, in which you can type the words being spoken, much like what traditional cel animation studios use (see Figure 6.10). Magpie Pro also includes a playback preview area, in which you can view the animation while you tweak the sequence.

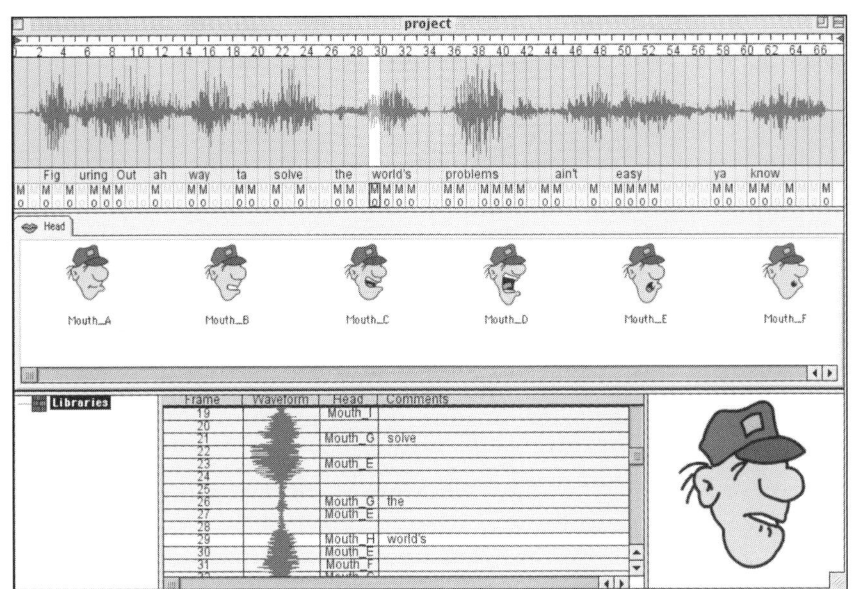

Figure 6.10
The Magpie Pro work area.

Magpie Pro doesn't work in vector graphics like Flash does. Instead, you must export a series of BMP files (or PICT files on the Mac) from Flash for use in Magpie Pro's Expression Set metaphor. Flash makes this process quite easy. Here's an outline of the steps you'll take to export files from Flash, work in Magpie Pro, and then import files back into Flash:

1. After you create your mouth shapes in Flash, simply choose **File|Export Movie**, and choose BMP (or PICT) Sequence as the output. This sequence will give you the necessary files that represent the art created in Flash for use in Magpie Pro's Previews and Expression sets.

2. Back in Flash, you then create a graphic symbol of each individual mouth position (or, in the demo's case, head position), named exactly the same as you named the exported BMP (or PICT) sequences (which you are using in Magpie Pro).

3. Then, nest these graphic symbols inside a new movie-clip symbol, with each of the graphic symbols sequentially ordered (as determined by the names you have given them)—see Figure 6.11—and open the file named *magpiepro.fla* for a look at how this part of the process is set up. Nesting the graphic symbols can be a bit complicated at first. But trust that, once you have all the various expression sets (in Magpie Pro) and corresponding movie clips (in Flash) set up, the time you'll save during production can be tremendous.

Figure 6.11
The movie-clip setup in Flash for accepting Magpie Pro-generated scripts.

4. Working in Magpie Pro, you'll simply drag the mouth (or head) positions you want to the frames in which you want the positions to occur.

5. When you're happy with the preview in Magpie Pro, you simply export an ActionScript text file (see Figure 6.12), for importing into Flash.

6. In Flash, set up the Timeline with the voice track on one layer, and set its Sync option to **Stream** (as we previously discussed in this chapter). On the same frame (but a new layer) on which the audio begins, create a keyframe, and place there the movie clip that contains the different mouth (or head) positions.

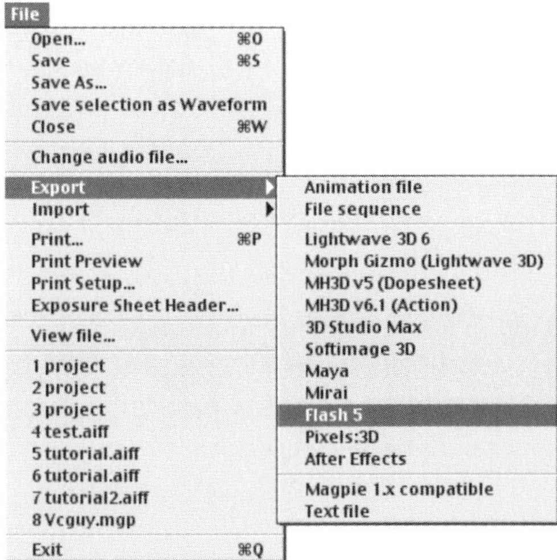

Figure 6.12
The Export menu for Magpie Pro.

7. Apply the ActionScript file (exported from Magpie Pro) directly to the movie clip by importing the text file. (Use the **Import From File** command from within the Object Actions panel, as you see in Figure 6.13.)

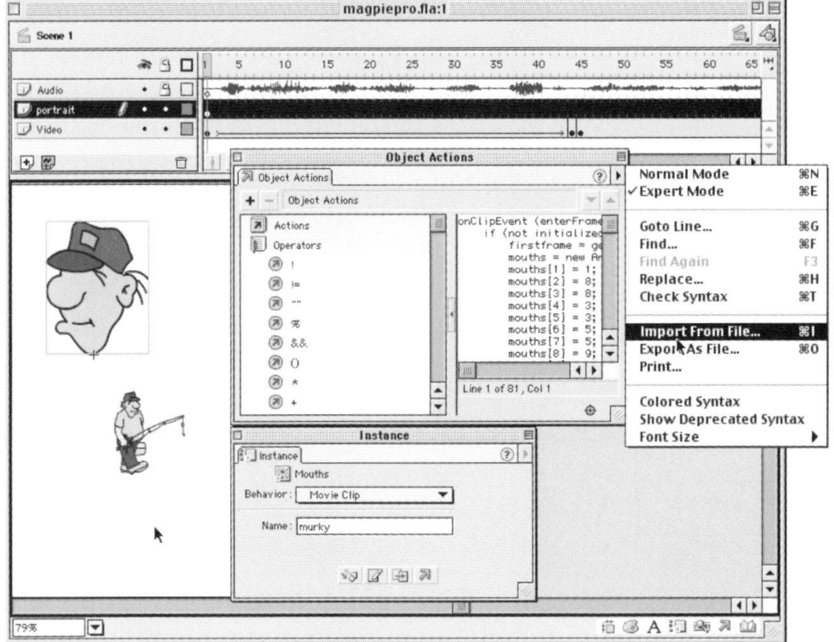

Figure 6.13
The **Import From File** command, which you access from the Object Actions panel.

After you export an SWF file, the movie clip will play back. The script attached to the movie clip will tell the clip what frames (your original mouth/head drawings) to play, and in what order they will play—in perfect synch with the voice track. This technique creates the smallest possible file size for your SWF file, because it reuses the symbols—over and over.

The above method using Magpie Pro has one drawback: This approach works only when the Web (SWF files) is your desired output destination. It will not work when you're exporting video from Flash. This limitation is not Magpie Pro's fault; it is because movie clips do not export when you're using video as a destination. When you're working for video output, however, a method for using Magpie Pro does exist that uses a file-linking setup. In short, you associate the Expression-set elements with Illustrator files created from the Flash export, thus creating a sequence of vector Illustrator files that Flash can import and use in video output. This technique makes much larger files that are not suitable for small-file Web destination. But in video, file size is of little concern. We'll leave the details of this method, together with a deeper explanation of the application, to the Magpie Pro documentation.

Mouth Shapes and Expressions

Now that you have a pretty good idea of what you need for producing convincing lip-synch, it's time to discuss some of the expressions that mouths can produce. We will caution that the use of symbols might be efficient, but you run the risk of monotony if you over use them. Unless you've pre-created every possible mouth shape in every possible emotion (happy, sad, angry, etc.), you might want to consider drawing the shapes as you need them. Creating each shape prevents you from being limited in what you can express at any given moment. Drawing custom mouths for a scene (even many frames of them) adds little to the final file size. But if small file size is an extreme concern, you might have to go with symbols (which, as repeated copies, take less file size) and give up some creative concerns.

Drawing the mouths themselves is relatively easy. You can render mouths with very few lines. A simple, straight, horizontal line can adequately express indifference, for example. Bending the line up slightly in the middle shows unhappiness. Making the line a zigzag connotes confusion, or even embarrassment, as you can see in Figure 6.14. The number of expressions you can create is endless. The slightest variations can evoke completely different moods in your characters.

Figure 6.14
Some basic moods a mouth can represent.

While you're animating the mouth in motion with lip-synch, you should keep in mind the emotions you want to portray. This awareness will help to further reinforce the emotion the character is feeling while speaking the words. For example, if, during speech, the character shows lots of teeth with the mouth turned down, he or she is expressing anger. If the character were speaking with lots of teeth showing, with the corners of the mouth turned up, he or she would be expressing a more jovial and happy emotion.

To give you a good example of how small adjustments can make big differences, open the *lipsynch3.fla* (or *lipsynch3.swf*) file on the CD-ROM, and play the animation. This file is the same one we used earlier in the lip-synching project, but this one has very slight adjustments to some of the mouth shapes (see Figure 6.15). In this file, the O and Oooo symbols have not been altered at all, and the E mouth has simply been flipped vertically. The rest of the mouths have been redrawn ever so slightly, mostly with the mouth corners turned down. With these changes, we now have a rather pessimistic man complaining about solving the world's problems.

Figure 6.15
By editing the mouths, even slightly, we have imposed an entirely different outlook on the character.

Certainly, if small adjustments can make big differences, huge changes can create extreme situations. Consider the character screaming at the top of his lungs, with the mouth outrageously wide open, tongue flapping like a flag in a hurricane, and saliva spraying in all directions. This character is disturbed beyond safety. Contrast that image, to the character that is just as angry, but instead mumbles under his breath with the mouth nearly closed, quivering with tension. He's a maniacal time bomb. As we've said, the possibilities are endless.

Eye Expressions

Of course, the eyes have a lot to do with expression and should not be simply staring into space (unless the character is a zombie). As with the mouth, slight variations of eye (more precisely, pupil) position and movement can have a dramatic effect on expressions. The eyes really are the windows to the soul.

Eyes have a universal language all their own. We all understand the eyes' ability to communicate; no matter what language a person speaks. This capacity is why you might ask someone, "Can you look me in the eyes and say that?" in trying to find the truth. When you're talking to someone, and their eyes are looking elsewhere (even slightly), you immediately know they aren't paying any attention to what you're saying. The eyes tell no lies...well, usually, they don't.

In the Weber character, we use the full area of the diving mask's glass for the pupils to do their thing. Doing this allows for lots of flexibility in the expressions we can use. In Figure 6.16, you can see how the eyes work with the mouth (and the words being sung), giving that "I've lost touch with reality and have entered this song I'm singing" expression.

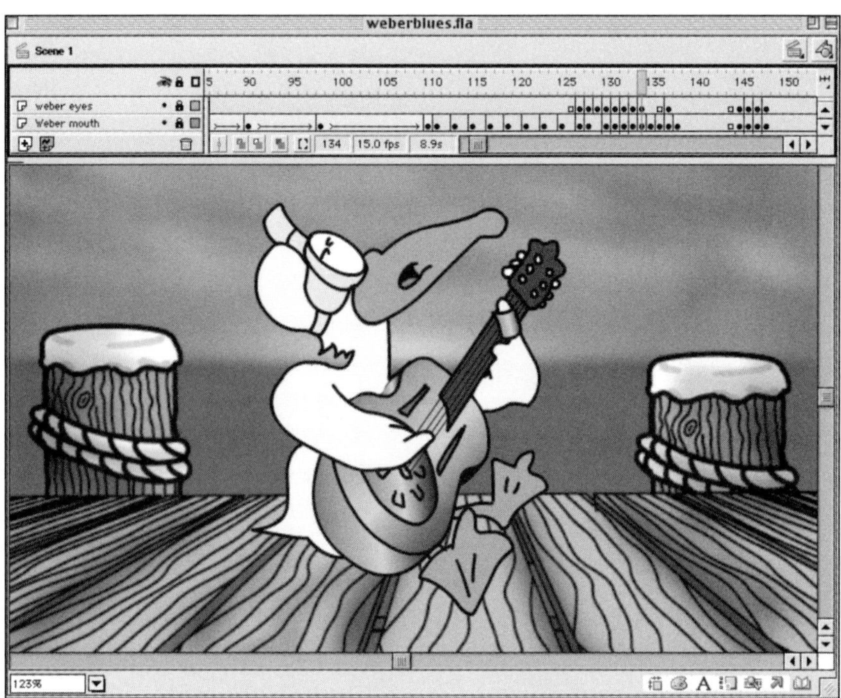

Figure 6.16
Weber is really getting into it. Notice the slits used for eyes, which make the eyes seem closed with passion.

Notice, too, in Figure 6.16, that the eyes are not only closed, but also closed with force. The slight wrinkles the closed eyes are making create this effect, and the wrinkles are what impart the passion of the expression. Generally, when a character's eyes are simply closed (no wrinkles or other distinguishing traits), they are in essence turned off, shut down, not functioning. The eyes command lots of power. See Figure 6.17 for some basic examples of eyes doing their thing.

Figure 6.17
Several examples of eye power. We intentionally left out the mouths so the focus is on the eyes.

PROJECT Creating Eye Expressions

Now that you have an appreciation for what eyes can add to your cartoon, let's make some eyes, hands on. We have supplied a Flash file on the CD-ROM with all the necessary elements. This file is a modified version of the project file you did earlier for lip-synching. We've left all the finished mouth shapes intact and synchronized to the voice track. We added the new eye-symbol elements; changed the character's face to one that faces forward; and moved his hat out of the way so we can see the eyes better (see Figure 6.18).

1. Open the *eyes.fla* file from the CD-ROM.
2. Make sure all layers except the **eyes** and **pupils** layers are locked.
3. First, we'll put in a blink sequence. Go to Frame 33 on the **eyes** layer, and add a keyframe (F6 shortcut).
4. Delete the eyes symbol that is there (**standardeyes**), and replace it with the **blinkeyes** symbol. You also can do this by using the Swap Symbol function in the Instance panel, and choosing the new **blinkeyes** symbol there.
5. Go to Frame 38 on the **eyes** layer. Create a new keyframe (F6), and swap back to the **standardeyes** symbol, using the method above.
6. Now the eyes will blink, but, because the pupils are on a different layer, they remain. So, we have to delete the pupils for a moment while the eyes are shut. On Frame 35, create a blank keyframe (F7 shortcut) on the **pupils** layer. This action deletes the **pupils** symbol. Now, go to Frame 37,

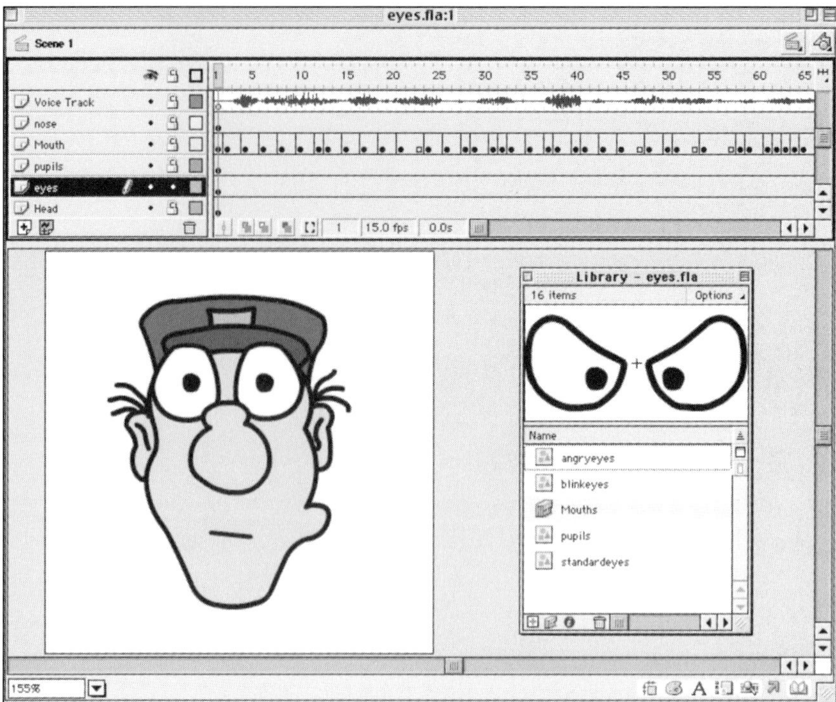

Figure 6.18
The eye expression project at the beginning of the project.

create another keyframe on the **pupils** layer, and drag the **pupils** symbol back into place. This step completes the blink.

7. We'll now set up the rest of the major eye-shape changes. Go to Frame 46 on the **eyes** layer, insert a keyframe (F6), and swap the **standardeyes** symbol with the **angryeyes** symbol. This change occurs at approximately the time the character is saying, "ain't easy," and the eyes' new shape imparts a bit of frustration.
8. On the same **eyes** layer, move to Frame 57, and insert a new keyframe (F6). Swap back to the **standardeyes** symbol. This change happens about the time the character is saying, "you know," and the eyes' softer look encourages understanding from the viewer.
9. Now, we'll deal with pupil movement. The remaining steps will deal only with the **pupils** layer, so you can now lock the **eyes** layer. Locking that layer will prevent you from accidentally moving the white parts of the eyes.
10. Select Frame 1 of the **pupils** layer. Via the Frame panel, set this frame to be a motion tween.
11. Move the playback head to Frame 5, and drag the **pupils** symbol to the lower left (from here on, when we refer to left or right, we mean *your* left or right, not the character's). This action will automatically insert a keyframe where the playback head is positioned in the tween area.

12. Move to Frame 16, and insert a new keyframe (F6). Do not move the pupils. This step causes the tween to pause with the pupils in the position you moved them to in Step 11 (lower left). This pupil position effectively breaks eye contact with the viewer and gives the impression that the character is contemplating something.
13. Move the playback head to Frame 20, and drag the **pupils** symbol back to a centered position, making an automatic keyframe at that position in the tween. This step brings eye contact back to the viewer.
14. Select Frame 37, and make it a motion tween via the Frame panel. This frame occurs right after the blink sequence you made earlier.
15. Put the playback head on Frame 43, and drag the pupils slightly upward (making another automatic keyframe). This step keeps the eyes from seeming like stone and gives them a subtle movement.
16. Move the playback head to Frame 46, and move the pupils slightly downward.
17. Move the playback head to Frame 52, and move the pupils to the right.
18. Move the playback head to Frame 56, and move the pupils to the left, past center.
19. Move the playback head to Frame 60, and move the pupils to center. The previous four steps created the back and forth movement one makes when shaking one's head in disagreement. This action occurs during the "ain't easy" part of the speech.
20. Now, for the finishing touch. Move the playback head to Frame 65, and move the pupils upward. This step completes the eye movement, giving a "look to the heavens for help" expression.
21. Export the file as an SWF file, and play it back. If you become stuck in any of the above steps, you can find the completed animation in the *eyes2.fla* file on the CD-ROM.

As you can now see, the possibilities for expression are within your grasp. Adding the little details such as eye movement and proper lip-synch can add dramatically to the quality of your cartoon. Spending time on these aspects (and we won't try to fool you—they *do* take time) will definitely give your cartoon production that professional look you need, to compete in today's market.

Moving On

Next up, we discuss some of the other aspects of your cartoon production: things such as preloaders and output decisions. Also, we'll provide a discussion about outputting to videotape, which is the new rage in Flash animation.

Flash™ 5 Cartoons and Games Studio

A book on Flash cartoons and games would not be complete without a space to show off the wonderful eye candy that can be created with this great software. On the following pages, you'll find examples of animations created for the Internet, TV, and film. You'll also find images of various games (included on this book's CD-ROM), as well as information about their respective cutting-edge Flash developers.

The Weber Cartoon

Bill Turner of Turnertoons Productions, Inc., shares a few stills from the Weber Show cartoon, *Human Blues*. The show is based on Weber and his ongoing environmental battle with humans. The entire Flash authoring file is included on the CD-ROM, which reveals the techniques used in long-form animation.

Here, we see the pre-loader that acts as a diversion; tickling Weber's feet keeps the viewer occupied while waiting for the show to download. The pre-loader also keeps track of the percentage of the file downloaded for good measure. The tickle feet animation is a movie clip that runs independently of the main Timeline, while the main Timeline looks to see how much of the file has loaded.

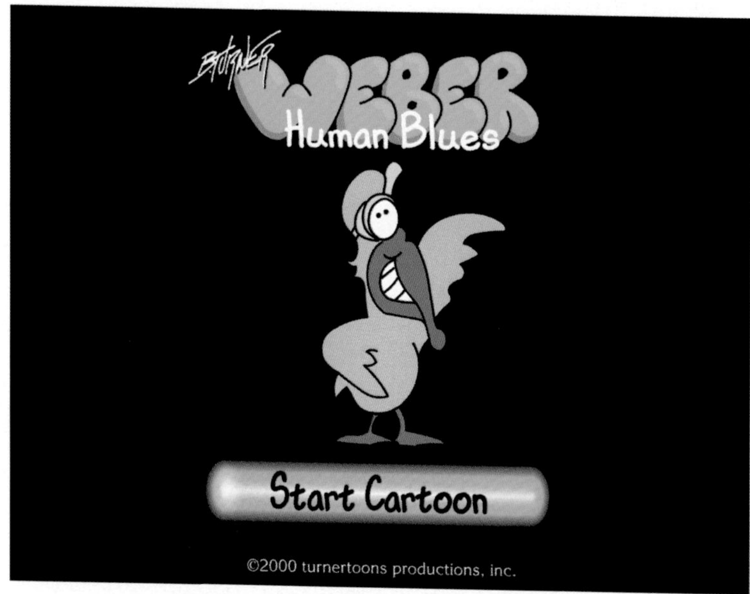

After the download is complete, the viewer is left with the Start Cartoon button. It's a good idea to have a "ding" sound attached to the appearance of this button in the event the viewer has stepped away during download time.

This is the opening scene that establishes Weber's location, and the beauty of the natural environment as the sun rises on a new day. Weber starts singing as he cranks up the bottle-neck slide guitar. Sound is discussed in Chapter 3 and background scenery in Chapter 4.

As Weber sings the blues, we cut to a scene describing what will be his predicament in trying to co-exist with humans as he dives for fish to eat. The singing and guitar playing continue uninterrupted. Notice the blurred lines that help simulate speed of motion.

Weber swims merrily along, filling his belly with fresh fish. The reason he wears his diving mask and snorkel will become abundantly clear. The underwater environment consists of many layers that are panned at different speeds to show depth.

Oh no! Pollution! Weber's daily feeding routine is abruptly cancelled because he accidentally swallows an abandoned truck axle lurking beneath the sea. The underwater environment's color palette shifts via Color Effects, and planning abruptly halts.

Who's responsible for this mess? Here, we cut to a panning scene that shows the culprits of disaster surrounded by tree stumps, desolation, and smoldering everywhere. Notice the shift in color palette to enforce the feeling of a hopeless wasteland. This scene is one huge animated symbol motion tweened across the view.

After personally dealing with an obnoxious human, the water turns murky, making it increasingly difficult for Weber to find his dinner. We wouldn't want to give away the humor as to why the water is now tainted. You'll have to watch the show on the book's CD-ROM for that. Again, Color Effects is used to achieve the animated palette shift.

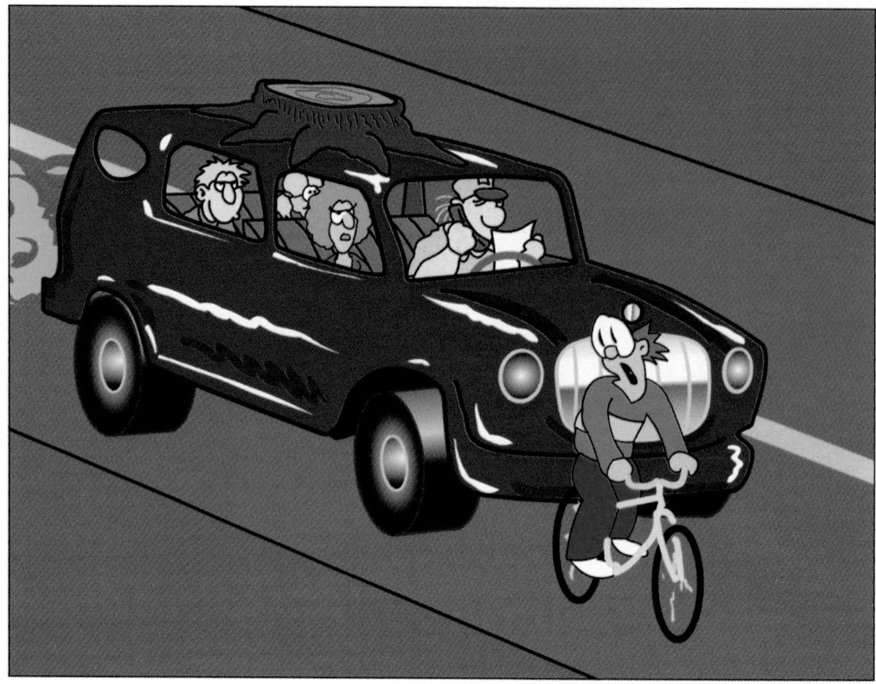

Here, we have the humans prowling the planet in their coveted "hillbilly limousine," with little regard for anything other than their personal comfort and wants. Nested animated symbols are scaled down by using Easing to achieve smooth zoom out effects.

Certainly, there's more than pollution forcing Weber to have an axe to grind with the humans. There's uncontrolled vanity, and unfettered gossip as well. Of course, Weber continues to sing the blues through all of these scenes. Using hand-painted Photoshop backgrounds makes the sky work wonders.

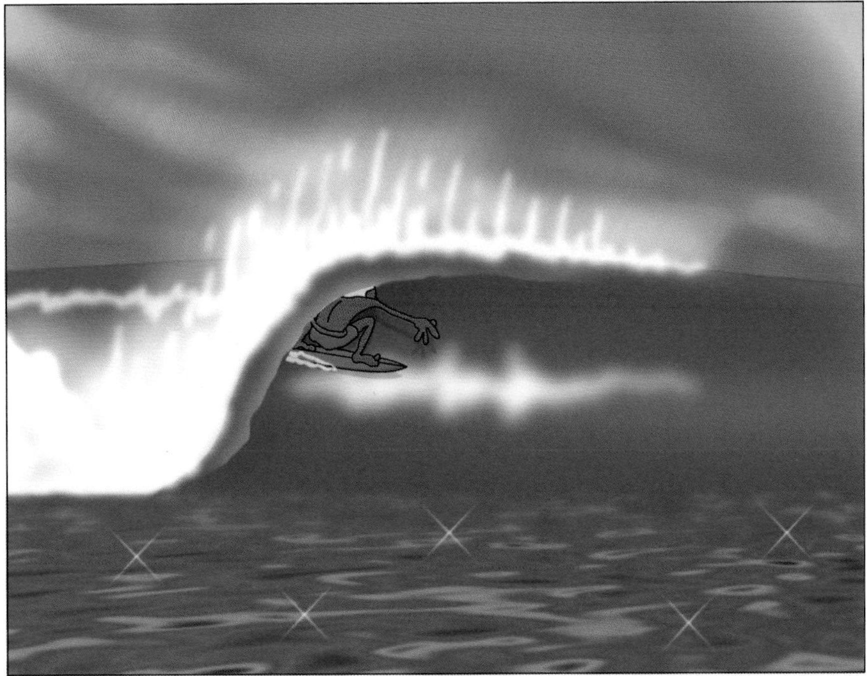

We cut to a surfing scene, as Weber explains that all he wants out of life is to survive and have a bit of fun. Can we really blame him for that? As this scene closes, Weber continues to sing about the humans' need to clean up their act. The wave animation sequence is painted by hand entirely in Photoshop and then merged with the Flash-drawn surfer animation.

As the tune ends with the final strum of the guitar, the screen cuts to the credits. This ends the episode, but gives the viewer the option to press the Play Again button, which will send the animation back to the first frame but bypass the pre-loader (see Chapter 7).

The Journal of Edwin Carp

Founder of Bazely Films (**www.bazelyfilms.com**), Richard Bazely, shares scenes from *The Journal of Edwin Carp*, created entirely in Flash. Narration is supplied by Hugh Laurie in this dry British tale. The project's final output is film. Richard's background as lead animator in various films, such as *The Iron Giant*, *Hercules*, *Osmosis Jones*, and many others, validate Flash's ability to do such high-end work. Some choice animation from the film is included on the CD-ROM.

As the pen travels across the page, the pre-written text art is revealed on a separate layer via an animated mask.

A simple zoom-in was established by creating an instance of the drawn background. The image would be largest in the first frame, but by the time the last frame appears, the image is scaled down to a smaller size, creating the illusion of a zoom. To add extra depth, the same effects were applied to the foreground objects. The nearer an object is to you, the quicker it will move.

This scene uses a combination of motion tweens and single-frame animation. The arms, body, hands, and feet are motion tweens, while the head is single-frame animation. Edwin Carp's head turns, and there is no other way to do this than to draw it, whereas the body parts move in a very simple way, which is suited for motion tweening.

Edwin Carp, clearly embarrassed at the indecency of the exposed model, covers it with a sheet. Another combination of motion tween: his body and head in this case, and single-frame animation: his arms and the sheet.

Here, Edwin Carp blows the dust off of an old moose head. The dust cloud uses the Alpha Effect, and is tweened from 30 percent to 0 percent, so that it starts out translucent and then disappears entirely.

It is easy to accomplish the staggering effect on Edwin Carp's mother by separating all of her body elements. Her arms, hands, tray, and teapot all shake incessantly. We created a motion tween first of her exiting, and then went back and added the shake by turning all the frames into single frames.

To get his mother's attention, Edwin Carp is about to drop "his creation" down below, where we find his unsuspecting mother. To create a crashing effect, we used what is called "camera shake." We moved the entire image up and down at random to create the feeling that there has been an almighty crash, and that this has caused the camera to shake.

Another example of a stagger. The moose is flying toward Edwin Carp's mother, and she is horrified. Her eyes get wider, and her mouth drops. A stagger is added to both eyes and mouth by first creating a smooth tween, then changing it to a jumpy single frame movement, so that the transition is no longer smooth, but jittery.

Edwin's mother is tearing down the stairs. This was achieved with surprising economy. Her body was drawn only once. A motion tween was made of her body, then, it was flipped horizontally for her second pass across the screen. For her third pass, her body was flipped back again (same with her head). Then, on a new layer, adding a single-frame animation will make the shawl flap in her wake. Techniques for conveying motion are discussed in Chapter 5.

In this case, Edwin's mother is running toward us, and the background moves way from us at the same time, creating the illusion of speed; quite a dynamic move. The mother is scaled up over time, while the room is scaled down.

Edwin's mother flies past Harrison. In doing so, Harrison's hair sticks up from the breeze as the mother passes by. At the end of the scene, his banana (with a little anticipation) topples off, creating the impression that the character flew by at an alarming speed.

Edwin Carp is rudely awakened by a dripping noise. A camera move was made by creating a motion tween of the background, and by sliding the background down. The dripping water was created with a slightly transparent color.

Spore Productions

Spore Cubes, a Flash game-developer's creation (**www.sporeproductions.com**), is a wonderful mind-boggling, puzzle-style game. Flash is a great tool for creating puzzle-style games; Spore Cubes is a great example of what can be done without heavy use of motion that can bog down game play. The object is to click on a colored square, which destroys that square and any others of the same color bordering it. The remaining squares drop down, filling the blanks left by departing squares. The rub lies in ridding the screen of all squares, which is quite difficult to achieve. The game is included on this book's CD-ROM.

Here, we see the starting screen, where you can read the instructions and choose the skill level.

The fully populated start of the Cubes game.

When you click on a cube, you destroy that cube, and any other cube of the same color that connects to it.

The object is to clear out all of the cubes, with the fewest number of clicks, therefore, you must look for the connecting color patterns and groupings.

Artifact Interactive

Flash Golf, from **www.artifactinteractive.com.au**, is a superb example of a Golf simulation completed entirely in Flash. To play, you select your club, check the wind speed and direction, and line up your shot. The timing of the mouse-click and release commands dictate the amount of force the ball is hit with and the distance it travels. Flash Golf is included on this book's CD-ROM.

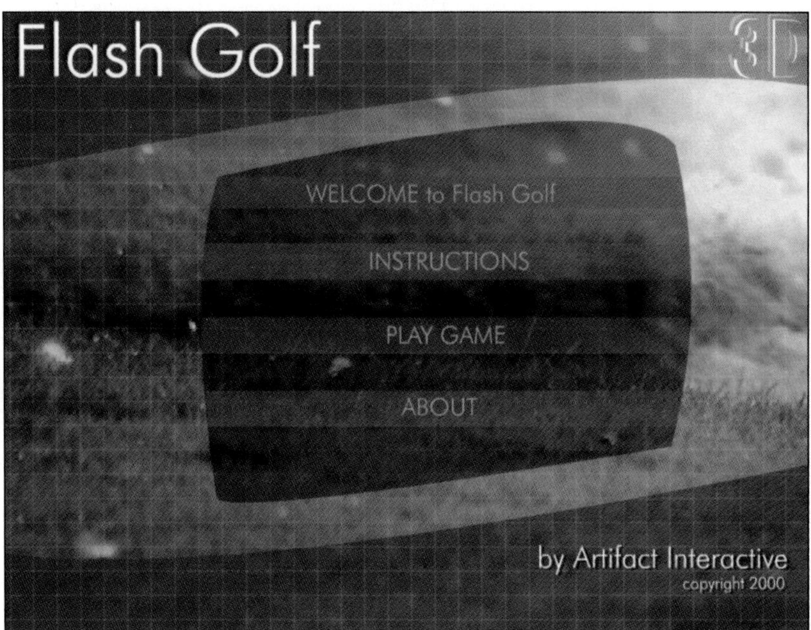

The opening screen from the Flash Golf game.

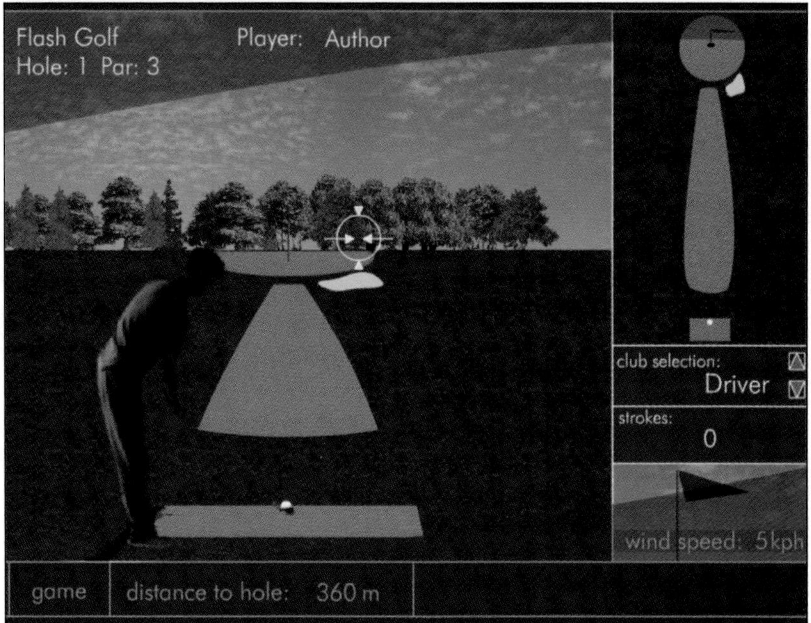

Here, we see the behind the player view, the overhead view, wind speed, direction, and club choice. You select the direction (target) and force of swing. By calculating these dynamics, the scripting determines where the ball will go once hit.

Ultimate Arcade, Inc.

Ultimate Arcade, Inc. (**www.ultimatearcade.com**) is a Flash game development company and online reference resource for Flash game designers. Here, we see some screen shots of Field Goal Frenzy, which is included on the CD-ROM for you to play. Ultimate Arcade's games not only use great graphics, but also complicated physics computations.

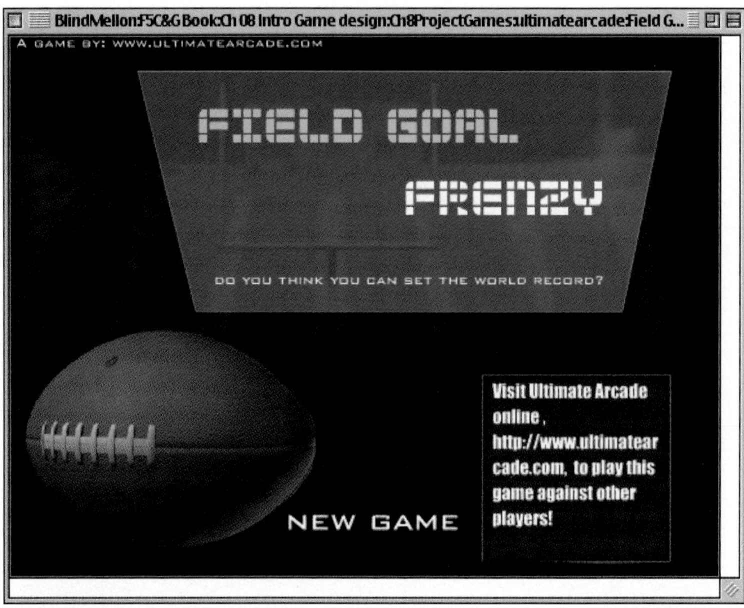

The splash screen. When played online, a running tally of the best Field Goal Frenzy player is displayed.

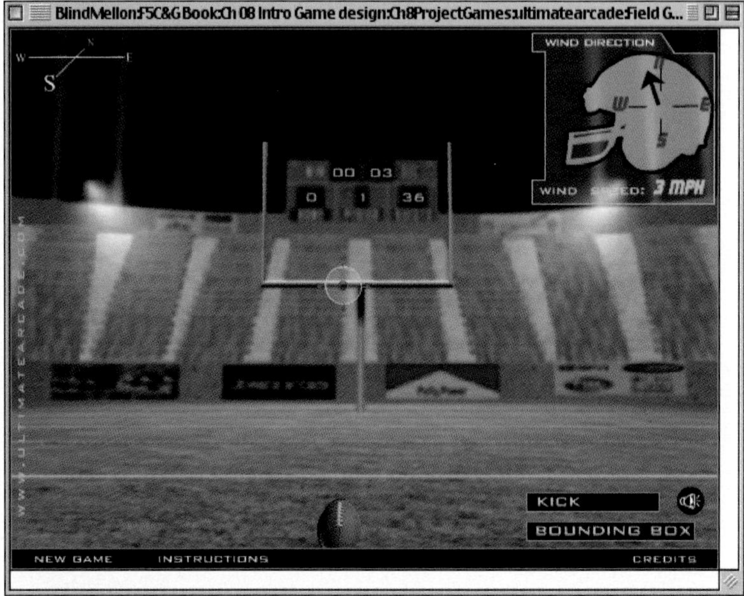

The game requires the player to consider the distance, wind direction, and speed to succeed in kicking the three-pointers.

Another Ultimate Arcade creation, Ultimate Nine Ball, is an excellent example of pushing Flash to the edge. The graphics are superb, and the engine that makes the game go is very sophisticated. There's a copy on the CD-ROM for you to play, but we'll caution that this game requires a pretty fast computer. Check Ultimate Arcade's Web site for updates at **www.ultimatearcade.com**. While there, you'll find that they have a healthy tutorial section in their Game Laboratory section.

The Ultimate 9 Ball game's splash screen.

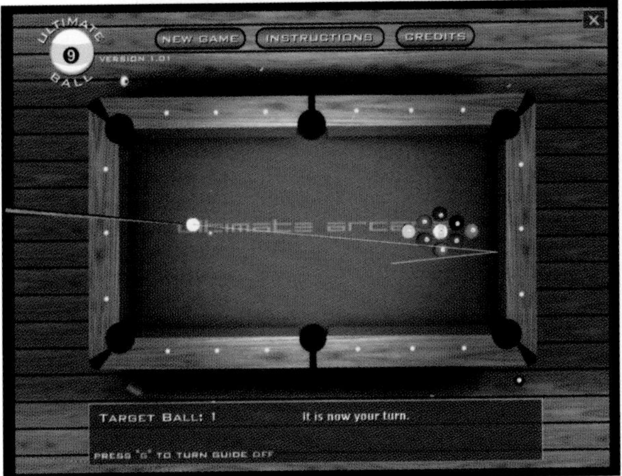

You can play using an overhead view, with yellow guides showing the ball's possible movement before shooting. This game uses incredibly complicated collision detection and physics. This is an experimental Flash endeavor.

Edesign.UK

Here, we see co-author and game designer James Robertson's version of Othello (included on the CD-ROM). This game features the basic devices needed to implement Artificial Intelligence. Appendix B explains some of the theories involved.

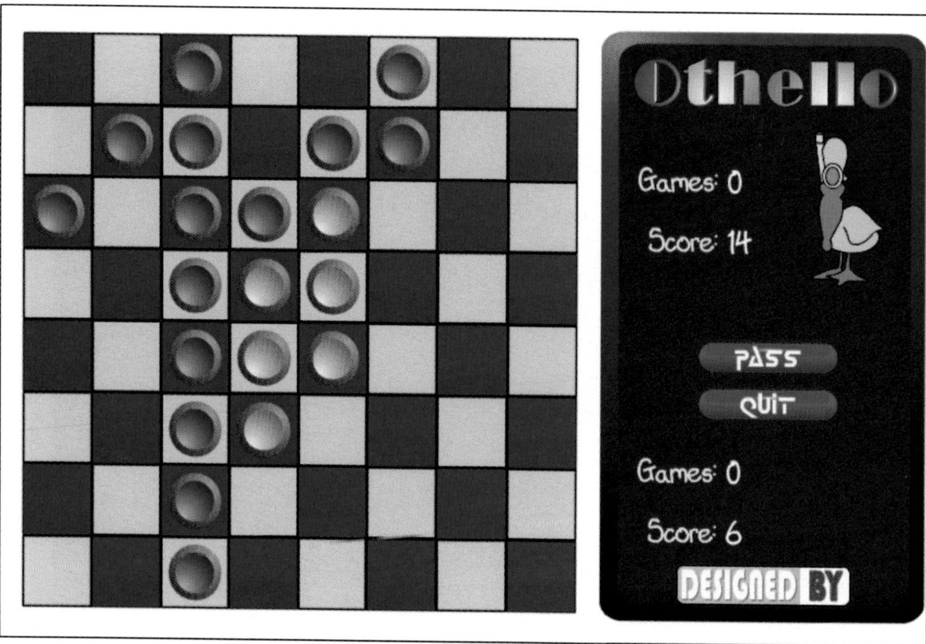

The main screen of the game, where you play against a computer-controlled opponent.

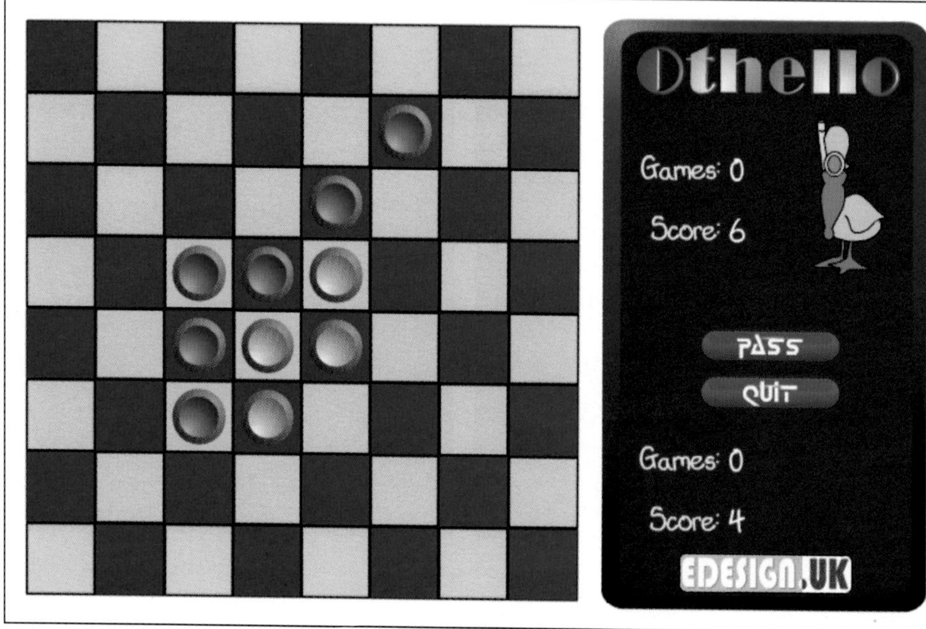

As discussed in Appendix B, the computer needs to "think" in order to be a worthy opponent.

SESS.NET

SESS.NET is a Flash game development site that creates some really cool games. One of these games, Arcade Animals Flying Squirrel, is included on the CD-ROM. SESS.NET also has several other cool Flash games: World-wide KO (a boxing game) and Simple Genocide (a shooter style game) are on their Web site.

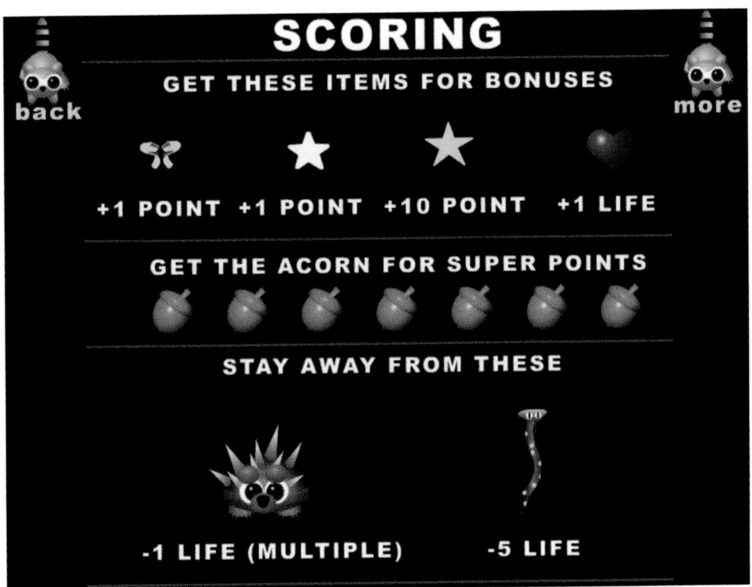

The splash screen lays down the law. It's always a good idea to keep the instructions as clear and simple as possible.

Here is the game in progress. You jump, fly, and scurry, in order to avoid the bad animals and collect good stuff. Simple to explain but hard to beat should always be a goal in game design.

Projects in the Book

The following pages show some of the projects included in the book. The full FLA authoring files for these projects are included on the CD-ROM.

Title

Scene# Shot# Date

Assigned To Duration : :

Min Sec Frms

Music

Sound Effects

Background

Dialogue or Narration

In Chapter 1, we supply the files needed for storyboarding directly in Flash. We have also supplied you with blank storyboard files in both NTSC (standard American television) and HDTV size formats.

Chapter 2 is a good place to experiment with the nuances of character creation. With the various elements supplied, you do not need to be a professional cartoonist to have a good time discovering what's possible.

Chapter 3 discusses the sonic aspect of your cartoon and game creation. Shown here is the clever interface of the Smart Sound application. A demo included on the CD-ROM allows nonmusicians to create professional custom music tracks and effects.

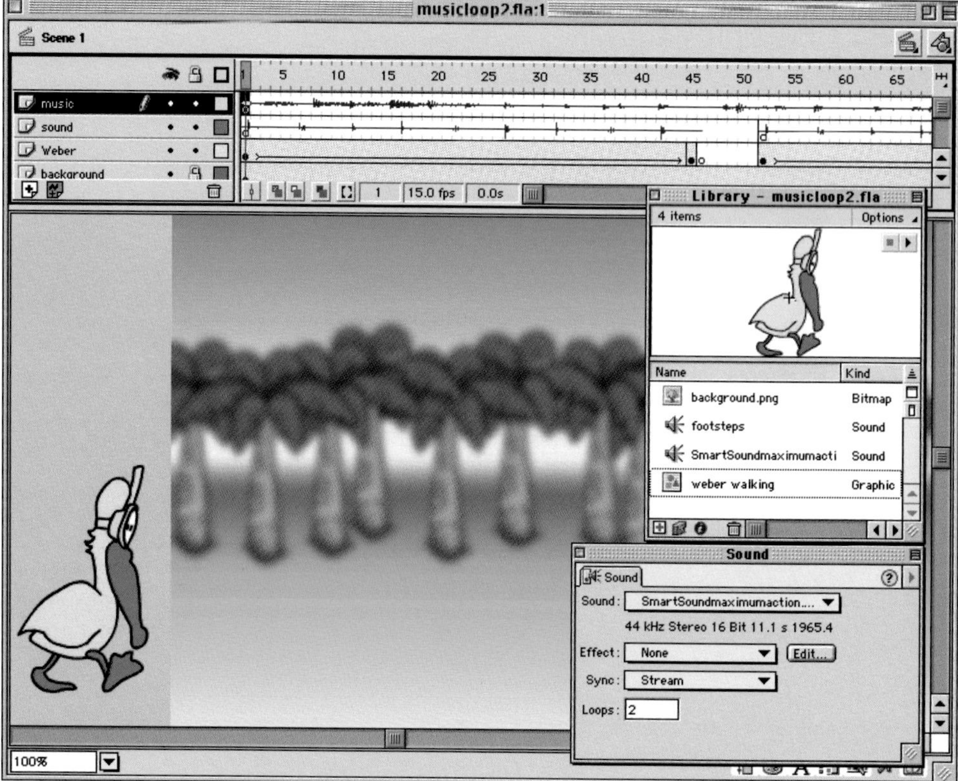

This project uses the seamless music loop created in Smart Sound and imported into Flash.

In Chapter 4, you'll find a project on backgrounds. Here, we see a project showing the lighting effect on the background.

This project shows how to use Photoshop to achieve a pull focus effect in your Flash cartoon or game.

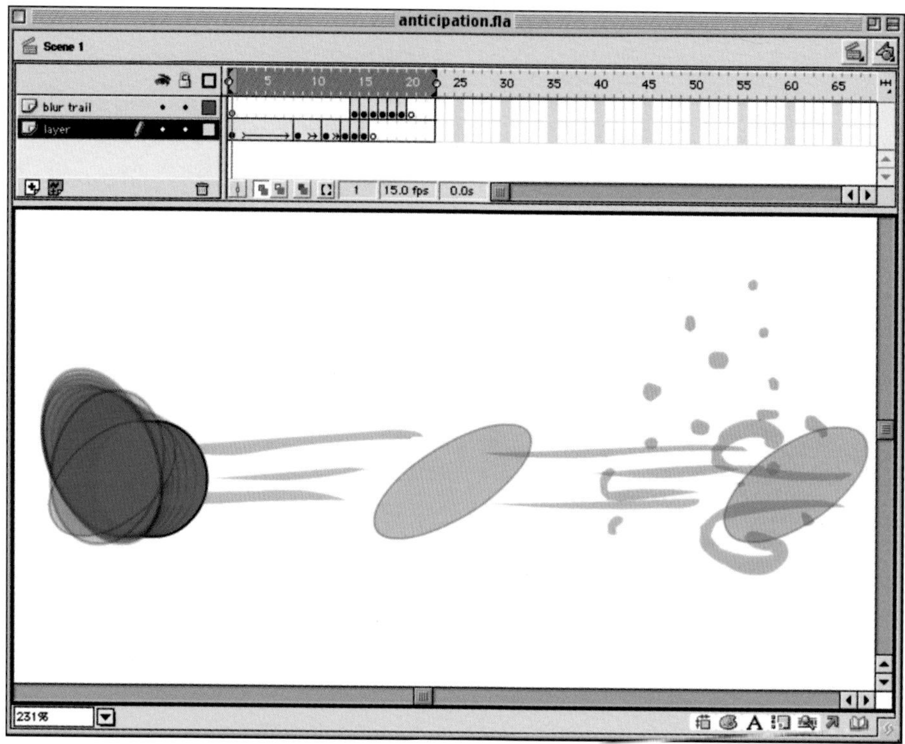

In Chapter 5, you'll find a project on motion study. Using a simple circle for clarity, we show how character motion, such as anticipation, can be achieved.

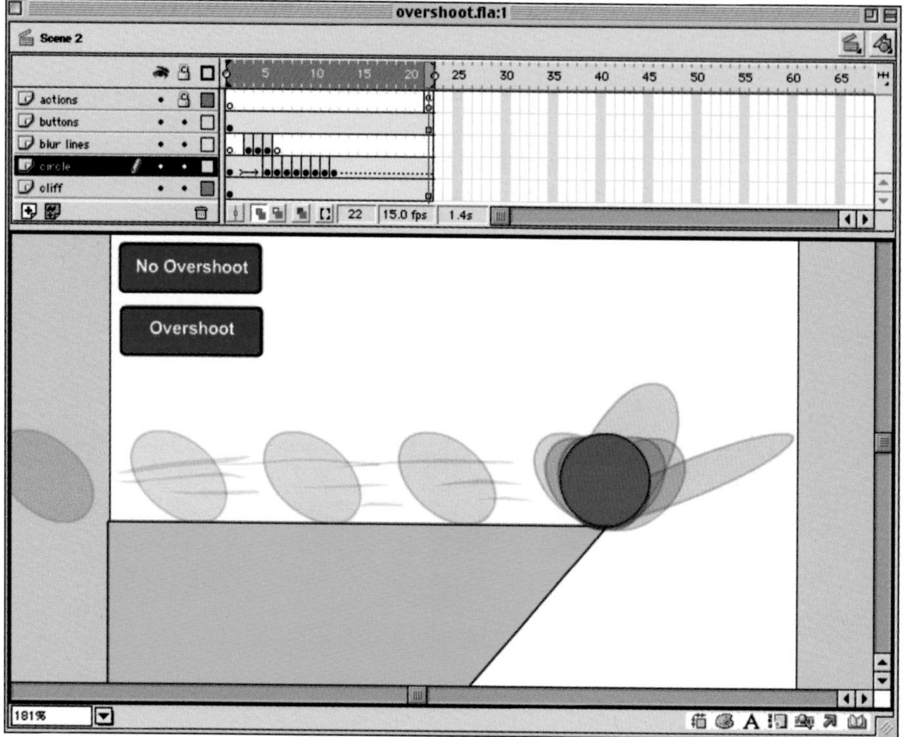

This project from Chapter 5 demonstrates the use of an overshooting motion, using our circle device. In the end, we put together several motion studies into a short cartoon.

Chapter 5 also covers the art of rotoscoping. We have supplied you with several videos that you can trace over in Flash to study human movement.

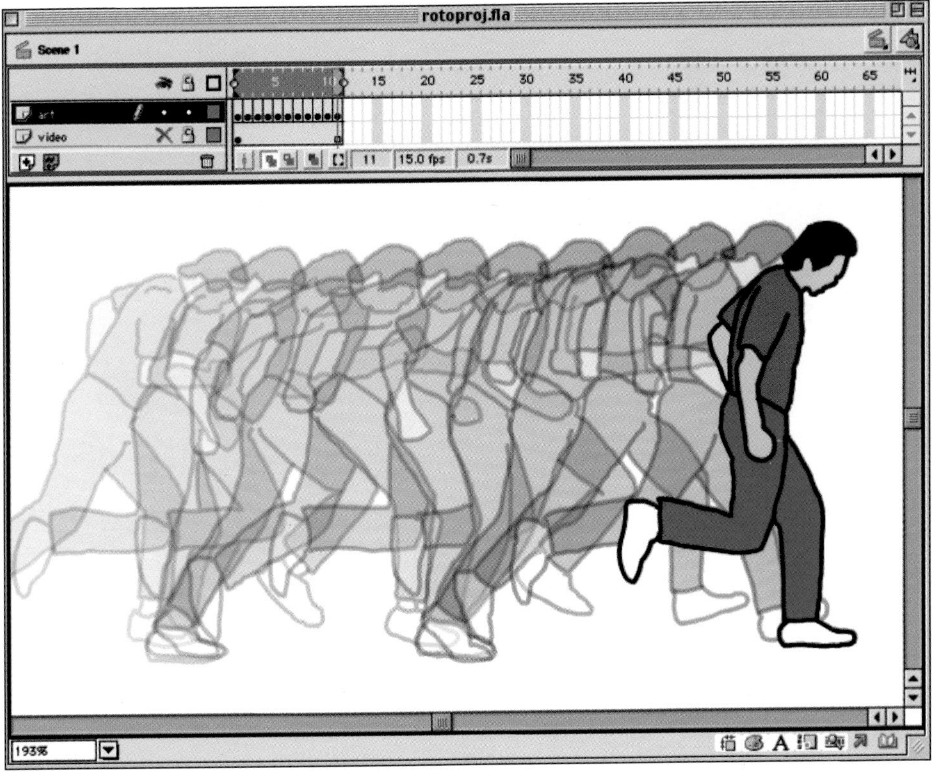

This is a finished rotoscoped sequence, drawn from the supplied video. The onion skin feature is turned on to reveal all the frames (see Chapter 5).

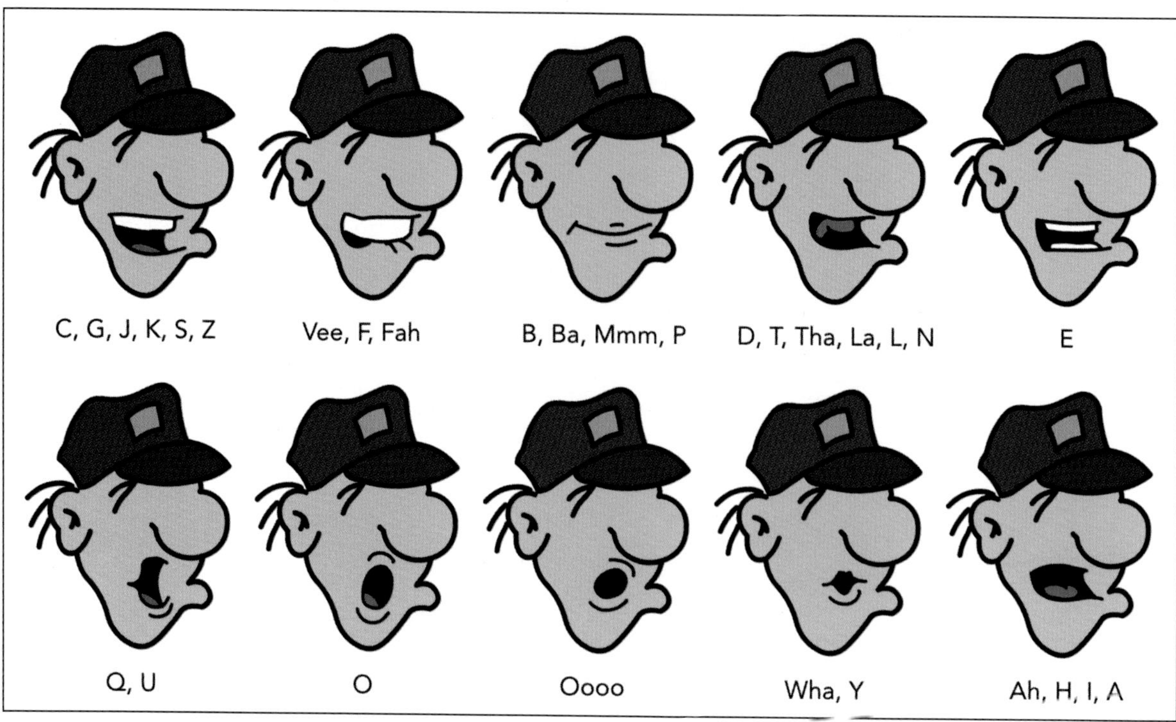

In Chapter 6, we discuss the art of lip-synching. Here, we see the broken down phonemes. In the chapter, there's a project that allows you to construct a lip-synched sequence.

Also in Chapter 6, we demonstrate eye expressions. This includes a project that allows you to compose an expression-filled animated cartoon.

Trivia Game

The CD-ROM includes the entire working authoring file for the Weber Trivia Game. The feature that separates this game from other trivia games is the addition of the "Ask The Idiots" section. This feature uses a rudimentary Artificial Intelligence technique that is fully explained in Chapter 9.

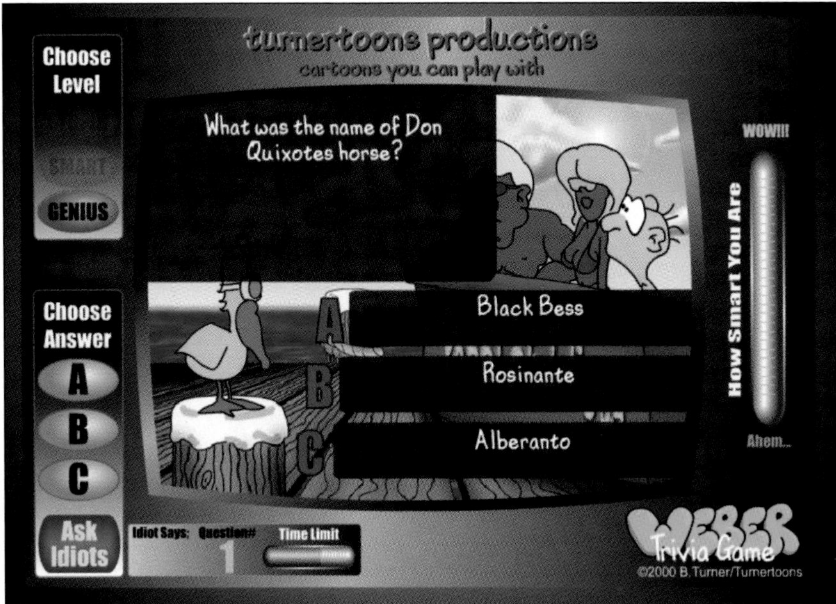

Here's the game's main interface on the Genius level. The game can be played entirely from this screen.

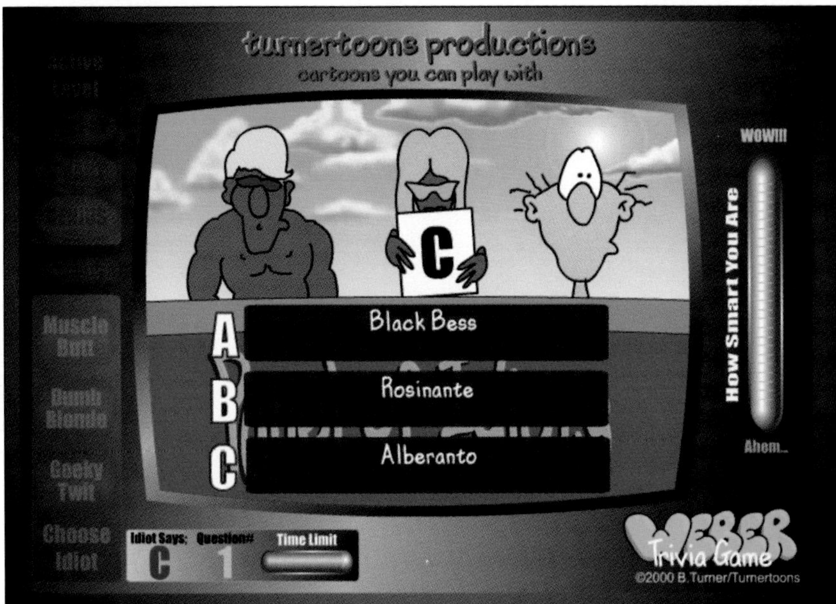

If you get stumped, you can ask the idiots for advice. Some idiots are better than others at answering questions on certain topics. This scripting technique is fully explained in Chapter 9.

Trivia Game Elements

Here, we have a sequence of elements that were re-purposed from the cartoon show's animation to use in the trivia game. Re-purposing graphic elements not only saves you time, but also gives the game a cohesive look. This allows you to offer an entire package of cartoons and games with a solid motif.

Adventure Game

The CD-ROM also includes the entire working authoring file for a project we call the Adventure Game. This is a very sophisticated isometric 3D Flash game. In the game, you control the character of Walter. Your quest is to find the lost map pieces that will lead you to the treasure. In the following pages, we break down some of the sequences, scenes, and various parts used in the game.

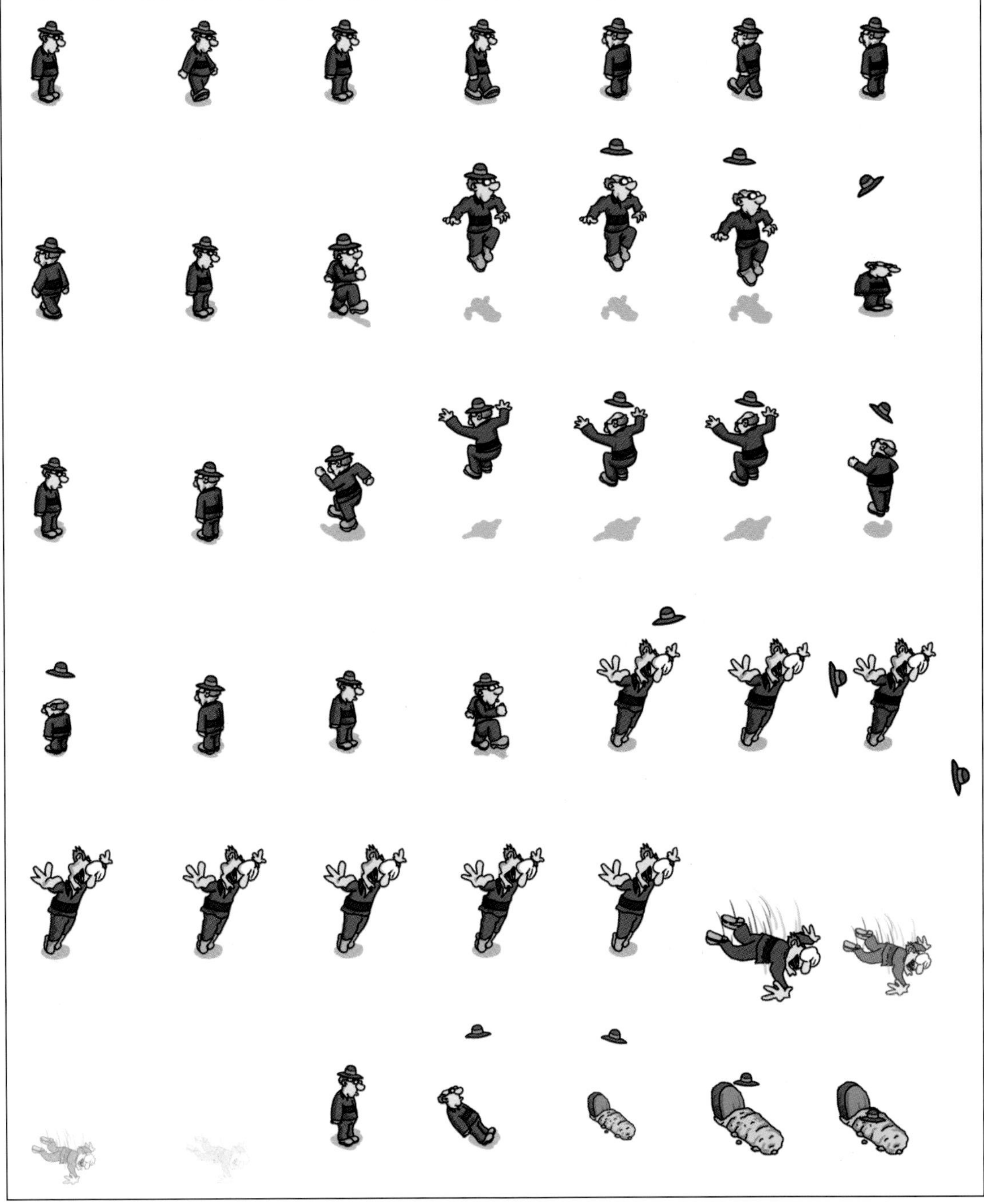

Here are all the drawings that are involved in creating the moves for the character of Walter in the Adventure Game.

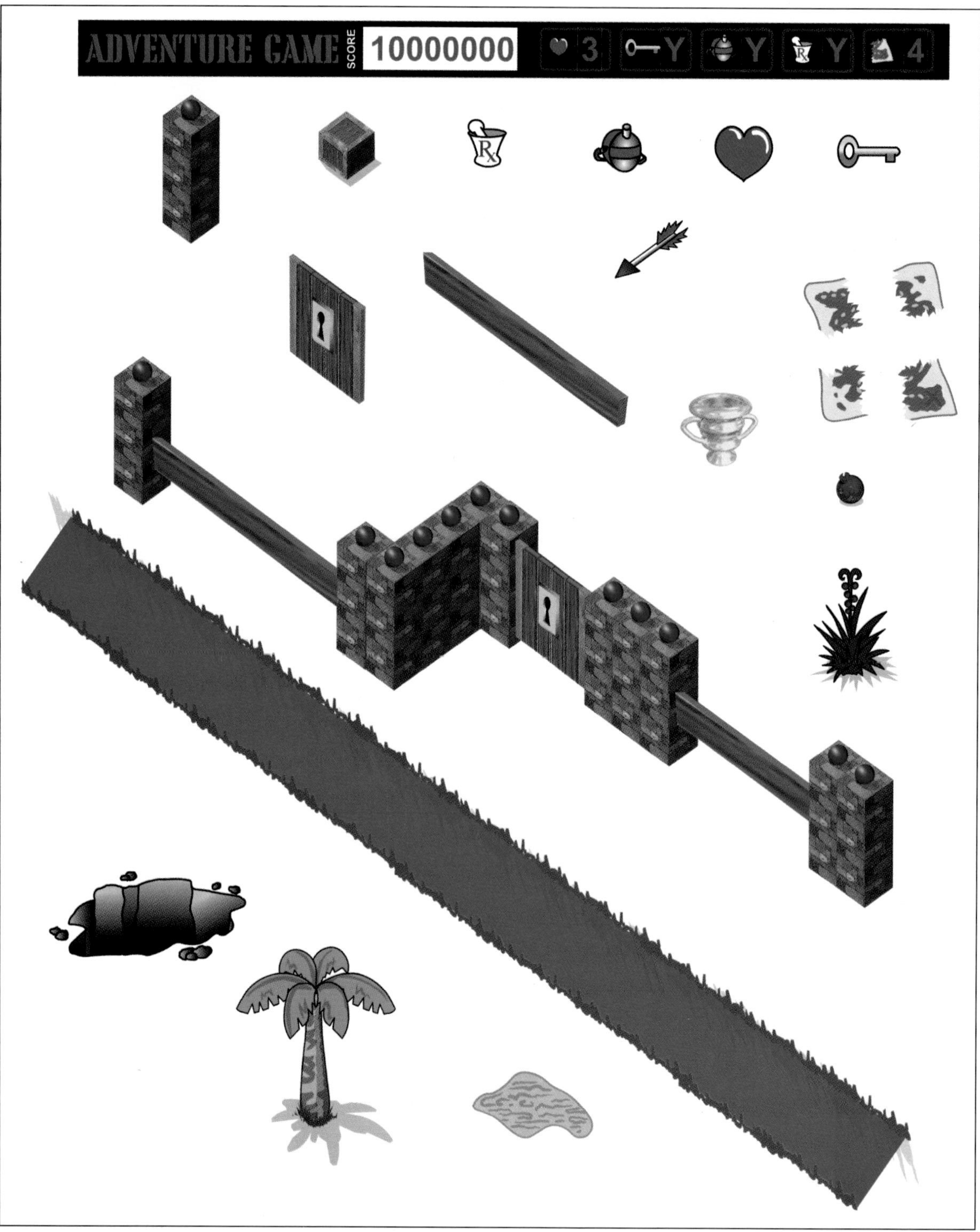

Here are drawings of all elements used in the Adventure Game.

More Adventure Game

The following pages show actual scenes from the Adventure Game. The game and the code that make it work are included on the CD-ROM and are fully explained in Chapter 10.

Here, Walter is faced with a locked gate for which he has no key. He must find the crate that contains the key in order to progress any further.

Walter falls into a hole and loses a heart (life). Sophisticated collision detection is used here.

Here, Walter is faced with the dangers of quicksand and poison bayonet bushes. He must get to the crates surrounded by the bushes, but how? Maybe he needs to find a bomb to blow them away. This is part of the game strategy.

Oops! Walter got too close to the poison bayonet bushes and has died. Too bad he didn't have the anti-poison, which may have helped sustain his life.

Chapter 7

It's a Wrap

Now that the animated cartoon is finished, you need to get it in front of an audience. To do that, you really have only three choices: the Web, video, and film. In this chapter, we'll discuss preparing your work for these mediums.

By Bill Turner

Destination: Internet

Because the Internet is where most Flash animators will be taking their work, we'll focus here first. As everyone knows, the Web is an immediate public information system. You can put an animation in front of many people within minutes of its completion. All you need is Web server space, and either your own domain name, or permission under someone else's domain. After that, you need only an FTP account and password (which usually come when you buy Web server space), and you can upload the animation files, which will become immediately available to the world.

Before we plow into world cartoon domination, we'll need to accomplish a few little details to make the viewer's experience everything we hope it could be—namely, we want to make the download wait as courteous as possible. Pre-loaders can help us do this.

Pre-Loaders

Because Flash is a streaming technology, it will attempt to begin playing the animation immediately, before all the data has been downloaded. This immediate response can be great in the respect that the end viewer's wait is much shorter. Unfortunately, the premature play can also seriously interrupt the flow of your cartoon if necessary items are not downloaded in time. The cartoon might need a certain sound for a frame, and that sound simply is not there yet, which causes the animation to abruptly halt to wait for it.

To prevent an animation from playing prematurely (before enough data has been downloaded), you can create a pre-loader. A *pre-loader* causes the cartoon to go through a looping mode on a few frames, while the software checks to see whether the needed data is loaded yet. When the specified frames are loaded, the animation begins to play, while the remainder completes downloading.

Most folks would rather wait a bit up front while the cartoon downloads, as opposed to having it play back in a stuttering, stop-and-go manner. But, as we all know, Web surfers are an impatient lot, likely to click away within moments of inactivity on a Web page. The trick is to give people something to view or do while they're waiting (see Figure 7.1).

At the very least, a pre-loader should give some indication that the download is progressing. At best, a pre-loader gives viewers something to do while they're waiting, such as a small animation to view, or maybe even a mini game they can play. The pre-loader should be very small (in bytes) so that it loads almost immediately. If the pre-loader takes too long to download, the delay will defeat the purpose of using the pre-loader.

To create a pre-loader, you'll be using a movie clip and two actions. The movie clip will contain the little distraction animation. Again, for these distractions,

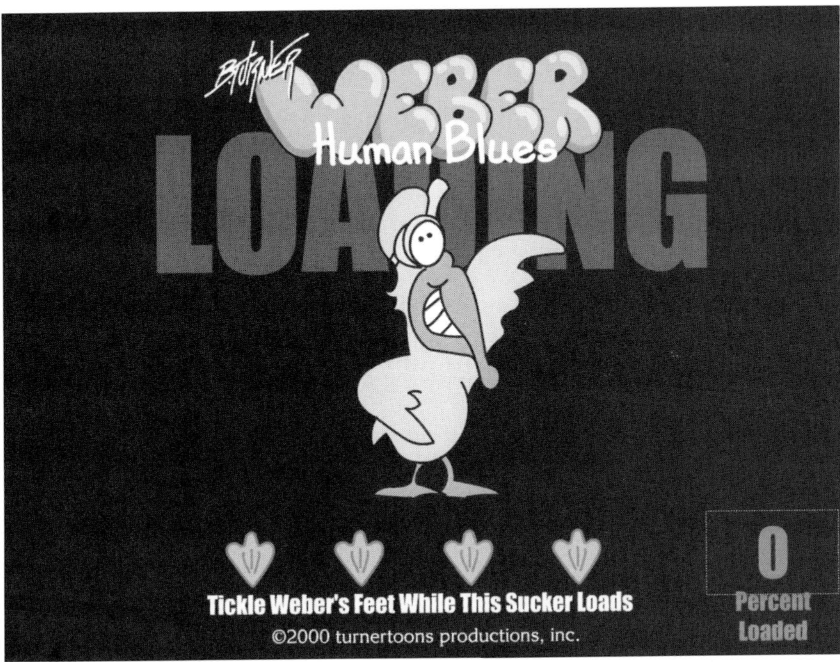

Figure 7.1
The pre-loader from the Weber *Human Blues* episode. The authoring file is included on the CD-ROM for your investigation.

make sure the file size of the movie clip animations is small, so that the pre-loader doesn't make the viewer wait. You can test out how long the download wait will be by using the Test Movie and Show Streaming functions.

The actions you need are quite simple. The first frame will have the **ifFrameLoaded** (where x=frame number the pre-loader looks for to be loaded) action that looks to see how much of the cartoon has loaded; the second frame will use the **GoTo** action to go back to the first frame to look again. If the file has not downloaded to the expectation of the first action, the two frames will continue in a loop until the first action is satisfied. While these actions are being performed, the small animation (movie clip) will play.

Note: Even though the **ifFrameLoaded** and **GoTo** actions use only two frames for the loop, the movie clip with the distraction animation is not limited to two frames. The movie clip can be as many frames as you want. Movie clip timelines play independently of the main Timeline the actions loop is working from.

This process can be a bit confusing to newcomers of actions and pre-loaders. The following project sheds light on how to make a simple pre-loader for your cartoons. If you are a more advanced reader, you might want to skip this one.

PROJECT Creating a Simple Pre-Loader

Now that you understand the need for pre-loaders, let's make one. We have set up a file with everything you'll need for this project. The file includes a movie clip for entertaining viewers while the animation is loading, and a soundtrack for mimicking the soundtrack of the cartoon itself. We've added this soundtrack because something actually needs to download for the pre-loader to work. Then, the words "Cartoon Plays" designate where the cartoon animation would take place (see Figure 7.2).

Figure 7.2
The pre-loader project.

1. Open the file named *simpleloader.fla*, located in the Preloader project folder.

2. Examine the Timeline, and notice that the mock cartoon actually starts on Frame 3, instead of Frame 1. We set it up this way because simple pre-loaders need two frames in which to operate the loop.

3. On the layer named **art**, insert a keyframe (press F6) at Frame 1. Then, from the Library window, drag the movie clip named **manshovel** to the stage, and center the clip comfortably there. We're using a movie clip for this animation because it contains more than two frames, but it will loop in its entirety within the two-frame loop we'll create on the main Timeline. (Movie clips operate on their own Timeline independent of the main Timeline.) On Frame 3, this animation will disappear because it will no longer exist on the Timeline.

4. Drag the symbol named **loading**, and center it below the **manshovel** symbol.

5. Now, here's the important part: Open the Actions panel (**Window|Actions**) and, on the layer named **actions**, select Frame 1 (which should already be a keyframe).

6. In the Actions panel, click the + sign in the upper-left corner (see Figure 7.3) to reveal the menu of actions. Choose **Basic Actions|If Frame Is Loaded**. Then, type **166** in the Frame field. This makes the frame's action look for Frame 166 to be loaded completely before the system executes the next command. Notice the scripting code added to the panel's Actions list:

```
ifFrameLoaded (166) {
```

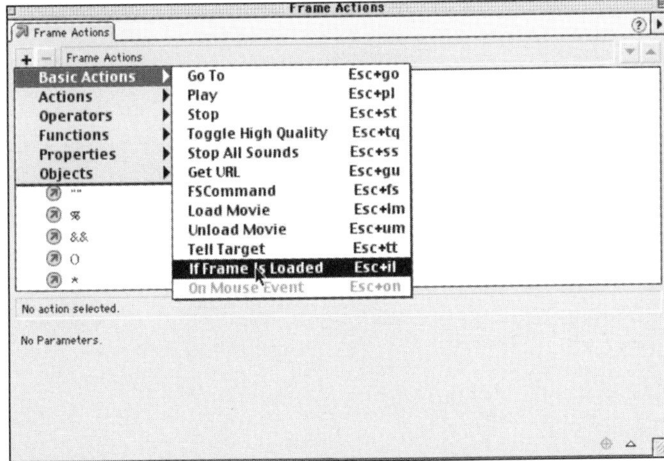

Figure 7.3
The Actions panel for the pre-loader.

7. Now, add the command to tell Flash what to do if this statement is true. In this case, we want the playback head to go to Frame 3 and start playing the animation. In the Actions panel, click on the + sign, and choose **Basic Actions|Go To**. In the Frame field, type **3**. Make sure that the Go To And Play checkbox is checked (it is checked by default). Notice the code added to the Actions list:

```
gotoAndPlay (3);
```

8. If the first statement is not true (if the frame is *not* loaded), we want Flash to keep checking. So, in Frame 2 in the **actions** layer, insert a keyframe (F6). With this frame selected, go back to the Actions panel. Click on the + sign; choose **Basic Actions|Go To**; and then, in the Frame field, type **1**. Make sure that Go To And Play is checked. This finishes the loop that looks for Frame 166 to be loaded before the system continues the animation.

```
gotoAndPlay (1);
```

9. Advance to Frame 170 (the animation's last frame), and insert a keyframe on the **actions** layer. In this frame, add the action that tells the animation to Go To And Play Frame 3. Now, the animation will loop after the first play-through, bypassing the pre-loader frames.
10. Save the authoring file.
11. Next, we'll test this pre-loader. Choose **Control|Test Movie**. This action builds an SWF file, then opens and starts playing the SWF immediately. Notice that you had no hint of the pre-loader. When such a small file loads from your hard drive, it happens so fast that the **If Frame Is Loaded (166)** action is satisfied immediately and jumps right into playing the "Cartoon Plays" section.
12. To see the pre-loader work, choose **Debug|56KB** (4.7Kbs). This will simulate a 56KB modem download.
13. Now, choose **View|Show Streaming**. You will now see what a person with a 56KB modem will see when he or she downloads your cartoon for the first time from the Internet.

This is a simple, but effective, pre-loader. Certainly, you can be more elaborate, as long as you take care not to add too much to the pre-loader section. By simulating streaming in Flash, you can get some idea of what your viewers will experience. In this project, we made the pre-loader wait until everything was loaded. Sometimes, you might not want to do this, however, because the wait might be excessive, and then you'd forfeit the benefits of streaming. The magic number to adjust is in the **If Frame Is Loaded** command (the number is 166 for this project). By changing this number to whatever needs to be loaded for the animation to play and stream smoothly, you can achieve an animation that starts playing as soon as it can, without the stuttering starts and stops that you want to avoid. Once you've finished the tweaking, you're ready to put your animation up for the world to see.

Domain Names

You might already have your own domain name, but if you don't, we'd like to point you in the direction for acquiring one. A domain name can be of vital importance, more so than where you buy Web space. With your own domain name, you can move your site to whichever Web server you want, without the fear of losing an audience you might have built. You cannot do this if you build an audience under someone else's domain name and then need to move the site. Because the Web is so changeable, you'll more than likely move your site sooner or later. Without getting into lots of technical details about domain name servers and such, suffice it to say that, as long as you own the name, your work can always be found, whether your cartoons sit on a server in New York City, or one in Bangkok. If your site is part of the Internet, the audience will always go to **www.(YourDomainName).com** and find the work.

As of this writing, domain names cost only $35 a year. Some registrars will let you buy one year at a time, and others require two years in advance. Either way, the price is a bargain, no doubt. You can buy a domain name online any time, even if you have not yet purchased Web server space. You can reserve the name for when you do set up shop with a Web space provider. Because you might not have the technical information about Web server IP addresses and such when you want to start your new domain name, you may want to just let the Web space provider set all this up for you.

Many providers will do the whole shooting match for you: They rent you Web space, acquire the domain name registered in your name, and set you up with an FTP account in one fell swoop. A good place to start in this search is the InterNIC's Accredited Registrar Directory, which you will find at **www.internic.net/alpha.html**. This directory is a listing of companies that can get you on the road to your own domain name and also supply many other services.

Your Site

After you have all the logistics of starting your Web site, you will, of course, have to create a site. This process can involve a great many issues beyond the scope of this book. If you're unfamiliar with HTML, DHTML, ASP, PHP, and any other form of alphabet soup used to describe Web practices, you might want to look into partnering with someone who does have the know-how. Probably a thousand books exist on the subject of making Web sites and, depending on how involved you want to be, finding one that suits your needs would be a good idea.

For simply publishing a cartoon to the Web, Flash itself will create the HTML (hypertext markup language) page that will allow your cartoon to be seen. This will be a no-frills page—Flash creates a page that simply contains the proper links and plug-in information for displaying the exported SWF file. This HTML page is created through the **File|Publish Settings** command in Flash.

As Figure 7.4 shows, the Formats tab of the Publish Settings dialog box is where you'll choose what you want Flash to publish. You can choose from a number of things but, mainly, you want a simple HTML page and the Flash SWF files to be created. You initiate this action by checking the box next to the formats, as Figure 7.4 shows.

Publish Settings

Formats | Flash | HTML

OK

Publish

Cancel

Type:	Filename:
☒ Flash (.swf)	anticipation.swf
☐ Generator Template	anticipation.swt
☒ HTML (.html)	anticipation.html
☐ GIF Image (.gif)	anticipation.gif
☐ JPEG Image (.jpg)	anticipation.jpg
☐ PNG Image (.png)	anticipation.png
☐ Windows Projector	anticipation.exe
☐ Macintosh Projector	anticipation Projector
☐ QuickTime (.mov)	anticipation.mov
☐ RealPlayer	anticipation.smil

☒ Use default names

Help

Figure 7.4
The Formats tab of the Publish Settings dialog box.

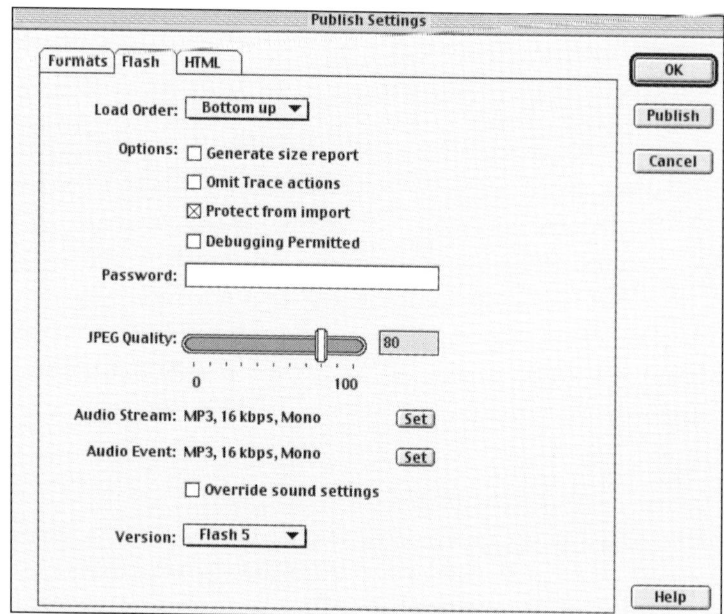

Figure 7.5
The Flash tab of the Publish Settings dialog box.

On the Flash tab of the Publish Settings dialog box (see Figure 7.5), you can make various global settings for the Flash SWF file that will be exported. We'll give you a quick run-through of the functions that concern animated cartoons:

- *Load Order*—Determines how the graphics will be displayed as they are loaded. Bottom Up means your cartoon artwork in the lowest layer in the stack will appear first when streaming into the Web page. This order can sometimes be unwanted—having artwork show up in strange pieces as the cartoon downloads. The pre-loader we discussed earlier eliminates this unwanted piecing together.

- *Options*—Gives you additional information about and control over your movie:
  - *Generate Size Report*—Creates a detailed text file that lists the size in bytes of each symbol, photo, sound, and font included in the exported SWF file.
  - *Omit Trace Actions*—Is for programmers, and is not relevant to linear cartoons that have no programming.
  - *Protect From Import*—Adds a bit of security to your exported SWF file, by preventing other Flash users from importing your artwork into their project files.
  - *Debugging Permitted*—Is for programmers, and is not relevant to linear cartoons that have no programming.
- *Password*—Is for programmers, and is not relevant to linear cartoons that have no programming.
- *JPEG Quality*—Determines the balance between image quality and file size. This is a global setting that affects all bitmap images, unless specified otherwise in the Library window. The higher the number, the better the quality—at the expense of larger file size.
- *Audio Stream and Audio Event*—Here, you set the global quality settings of the soundtracks in your cartoon. The higher the Kbps (1,000 bits per second), the better the sound quality at the expense of larger file size. The Override Sound Settings checkbox lets you have these settings override any sound settings you might have made in individual sound files in the Library window.
- *Version*—Lets you choose between the versions of Flash plug-ins required to play the SWF file. You can choose from Flash versions 1 through 5. Beware that if you use functions the older versions do not support, those functions will not work. Flash 3 will not handle MP3 sound, for example.

The next tab is the HTML information that you can customize, as you can see in Figure 7.6. Here, you can choose the various settings with respect to how Flash will create the HTML file that will contain your cartoon. We'll give a brief rundown of these settings as they concern your cartoon.

- *Template*—Here, you can choose to have alternate forms of the Web page, to be viewed by Web surfers who do not have the Flash plug-in. You probably will never change this pop-up window (the default setting demands the presence of the Flash plug-in), because your cartoon will need to be viewed with the Flash plug-in.
- *Dimensions*—Match Movie is the usual choice, because this option informs the HTML page to display the cartoon just as you created it in Flash. You

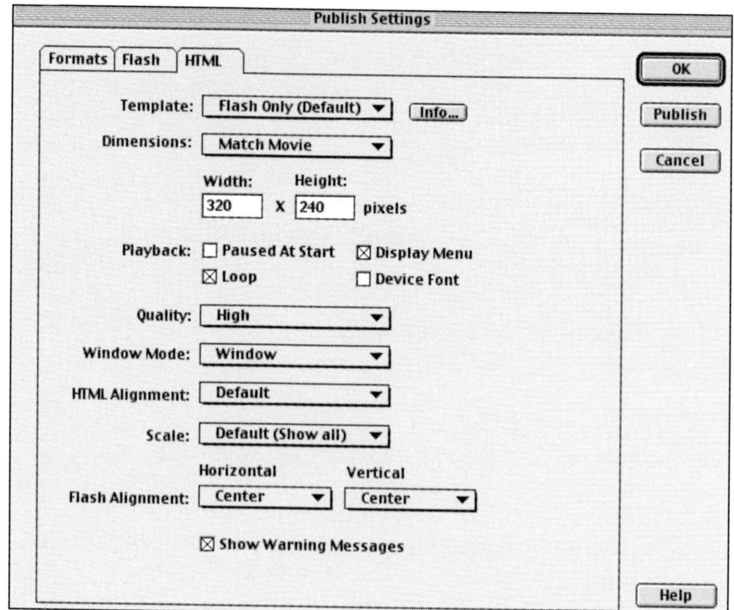

Figure 7.6
The HTML tab of the Publish Settings dialog box.

can change this pop-up window to Pixels, which will let you scale up or down the cartoon's display size by typing the pixel dimensions in the Width and Height boxes. Or, you can choose Percent to use a percentage relative to the browser window.

- *Playback*—This setting provides four options. The Paused At Start option pretty much explains itself. When this option is checked, the cartoon will not play unless you have a programmed button in the cartoon itself telling it to play. Otherwise, the cartoon will begin playing as soon as it can. The Display Menu option provides the menu you can pop up by control-clicking (on the Mac), or right-clicking (on the PC) the movie itself in the Web page. This menu contains such functions as Play, Rewind, and Zoom In and Out. Loop allows the cartoon to loop forever, as long as the page is active. The Device Font option substitutes anti-aliased (smoothed line edges) system fonts for fonts not installed on the user's system (Windows only). This option is usually of little consequence in cartoons, because you will most likely be embedding fonts as you create animated art.
- *Quality*—This setting dictates the various levels of anti-aliasing (smoothing of line edges) applied to the art. The Low setting provides no anti-aliasing and permits faster performance on slower computers. The Medium setting applies some anti-aliasing, but ignores smoothing bitmaps. The High setting smoothes all vectors, regardless of performance, but it does not smooth moving bitmaps. The Best setting anti-aliases everything, no matter what, and provides the highest quality—at the expense of frame rate on slower computers. The Auto Low and

Auto High settings let the Flash plug-in determine whether the computer the animation is playing on can keep up with the demands of the quality mode; the plug-in adjusts itself automatically by taking away or adding anti-aliasing to the art as it plays.

- *Window Mode*—Leave this at its default (window), unless you want only your HTML page to be viewed by the Windows only (not Mac) version of Internet Explorer 4.0 with Flash Active X control. This choice allows for Dynamic HTML authored pages to show through the transparent portions of your Flash movie but can slow performance. We recommend leaving this at the default.
- *HTML Alignment*—Default centers the Flash movie on the page. The remaining choices (Right, Left, Top, and Bottom) explain themselves.
- *Scale*—Default (Show All) is the most common choice here for cartoons, because the default simply shows the movie at the size you've specified in the Dimensions.
- *Flash Alignment*—This setting determines how the movie is placed within the movie window and how it is cropped.
- *Show Warnings*—When checked, will show a warning message if there is an HTML tag conflict.

After you have established all these settings, you can simply click the Publish button for Flash to create the necessary HTML and SWF files for uploading the animation to your Web site. The file will be written to the folder where the authoring (FLA) file exists. The HTML and SWF files are the two files you will put on the Web. The authoring file need not go, nor would it play even if you did put it on the Web. The authoring file, once saved, will maintain all these publishing settings so that you won't have to keep inputting them each time you publish from that authoring file.

This process will make a rudimentary Web page. We recommend that you go further in your Web site development with applications such as Macromedia's Dreamweaver, which contains excellent support for Flash, as well as for many other Web elements you might want to include in your HTML pages.

Destination: Video

Video output from Flash is a hot new topic—well, not really; we've been doing video animation from Flash for years. Video output from Flash has just been a well-kept secret. Even the first version of Flash (actually named Future Splash Animator back then) could export to QuickTime video. Because QuickTime video is so versatile—it's being used in everything from live, streaming Web video to high-end, broadcast-quality video for television—it makes a strong partner with Flash as an animation tool.

We spoke of QuickTime earlier in Chapter 5's rotoscoping section, but if you missed that, we'll mention it again here. All Macintosh computers come with QuickTime as a standard component, and most PCs will have the software as well. If you do not have QuickTime, you can download it, free of charge, from Apple at **www.quicktime.com**. Apple also offers a Pro version for $29.95 that adds some editing functions to the QuickTime Player, but that version is not necessary for outputting to video from Flash. As of this writing, the latest official version of QuickTime is 4.1.2.

Note: MiniDV is a new, purely digital, video-recording and playback-tape format. The tapes themselves are quite small (about 2.75×2 inches). Unlike your home VCR, which records an analog signal, MiniDV records video as digital data, much like a hard drive does, but MiniDV writes the video data to tape. As a result, you can take video data from the MiniDV tape into the computer and back out to tape again with little to no loss in picture quality.

MiniDV

Many professional systems can record QuickTime video to tape, such as BetaSP and DigiBeta, which are high-end, videotape formats television broadcasters use. Frankly, any tape-format recorder that can interface with a digital video card can record QuickTime—and, therefore, Flash-generated animation. But, for the purposes of this discussion, we'll come down out of the high-priced stratosphere of DigiBeta, into the high-quality, reasonably priced world of MiniDV.

We mentioned MiniDV in Chapter 5, and how reasonably priced the equipment is. What we didn't mention there was how good the quality of MiniDV is. We're sure some BetaSP (a standard in television broadcasting) users out there will disagree, but we think the quality of MiniDV nearly parallels that of its much pricier big brother. MiniDV is so good, in fact, that a new legion of independent filmmakers is working solely in MiniDV. It's that good, and certainly good enough for running out cartoons from Flash. If you really need BetaSP, or higher output, that's certainly possible, too. In fact, we've actually taken MiniDV-recorded Flash animations and duped them to BetaSP through the S-Video output of the prosumer deck—and even the video tech, who really knows his stuff, thought the final output looked great.

The sound of MiniDV is also quite good. At 16-bit, 48kHz stereo, its quality is slightly above that of CD quality. So, when you're outputting to MiniDV from Flash, you'll want to make sure your sound is of the highest fidelity, with no compression in between to taint it.

Here are some links to consumer and prosumer MiniDV equipment. Unfortunately, the addresses are quite long. The first link is for MiniDV cameras; the second is for decks and accessories:

- ***www.sel.sony.com/SEL/consumer/ss5/generic/digitalvideo/minidvcamcorders/index.shtml***
- ***www.sel.sony.com/SEL/consumer/ss5/generic/digitalvideo/minidvdecksandperipherals/index.shtml***

You will also need an interface for your computer to hook up to MiniDV video equipment. This means you'll need an IEEE 1394 interface (also known as

Apple Computer's FireWire, or Sony's iLink). Nearly all new Macintoshes come with this interface as standard equipment. If you have an older Mac or PC without the interface, you can add a relatively inexpensive PCI card to add this functionality. Once you have FireWire installed, you can hook up not only MiniDV, but a host of hard drives, DVD, and CD-ROM burners as well. The real beauty of FireWire is its high-speed transfer rate over a very simple connection. The wiring FireWire uses does not have the length and termination problems of SCSI, and it is thin and easy to route. You can find out more about FireWire at **www.digitalorigin.com**. Digital Origin markets FireWire (or IEEE 1394) boards and software for both PC and Mac. Also, you can visit the parent company, Media 100 Inc., at **www.media100.com**; Media 100 Inc. markets many goodies related to digital video hardware and software in general.

Certainly, you'll want to shop around for prices. Like any other technology, as these products become widespread, the prices will come down. MiniDV is poised to become widespread in the near future, so shop around.

Preparing Your Cartoon for Video

You need to keep a few things in mind when you're creating video from your Flash animations. Some of these things we referred to earlier, such as aspect ratio (the dimensions of the frames) and frame rate. We'll review these considerations next, in some detail, to reinforce this knowledge.

Frame Rate

Videotape always plays at 30fps (frames per second)—actually, 29.97fps, but because Flash cannot specify this rate, we go with 30fps—or an evenly divided segment thereof. On the issue of frame rate, the actual playback speed is 29.97fps and, if you were doing video animations longer than about seven minutes, this frame rate would be an important distinction. In longer animations done at 30fps and played at 29.97fps, a slight drifting of the audio synchronization would occur at around the six- to seven-minute point. Because most cartoons will run under this time limit (i.e., before drifting), you need not worry about it. If you have longer cartoons that require perfect audio synchronization, you should consider doing the animation in segments, and piecing it together in an application that can deal with the 29.97 frame rate, such as Adobe After Effects.

Most of the time, you will not want to animate at 30fps; as we discussed in Chapter 5, 15fps seems to be ideal. When your animation is created at 15fps, the video will simply show one animation frame for every two video frames, and everybody's happy. If you were to make your animation at 13fps, 26fps, or some other number not evenly divisible into 30fps, the animation would end up with serious stuttering problems when it was played back from tape.

Dimensions

The dimensions of the animation are also important. Frame dimensions for video can vary slightly from format to format, but a standard for computer-generated, square pixels is 640×480, and these are the dimensions you should use. Because your computer monitor uses a square-pixel format, this format will scale nicely into the format required for MiniDV. The MiniDV format is actually 720×480 pixels, but this is a rectangular pixel format, as is all NTSC TV video. You might wonder, why not work at 720×480 pixels in the first place? Good question. The answer is that because the computer deals in square pixels, anything you draw that needs to be circular, such as the tires on a car, will appear squished and distorted on TV. If you work at 640×480 pixels on the computer, the circles will be elongated when they're scaled to the 720×480-pixel video file. The circles will look strange on a computer, but they'll look perfectly fine on a TV screen. This concept can be confusing if you're new to video; refer to Figure 7.7 for a visual explanation.

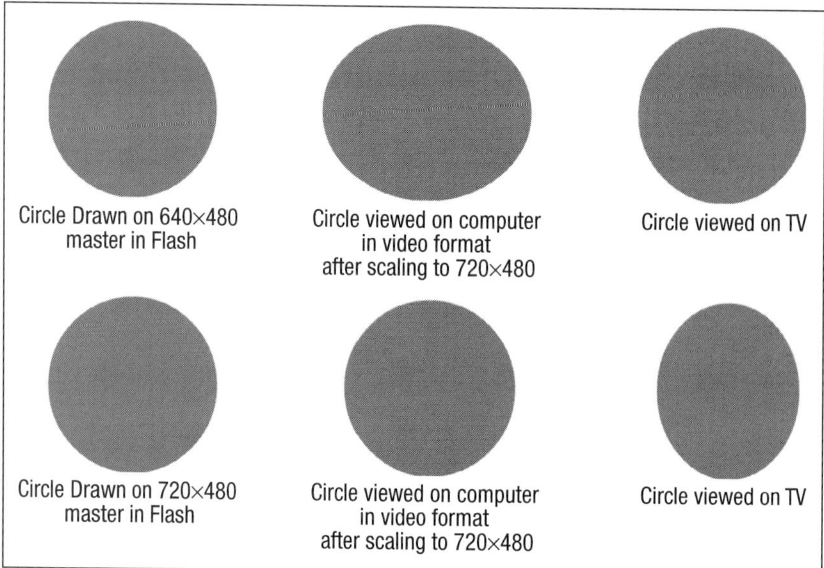

Figure 7.7
The video circle problem.

An issue those new to video might miss is the action- and title-safe area. Your standard TV screen is quite unlike computer monitors. While the computer monitor shows you *everything*, the TV screen cuts out a good portion of the view around the edges. This area is a No Man's Land, and you will not want something important in the animation to fall into this area. Included on the CD-ROM is a file named *NTSCsafeareas.fla*, and this file has a grouped graphic that designates which areas are safe for art to exist in. Notice the two rectangles (see Figure 7.8), one inside the other. The inner rectangle designates Title Safe, the outer area designates Action Safe. Title safe is where you'll want to confine important text. Action Safe is where you'll want to confine important graphic elements. This delineation is not to say that art cannot exceed these areas, just that, if it does, it might not be visible on a TV screen.

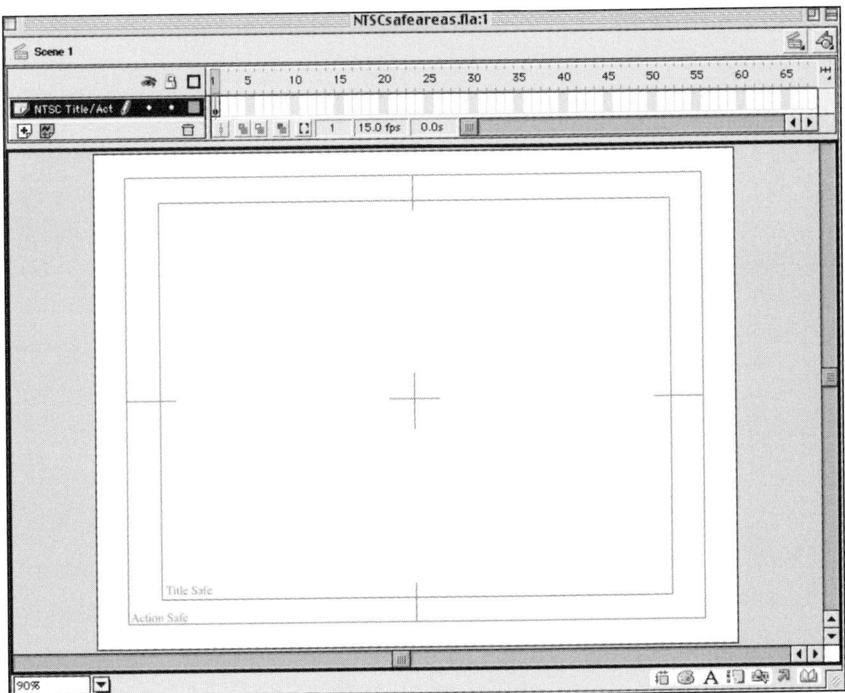

Figure 7.8
Action- and title-safe areas.

Interlacing

Another major difference between computer monitors and TV screens is the way each medium draws an image. Computer monitors are noninterlaced, which means that the cathode ray scans each horizontal line of phosphors every cycle to create an image. A TV screen is interlaced, which means that the ray scans every other horizontal line of phosphors with each cycle. A cycle is a complete image on the screen. Without being terribly technical about this, what it means to your animation is that a TV drops out a one-pixel line every 1/60th of a second. So, if you have horizontal lines of one pixel in your art, the art will flicker, or vibrate, on a TV screen—something you'll want to avoid when you're creating art for video output. You might have noticed this phenomenon while you were watching a TV weatherman who was wearing a tie with thin horizontal stripes on it; the tie probably vibrated like mad. Usually, news people avoid wearing any clothing that has small horizontal stripes, but every now and then, something sneaks in. Generally speaking, the TV screen's quality is much lower than a computer monitor's, so avoid tiny details in your animation, because they simply won't show up very well.

Color

Color is another issue with TV display. Your computer monitor shows many millions of colors (at 24-bit resolution), TV does not have as wide a color range. TV has a particularly tough time showing bright reds, yellows, and light blues without having what's called "bleeding". Colors that bleed, such as the ones just mentioned, will have the unwanted look of a spiked horizontal blurring where the color meets a different color. The standard color palette in Flash is really not the best for video. If you've already created an animation in Flash, and you don't really feel like re-coloring it, help's available: Adobe After Effects and Adobe Premiere both have a video filter for enforcing NTSC colors on the video clip you've exported from Flash.

You can purchase a software extension for the Macintosh (only) that helps remove this problem while you're creating the art. Synthetic Aperture makes a great solution called Echo Fire, which you can find at **www.synthetic-ap.com**. The Echo Fire package comes with a custom Color Picker you can access from Flash's color-selection palette (when you choose the system color picker—see Figure 7.9). If you choose your colors here, the software will inform you of the color's legality in video, and it will give you a chance to click the Legalize button, which takes you to the best color that video can display. The Echo Fire software also comes with a FireWire DV video player application, and another small application that lets whatever you have on your computer screen (Flash included) be routed through FireWire and viewed on your TV screen while you create the art. This function gives you the capability to see exactly what the colors and art will look like on the TV.

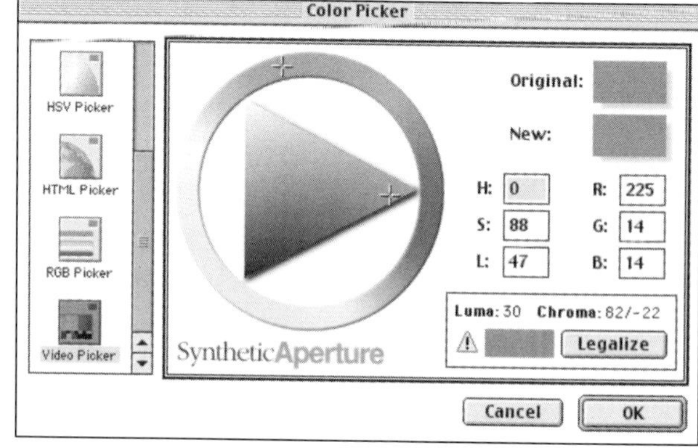

Figure 7.9
Synthetic Aperture's video-safe Color Picker.

PROJECT Preparing Video Output

Now, we'll do a short video-output exercise. In the Video Project folder, you'll find the file named *surfing.fla* (see Figure 7.10). Unfortunately, this is a Mac-only project because Flash doesn't output QuickTime video directly on a Windows PC. You can, however, do the various steps, applying the QuickTime settings to AVI output instead, with the exception of codec choice (*codec* is short for the compression/decompression scheme the software uses to create the video file). You will then have to convert your video file to DV format to play it through FireWire or IEEE 1394.

1. Open the *surfing.fla* file.
2. Notice the layer that contains the action- and title-safe-designating graphic (named NTSC Title/Action safe). You want to remove this graphic before you export to video, or the graphic will show up, too. Simply delete the layer it's on.

Figure 7.10
The video-output project file.

3. Choose **File|Export Movie** and, in the Save As Type list, select QuickTime Video. (Simply choosing QuickTime will not make a video file, but rather will make a Flash track in a QuickTime movie, which is not what we want here.) Type a file name, and click on Save.

4. In the Export QuickTime dialog box, enter 720×480 (you will have to uncheck Maintain Aspect Ratio). This action stretches the 640×480-pixel image, as we discussed earlier (see Figure 7.11).

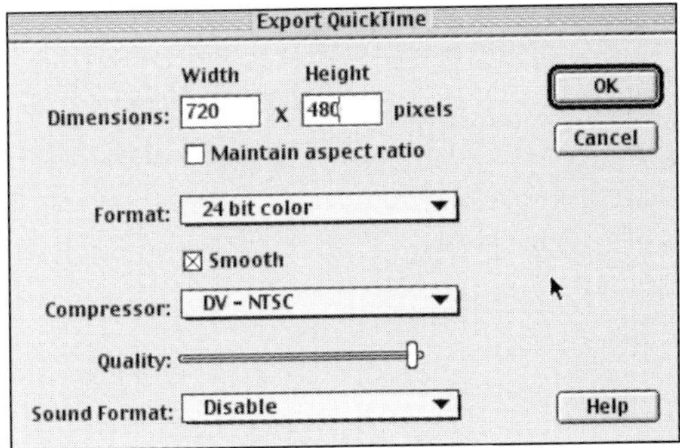

Figure 7.11
The Export QuickTime dialog box.

5. Set the Format pop-up (or pull down) window to 24-bit color depth, and check the Smooth checkbox.

6. The next pop-up window, Compressor, is where you choose the codec. Select DV-NTSC. Move the Quality slider all the way to the right (for Best). For Windows users, select Full Frames Uncompressed.

7. For this example, you can disable sound, because there isn't any. If there were sound, you'd want to make it the highest quality possible by using 44kHz, 16-bit Stereo.

8. Click OK, and Flash will commence to rasterize the vector art into a pixel-based video file. Beware—these files can become quite large, running into the hundreds, and even thousands, of megabytes (gigabytes). This project creates about a 20MB, DV video file.

Note: Remember that choosing **Export Movie|QuickTime** (rather than QuickTime Video) will not make a pixel-based video file. Instead, it will simply make a Flash track that the QuickTime player and browser plug-in can read. It will not play back to MiniDV tape.

Windows users, to convert your video file to DV format, you will need to convert the file using QuickTime Pro, Media Cleaner (**www.mediacleaner.com**), or any other such video file format conversion applications.

After you have a video file, you can edit it with any other video-editing software. Applications such as Adobe Premiere and After Effects can add an army of plug-in effects and options to your animated cartoon once it's in video format.

If you export the video from Flash using the None codec option (None is uncompressed and, therefore, no codec at all), or using the Animation codec at its highest quality, and then use the Format pop-up window's 32-bit color (alpha channel), the result will be a video clip with an alpha channel. The alpha channel will allow whatever art is in your animation to composite over other elements in a video-editing application (such as After Effects).

Note: You will need to make sure the background color of the Flash animation is set to a color of 0% opacity to get the alpha channel to work with video export.

Even though the Web is a Flash animation's main destination, some of you might want to at least experiment with video output. Watching your cartoon on a big-screen TV with a booming sound system can be quite a lot of fun. Others might find the value of this form of output in a commercial sense. As we said earlier, you *can* do broadcastable animations from Flash, and we think that's a pretty neat trick from such an affordable animation program.

Destination: Film

Because Flash is a vector-format application, you can scale up your animation art without inducing unwanted jaggies (aliased or stair stepped looking edges); you can actually output a sequence of high-resolution files that you can then print to film via a film recorder. If all your art is in a Flash animation vector (drawn in Flash or imported from Illustrator or Freehand), you can output very high-quality frames. Imported bitmaps (such as Photoshop files), however, will become jaggy and unattractive unless you use originals with high enough resolution when you're importing into Flash.

You will need to find out what format the film recorder that you're sending to requires. You can export a numbered sequence—via **File|Export Movie** and choosing a file type of PICT (Mac), or PNG (PC or Mac) files—that can then be batch-process converted with an application such as Photoshop to the format you need. Because there are different companies using different film recorder systems, find out what digital format they can use before you go through exporting what could be thousands of large files that take up many gigabytes of disk space. Most systems can take a sequence of Mac PICT files or PC Targa files, but do find out first. You would also need to figure out the mammoth task of how to transfer these files. Generally, a high-capacity tape drive is the solution for moving large amounts of data, but find out first from the folks running the film recorders as to what data tape formats they use.

Note: Images for film output need to be very high resolution. Starting at about 4,096 pixels wide for each frame. Scaling up a pixel-based image that starts off at 640 pixels wide would become quite broken up and jaggy.

Outputting to film is not for the faint of heart or wallet. We discuss this option here only to alert those of you who might want to do it that you can. You will have to research the issues above, and maybe others as well, but you can do it. With the help of other applications, maybe Flash can be the engine of that next animated feature film.

Moving On

Well, that pretty much wraps up the animated-cartoon-creation section of this book. Open up your mind, because it's time to program games. As you'll discover, animated cartoons can play a significant role in games, too.

Chapter 8

Introduction to Game Design

By James Robertson
and Bill Turner

As game developers, we are often asked, "How do I make a game?" This question is tough to answer because it's like being asked, "How do I build a house?" Many factors are involved, and each one can be complex. This chapter will help you get started.

Choosing a Genre

You need to consider everything we discuss in this chapter *before* you go anywhere near your computer and open your copy of Flash. When you build a house, you need to turn your ideas into detailed plans before you start any building work, and designing a game is no different.

First, you need to pick a game genre. What type of game will you create? Will it be a puzzle game, a card game, a racing game, a shooting game, a strategy game, a role-playing game, or an adventure game? You can employ a whole host of game genres for your game. If you are developing a game for a customer, the game genre likely will already have been chosen. However, if you are writing a game for your own enjoyment or portfolio, it's best to choose a game genre that *you* personally like playing. If you enjoy playing puzzle games, you'll understand what makes a good puzzle game, and you'll be more motivated to make your game the best it can be.

Note: Coming up with an original game genre can be difficult (computer games have been around for more than 20 years), so don't panic if the genre has been used before. Do, however, try to add something new. After all, if you simply re-create an old game, how will you persuade people to play your version and not the original one?

So, rather than asking, "How do I make a game?" you should first ask yourself something like, "How do I make a driving game?" Now, the question is slightly more focused, but it's still difficult to answer. What type of driving game? Will the game use an in-car view, a behind-the-car view or, perhaps, an overhead view? Will you be racing against the clock, or against computer-controlled opponents? You need to get even more specific and decide on all the aspects of the game. This set of factors is called the *game strategy*.

Coming Up with a Game Design

When you've decided on your game genre, you need to start working on the game design principles, where your game really comes to life. When you develop these principles, you are defining exactly how the game works. For example:

- *Who are the player's opponents?* Will you have computer-controlled opponents, or will you implement a high-score table so players can compete with other players around the world?
- *What's the purpose of the game?* Is the game simply win or lose, such as Solitaire or FreeCell? Are players searching for something (buried treasure, a way out of a maze), or for a character (as in "Where in the World Is Carmen Sandiego?")? Or, is the game something at which players can improve over time, as in snowboarding games for Sony Playstation? Are players racing the clock, learning tricks to gain points, or doing both (racing the clock and trying to score extra points)?
- *Does the game have a time limit?* What happens when the limit is reached? Can players start again with no penalty and just keep trying until they win the game (FreeCell works like this)? Or will penalties accumulate for every retry?

- *Do players have "lives" or "continues" that will let them keep playing after they've run out of time, crashed, or died?*
- *How many levels of difficulty does the game have?* What sorts of obstacles and rewards are there?
- *Can the player customize any part of the game?* For example, at the beginning they could choose to play either a male or female character. Maybe the characters looks and clothing are selectable too.

The game design principles also involve creating the extra elements that make your game more interesting and therefore more appealing to game players. For example, consider adding a high-score table, which will keep track of the top scores achieved in the game. This addition will encourage people to replay the game and try to get to the top of the list. Consider adding a "Save Game" feature so that players can leave the game for a while and then later pick up where they left off. Consider how you can leave room for expanding the game later (with extra levels, new locations, and so on). Elements such as these can enhance almost any game.

Rushing the strategy part of game development is easy. But, ultimately, strategy is one of the most important parts of your game, so please take your time and think it through. Terrific graphics are fun to create and fun to look at, but graphics alone won't be enough to keep players interested for long.

Example: Compare Two Driving Games

Let's take a quick look at a game idea for which the strategy hasn't been developed properly, and compare that idea with a fully developed game. Here's the under-developed version: The Super Flash Driving Game. The Super Flash Driving Game is a racing game that uses an overhead view. You race against three computer-controlled opponents on five tracks. You steer the car by using the left and right arrow keys, and you accelerate by pressing and holding the spacebar. Each race consists of five laps, and at the end of the race, prize money is awarded to the first three drivers ($10,000 for first place, $5,000 for second place, and $2,000 for third place). After you complete a race, you move on to the next track and play again.

Here's the same game idea with a more developed strategy: The Super Flash Driving Game II. This game is like the first game in the following ways: It's a racing game that uses an overhead view. You race against three computer-controlled opponents on five tracks. You steer the car by using the left and right arrow keys, and you accelerate by pressing and holding the spacebar. Each race consists of five laps and, at the end of the race, prize money is awarded to the first three drivers ($10,000 for first place, $5,000 for second place, and $2,000 for third place).

Game II has some variations and improvements, however. In addition to steering and accelerating, you can also brake (by using the down arrow key). And, at the beginning of the game, only one track is available. The other tracks are "locked" until you win a race—when you win on Track 1, Track 2 becomes available; when you win on Track 2, Track 3 becomes available; and so on. When all five tracks have been "unlocked," you can enter the Super Grand Prix, which consists of a 10-lap race on each of the tracks. To be crowned the Super Grand Prix champion, you must get more points than the computer-controlled cars.

And there's more: After completing a race, you can enter the garage and use your prize money to buy upgrades for your car—upgrades include engine improvements, gearbox improvements, and chassis improvements. By improving your car, you'll be able to go faster and unlock the other tracks. You'll also be able to personalize your car by changing the look of various things like the car color, adding custom logos, changing the style of the wheels and so on. Every track will have a high-score table that shows the fastest lap and the fastest race (a total for five laps). Throughout the racing section of the game, bonus money will randomly appear on the track (values of $100, $200, and $500), and you can collect the money by driving over it. But you'll have to be quick—the bonus money stays on screen for only a few seconds. Hazards such as oil patches, stray animals, and potholes will also randomly appear on the track. You'll have to avoid these hazards; otherwise, your car will spin and crash, losing you valuable time.

Now let's analyze these two game ideas, so you can see how important properly developing your game strategy is before you start working in Flash. The first driving game would quickly become tiresome because you have no reason to keep playing the game—you've seen all the tracks, so there's nothing new to keep you interested. We prolong Game II, however, by giving you access to the tracks only after you've reached a certain level. By withholding tracks, we give the players a reason to come back and play again. Even when they've unlocked all the tracks, the Super Grand Prix gives players another reason to keep playing. The addition of an "upgradeable" car adds another element to the game, as do the hazards on the track. All of these little features add up to make the game more playable, and more fun.

When you create the strategy for your game, you'll want to develop your ideas as completely as possible and include as much detail as possible. At this stage, sharing the game strategy with other people is a good idea—to see whether they can suggest any changes or additional ideas.

Deciding What's Possible and What's Not

Before you start work on the Flash version of Quake or Formula 1 Grand Prix (or whatever your favorite game happens to be), you must decide what's possible and what's not possible. You need to consider two things when you're deciding this:

- What are you capable of?
- What is Flash capable of?

Let's address these questions.

What Are You Capable Of?

Before you jump into developing a game, assess your skills. For example, consider the following:

- Do you have enough artistic ability to create the graphics you have in mind?
- How much programming or scripting do you know, or need to learn?
- If your game will have music or sound effects, do you need music composition skills, or access to a royalty-free library of effects?
- Have you played many games, and do you have a sense of what's fun and interesting for you as a player?

Depending on your answers to these questions, you might decide to scale back on the game, to develop some of your skills, to recruit a co-developer whose skill set complements yours—or to go full-speed ahead with your game plan.

Keep in mind that large-scale, complex games are often built by teams of designers, not by one person. Quake and Formula 1 Grand Prix, for example, are high-budget games that cost great sums of money to produce, and a team of experienced artists, programmers, and musicians developed them over a long period of time. Figure 8.1 shows a scene from Quake 2, and you can see a great deal of complexity in it. The characters and scene are three-dimensional; you see the protagonist's hands and gun, the villains, a stage, crates, a staircase, curved walls of varying textures, a sky, mountains in the background, and a scoreboard in the corner. You can be sure that this is *not* the first game the designers produced.

As a game designer, you have to "learn to walk before you can run." You accomplish this goal by creating some simple games first. Creating games in Flash is an ongoing learning process; you need to start with something simple and build your way up to the larger, more complex games. In the next chapter, we look at how to design a quiz game—the ideal place to start if you're new to Flash game programming. After you've mastered the quiz game, try tackling some other simple games, such as a tic-tac-toe game; then, you might try a Ping Pong-style game, and then, perhaps, a simple shooting game. These games will teach you some important basic techniques such as how to use arrays, work with collision detection, add intelligence to games, and control movie-clips—and lots of other techniques, too. With every game you create, you'll learn something new. When you've completed these games, not only will you have more knowledge about game design, but you'll also have more confidence to attempt the larger, more complex games.

Figure 8.1
A scene from Quake 2 by ID Software. Notice the three-dimensional characters and environment.

What Is Flash Capable Of?

Okay, so now that you've created a few games and built up your knowledge and confidence, you can start working on that Flash version of Quake. Right? Well...probably not. At the moment, the Flash player is simply not powerful enough to display the 3D environment that makes up the Quake world. Quake is built around a highly sophisticated 3D engine that has been specifically designed for this type of game. In general, Flash is not suited to games that require fast moving graphics. However, don't let that limitation deter you. There's no reason your game *has* to use the kind of first-person perspective and three-dimensional view that many modern games use. If you want to develop a game like this, why not consider using an overhead view, or perhaps a two-dimensional, side view, or even an isometric 3D view? Using Flash, you should be able to produce almost any game you care to imagine. Of course, you will not be able to do some things (such as use a Quake-style 3D engine), but you can implement a clever strategy to work around this restraint and still create a game that is as entertaining and fun to play as any game currently available. If you are designing games for the Web, you also need to bear in mind the total file size of your game. The majority of people still access the Internet via a dial-up modem, so try and keep your file sizes as low as possible.

Keeping It Real

An important aspect of your game design is realism. On some occasions, a realistic game is important; but, at other times, breaking the rules and taking your game into a fantasy world is good. Let's look at a few examples where you should use realism.

First, let's consider the Super Flash racing game that we mentioned in the previous section. In a car, when you accelerate, the car gradually speeds up until it reaches a maximum speed; when you brake, the car gradually slows down until it stops. So, why not make the car in your games do exactly the same thing? We see many car games in which you press the acceleration key and the car instantly reaches the top speed; and then, as soon as you release the key, the car instantly stops. Adding small features that make the game more realistic will make the game more enjoyable too.

This book's companion CD-ROM contains a small demonstration of an accelerating and braking car (see Figure 8.2). All the values (braking, acceleration, and maximum speed) can be changed, so you can see how they affect the car.

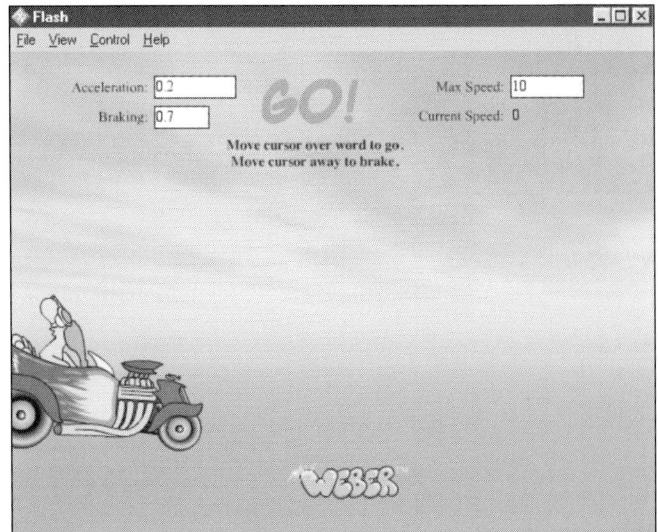

Figure 8.2
Accelerating and braking.

If you're re-creating a real-life situation in your game, bear in mind the laws of physics (more precisely, the laws of classical mechanics), including the rules concerning acceleration and gravity. This realism makes the game more enjoyable, and it also means you don't need to explain exactly how everything in the game works.

As an example of Newton's laws of motion, look at Figure 8.3, which shows a freeze-frame image. In this image, a bowling ball is hanging in the air above a seesaw; on the other side of the seesaw are a pair of scissors and a balloon on a string. What do you think will happen when we unfreeze time and allow the bowling ball to drop? Hopefully, you can work out the solution by just looking at the picture. But, if you can't, try the demonstration called "Gravity" on the CD-ROM.

All of the objects in the demonstration are familiar to you, and they follow simple physical rules, so you can work out exactly what will happen without being given any additional information. This built-in knowledge of how things

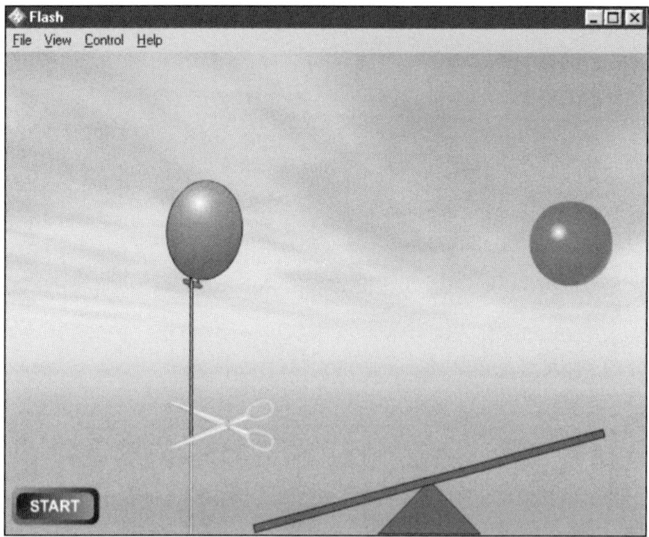

Figure 8.3
What happens next?

work is very important in a game because it allows people to instantly pick up your game and start playing without having to read pages and pages of instructions (nobody likes doing that). Game design uses this built-in knowledge extensively. For instance, if you play an adventure game and find a locked door, what do you do? You think to yourself, "Where's the key?" If you are playing a platform game, and you come across a small gap or a hole in the ground, what do you do? You try to jump over it.

Balancing Realism and Surprises

Having just discussed the importance of realism and the benefit of taking advantage of players' built-in knowledge, we're now going to go the other way for a minute: Don't let this built-in knowledge turn your game into a cliché. It's important to give players something new and unexpected, and a good way to do this is to exploit the players' built-in knowledge. For example, imagine that you're playing an adventure game set in a large mansion; you're faced with a locked door, and scattered around the mansion are 10 different keys. You can be fairly sure that most people will gather up all these keys and try to

Isaac Newton's Three Laws of Motion

Newton's first law—the law of inertia—states that, unless acted upon by an external force, an object at rest remains at rest, and an object in motion continues to move in a straight line with constant speed.

Newton's second law states that the net force on an object is equal to its acceleration (the rate of change of velocity), which is the product of a body's mass and its velocity. (You might have learned this formula in high school: $F=ma$, or Force equals Mass times Acceleration). Acceleration is directly proportional to the force F, and inversely proportional to the mass m of the body. So, the larger the force, the larger the acceleration; the larger the mass, the smaller the acceleration.

Newton's third law, that of action and reaction, states that the actions of two bodies upon each other are always equal and directly opposite—that is, reaction is always equal and opposite to action.

open the door with them. But this game is different; maybe you can make the door open another way. Perhaps you could force it open with a crowbar or a credit card. Or maybe the key is actually in the lock on the other side of the door, and you can retrieve it by sliding a piece of newspaper under the door and knocking the key out in a Rube Goldberg style situation. The key falls onto the paper, then rides on the paper as the player pulls it under the door back to his or her side, thus giving him or her access to the key needed to proceed. Use your imagination, and give the player something unexpected. Giving people something unexpected can increase their enjoyment of the game—and that leads us to the next section.

Keeping It Unreal

We've just looked at some examples where realism is important—other examples include sports games such as golf, track and field, and billiards. But remember that you are creating a game world here, so breaking the rules is perfectly acceptable. In fact, we strongly recommend that you do break them. Ultimately, games are about having fun, and you can make them more fun by breaking some of the realism rules.

Let's consider our Super Flash racing game again. The game involves racing your car around the track at high speeds, which, in reality, is very dangerous. What happens if you crash? If the game were totally realistic, the race would be stopped. The car would be damaged beyond repair, and the driver would be taken off to the hospital—or the morgue. It doesn't sound like much fun, does it? So, in the game, we simply make the car go into a spin and slow down—this action costs the player a bit of time, but no real harm's done. In a situation such as this, breaking the rules is common sense. But we can do better than that.

Rather than just breaking the rules, why not completely smash them apart? Many of the driving games available try to be accurate simulations, but why not make them more fun? Perhaps you can give special add-ons to the car, such as rocket boosters; bladed tires with which to attack your opponents; smoke canisters to confuse the people behind you; built-in machine guns so you can shoot your opponents; or even an anti-gravity device so your car can hover just above the ground and not be troubled by holes, oil slicks, or other nasty items. You can add a whole host of fun things.

Doing Research

The final part of designing your game is *research*. In other words, get out and play some games. If you're designing a driving game, play as many other driving games as possible to see how other people have done it. We're not suggesting that you copy any ideas you see; in fact, you should do just the opposite. Look at the games and see what features are missing, and which features could be improved. When you're playing games, stop to think, "Wouldn't it be good if I could just do...." As a game developer, you can add that new feature or idea that will make the game better. After you've done your research (and everything else mentioned in this chapter), you should be ready to start designing your own games.

PROJECT Let's Play

On the CD-ROM, we have included a number of games from some of the top Flash game designers around the world. For this chapter's project, we would like you to play these games and take some time to do the following:

- *Consider how the designers could have approached the design of their games*—Make a few notes on the features of each game that really add to the playability and enjoyment, and try to find some areas where the game could be improved. Maybe something doesn't work as you would like it to, or perhaps you'd like to see some additional features.
- *Take at look at the technical side of the games*—Have the designers left things out because they can't be done in Flash? Or maybe the designers *have* managed to do something you thought was impossible.
- *Look at the realism of each game*—Have the designers used concepts such as gravity or acceleration anywhere in the game? Or maybe the designers have broken the realism rules and added something that wouldn't be possible in a real-life situation. In Figure 8.4, you can see a scene from the Flash Golf game by Artifact Interactive. This game is a great example of how to use realism in your game, so take a look at some of the features the designers have included.

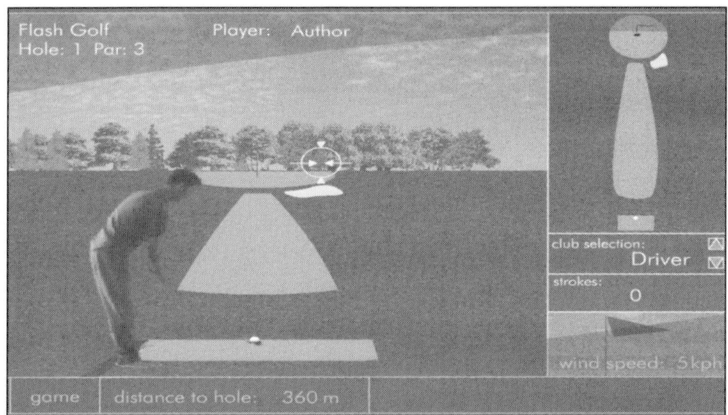

Figure 8.4
A scene from Flash Golf by Artifact Interactive.

Whatever you see or find, remember that these are successful games that have been sold to commercial sites around the world. Hopefully, you'll be able to identify why these games have been so successful—and, more importantly, you'll be ready to develop your own ideas into some great games.

Moving On

Next, we'll tackle an actual Flash trivia game with an intelligence twist. Chapter 9 will provide and explain the coding necessary for creating this trivia game.

Chapter 9

Designing Trivia Games

In this chapter, we're going to look at using Flash to create your own trivia game. In each section of this chapter, we'll concentrate on one particular element of the game. At the end of the chapter, we'll combine all the techniques to build the Weber trivia game.

By James Robertson
and Bill Turner

Overview of the Weber Trivia Game

Trivia games have been around probably as long as there's been knowledge to play with. The premise is simple: ask a question, then, give the correct answer, which is simple to understand, but difficult to beat. This makes a classic gaming environment. Everyone wants to be king of the knowledge hill.

With the Weber Trivia Game, we've added a fun twist to what could be just a boring screen of text questions. A screen of text only questions would work just fine as a trivia game, but then which one would you rather play, the graphically appealing game with a humorous twist, or the boring old plain text game? By giving the game a colorful atmosphere and fun characters it invites you to play.

The questions, however, can be as difficult, or easy, as you desire to make them. This is why we designed the game with three levels, stupid, smart, and genius. Hopefully, anyone could answer the stupid ones, but then answering the smart and genius levels gives you bragging rights, and a reason to play the game over and over.

Another twist in the game's design is the "Panel of Idiots". For this we've played no favorites, by using a cross section of cliché beach going characters (who are generally not known for being too bright) to get help from when stuck on a question. The reason we choose to call the panel "Idiots" is to make the player reluctant to ask for their advice. We really want the *player* to answer the questions. Even with this thought in the player's mind, "should I ask them, they're idiots, how should they know?" we give the player a chance when totally stumped. Human curiosity dictates that players will use the idiots. We do leave an "out" in the design when using the idiots. You can override an idiot's suggestion when you give your answer.

It may be a mixing of definitions, but the "Idiots" actually have a level of artificial intelligence. Some do better at getting the correct answer on certain subjects than the others. If you play using the idiot's advice long enough, a pattern will emerge. But then you will probably lose to those who really know the answers to the questions. This makes the "Panel of Idiots" a novel distinction to the Weber Trivia Game.

Re-Purposing Graphics

In the Weber trivia game, we'll be uncovering the engine that makes it all work—the brains, if you will. The eye candy is art that we are re-purposing from full-length animations, using techniques we discussed earlier in the book. The capability to take what was a linear animation and turn it into a highly interactive game is one of the real beauties of working in Flash—and it makes Flash a truly versatile environment for creating such games.

With a little tweaking, you can incorporate the symbols of animated loops you've used in other projects into your next game. In the case of the Weber trivia game, we've simply used various symbols (or animated loops) from earlier animations. As you can see in Figure 9.1, we've reused an animation loop of Weber the pelican sucking down fish as a prize for answering a question correctly during play.

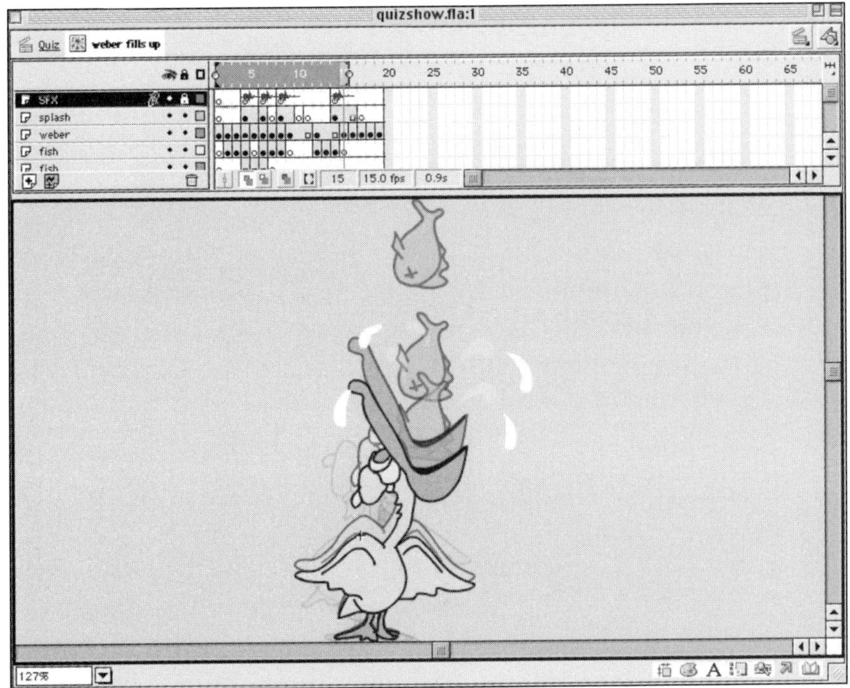

Figure 9.1
Weber is happy at the announcement of a correct answer.

By tweaking the symbol's size, rotation, and placement on the screen—that is, by not re-creating the entire sequence—we saved precious time. The sequence in Figures 9.2 and 9.3, in which Weber sits and becomes impatient waiting for the player's response, is a reuse of the symbol we used in the pre-loader, where Weber sighs and wonders what is taking so long. This symbol works well with the design of the game. As Weber becomes impatient, he looks to the buttons that say "Choose Level" (these buttons start the game) as a little hint to the player of what he or she needs to do next. Then, Weber proclaims in audible voice, "Gosh, it is *boring* being a pelican," to further solidify the hint that the player should choose a level and get started. Designing with reuse in mind is not cheating. In fact, creative reuse of elements is mandatory to create the smallest possible files and keep a graphically rich experience.

Not only the character animations, but also the backgrounds and props (such as the dock) are re-purposed from earlier shots in a linear animation. For the purpose of the game, we had to add the desk where the "Panel of Idiots" resides. The idiots themselves came from other animations; we adapted them to the situation via scaling, rotating, and eliminating extraneous parts. To save file size, we removed things such as the lower body half that'll never be seen.

Figure 9.2
Weber looks at the buttons as a subtle hint to get the game started.

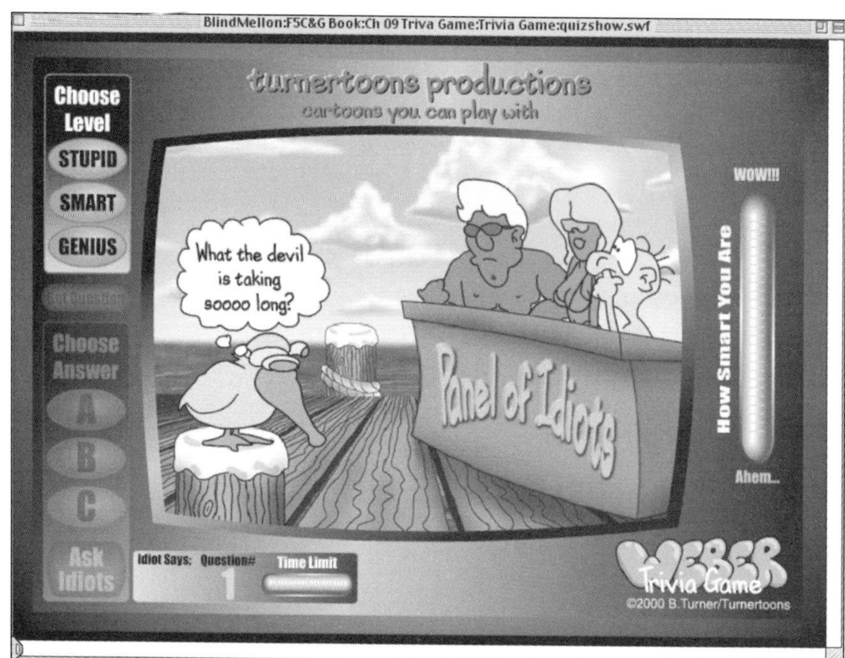

Figure 9.3
This loop makes it to the point where, after a few moments of no response from the players, Weber thinks, "What's taking so long?"

The scene in which the player asks the idiots for advice is the only place in the entire game where we made original animation specifically for this game. In this case we did not have suitable animations of character expressions already in hand. We created three special loops for the idiots to plead "Pick Me!" The loops include special stopping points at which they hold up the answer they've picked—A, B, or C—as you can see in Figure 9.4.

Figure 9.4
The symbol in which one of the idiots gives advice.

The key to successful re-purposing of graphics is making sure they fit with the needs of the game at hand. This fit can go a long way toward creating games with themes that interlock with cartoon shows you might be working with. Having playable games that relate to the story line of the cartoon can dramatically enhance the cartoon show itself. People generally stay much longer on—and will revisit more often—a Web site that has games than a site that contains only cartoon shows. They watch a cartoon show once, maybe twice. They might play a game indefinitely if it's entertaining. In some cases, a game can hold the player's attention for many hours, thus enhancing the cartoon show and the Web site itself.

Be aware that circumstances will arise that call for the creation of new graphics for the game only. You can usually accomplish this requirement easily by using the base art from other animations and customizing those animations to fit the game's needs. But don't hesitate to create new art. If you think you need new art for something, you probably do. The time you have saved in re-use elsewhere should give you plenty of time to create what you need.

Overview of Game Scripting Requirements

Before we dive into discussions of scripting, let's take a quick look at the steps you'll need to complete to develop a trivia game. You'll need to do the following:

1. Create the questions for the game. In addition to coming up with the content, you'll need to decide how you will store the questions and

answers. You'll also need to decide the format for your questions (such as multiple choice), how many possible answers each question will have, whether your questions will fall into different categories, and so on.

2. Load the questions and answers into the Flash movie, and display them on the screen.
3. Create scripts for determining whether players have answered questions correctly.
4. Create scripts for keeping score and for displaying the score on screen.
5. Create scripts for other aspects of the game, such as adding a collection of hints for players, or creating several levels of difficulty for the game.

Let's start now with creating scripts for questions and answers.

Creating Questions

When you're creating a trivia game, one of the first things you need to consider is the storage method for the trivia questions. You need to make sure that the game is easy to update with new questions, and that these questions are in a format that can work on different systems. You can store the questions for your game in one of three main ways:

- *Write the questions in ActionScript variables,* and store them as part of your movie.
- *Store the questions in external text files,* which you can load into your movie.
- *Store the questions in a database file,* which you can query and load into your movie.

Each of these methods has its good and bad points, and you will have to decide which approach is best for your particular project. We'll look briefly at each method, and then we'll choose a method for this chapter's project game.

Storing Questions in Variables in the Movie

If you store your questions in ActionScript variables within the Flash movie, the questions will be harder to update; to do so, you'll need to refer to the source code, enter some new questions, and republish the movie. However, if you want to distribute the game as a single file, and it's a one-off game that you won't update—perhaps as a demonstration version to be used on a CD-ROM—storing the questions as variables might be good.

For each trivia question, you will need several variables to store the information. Our chapter project game uses multiple-choice questions, so we need one variable for the question and another variable for each possible answer. If you do the same for your project, you must repeat these variables for every trivia question you want to include in your game. Storing the question data as variables in your movie would look something like this:

```
question1 = "Who was the first man on the moon?";
a1="Buzz Aldrin";
a2="Neil Armstrong";
a3="Buzz Armstrong";
```

Flash 5 Arrays

One of Flash 5's new features is support for arrays. An *array* is simply a list of items stored under a single variable name. For example, you could store a quiz question and three possible answers using the following array statement:

quiz = new Array("Who was the first man on the moon?", "Buzz Aldrin", "Neil Armstrong", "Buzz Armstrong");

The quiz question is stored in variable quiz [0], answer 1 is stored in variable quiz [1], answer 2 is stored in variable quiz [2], and so on. We'll cover arrays more fully in Chapter 10.

Storing Questions in External Text Files

If you store the questions in external text files, updating the questions will be much easier than if you store them as variables—you can update questions stored in external text files without modifying the original source code, but you should also bear in mind that somebody else could also easily update the questions. You wouldn't want a game to be open to theft by others. You also need to remember that with the questions in this format, somebody could easily look at the text files and determine the correct answer for each question. That's not a problem if your game is just a fun addition to your Web site. But, obviously, it would be a problem if you were offering a prize to the first person to answer all the questions correctly.

When you store questions in external text files, you still store your questions and answers in variables, but you store those *variables* in text files. You can load the text files into Flash by using the **loadVariablesNum** command, specifying the name of the text file that contains the variables, and specifying the movie level the variables should be loaded into. The code for this action looks like the following sample (the file name in this example is **q1.txt**, and the level is zero):

```
loadVariablesNum ("q1.txt", 0);
```

Note: In this example (and all the others mentioned in the book) we are loading the variables into level 0 and this requires the **loadvariablesNum** command. The **loadvariables** command is used when loading variables to a target rather than a level number.

You can store all the quiz questions in a single file and load that file into the game. But if you are creating a large trivia game with, say, 100 questions, or maybe even 200 questions, this single file would be quite large. If the game will be used offline, the file size is not a problem; but if you want to have the game on your Web site, remember that many visitors will be accessing your site with relatively slow modems. Therefore, to reduce load times, storing each question (with its answers) in a separate text file is better than using one large file.

You must create the text files in a format that Flash can understand. The text must be in the standard MIME format, **application/x-www-urlformencoded** (this is the standard format CGI scripts use). You can load multiple variables into Flash; each new variable must be preceded by the ampersand character (&). Here's an example:

Variable1=testing&Variable2=testnumber2&Variable3=Finalvariable

We'll discuss formatting requirements in more detail later in the chapter (see "Choosing Question Types for the Project Game").

Storing Questions in an External Database

If you store the questions in a database file, you will also need knowledge of an additional, server-based, scripting language, such as Microsoft's Active Server Pages (ASP) or Personal Home Page (PHP). As the name suggests, server-based scripting languages can be run only from a Web server, and will therefore not be suitable if your game needs to run in an offline format (such as on a CD-ROM). These additional scripts are required because Flash cannot read information directly from a database file. You have to use another scripting language to read questions from the database and then feed that information to your Flash movie. The server-based scripting language and database format you use will vary greatly depending upon which Web server you have. Which language/database you use is unlimited, as long as it can return text variables in a suitable format. The most popular choice is Microsoft's Active Server Pages/Microsoft Access. Using an ASP script, reading information from a database and returning the information to Flash via the **loadVariablesNum** command is relatively easy. See Chapter 10 for more details about this.

Loading External Variables into Flash

For security reasons, you can load variables only from the same sub-domain as your Flash movie. So, if your Flash movie is stored on **mydomain.com**, the variable file that you are loading into Flash must also be on **mydomain.com**.

The database option offers more security than the previous methods do because, when you store questions in a database, other people cannot change the questions or intercept them to find the correct answers. However, this method works only from a Web server; you cannot use the game on a standard desktop computer or run it from a CD-ROM as a standalone game.

Choosing a Storage Method for the Project Game

For the Weber trivia game that we're building in this chapter, we have two main aims:

- *We want to be able to update the questions without having to modify the movie's source code.* That requirement rules out storing questions in variables within the Flash movie.
- *We want the game to work in an offline format, from CD-ROM.* That requirement rules out storing questions in an external database.

So, for our end-of-chapter project, we will use the second method and load our questions from external text files. We'll use one text file for each question and its answers.

Choosing Question Types for the Project Game

Now that we've decided on the best format for the questions, we have to decide what kind of information we need to store in these text files. Trivia games come in all shapes and sizes, so the information will vary from game to game. In the Weber trivia game, we will have a series of multiple-choice questions; we've decided to have three choices for each question, plus a category for each question (we'll explain why later). So, for each question, we need to know six pieces of information (the question, the three possible answers, the correct answer, and the category), and we'll store each piece of information in a variable. We'll have a **question** variable, three possible-answer variables (**a1**, **a2**, and **a3**), a correct-answer variable (**ca**), and a **category** variable. The variables look like this:

```
question=Who was the first man on the moon?
a1=Buzz Aldrin
a2=Neil Armstrong
a3=Buzz Armstrong
ca=2
category=science
```

To store these variables in a text file that can be loaded into Flash, we need to store all the variables on a single line and use the ampersand character (&) *between* the variables.

Note: You cannot insert any spaces or line breaks between the variables; otherwise, Flash will misinterpret the information. The final text file will look like this (except that the code will be all one line).

```
question=Who was the
first man on the
moon?&a1=Buzz
Aldrin&a2=Neil
Armstrong&a3=Buzz
Armstrong&ca=2&category
=science
```

You can save this file as **q1.txt**—remember to save the file in text-only format; otherwise, you won't be able to load the file back into Flash. You can save new questions as **q2.txt**, **q3.txt**, **q4.txt**, and so on.

Loading and Displaying the Questions and Answers

Now that you've created your first quiz question, how can you use it in your quiz game? Well, the answer is remarkably easy. First, you load the variables from the text file into the movie. Then, you display the questions and answers on the screen.

To load the variables, use the following code:

```
filename="q1.txt"
loadVariablesNum (filename, 0);
```

This command loads variables from the file called **q1.txt** into Level 0 of your movie. If you were using a language such as ASP or PHP to query a database, you would use the same command but simply change the file name to the name of your script file. For example, if your script file was called **getquestion.asp**, you would use the following code:

```
filename="getquestion.asp"
loadVariablesNum (filename, 0);
```

After you have loaded the question data into Flash, you then want to display the questions and answers on the screen. To do this, you just need to set up some dynamic text fields with names that match the variable names you've used in your text file. A *dynamic text field* is a text box that can be updated using ActionScript. You must give the dynamic text field a variable name, and then you can change the contents of the text field by changing that variable name in your ActionScript. Using the example **q1.txt** file we showed previously, you need text fields called **question**, **a1**, **a2**, and **a3**. You can see the dynamic text boxes in Figure 9.5, or you can access the source file on the CD-ROM in the file named *demo1*.

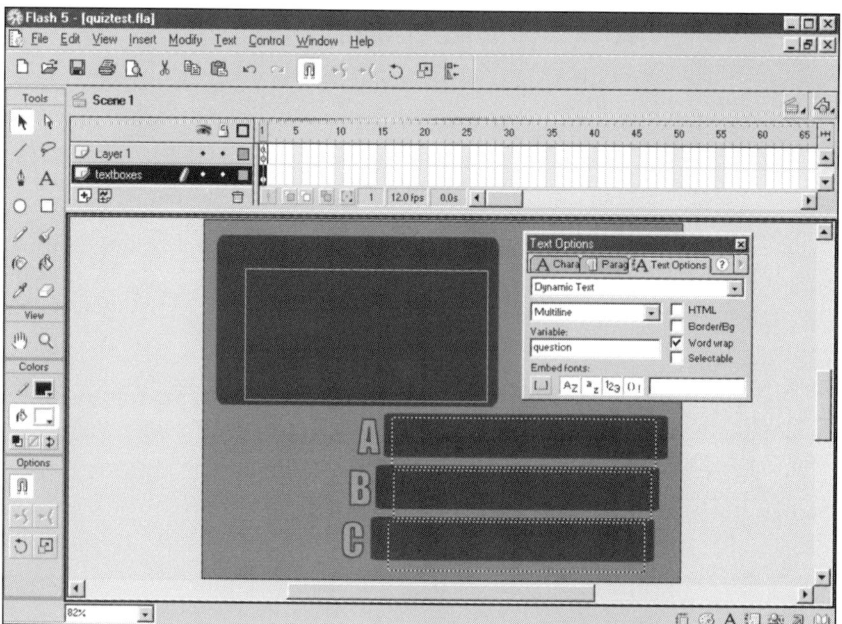

Figure 9.5
Setting up the dynamic text fields.

One thing you must remember is that when you're testing this game offline, the **loadVariablesNum** command can load the data instantly into your movie. However, if you store the movie online, a loading delay of a few seconds (depending upon the reliability and speed of your Internet connection) will occur. If the data hasn't fully loaded, your game will not function correctly, so you need to make the game pause until you are sure the question file has finished loading. You create this pause via the following program loop on the next page, which checks to see whether the data has been loaded.

```
Frame 1:
question = "Loading...";
loadVariablesNum ("q1.txt", 0);

Frame 2:
(leave this frame empty)

Frame 3:
if (question eq "Loading...") {
    gotoAndPlay (2);
}
```

We set the **question** variable equal to "**Loading...**", and then this small loop simply keeps rechecking the value of this variable. If **question** equals "**Loading...**", the question file has not been loaded yet, so we simply repeat the loop. As soon as the question file has been loaded, the variable **question** will contain the next quiz question, and the game can continue.

Note: There are a couple of reasons for the use of **eq** rather than **==** in the code used throughout here. Even though Flash 5 recommends the use of **==**, if you use Flash 5 to convert a Flash 4 movie it will use **eq**. Also, when comparing strings, some people have reported that **==** doesn't always work (that is, it's a bit buggy).

Determining the Correct Answer

We've managed to load the question into our quiz game; now, we need to give the player an option to choose the correct answer. To do this, we need to create three buttons labeled A, B, and C, and then the player can click on them to choose an answer. One variable we set in our question file was the correct-answer (**ca**) variable. We can now use this variable to determine whether the player has chosen the correct answer. The variable **ca** has a value of 1, 2, or 3, corresponding to answers A, B, or C. Determining whether a player has chosen the correct answer requires just a simple check—if the player chooses answer A, and variable **ca** equals 1, the answer is right; otherwise, the chosen answer is wrong.

Here's the code for the first button (answer A):

```
Button "A"

on (release) {
    if (ca == 1) {
        gotoAndPlay ("right");
    } else {
        gotoAndPlay ("wrong");
    }
}
```

For the other buttons, we compare the variable **ca** with a different number. Here's the code for buttons B and C:

```
Button "B"
```

```
on (release) {
    if (ca == 2) {
        gotoAndPlay ("right");
    } else {
        gotoAndPlay ("wrong");
    }
}

Button "C"

on (release) {
    if (ca == 3) {
        gotoAndPlay ("right");
    } else {
        gotoAndPlay ("wrong");
    }
}
```

For each button, we've used the **gotoAndPlay** command twice:

```
gotoAndPlay ("right");
gotoAndPlay ("wrong");
```

To make this code work in your quiz game, you will need to create a frame labeled **right** and a frame labeled **wrong**. Each frame can display either a simple graphic or a text message to tell the player whether he or she chose the right or wrong answer. In Figure 9.6, you can see how we've attached the ActionScript to the answer button, or you can access the source file on the CD-ROM in the *demo2* file.

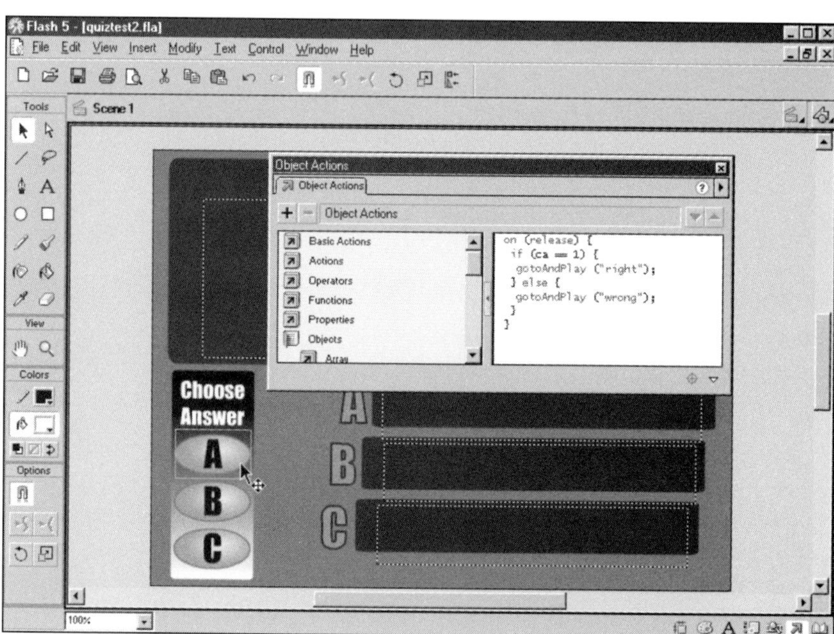

Figure 9.6
Here, we see the scripting needed to determine whether the selected answer is right or wrong.

Keeping Score

Two elements are necessary for keeping score:

- Keeping track of the current score
- Displaying the current score on screen

In our Weber quiz game, we want to give two points for every correct answer, and subtract one point for every wrong answer. We are also going to give each player three lives in the game and, every time a player chooses the wrong answer, he or she will lose a life. When a player loses all three lives, the game is over. Obviously, you can vary this point scheme, depending upon how you want your own game to work. To implement this point scheme in your game, all you need to do is add the following code for when the player chooses the correct answer:

```
score = score+2;
```

Easy, isn't it? And, if the player chooses the wrong answer, the code is this:

```
score = score-1;
lives = lives-1;
```

Compound Operators

Flash 5 supports compound assignment operators to combine operations. For example, the following two statements give the same result.

```
score += 2;
score = score + 2;
```

Displaying the score on screen is slightly more difficult, but only slightly. Decide what the maximum score for your game will be, and then create a movie clip that displays a score value from 0 to your maximum score. Give the movie clip an instance name. Add a **Stop** action in the first frame (to keep the entire clip from playing at once). And then (as we did in our game), use the **gotoAndStop** command to display the player's current score.

Let's look at our example again. For the project game, we've created a movie clip with the instance name **gmeter**. This movie clip consists of a 25-frame animation that shows the score rising from value 1 to value 25. To ensure that this movie clip doesn't automatically play and keep rising, we need to add a **Stop** action in the first frame. To use this movie clip to display the player's score, we just need to show the relevant frame number. Remember, our scoreboard movie clip starts at Frame 1, and this frame represents a score of 0; so, to represent any score, we display the frame number that equals the score+1. For example, to indicate a score of 15, we show Frame 16 (the value of score+1) in the **gmeter** instance.

In the previous version of Flash (Version 4), we would do this using a **tellTarget** command, which would look something like this:

```
tellTarget ("/gmeter") {
    gotoAndStop (score+1);
}
```

The **tellTarget** command is still available in Flash 5, but it is included only to ensure compatibility with older Flash movies. Flash 5 uses a new dot syntax, in which the code looks like this:

```
gmeter.gotoAndStop( score+1 );
```

To use the dot syntax method, we simply precede the **gotoAndStop** command with the instance name of our movie clip, remembering to separate the two commands with a dot (or period). This new method is much simpler and certainly easier to understand. If our movie clip was called **weber**, and we wanted to make it **goto** Frame 15 and stop, the code would look like this:

```
weber.gotoAndStop( 15 );
```

The new syntax used in Flash 5 ActionScript is very similar to the core JavaScript programming language and in fact, ActionScript is based on the ECMA-262 specification. This specification was derived from JavaScript to serve as the international standard for the JavaScript language. You don't need to know JavaScript to use and learn ActionScript, but if you are already familiar with JavaScript then ActionScript will appear very familiar to you.

Naming Your Movie-Clip Instances

Before we move on, we need to make one important note about naming your movie clips. You must avoid using spaces in the instance name. The dot syntax shown above will *not* work if your movie-clip instance name includes a space. If you are converting an older Flash 4 movie to Version 5, and some of the movie clips already have spaces in the instance names, you can access the clips using the following (slightly more complex) command:

```
_root["old name"]".gotoAndStop( 15 );
```

This code's not as nice as the previous example, is it? So, to make the programming much easier, remember to avoid using spaces in your instance names.

Setting the Range of Scores

In our project game, the scoreboard movie clip shows scores from 0 to 24 (because the clip has 25 frames). So, before we show the score, we need to check that the current score is not more than 24—otherwise, we'll be trying to display a frame that doesn't exist. We also need to make sure that the score has not dropped below 0 because, if it does, we'll have the same problem. So, using our **gmeter** instance, the entire code for checking the score and displaying it on screen will look like this:

```
if (score > 24) {
    score = 24;
}
```

```
if (score < 0) {
    score = 0;
}
gmeter.gotoAndStop( score+1 );
```

You can see a demonstration of this code on the CD-ROM in the demo3 file.

Adding Intelligence

Many quiz games are available on the Internet, so to make your quiz game stand out in the crowd, you need to add some kind of interesting or original feature. In the Weber quiz game as I have mentioned earlier, we've decided to add a feature called "Panel of Idiots": If players get stuck on any question, they can ask the panel of idiots for advice (see Figure 9.7).

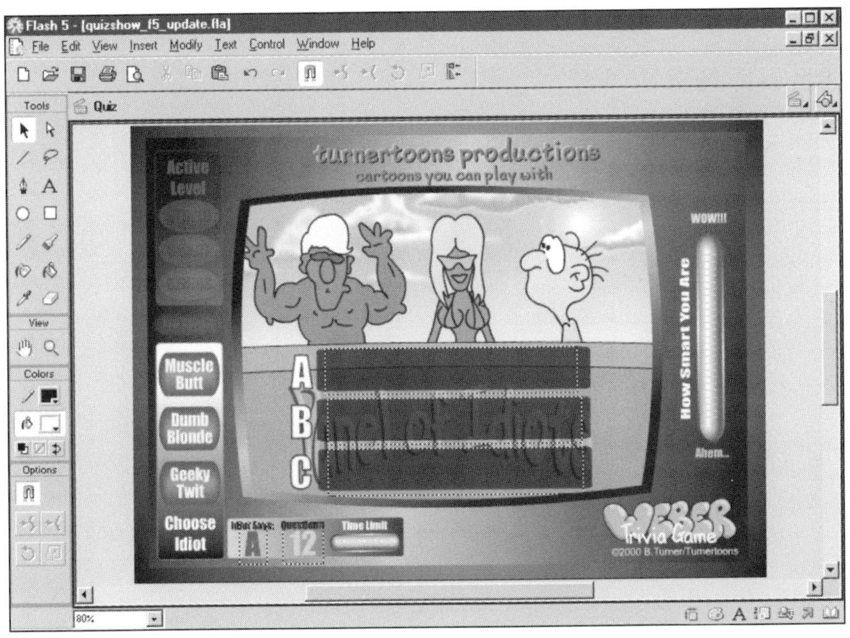

Figure 9.7
We'll be adding intelligence to the project game via a mechanism to ask the "Panel of Idiots."

The idea is that the idiots will recommend an answer (either A, B, or C), and then the player can choose whether to follow their advice. We *could* have just programmed our idiots to choose an answer randomly, but we thought it would be more fun if our "idiots" were given some intelligence. Next, we'll explain how you can do this.

Using the random Command with the limit Variable

To give the impression of some kind of intelligence, you will use the **random** command to generate a random number and, if this random number is above a set limit, the idiot will recommend the correct answer. The code will look like the example on the next page:

```
limit=50;
test = random(100);
if (test > limit) {
    guess = ca;
} else {
    guess = random(3)+1;
    }
}
```

This code chooses a random number from 0 to 99 and stores it in the variable **test**. If the value of **test** is *more* than your limit (which we have set to 50), the idiot will recommend the correct answer. Otherwise, the idiot just chooses a random answer (which *might* be correct).

You can modify this code slightly to ensure that, when the idiot chooses a random answer, he or she can choose anything *except* the correct answer. You simply add a loop that will keep choosing a random answer if the current guess is equal to the correct answer. The new code looks like this:

```
limit=50;
test = random(100);
if (test > limit) {
    guess = ca;
} else {
    guess = ca;
    while (guess == ca) {
        guess = random(3)+1;
}
```

When you use this code, if the random number (from 0 to 99) is more than 50, the idiot will get the correct answer. There are 49 numbers above 50, so the idiot has a 49 percent chance of getting the right answer.

Setting Up Three Levels of Difficulty

Our Weber quiz game will have three difficulty levels—Stupid, Smart, and Genius. We want to make sure that, on the harder levels, the idiots are *less* likely to give you the correct answer. After all, they are idiots. To do this, we need to make the **limit** variable higher for the harder levels. If we increase the **limit** to 70, the idiot has a 29 percent chance of getting the right answer and, if we increase the **limit** to 90, the idiot has only a 9 percent chance of getting the right answer. So, the higher this variable, the less likely it is that the idiot will provide the correct answer. The code for these levels of difficulty is shown below:

```
if (gamelevel eq "stupid") {
    limit = 50;
}
if (gamelevel eq "smart") {
    limit = 70;
```

```
}
if (gamelevel eq "genius") {
    limit = 90;
}
```

Setting Up Question Categories

In the first section of this chapter, we looked at the variables in the text question files, which we load into our quiz game, and we mentioned that we'd include a variable called **category** that would be explained later. Well, now you'll find out why we've included that **category** variable. We have assigned the questions to one of six categories (Children's, Games, Miscellaneous, People, Science, and Natural History), and we're going to make each idiot a specialist in two of these subjects. When players ask an idiot a question from his or her specialist category, we want to increase the likelihood that the idiot will give players the correct answer.

To do this, the code must do the opposite of the code we showed previously—it must decrease the **limit** variable. We can do this very simply with the following code:

```
if (category eq "childrens" or category eq "games") {
    limit = limit-20;
}
```

For each idiot, we specify different categories, so that each one specializes in different quiz subjects. Reducing the **limit** variable by 20 makes it 20 percent more likely that the idiot will give the correct answer. See Figure 9.8 for a look at the main screen of the Weber trivia game.

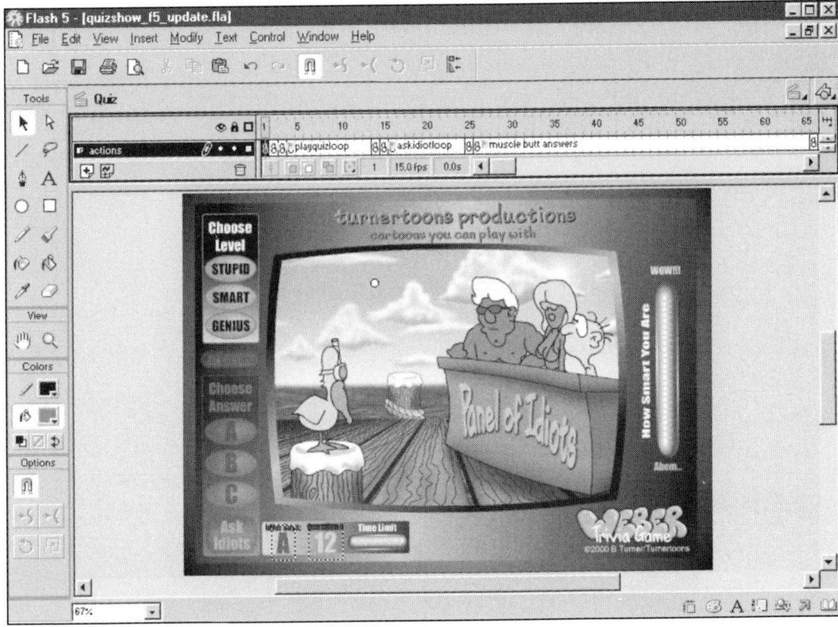

Figure 9.8
The main screen of the Weber trivia game featuring the "Panel of Idiots."

PROJECT Putting It All Together and Publishing Your Game

We've now looked at all the aspects of scripting a quiz game. The final thing you will need to do is publish your Flash movie in a format that other people can view. To do this, go to the File menu in Flash, and select Publish Settings. In the Publish Settings section, you'll see three tabs labeled Formats, Flash, and HTML. In the Formats section, you can choose the file type of your published movie. If you are publishing the movie for the Web, you need to choose HTML and SWF formats. Flash will automatically create the necessary HTML file to display your movie on your Web site. You can edit the HTML file in your favorite HTML editor, but we recommend that you use Macromedia's DreamWeaver because it has direct support for Flash movies. And with the use of Macromedia's latest JavaScript Integration kit, you can control the movie using JavaScript programming. When you've finished editing the file, you simply upload the HTML and SWF files to your Web server.

If you want to send the movie to somebody who doesn't have the Macromedia Flash plug-in, you should choose the projector format. The projector format is an executable file format that is ideal for distribution on CD-ROM. Flash gives you the choice of creating either a PC- or Macintosh-format projector.

Using Flash 5 Panels

When you're working in Flash 5, you'll be using the Actions panel frequently. Rather than closing or moving the panel when it's not in use, you can simply double-click the title bar to collapse the panel and create more on-screen space. This option works with all the Flash panels. To reactivate the panels, simply double-click the title bar again.

Weber Quiz Game

On the CD-ROM, we've provided the full Weber quiz game, which uses all the methods we've mentioned in the previous sections. The entire code is shown below, with additional comments to explain what's going on.

First, we have split the game into two scenes called **loader** and **quiz**. The **loader** scene loads the rest of the game and lets you play the quiz only after the whole file has been downloaded. The code is very simple. In Frame 1, we check to see whether Frame 230 from the scene **quiz** has been loaded (Frame 230 is the last frame of the movie). If the last frame has been loaded, we start the quiz; if it has not, we simply go back to Frame 1 and recheck to see whether it has been loaded.

```
Scene loader
   actions for frame 1
      ifFrameLoaded ("Quiz", 230) {
         gotoAndStop ("Quiz", "Start Quiz");
      }

   actions for frame 2
      gotoAndPlay (1);
```

Here's the **quiz** scene. In the first frame, we set up an array called **qarray**, which we will use to create a list of random, nonrepeating questions. To do this, we have added a loop, which increments the variable **count** from 1 to 15. In each loop, we choose a random array element (from 1 to 15) and check the value of this element—if the element value equals 0, we put the variable **count** into the array. If the value is not 0, the array element has already been used, so we go back and choose another, random array element until we find an unused one. The process sounds a bit complicated, but if you follow it through, step-by-step, it will soon become clear—honest. In this first frame, we also set various game variables such as the score (questions answered correctly), number of lives (or the number of times the player may choose a wrong answer), and so on. In this section of code, we are also loading a file called "**webertho.txt**", which is a text file containing comments/phrases that Weber will say during the game. You'll see this speech when you choose the correct answer to any of the quiz questions.

```
Scene Quiz
   actions for frame 1
      loadVariablesNum ("webertho.txt", 0);
      qarray = new Array();
      total_questions = 15;
      array_length = total_questions;
      count = 1;
      while (count <= array_length) {
         qarray[count] = 0;
         count = count+1;
      }
      // Create an array of non-repeating random numbers
      count = 1;
      while (count <= array_length) {
         item = (random(Number(total_questions)))+1;
         while (qarray[item] > 0) {
            item = (random(array_length))+1;
         }
         qarray[item] = count;
         count = count+1;
      }
      // Set game variables
      getquestion = false;
      total_questions = 15;
      lives = 3;
      score = 0;
      currentq = 1;
      idiotsays = "";
      askidiot = false;
      num_questions = 10;
      level1_limit = 50;
      level2_limit = 70;
      level3_limit = 90;
      knowledge_factor = 20;
      stop ();
```

```
actions for frame 2
   // In this section we change the level selector
   // to display the current game level
   if (gamelevel eq "smart") {
      levelselector.gotoAndStop(2);
   }
   if (gamelevel eq "genius") {
      levelselector.gotoAndStop(3);
   }
   stop ();
```

The following section of code does two things. First of all, it resets the Weber animation to Frame 1. Then, it checks to see if **askidiot** equals true—if it does, then the player has just been to the "Ask the Idiot" section of the game so we need to re-display the question slate and continue the game (the game timer is not altered, otherwise the "Ask the Idiot" feature could be used to gain more time to answer the question). If **askidiot** is not true, then this is the first time that the player has seen the current question, and we need to reset the timer feature to 0 before we continue.

```
actions for frame 3
   Weber_waiting.gotoAndStop(1);
   if (askidiot == true) {
      questionslate.play();
   } else {
      timelimit = 0;
      time_meter.gotoAndStop(1);
   }
```

The following section of code is a loop that keeps track of how long a player takes to answer a question. If the time limit is more than 25, the player runs out of time.

```
actions for frame 14
      // This section increases the timer…
      if (getquestion == true) {
         timelimit = timelimit+1;
         time_meter.nextFrame();
      }
      // If timelimit > 25 then we're out of time!
      if (timelimit >= 25) {
         gotoAndPlay ("wrong");
      } else {
         gotoAndPlay ("playquizloop");
      }
```

The next section sets up the **limit** variable, which is used to add intelligence to the "Panel of Idiots" part of the game. You'll see that the limit varies depending upon which game level we are playing (Stupid, Smart, or Genius level):

```
actions for frame 15
      answera = a1;
      answerb = a2;
      answerc = a3;
      test = random(100);
      // This sets the knowledge limits. If we are playing
      // a harder game level then it's LESS likely that the
      // idiots will recommend the correct answer.
      if (gamelevel eq "stupid")
         limit = level1_limit;
      }
      if (gamelevel eq "smart") {
         limit = level2_limit;
      }
      if (gamelevel eq "genius") {
         limit = level3_limit;
      }

actions for frame 25
      // This section is where we update the timer when
      // we are in the "ask the idiot" section of the
      // game.
      timelimit = timelimit+1;
      time_meter.nextFrame();
      // If time>25 then time is up!
      if (timelimit >= 25) {
         gotoAndPlay ("wrong");
      } else {
         gotoAndPlay ("askidiotloop");
      }
```

The next section of code is the part of the "Panel of Idiots" section used when the player asks the "muscle butt" character. This section is where we've added the "intelligence" factor, which we discussed earlier in the chapter. You'll see that if the question category equals **childrens** or **games**, the **limit** variable is reduced by 20 (the value of **knowledge_factor**). These two categories are the specialist categories for this particular "idiot." The **knowledge_factor** variable determines how "intelligent" the game character is—a higher value means the character will be *more* likely to give you the correct answer.

```
actions for frame 26
// This section is where Muscle Butt answers
// First of all we stop the animations of the other characters
      _root ["dumb blonde answers"].gotoAndStop(1);
      _root["geeky twit answers"].gotoAndStop(1);
// Then we check to see if the current question is on one
// specialist categories. If it is then we reduce the limit
// variable, which means he is MORE likely to recommend the
// correct answer.
      if (category eq "childrens" or category eq "games") {
         limit = limit- knowledge_factor;
```

```
        }
        if (test > limit) {
// The idiot has guessed the correct answer
            guess = ca;
        } else {
// The idiot will guess the wrong answer. We choose
// a random answer and if the guess is EQUAL to the
// correct answer and we choose another answer. This
// ensures that they don't have a lucky guess and
// recommend the correct answer.
            guess = ca;
            while (guess == ca) {
                guess = random(3)+1;
            }
        }
// This following section displays the correct
// animation depending upon which answer he
// recommends.
        if (guess == 1) {
            idiotsays = "A";
            _root["muscle butt answers"]
             .gotoAndStop("muscle answers a");
        }
        if (guess == 2) {
            idiotsays = "B";
            _root["muscle butt answers"]
             .gotoAndStop("muscle answers b");
        }
        if (guess == 3) {
            idiotsays = "C";
            _root["muscle butt answers"]
             .gotoAndStop("muscle answers c");
        }

actions for frame 66
        gotoAndPlay ("playquiz");

actions for frame 67
// This section is where Dumb Blonde answers
        _root["muscle butt answers"].gotoAndStop(1);
        _root["geeky twit answers"].gotoAndStop(1);
        play ();
        if (category eq "misc" or category eq "people") {
            limit = limit- knowledge_factor;
        }
        if (test > limit) {
            guess = ca;
        } else {
            guess = ca;
            while (guess == ca) {
                guess = random(3)+1;
            }
        }
```

```
      if (guess == 1) {
         idiotsays = "A";
         _root["dumb blonde answers"]
          .gotoAndStop("blonde answers a");
      }
      if (guess == 2) {
         idiotsays = "B";
         _root["dumb blonde answers"]
          .gotoAndStop("blonde answers b");
      }
      if (guess == 3) {
         idiotsays = "C";
         _root["dumb blonde answers"]
          .gotoAndStop("blonde answers c");
      }

   actions for frame 105
      gotoAndPlay ("playquiz");

   actions for frame 106
// This section is where Geeky Twit answers
      _root["dumb blonde answers"].gotoAndStop(1);
      _root["muscle butt answers"].gotoAndStop(1);
      play ();
      if (category eq "science" or category eq "nat hist") {
         limit = limit- knowledge_factor;
      }
      if (test > limit) {
         guess = ca;
      } else {
         guess = ca;
         while (guess == ca) {
            guess = random(3)+1;
         }
      }
      if (guess == 1) {
         idiotsays = "A";
         _root["geeky twit answers"]
          .gotoAndStop("geek answers a");
      }
      if (guess == 2) {
         idiotsays = "B";
         _root["geeky twit answers"]
          .gotoAndStop("geek answers b");
      }
      if (guess == 3) {
         idiotsays = "C";
         _root["geeky twit answers"]
          .gotoAndStop("geek answers c");
      }

   actions for frame 146
      gotoAndPlay ("playquiz");
```

The next section of code is the "right answer" part of the game. In Frame 155, we choose a random thought for Weber, which was loaded from a text file at the beginning of the quiz game. This thought will be displayed after the "right answer" animation. The Weber thoughts are stored in a series of variables from **mthought1**, **mthought2**, through to **mthought21**. We are using the command **eval("mthought" add x)** to access these variables, which simply adds the value of **x** to "**mthought**"—if **x** equals 12 then we are looking at variable "**mthought12**". In Frame 198, we reset some of the game variables, increase the **currentq** (current question) variable, and add two to the player score.

```
actions for frame 155
      x = random(21);
      mthought = eval("mthought" add x);

   actions for frame 198
// Reset some of the game variables
      askidiot = false;
      getquestion = false;
      idiotsays = "";
// Increase the current question variable
      currentq = currentq+1;
// Increase the score
      score = score+2;
// Have we got the maximum score?
      if (score > 24) {
         score = 24;
      }
      gmeter.gotoAndStop(_root.score+1);
// Check to see if the quiz has finished
      if (currentq > num_questions) {
         gotoAndStop ("Quiz", "Start Quiz");
      } else {
         gotoAndPlay ("Get question");
      }
```

The next section of code is the "wrong answer" part of the game. We reset some of the game variables, increase the **currentq** (or current question) variable, subtract one from the player score, and subtract a life.

```
   actions for frame 230
// Reset some variables
      askidiot = false;
      getquestion = false;
      idiotsays = "";
// Lose a life and reduce the score
      lives = lives-1;
      score = score-1;
      if (score < 0) {
         score = 0;
```

```
      }
      gmeter.gotoAndStop(_root.score+1);
      currentq = currentq+1;
// Check to see if the quiz has finished (we've had
// all the questions or we've run out of lives)
      if (currentq > num_questions or lives <= 0) {
         gotoAndStop ("Quiz", "Start Quiz");
      } else {
         gotoAndPlay ("Get question");
      }
```

The answer buttons (A, B, and C) use the following code. This is where we check whether the player selects the right or wrong answer.

```
 actions for Answer A
      on (release) {
         if (getquestion == true) {
            if (ca == 1) {
               gotoAndPlay ("right");
            } else {
               gotoAndPlay ("wrong");
            }
         }
      }

   actions for Answer B
      on (release) {
         if (getquestion == true) {
            if (ca == 2) {
               gotoAndPlay ("right");
            } else {
               gotoAndPlay ("wrong");
            }
         }
      }

   actions for Answer C
      on (release) {
         if (getquestion == true) {
            if (ca == 3) {
               gotoAndPlay ("right");
            } else {
               gotoAndPlay ("wrong");
            }
         }
      }
```

In this next code segment, the “question clip” is the movie clip, which loads and displays the quiz questions. In Frame 2, we get the next question from the array called **qarray**, and then we use the **loadVariablesNum** command to load the question file into our game.

```
   Question clip
      actions for frame 1
         stop ();

      actions for frame 2
// Get the current question number
         question_num = _root.qarray[_root.currentq];
// Calculate the filename for the current questions
         filename = _root.gamelevel add "/q" add question_num add
".txt";
         question = "Loading...";
// Start loading the question…
         loadVariablesNum (filename, 0);
// If question hasn't loaded then keep looping
      actions for frame 4
         if (_root.question eq "Loading...") {
            gotoAndPlay (3);
         }
// Display the question and possible answers.
      actions for frame 5
         quizquestion = _root.question;

      actions for frame 16
         answera = _root.a1;

      actions for frame 19
         answerb = _root.a2;

      actions for frame 22
         answerc = _root.a3;

      actions for frame 34
         stop ();
```

Moving On

This chapter featured a relatively simple quiz game. Now that you've completed the code for that game, you should be ready to tackle a more complicated game. In the next chapter, we'll be going into the third dimension and creating a fully featured, 3D adventure game with some advanced ActionScripting.

Chapter 10

Designing Adventure Games

In this chapter, we will take you through the complete development of a complex, isometric 3D adventure game. In each section, we'll be adding new features or functionality to the game, and we'll discuss the theory behind the ideas. And then we'll take you through the programming required to make it all happen. Have fun.

By James Robertson

Game Overview

The game that we'll develop in this chapter revolves around a character named Walter. Walter's objective (and the player's), is to find map sections, and put them together to find a golden chalice. Of course, Walter has to overcome obstacles and dangers to find these map pieces, and then survive to the end of the game. The game will be set in an isometric 3D environment, and many traps and pitfalls will be aimed at killing poor Walter.

In each section of this chapter, we'll be adding new features or functionality to the game. Each section will have its own source code so that you can play with the game and learn the techniques we've discussed. This book's companion CD-ROM also contains Flash files with the code for each stage of game development. At the end of each section, we encourage you to play with the source code, and to try to modify and develop it further. Doing so, will ensure that you fully understand the process, and it will make the next section easier to understand.

While developing this game, we'll write ActionScript code for such things as having Walter walk around the screen, and in front of, behind, and between objects; hop up and down; smash crates to find bonus objects; and avoid dangers such as quicksand and bottomless pits. We'll also build in collision detection (so Walter doesn't walk right over objects in his path), and we'll create several layers and assign depth values to them (to help create the illusion of a 3D environment). We'll need to add code for various animations (movie clips) depending on the circumstances (such as Walter walking, Walter hopping, Walter falling into quicksand and perishing, and Walter winning the game). We'll add various bonus objects for Walter to find and use to protect himself, to gain an extra life, to open locked doors, and so on. As we add complexity to the game by adding difficulty, and more scenes for Walter to wander in, we'll also need to add code for saving Walter's status at any given point. And we'll add code for restarting the game when it ends prematurely (when Walter runs out of lives before collecting his trophy).

What Is Isometric 3D?

In computer graphics, an *isometric view* is a rendering that shows three-dimensional objects with height and width, but without the perspective change that would be added by including depth. An isometric view provides the *illusion* of depth, but maintains the object's dimensions (which a *perspective* view would distort by showing an object's height becoming smaller with increasing distance).

Adding a Walking Character

Now, we're ready to start developing the game. The first thing we want to do is to get our Walter character to walk around the screen. This is one of the most exciting parts of the game, because for the first time, you really see your graphics come to life. In the 3D environment we're building, we have two animations for every movement that Walter makes—one animation is facing toward us, and the other is facing away from us. But, ultimately, we need to have four animations because Walter can move in four directions (up, down, left, and right). We create the two additional animations by "mirroring" the original ones, using the Flip Horizontal transformation, which you will find in the Modify menu in Flash. You can see these mirrored animations in Figure 10.1. Notice that the bottom two versions of Walter are mirrored images of the top two animations.

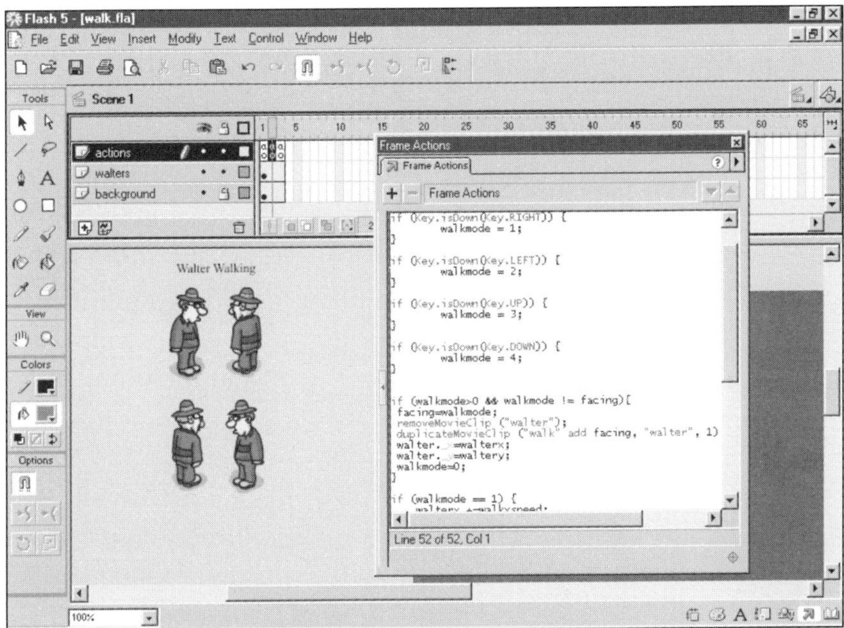

Figure 10.1
The mirrored animations of the walk.

To mirror the animations in this way, do the following:

1. Start Flash, and open the file named X. Create a new layer in your movie.
2. Drag the two walk animations (called **waltwalktoward** and **waltwalkaway**) from the library and onto the stage area.
3. Place the two movie clips offstage, and give them the instance names of **walk1** (for the **waltwalktoward** movie clip), and **walk2** (for the other movie clip).
4. Highlight both movie clips, copy them, and paste them just below the original movie clips. On these duplicates, use the Flip Horizontal transformation, which you will find in the Modify menu. Name these duplicates **walk3** and **walk4**.

   The numbers we've used for these animations are very important, and we will use them throughout the game to indicate the direction in which Walter is moving (1=right, 2=left, 3=up, and 4=down). Throughout this chapter, we will refer to these numbers as the "direction values."

We also need to add some code to these movie clips to keep them from playing automatically, and to ensure that we can control them correctly. First, we need a **STOP()** action in each frame so that we can control the walk animation using ActionScript (we don't want the whole animation to play on its own). In the first frame, we need to set the variable **/:walkmode** equal to 0. The **walkmode** variable indicates which direction Walter is currently walking—a value of 0 indicates that he is not moving. Prefixing the variable name with /: tells Flash that this variable is available from the main Timeline, and not just as a local variable in our Walter movie clip. Finally, at the end of the animation, we need to add a frame that simply says **gotoAndStop (1)**; this frame makes sure that our animation loops back to the beginning when it reaches the final frame.

Adding the Initial Variables

The graphics are ready to use, so we can start adding the ActionScript that will control the animations. The first thing we need to do is set up the initial variables, which we'll use for the walking speed, Walter's starting position, and the direction that Walter is facing.

Use Variables for Flexibility

Always make sure that you specify the walking speed using variables at the beginning of your movie, rather than numerical values deep inside your game, because you might need to change these variables later on.

Variables for Walking Speed

In an isometric game, our character will move in both the x direction (along the horizontal axis), and the y direction (along the vertical axis) when he walks, so we need to have separate variables—**walkxspeed** and **walkyspeed**—for the two axes. The speed dictates *how many screen pixels* the character moves when he walks, and this number will vary depending on the number of frames in your walk animation, and on the size of your in-game graphics.

Variables for Walter's Coordinates and "Facing" Direction

We'll use two variables (called **walterx** and **waltery**) to keep track of the character's current x,y-coordinates. At the start of our movie, we'll set these to the center of the screen—our movie size is set to 640×480 pixels, so the center of our screen is 320 pixels across, and 240 pixels down the screen. To display Walter in the middle of the screen, we have to duplicate one of the "walk" movie clips that we created earlier, and set the x,y-coordinates of this duplicated movie clip to **walterx** and **waltery**, respectively. We'll use the **facing** variable to keep track of which direction Walter is currently facing, and this direction determines which movie clip we need to duplicate. Let's take a look at the code that sets up these variables and places Walter in the middle of the screen:

```
walkxspeed = 6;
walkyspeed = 3;
// Have Walter face right
facing = 1;
// Set Walter's position
walterx = 320;
waltery = 240;
duplicateMovieClip ("walk" add facing, "walter", 1);
```

```
walter._x=walterx;
walter._y=waltery;
```

Variable for Walking Direction

We will be also using a variable called **walkmode** to indicate which way we want to make the character move, so when the player presses one of the arrow keys (left, right, up, or down), we simply need to set the **walkmode** variable equal to the direction values that we set up earlier. The code looks like this:

```
if (Key.isDown(Key.RIGHT)) {
        walkmode = 1;
}
if (Key.isDown(Key.LEFT)) {
        walkmode = 2;
}
if (Key.isDown(Key.UP)) {
        walkmode = 3;
}
if (Key.isDown(Key.DOWN)) {
        walkmode = 4;
}
```

We will be using the **walkmode** variable with the **facing** variable, to make the Walter character turn around on the spot without actually moving. This means that if the character is walking to the right, and you try to move the character left, he will first stop walking, and then face left, before he starts walking in that new direction. This combination just adds a small touch of realism to the game, and it will be useful later in the game, when we need to make Walter turn and face a particular direction, without moving from his current position.

The code below will check to see whether **walkmode** is greater than 0 (that is, if the player has pressed a direction key). If the direction specified in **walkmode** is *not* equal to the direction that Walter is currently facing, we must remove the current Walter animation and replace it with one that is facing the correct way. Here's the code:

```
if (walkmode>0 && walkmode != facing){
 facing=walkmode;
 removeMovieClip ("walter");
 duplicateMovieClip ("walk" add facing, "walter", 1);
 walter._x=walterx;
 walter._y=waltery;
 walkmode=0;
}
```

Moving Walter

We're nearly there. The final thing we need to do is actually move Walter on the screen. If Walter walks right, in our isometric environment, he will actually move *across* and *down* the screen, so we need to increase both the x- and y-coordinates by the walking-speed variables that we set up at the beginning of the movie. If Walter walks left, the opposite happens, and we have to decrease both the x- and y-coordinates by the walking-speed variables. If Walter walks up, we increase the x-coordinate and decrease the y-coordinate and, finally, if Walter walks down, we decrease the x-coordinate and increase the y-coordinate. In ActionScript, we handle this movement by the following four **IF** statements (one for each direction):

```
if (walkmode == 1) { walterx +=walkxspeed;
 waltery +=walkyspeed;
}
if (walkmode == 2) {
 walterx -= walkxspeed;
 waltery -= walkyspeed;
}
if (walkmode == 3) {
 walterx += walkxspeed;
 waltery -= walkyspeed;
}
if (walkmode == 4) {
 walterx -= walkxspeed;
 waltery += walkyspeed;
}
```

Now that we've modified the x,y-coordinates, we need to actually move the current movie clip to this new position, and play the next frame in the walk animation.

```
if (walkmode>0) {
 walter._x = walterx;
 walter._y = waltery;
 walter.nextFrame ();
}
```

Note: The code for this game relies on many variables, which might become difficult to keep track of after awhile.

That's it. We've now created our walking character. Load the **walk** demo from the CD-ROM to try it out.

Displaying Isometric Graphics Using a Grid System

To display the isometric graphics on screen, we are going to use a grid system. The grid system divides the game screen into a number of imaginary squares, and we plot our graphics in the center of these squares. Obviously, in the real game, you don't actually see these grid squares; you see only the objects that are placed inside them.

The size of each square in this grid (and the number of squares in the entire grid), will vary depending upon the size of the graphics you use in your game. You need to create these graphics in such a way that you can tile them, so you can join them together to create different scenes. This process is a bit like using building blocks—you can assemble the building blocks into all kinds of different shapes and sizes. Our grid size will be the same size as these tileable graphics. For the Walter adventure game, we are basing our grid system on the size of our brick tower graphic—the base of this object is 48×34 pixels. When we plot graphics in an isometric 3D view, we plot the objects diagonally on the screen, with a 50 percent overlap between each graphic. This means that if our object is 48×34 pixels, our individual square size is 24×17 pixels (each dimension is halved). So, in our grid, each square will be 24×17 pixels.

When we write the routine that plots the isometric graphics on screen, we need to define the dimensions of our grid and the individual squares within that grid as different variables. The dimensions of a square in our grid are stored in the variables **plotxsize** and **plotysize**. The dimensions of the entire grid are stored in the variables **gridx** (number of squares across) and **gridy** (number of squares down). In our Walter adventure game, we'll be using a 13×15 grid, and each square in this grid is 24×17 pixels in size. When plotting isometric graphics on screen, we must centralize the graphics on the screen, and we do this by creating a variable called **plotxoffset.** This offset variable is equal to the width of our movie, divided by 2—in our case, the movie is 640 pixels, so **plotxoffset** is set to 320. Here's the code that defines all of these variables:

```
gridx = 13;
gridy = 15;
gridsize=gridx*gridy;
plotxsize = 24;
plotysize = 17;
plotxoffset=320;
```

We give a number to all of the objects that we want to plot on screen. For example, in our adventure game, item1 is the brick tower, item2 is the dangerous bush, item3 is the crate, item4 is a locked door, and item5 is a palm tree. We use these item numbers to determine which object is plotted at which position on the screen. We define the object locations by creating a string of numbers (one number for each square in our grid). Here's an example string for a grid that is 13 squares by 15 squares. Each row has 13 entries, and the grid has 15 rows. If we don't want to plot an object at any particular grid position, we place a 0 there. So, in the following code, the first row is empty, the brick tower takes up the entire second row, and so on:

```
0000000000000
1111111111111
0000001000000
0000001000000
0000011100000
0000000000000
0000000000000
0020000000200
0000000000000
```

```
0000003000000
0000000000000
0040000000400
0000000000000
0000000000000
0050000000500
```

Figure 10.2
The Walter adventure game plotted on screen.

Just by looking at this example, you might be able to imagine how this graphic will look when it's plotted on screen (see Figure 10.2). Remember that every 0 represents a space, 1 represents a brick wall, 2 represents a bush, and 3 represents a crate. In this example, We've made the code clearer by adding line breaks at the end of every row, but when you write this code in ActionScript, you must use one long string that will look something like this:

```
tempobjects =
"000000000000
0111111111111
1000000100000
0000000100000
0000001110000
0000000000000
0000000000000
0002000000020
0000000000000
0000000300000
0000000000000
0004000000040
0000000000000
0000000000000
00050000000500";
```

Converting the Grid Positions to an Array

We create the grid using a string of numbers because that format is relatively easy for us to use and understand. However, using this format throughout the game would make the programming side more difficult; so, to make the programming easier, we need to convert this string to an array. An *array* is simply a list of items that are accessible under a single variable name. Each item in the list is known as an *element*, and you can access an element using this syntax: **Arrayname[element number]**. For example, if our array is called "objects", and we want to access item6 in the list, we use the command **objects[6]**. The following code uses the **substr** command to extract each object from our original string and place it into an array called **groundobjects**:

```
groundobjects = new Array();
for (i=0; i<gridsize; i++) {
 groundobjects[i] = tempobjects.substr(i, 1);
}
```

Plotting the Objects on Screen

Now that we've converted our grid positions into an array, we are ready to plot the objects on screen. To do this, we set up a loop that looks at each item in our grid, and then plots the appropriate object on the screen in the correct grid position. We do this by using the **attachMovie** command, which is a new command in Flash 5. This command lets us retrieve a movie clip from our library and duplicate it on the screen.

Before you retrieve and duplicate the movie clip, you need to set up your library correctly. Select an item in your library and choose Linkage from the Library window's Options menu. In the Symbol Linkage Properties dialog box, choose Export This Symbol, and then give the symbol an identifier. This identifier is the name you use in your ActionScript to access that particular symbol. So, for example, in our game, we have a graphic symbol called **bricktower**, and we have set the identifier of this symbol to **item1**. We can now use this symbol in our movie by adding the following ActionScript:

```
attachMovie( "item1", "newobject", depth )
```

The above command will duplicate our **bricktower** symbol (with the identifier of **item1**), give the new duplicated movie clip the name of **newobject**, and place the duplicated clip at a depth level defined in the variable **depth**.

The depth setting is very important in our isometric 3D environment. In Flash, you can assign a *depth value* to each movie clip, and when two-movie clips overlap on the screen, the movie clip with the *highest* depth value will appear on top of the other clip. Remember, you cannot have two movie clips at the same depth level. If you try to use a depth level that already exists, your new movie clip will replace the original one. For now, we will give each of our objects a depth value that is the same as the object's grid position—that is, if the object is at position 10 in our grid, we will give it a depth value of 10.

Here's the code that loops through our array of objects and plots them at the correct positions on the screen:

```
x=1;
y=1;
for (i=0; i<gridsize; i++) {
 itemtype=groundobjects[i];
 attachMovie( "item" add itemtype, "object" add i, i )
 plotx=plotxoffset+(x*plotxsize)-(y*plotxsize);
 ploty=(x*plotysize)+(y*plotysize);
 _root["object" add i]._x = plotx;
 _root["object" add i]._y = ploty;
       x+=1;
        if (x>gridx){
         x=1;
         y+=1;
       }
}
```

That's all you need to do. You can try this demo on the CD-ROM in the file called *plotiso3d*, or refer to Figure 10.3 to see how the graphic looks.

Figure 10.3
Displaying part of the game screen on the grid system.

Depth Sorting and Simple Collision Detection

Okay, so now that you've played with that demo, you'll notice that the graphics look three-dimensional. However, when your character goes near the objects, he just walks right over the top of them and spoils the illusion of depth. When we plotted the graphics on screen, we gave each item a depth value based upon its position in the grid. To make everything work correctly, we need to do exactly the same thing with our Walter character, and change his depth value depending upon where he is on the screen. We have just one small problem: At the moment, we have no idea which grid position Walter is currently standing in. So, we have to add some code to keep track of this information.

Knowing which grid square Walter is in (or is walking toward) let's us set the correct depth value for our character, so that he can walk behind, around, and in front of the various objects; what's more, we can also use the information to do some simple collision detection. We are using a 13×15 grid, which is numbered consecutively from left to right. So, the first row of our grid contains grid positions 1 through 13, the second row contains grid positions 14 through 26, and so on. If Walter is currently in grid position 5, and we press the right-arrow key to move Walter to grid position 6, we can check to see whether an object is already at that grid position—if so, depending upon what object is there, we can make Walter react to it.

Variables for Current Position and Destination Position on the Grid

To keep track of the Walter grid position, we need to make some amendments to our current code. Let's start by taking a look at the code we must have to initialize the various settings for how Walter moves, and where he starts on the screen. First, we'll be using two new variables to store Walter's *current* grid position, and we'll call these variables **waltergridx** and **waltergridy**. We'll have two other variables to store Walter's *destination* grid position; we'll call these variables **destinationgridx** and **destinationgridy**. The destination position is calculated when the player presses an arrow key to move Walter. We need to know the destination grid position because Walter cannot walk in some squares (for example, if a wall or door is already at that position), so we need to check this limitation before we start the walking animation. In the previous section, we used the following formulae to calculate the physical x,y-coordinates from the grid position:

```
plotx=plotxoffset+(x*plotxsize)-(y*plotxsize);
ploty=(x*plotysize)+(y*plotysize);
```

And we use exactly the same formula to calculate Walter's x,y-coordinates, but we replace the variables **walterx** and **waltery** with **waltergridx** and **waltergridy**, respectively. The code looks like this:

```
walterx=plotxoffset+(waltergridx*plotxsize)-
(waltergridy*plotxsize);
waltery=(waltergridx*plotysize)+(waltergridy*plotysize);
```

Linking Walking-Speed Variables to Grid-Square Size

We need to make one final change to the initial variables, and that change is the walk-speed variable. If you remember, this variable determines how many pixels Walter moves when you press one of the arrow keys. Previously, we just used a **walkxspeed** of six pixels and a **walkyspeed** of three pixels. Now that we are trying to calculate Walter's correct current grid position, we need to make sure that, when he walks in any direction, he moves *exactly* one square in that chosen direction. If we don't do this, we won't be able to accurately detect whether Walter has walked into a grid position that already contains an object. To achieve the result we want, we now need to link the **walkspeed** variables to the size of each square in our grid. The walk animation that we use for Walter is four frames long, so, in each frame of this animation, we need to move Walter a quarter of the way across the square. Here's the code:

```
walkxspeed = plotxsize/4;
walkyspeed = plotysize/4;
```

So, our initialization code for Walter now looks like this:

```
facing = 1;
waltergridx = 6;
waltergridy = 15;
destinationgridx=waltergridx;
destinationgridy=waltergridy;
walterx=plotxoffset+(waltergridx*plotxsize)-
(waltergridy*plotxsize);
waltery=(waltergridx*plotysize)+(waltergridy*plotysize);
duplicateMovieClip ("walk" add facing, "walter", 500);
walter._x = walterx;
walter._y = waltery;
walkxspeed = plotxsize/4;
walkyspeed = plotysize/4;
```

Now that we've looked at the initialization code, let's take a look at the main code.

Checking Walter's Walking Mode and the Destination Position's Availability

The first thing we need to do is modify the "keypress" routine in a couple of ways: When a player presses a key to move Walter, we want to check whether or not Walter is walking, and we want to check the availability of the destination square. (We want to calculate the destination grid's position so that we can check to see whether it's a square that Walter can go to.)

Let's first look at the mode check. If Walter is partway through the walking animation, we don't want the player to suddenly press another key and try to move Walter in another direction. So, we need to add some code to check whether Walter is currently walking or stationary. We can do this quite easily by checking the value of the **walkmode** variable—if **walkmode** equals 0, Walter is not walking.

We'll add a new variable called **destinationcheck**, which we use to determine whether we have to check the destination grid position. We use this variable because we need to check the destination only once (when Walter *starts* walking) for each time Walter is moved, and we don't want to check in every frame of our game.

Here's the new code to handle the keypress for the right-arrow key:

```
if (Key.isDown(Key.RIGHT)) {
        if (walkmode == 0) {
              destinationgridx = waltergridx+1;
              destinationgridy = waltergridy;
              destinationcheck = true;
              walkmode = 1;
        }
}
```

Run Code Only When Necessary

To ensure that your game runs at an acceptable speed, be careful to add features that run particular code only when the code is really necessary. If you constantly run unnecessary code, your game will quickly become slow and unusable.

The code for the other keys uses exactly the same format, and it looks like this:

```
if (Key.isDown(Key.LEFT)) {
       if (walkmode == 0) {
              destinationgridx = waltergridx-1;
              destinationgridy = waltergridy;
              destinationcheck = true;
              walkmode = 2;
       }
}
if (Key.isDown(Key.UP)) {
       if (walkmode == 0) {
              destinationgridy = waltergridy-1;
              destinationgridx = waltergridx;
              destinationcheck = true;
              walkmode = 3;
       }
}
if (Key.isDown(Key.DOWN)) {
       if (walkmode == 0) {
              destinationgridy = waltergridy+1;
              destinationgridx = waltergridx;
              destinationcheck = true;
              walkmode = 4;
       }
}
```

Adding Collision Detection

Now, let's try some simple collision detection. The first thing we need to check is that Walter has not tried to walk off the edge of our grid. If he does, we set the variable **walkmode** to 0, which stops the walking action. Here's the code:

```
if (destinationgridx>gridx or destinationgridx<0 or destination
gridy>gridy or destinationgridy<0) {
 walkmode = 0;
}
```

If Walter hasn't walked off the edge of the grid, we need to check the destination grid position to see whether it contains an object. If we know the destination x- and y-coordinates, we can calculate the destination grid position with the following formula:

```
gridpos = (destinationgridy-1)*gridx+(destinationgridx-1);
```

At the beginning of our movie, we put all the items into an array called **groundobjects**. To check what item is stored in our destination grid position, we can simply check the element **gridpos** in the **groundobjects** array. We do this with the following statement:

```
item = groundobjects[gridpos];
```

The variable **item** will now contain a number that refers to an object. If **item** equals **0**, the square is empty; if **item** equals **1**, the square contains a brick tower. If **item** equals **2**, the square contains a dangerous bush, and so on. For now, we just need to know whether the square is empty (that is, the variable **item** equals **0**). If it is (and does), Walter can safely move to that square, so we set the variables **waltergridx** and **waltergridy** to equal **destinationgridx** and **destinationgridy**, respectively. That part of the code will handle the simple collision detection.

Changing Walter's Depth Value

In addition to adding collision detection, we can change the depth value of our Walter character. By doing this, we will make the game truly three-dimensional, because Walter will then be able to walk in front of, behind, and around objects (rather than walking through them or over them). We need to set Walter's depth value to the same value as the destination grid position—and, luckily, we've already calculated the grid position (it's stored in the **gridpos** variable), because we used this variable to check whether an object was stored at this location. To change Walter's depth value, we use a command (new in Flash 5) called **swapDepths**—to use this, we specify the movie-clip name and the new depth value. Here's the code that changes Walter to the depth value specified in the **gridpos** variable:

```
walter.swapDepths(gridpos);
```

That's it. We need to make just one final addition to this piece of code. We've already specified what happens if the destination square is empty. If the square is *not* empty, however, we need to set the **walkmode** variable to 0 (this setting stops the walk animation). Here's the complete code for this section:

```
if (destinationcheck == true && walkmode == facing) {
 if ((waltergridx != destinationgridx)
 or (waltergridy != destinationgridy)) {
             gridpos = (destinationgridy-
```

```
1)*gridx+(destinationgridx-1);
              item = groundobjects[gridpos];
              if (item == 0) {
              waltergridx = destinationgridx;
              waltergridy = destinationgridy;
              gridpos = (waltergridy-1)*gridx+(waltergridx-1);
            walter.swapDepths(gridpos);
              } else {
                    walkmode = 0;
              }
      }
       destinationcheck = false;
}
```

The above code checks and sets the depth value as Walter starts walking. We have to change the depth value in two other places. The first place is the code where Walter turns around on the spot (without walking). Previously, we used the following code:

```
if (walkmode>0 && walkmode != facing){
 facing=walkmode;
 removeMovieClip ("walter");
 duplicateMovieClip ("walk" add facing, "walter", 500);
 walter._x=walterx;
 walter._y=waltery;
 walkmode=0;
}
```

This old code just sets the depth value to 500, regardless of the current grid position. We need to amend the code slightly, to the following code (the amendments are highlighted):

```
if (walkmode>0 && walkmode != facing){
 facing=walkmode;
 removeMovieClip ("walter");
 gridpos = (waltergridy-1)*gridx+(waltergridx-1);
 duplicateMovieClip ("walk" add facing, "walter", gridpos);
 walter._x=walterx;
 walter._y=waltery;
 walkmode=0;
}
```

The other place where we must change the depth value is in the code for when Walter stops walking. We find this code—which updates Walter's current x,y-coordinates and moves the walk animation to the next frame—at the end of the code in Frame 2.

```
if (walkmode>0) {
 walter._x = walterx;
 walter._y = waltery;
 walter.nextFrame();
}
```

At the end of this code, we add the following, which will be run when the variable **walkmode** equals **0** (that is, Walter has stopped walking).

```
else {
 gridpos = (waltergridy-1)*gridx+(waltergridx-1);
 walter.swapDepths(gridpos);
}
```

And that's it. You can see this code in action on the CD-ROM in the file called *depth*.

Tidying Up

If you've tried the demo on the CD-ROM, you'll notice two little glitches that slightly mar the performance of our game. Before we go any further, we need to fix those glitches. In case you haven't already noticed the problems, here they are:

1. The collision detection works only if you walk through the *center* of the door object. The current version of the game lets you walk through the side of the door without any problems.
2. If your character walks "down" (on the screen, this is down and to the left), and passes an object on his left side, a small graphical glitch causes the character to appear to walk through the object.

So, what causes these problems? The first problem occurs because our door graphic is wider than our grid system of 24×17 pixels. The collision detection works in the center of the door because that location is positioned over one of our grid squares. The second problem is caused by the way we change Walter's depth when he moves. As soon as he starts moving, we change his depth value to that of the destination square. If Walter is walking "down," the depth value of the destination square is higher than the current square, which means that if he's standing next to an object, he will briefly be displayed on top of that object as he walks from the current square to the destination square.

Adding Objects to the Sides of the Door Object

Let's look at the first problem. We can easily fix this problem by modifying our grid system that defines the location of all of our objects. All we need to do is add an object to the squares on either side of our door graphic. It's important to note that we are not going to plot a new graphic in these squares—we simply must add a non-zero value to our grid, so that our collision detection system will stop Walter from walking through those squares. Here's our original grid system:

```
0000000000000
1111111111111
```

```
0000001000000
0000001000000
0000011100000
0000000000000
0000000000000
0020000000200
0000000000000
0000003000000
0000000000000
0040000000400
0000000000000
0000000000000
0050000000500
```

In this grid system, the number **4** represents the door graphic. So, all we need to do is add a non-zero value before and after each 4 in our grid. You can use any non-zero value that is currently unused (we recommend that you use a "z" character). Because no object is associated with the "z" character; the z acts like an invisible object. You won't be able to see anything, but Walter will not be able to walk onto that square. You can, of course, use this technique in other situations; maybe you need to create some kind of invisible barrier such as a glass wall, or perhaps a force field.

Checking Depth Values

The second problem is slightly harder to fix, and because it's only a small graphical glitch, you might think it's not worth the effort. However, fixing these apparently small problems makes the difference between an average game and a good game; so, if you see a small problem in your game, you should definitely try to fix it. You can be sure that, if you've spotted this problem, other people will spot it, too. As we said earlier, this problem occurs when we set Walter's depth position. If Walter is walking from Square 10 to Square 25, his depth must change from a value of 10 to 25, as well. This value becomes a problem only if Walter is standing next to an object at the moment you change the depth setting. If you look at Figure 10.4, you'll see "before" and "after" images, as Walter walks from one grid square to another.

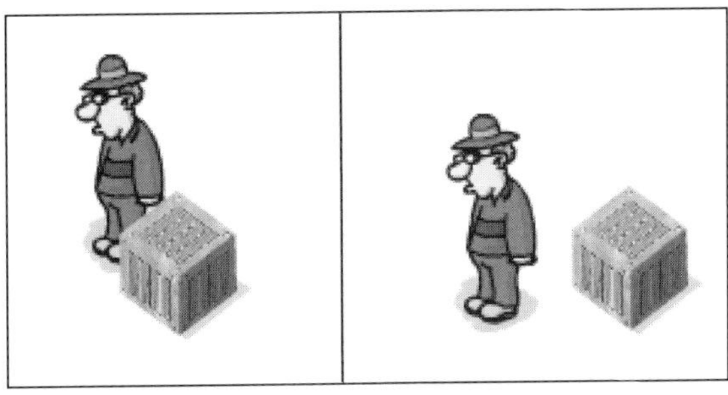

Figure 10.4
Walter walking in the depth grid.

In the first section of the figure, Walter is in Square 10 (and has a depth value of 10), and the crate is in Square 11 (and, therefore, has a depth value of 11). Because the crate has a higher depth value than Walter does, the crate is drawn on top of the Walter graphic, thus giving the impression that Walter is behind the object. As Walter walks "down," his movement takes him to square 25, and so we must set his depth value to 25. We change the depth setting as soon as Walter *starts* walking, and because this setting is higher than the crate, Walter appears on top of the crate graphic. This variation in settings gives us the graphical glitch we are seeing.

To solve this problem, we start by checking to see whether Walter is standing next to an object when he starts walking "down." If he is, rather than setting his depth value to the destination square, we leave his depth value at the current setting. So, in the example above, we will *not* change his depth setting to 25 when he starts walking. Instead, we will leave the value at 10, and he will, therefore, not "walk over" the crate. This rule has an exception, however, and Figure 10.5 shows this exception.

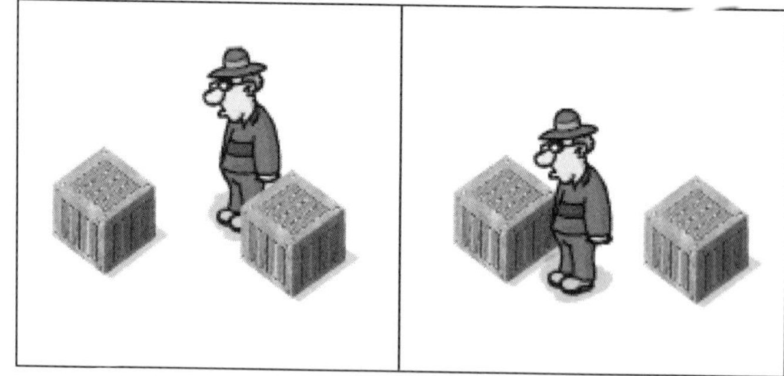

Figure 10.5
Avoiding depth graphical glitches.

In this figure, a crate is next to the destination square (Square 24). So, if we leave Walter's depth at 10, when he starts walking, he will have a lower depth value than this new crate; he will, therefore, be plotted below this graphic, which would also cause a graphical glitch. In this particular situation, which depth value we use for Walter doesn't matter—at one point in the animation, Walter will always be plotted either above the original crate, or below the new crate. To make the graphic work, we would need a depth value that is less than 11, but more than 24—and that is just not possible. The only possible solution is that, when you build your own grid system that plots the objects on screen, you avoid placing objects in this particular configuration.

We've already mentioned the glitch that you see when a character is walking "down," and an object is on the character's right side. A similar problem occurs when the character is walking "up" the screen and has an object on his left side. Again, we must add some code that checks for this situation and then modifies the depth settings accordingly.

Okay, we've spoken about the theory; now, let's take a look at the code. First, you need to calculate the current depth value, and the depth value of the destination square. We will place our code in the section where we change Walter's depth value; so, at this point, we already have a variable called **gridpos** that holds the depth value of the destination square. We want the default depth to be whichever variable holds the highest value. We can then check for each situation mentioned above, and modify the depth setting as required. Here's the code that we'll be using:

```
// Calculate depth of current square and destination square
 depthval = (waltergridy-1)*gridx+(waltergridx-1);
 destdepthval=gridpos;

// Set default depth setting
 if (depthval>destdepthval) {
 newdepth = depthval;
 } else {
 newdepth = destdepthval;
 }

// This is for when we're walking down
 if (facing == 4) {
// Check the item to the left of the destination square
 item = groundobjects[destdepthval-1];
// If item==0 (i.e., Square is empty) then continue check
 if (item == 0) {
// Check the item at position to the right of the current square
 item = groundobjects[depthval+1];
// If item!=0 (i.e., Square is NOT empty) then do the fix.
 if (item != 0) {
 newdepth = depthval;
 }
 }
 }

// This is for when we're walking up and is the opposite of the
// previous code
 if (facing == 3) {
// Check the item at position to the left of the current square
 item = groundobjects[depthval-1];
// If item==0 (i.e., Square is empty) then continue check
 if (item == 0) {
// Check the item to the right of the destination square
 item = groundobjects[destdepthval+1];
// If item!=0 (i,e., Square is NOT empty) then do the fix.
 if (item != 0) {
 newdepth = destdepthval;
 }
 }
 }
```

That's the end of the fix. You can see this code in action in the demo called *depth_v2*, which is on the CD-ROM.

Adding Depth Layers

In our final game, we want to have some objects such as holes, rivers, and so on, which are actually slightly *below* ground level. With our current grid system, these items would be quite difficult to implement, so we have to improve the system by adding more layers. At the moment, we use our grid to place objects on the ground. We will now add two more grid systems, which will let us place objects at (or below) ground level, and above ground level. So, we'll now have three layers:

- *The* ***baseobjects*** *layer* is for items that are at the same level as Walter's feet, and it includes holes, rivers, and pits.
- *The* ***groundobjects*** *layer* is for all objects that are placed on the ground, but that rise above ground level; this layer includes crates, brick walls, and palm-tree trunks.
- *The* ***skyobjects*** *layer* is for objects that are placed above Walter's head, and it will be used for the palm frond, and will be available for future objects such as archways, etc.

Figure 10.6 gives a view of how these levels will work. These multiple layers will give us much more flexibility and realism when we are creating our final levels for the adventure game.

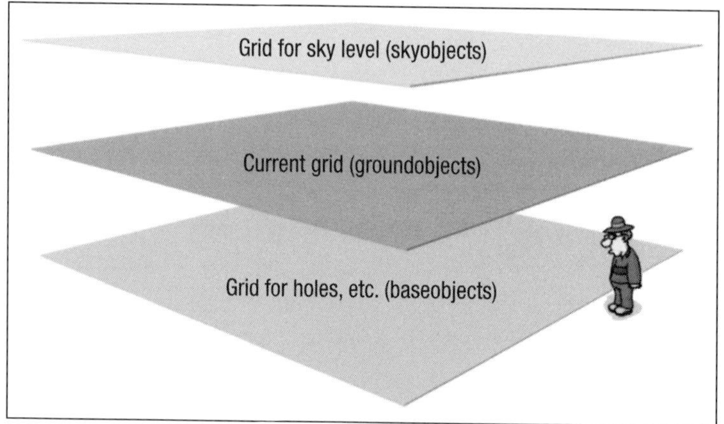

Figure 10.6
Various grid layers, graphically explained.

Before we start explaining the ActionScript, we will quickly show you the new graphical objects that we'll be adding into this section of the game. First, we will add a bottomless pit, some quicksand, and a plank of wood, and we'll split the existing palm-tree graphics into three separate items (a shadow, the trunk, and the frond). We are modifying the palm-tree graphic because, in our new layer system, different parts of the tree will be in each layer—the shadow will be in the base layer, the palm trunk will be in the ground layer, and the frond will be in the sky layer. Our list of objects now looks like this (the number next to each object relates to the number that we use in our grid system):

- *0*—Empty square
- *1*—Stone pillar
- *2*—Killer bush
- *3*—Crate
- *4*—Locked door
- *5*—Palm tree (trunk)
- *6*—Bottomless pit
- *7*—Quicksand
- *8*—Plank
- *9*—Palm tree (shadow)
- *a*—Palm tree (top)

Let's now look at how we will implement this newly layered grid system. Previously, we defined a single grid, which contained details of where the graphics would be placed on the screen. We now have to define three of those grids:

- Grid 1, called **tempobjects**, will contain items such as stone pillar, dangerous bush, crate, locked door, and palm tree trunk.
- Grid 2, called **tempbaseobjects**, will contain items such as the bottomless pit, quicksand, and the palm tree shadow.
- Finally, grid 3, called **tempskyobjects,** at the moment contains only the palm treetop (or frond).

We define these grids as a string variable (in exactly the same way as we did in the previous sections). Here's the code:

```
tempobjects =     "0000000000000111111111111100000010000300020001
000000000001110000
00000001000000100000100020010000010000001000000000000103000300000
01000000000000100050000050000000000000000000000000000000000011000
0";
tempbaseobjects = "0000000000000000000000000000000000000000000000
000000000000000000
00006000000000000000000000000000000000000000000000000700000000000
00000000000000000090000090000000000000000000000000000000000000000
0";
tempskyobjects =  "0000000000000000000000000000000000000000000000
000000000000000000
00000000000000000000000000000000000000000000000000000000000000000
000000000000000000a00000a0000000000000000000000000000000000000000
0";
```

As before, we need to convert these strings into an array to make the game programming slightly easier. We use the same program loop to convert the strings, but we have to add a few additional lines to convert our new grids, as well as the existing one.

```
// Convert to array
groundobjects = new Array();
baseobjects = new Array();
skyobjects = new Array();
for (i=0; i<gridsize; i++) {
 groundobjects[i] = tempobjects.substr(i, 1);
 baseobjects[i] = tempbaseobjects.substr(i, 1);
 skyobjects[i] = tempskyobjects.substr(i, 1);
}
```

Again, we plot these grids onto the screen using the same program loop as before, but with some additional code to plot our new grids, as well. We also have one other important change, which will affect the rest of our programming: We need to assign a depth value to each layer.

Assigning Depth Values to the Layers

We give each layer in our grid system a depth level. Previously, we simply calculated the current grid position and used that as our depth value—that is, if Walter was at grid position 25, his depth value was also set to **25**. This approach will now change. Everything in the **baseobjects** layer (the layer that contains holes, shadows, and so on) must *always* be below Walter. So, if Walter walks over a shadow or a hole, he should also be drawn above them. Everything in the **skyobjects** layer (which contains palm tree tops and any flying objects), must *always* be above Walter. So, if Walter walks under a palm tree or flying objects, he must be drawn below them. To achieve this, we assign a depth value to each of our layers. The **baseobjects** layer has a depth value of **0**, our **groundobjects** layer has a depth value of **500**, and our **skyobjects** layer has a depth value of **1,000**.

Whenever you move or create an object on a layer, you must use the depth values to set the correct depth for your graphic. So, whenever we draw or move anything on the **groundobjects** layer (this is our original layer that contains most of the objects, and is where Walter is displayed), we have to calculate the object's current grid position and add the depth value for that particular layer. If Walter is at grid position 25, his depth value will now be **25+500**. Here's the code that draws all of the grid layers onto our game screen:

```
// Set depth levels for each layer
groundlevel = 500;
skylevel = 1000;
// The sky height indicates how high
// above the ground our sky layer is
skyheight = 100;
```

```
// Draw Grid
x = 1;
y = 1;
for (i=0; i<gridsize; i++) {
 // Plot base objects
 plotx = plotxoffset+(x*plotxsize)-(y*plotxsize);
 ploty = (x*plotysize)+(y*plotysize);
 itemtype = baseobjects[i];
 depthval = i;
 attachMovie("item" add itemtype, "base" add i, depthval);
 _root["base" add i]._x = plotx;
 _root["base" add i]._y = ploty;

// Plot ground objects
 itemtype = groundobjects[i];
 attachMovie("item" add itemtype, "object" add i,
depthval+groundlevel);
 _root["object" add i]._x = plotx;
 _root["object" add i]._y = ploty;

// Plot sky objects
 itemtype = skyobjects[i];
 attachMovie("item" add itemtype, "sky" add i, depthval+skylevel);
 _root["sky" add i]._x = plotx;
 _root["sky" add i]._y = ploty-skyheight;

 x += 1;
 if (x>gridx) {
 x = 1;
 y += 1;
}
}
```

One final addition to this section is in the main code, where we set or change Walter's depth. We have to add the **groundlevel** value to his depth value. You can view the source code, and see it in action, in the file called *layers* on the CD-ROM.

Detecting Complex Collisions

If you've played the previous demo, which shows the newly layered grid system, you'll notice that Walter can quite safely walk across the quicksand and bottomless pits (which he should fall into). He can do this because we haven't added the collision detection for these items yet, and that's what we will do now.

In a previous section, we looked at simple collisions, and we used the grid system to detect whether Walter had collided with an object. That method worked by checking the grid position that Walter was trying to move to—if Walter tried to move to a grid position that already contained an object, we stopped him from moving in that particular direction. That approach works fine for the objects we've been using so far (crates, brick walls, palm trees, and so on). However, for our quicksand and bottomless pits, we can't use this technique, because these objects are both larger than a single grid square, and they are an irregular shape (that is, not square). So, to detect collisions with these objects, we will use a new technique. Flash Version 5 has a new ActionScript command called **hitTest**, which we can use to determine whether two objects have collided. If you wanted to test whether Walter had hit (or touched) an object called **quicksand**, you would use the following command:

```
walter.hitTest(quicksand);
```

That code seems simple enough. However, this command has a problem. When we use it in this format, the command uses a *bounding box* to detect collisions. A bounding box is the smallest rectangular area that your object(s) can fit into—so, even if you are not actually standing on the quicksand, but you are within the bounding box area, Flash will believe that the two objects are touching. In many cases, this conclusion would be perfectly acceptable, but in our adventure game, we want Walter to be able to walk right to the edge of the quicksand or the bottomless pit—and fall in only if he actually walks over the graphic, not just when he is *near* the graphic. In Figure 10.7, you can see two examples of Walter standing next to the bottomless pit; the box around each object is the bounding box. In both examples, Flash would detect a collision between these two objects, even though Walter is not actually standing on the bottomless pit graphic.

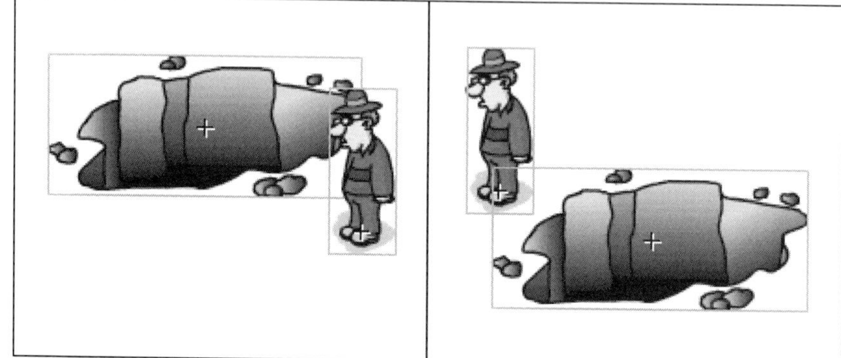

Figure 10.7
Complex collisions. Even though Walter is not standing over the bottomless pit, Flash thinks he is because the bounding boxes overlap.

The **hitTest** command does support another syntax, and we will be using that syntax to detect our collisions. This syntax lets us detect whether any object overlaps our specified x,y-coordinates, and we can also define whether we want to use the bounding box area, or the actual object shape as our collision area. The syntax looks like the following:

```
anyMovieClip.hitTest(x, y, shapeFlag);
```

The **shapeflag** variable is a Boolean value (that is, **true** or **false**), and determines whether we use the object's true shape (**true**), or the bounding box (**false**) for our collision detection.

In our game, we already know the x,y-coordinates of our Walter character (they are stored in the variables **walterx** and **waltery**), so our collision detection will look something like the following:

```
collision = bottomlesspit.hitTest(walterx, waltery, true);
```

Adding a Movie Clip for Refined Collision Detection

To make our collision detection completely accurate, we do need to make an addition to our graphics. In Figure 10.8, you can see two examples of Walter standing next to the bottomless pit. In the left-hand section, note the small, graphical details around the pit (small pebbles, pieces of dirt, etc.). If we use the collision-detection command shown above, the code will also detect when Walter touches one of these details, and we don't really want to do that—we just want to know whether Walter is touching the actual pit. In the right-hand section of Figure 10.8, you can see the pit itself as a black object—this is *an additional movie clip* placed under the bottomless pit graphic (this movie clip is called **nastyholebase**), and it is the exact size/dimensions of the pit, but without the graphical details around the edge (these are shown as outlines). This new movie clip is the one we will use for our collision detection. By detecting collisions with this movie clip, and not the original graphic, we will detect a collision only when Walter is walking directly on the pit, and not when he is touching one of the graphical details around the pit. Our new collision-detection command will now look like the following:

```
collision = bottomlesspit.nastyholebase.hitTest(walterx, waltery,
true);
```

Figure 10.8
Using the actual pit outlines for collision detection.

Notice that we simply add the name of our new movie clip after the original movie clip name. This command is now doing a **hitTest** on the movie clip called **nastyholebase**, which is stored in the movie clip called **bottomlesspit**.

In Figure 10.8 (on the right side), you can also see the center point of the Walter character (the small cross shown between his feet). The center point of an object is very important and, in this case, is the exact point that must touch the **nastyholebase** clip before a collision is detected. If Walter's center point was actually in the center of our Walter graphic, that point would have to cross the **nastyholebase** clip before the program detected a collision.

Changing the Plotting of the Base Objects

We've covered the theory of how this collision detection works, so now let's look at the modifications we need to make to the ActionScript. First, to make the collision detection routine easier, we need to change the way the base objects are plotted onto the screen. At the moment, we are using a **for..loop** to work through the grid and plot the objects at their correct position on the screen. As we do this, we are creating new movie clips, which we name according to their position on the screen. For example, if we are plotting two objects on our base level at grid positions 25 and 47, our two objects on this level will be called **base25** and **base47**. If we had to detect collisions on these objects, we would have to write a routine that checked every grid position to see whether an object was there.

To make life easier, we will change the routine so that the first object is called **base1**, the second object is called **base2**, and so on. Then, we simply need to know how many base objects we have, and then we can use a **for..loop** to check collisions with each of these objects. Please note that we are changing only the plot routine for the base objects. To do this, we first (before we start our **for..loop**) set a variable called **baseitems** to **0**. Then, when we are plotting an object on the base level, we simply increment this variable, and use that as the new name for our object. Here's the code to do this, and we've highlighted the lines of code that have changed since the previous section:

```
// Plot base objects
 plotx = plotxoffset+(x*plotxsize)-(y*plotxsize);
 ploty = (x*plotysize)+(y*plotysize);
 depthval = i;
 itemtype = baseobjects[i];

 if (itemtype != 0) {
 baseitems += 1;
 attachMovie("item" add itemtype, "base" add baseitems, depthval);
 _root["base" add baseitems]._x = plotx;
 _root["base" add baseitems]._y = ploty;
 }
```

Adding Animations for Walter's Demise

As part of our collision detection, we are also going to add the code that shows the appropriate animations when Walter is killed. He will be killed if he walks into quicksand, a bottomless pit, or a dangerous bush. The code for detecting whether Walter walks into a dangerous bush is almost in place already—we used it to determine whether Walter can walk to a particular grid position. At the moment, we simply check to see whether Walter is walking to an empty square. We can just modify this slightly by specifically checking for the dangerous bush. Here's the code to do this:

```
// Did we hit the bush??
if (item == 2) {
 dangerbush = true;
} else {
 dangerbush = false;
}
```

For now, we will simply set variable **dangerbush** to either **true** or **false** to indicate whether or not we have hit the bush.

Next, we'll look at the main collision-detection routine. You must be aware that routines like this will have an impact on the speed of your final game, and if you are doing collision detections on a large number of objects, your game might become unbearably slow. For this reason, deciding when you will run your collision-detection routine is important. In some games, you might be able to minimize how often you calculate collisions, but in our game, we need to check for collisions in every frame. To detect collisions, we are using the following routine:

```
// Complex hit detection....
for (i=1; i<=baseitems; i++) {
// Check for collision with quicksand
 sinkingsand = _root["base" add i].
quicksandbase.hitTest(walterx, waltery, true);
// Check for collision with bottomless pit
      nastyhole = _root["base" add i].
nastyholebase.hitTest(walterx, waltery, true);
// If quicksand, dangerbush, or bottomless pit collision has
// happened, then we stop Walter from walking and set the variable
// dead equal to true
 if (sinkingsand == true || dangerbush == true
|| nastyhole=true) {
 walkmode = 0;
 dead = true;
 }
}
```

This code is just the basic code, and we are going to improve it slightly. When Walter falls into the bottomless pit, we want to make him fall toward the center of the pit—that just looks more realistic. Here's how we do this:

```
 if (nastyhole == true) {
// Get the x,y coordinates of the center of the hole
 holex = _root["base" add i]._x;
```

```
 holey = _root["base" add i]._y;
// Calculate which way Walter needs to fall to make him face the
// center of the hole
if (walterx>holex) {
 if (waltery>holey) {
 facing = 2;
} else {
 facing = 4;
}
} else {
 if (waltery>holey) {
 facing = 3;
} else {
 facing = 1;
}
}
// The fall animation is 14 frames long, so we
// calculate the distance
// between Walter and the center of the hole, then divide the
 result
// by 14. The resulting figure (stored in movex and movey) is the
// distance that we move the fall animation to make it look like
// Walter is falling toward the center of the hole
 movex = (walterx-holex)/14;
 movey = (waltery-holey)/14;
 walkmode = 0;
 dead = true;}
```

Now, we need to add some code to display an animation when Walter dies. We've created two animations for this. When Walter walks into a bottomless pit, we display an animation of him falling, and when he hits either quicksand or a dangerous bush, we display an animation of Walter disappearing underground and being replaced with a gravestone. Each of these animations can be displayed in one of four directions, which will match the direction that Walter was facing when he was killed. These four directions match the direction values that we defined at the beginning of the chapter (1=right, 2=left, 3=up, and 4=down). The "fall" animations are called **fall1**, **fall2**, **fall3**, and **fall4**. The "die" animations are called **die1**, **die2**, **die3**, and **die4**.

At the end of each of these animations, we set a variable called **crashland** equal to **true** to indicate that the animation has finished. Following the previous collision-detection code, if the variable **dead** equals **true**, we need to remove the current "walter" movie clip and replace it with the appropriate animation. Here's the code that does this:

```
if (dead == true) {
// Calculate current grid position
 gridpos = (waltergridy-1)*gridx+(waltergridx-1);
```

```
// Calculate depth value
 depthval = gridpos+groundlevel;
// Remove current "walter" movie clip
 removeMovieClip ("walter");
// If we've hit the bottomless pit, then show the falling animation
if (nastyhole == true) {
 duplicateMovieClip ("fall" add facing, "walterfall", depthval);
}
// …otherwise show the standard dying animation
if (dangerbush == true || sinkingsand == true) {
 duplicateMovieClip ("die" add facing, "walterfall", depthval);
}

// Set the correct x,y coordinates of the animation
 walterfall._x = walterx;
 walterfall._y = waltery;
// Start playing the animation
 walterfall.gotoAndPlay(2);
}
```

Ending the Loop

Normally, the game keeps running in a loop, but, when the character has died, we don't want to run this loop anymore. In Frame 3 of our movie, rather than simply repeating the loop, we will now have the following code, which ensures that the game continues to loop only while Walter is still alive:

```
if (dead != true) {
gotoAndPlay ("gameloop");
}
```

Following this code, we have another small loop, which simply waits for the **crashland** variable to be set to **true** (this happens when the dying animation has been completed). During this loop, we move the animation by the variables **movex** and **movey**. These variables are used *only* when Walter is falling down the bottomless pit, and they are used to make him fall toward the middle of the hole. When **crashland** equals **true**, we can simply restart the game by going back to Frame 1. Here's the code for these two frames:

```
Frame: 4 labeled "dead"
walterfall._x -= movex;
walterfall._y -= movey;

Frame: 5
if (crashland != true) {
    gotoAndPlay ("dead");
}
```

That's all the code we need for this section. You can find a demonstration of this section on the CD-ROM, and it's called complex *collisions*.

We're Hopping Mad

To make our adventure game even more interesting, we've decided to give Walter the ability to hop around the screen. This action isn't just for fun; ultimately, Walter will use this hopping technique to smash open crates and pick up the bonus objects, which we've hidden inside the crates. The first thing we need is a hopping animation. As before, we need Walter to be able to hop in four different directions, so we've created four movie clips, called **hop1**, **hop2**, **hop3**, and **hop4**. The hopping animations work in the same way as our previous Walter animations—Frame 1 contains a **stop()** command, and the final frame resets the **walkmode** variable to **0**. In addition to this, with the hop animations, we will also set an additional variable called **endhop** to **true**. As the name suggests, this variable will let us know when the hop has finished.

```
/:endhop = true;
/:walkmode = 0;
```

To make Walter hop, we are going to use the spacebar. But, we want Walter to be able to jump in a particular direction, so we are going to use the spacebar with the arrow keys. So, to make Walter hop to the right, you need to press the spacebar *and* the right-arrow key. The ActionScript used to detect multiple key presses and make Walter hop is very similar to the code we are using for single key presses. Let's take a look at the original code:

```
if (Key.isDown(Key.RIGHT)) {
 if (walkmode == 0) {
 destinationgridx = waltergridx+1;
 destinationgridy = waltergridy;
 destinationcheck = true;
 walkmode = 1;
}
}
```

With the walking script above, we need to ensure that Walter is not currently walking before we set the new values, which is why we check the value of **walkmode** first. The same is true for the hopping script that follows below, but we also need to check that the character is not hopping, either. To do this, we check a variable called **doinghop**. The rest of the script should look familiar, except for the value of **walkmode**. When Walter is walking, we give him a value from 1 to 4 (depending upon which direction he is walking), and when he is hopping, we assign a value of 6 to 9, to indicate that he is hopping in a particular direction. The value of 5 is currently unused, but we have reserved that value in case we want to make Walter hop on the spot without moving in a particular direction.

The following code detects when the user presses the appropriate keys to make Walter hop, and it sets a variable called **starthop** to **true**, so that we know the hop has started:

```
if (Key.isDown(Key.RIGHT) && (Key.isDown(Key.SPACE))) {
    if (doinghop != true && walkmode==0) {
      depth = true;
        destinationgridx = waltergridx+1;
        destinationgridy = waltergridy;
        starthop = true;
 facing=1;
        walkmode = 6;
    }
}
```

This code is repeated for the other directions, which you can see here:

```
if (Key.isDown(Key.LEFT) && (Key.isDown(Key.SPACE))) {
      if (doinghop != true && walkmode==0) {
        depth = true;
        destinationgridy = waltergridy;
        destinationgridx = waltergridx-1;
        starthop = true;
 facing=2;
        walkmode = 7;
    }
}
if (Key.isDown(Key.UP) && (Key.isDown(Key.SPACE))) {
      if (doinghop != true && walkmode==0) {
        depth = true;
        destinationgridy = waltergridy-1;
        destinationgridx = waltergridx;
        starthop = true;
 facing=3;
        walkmode = 8;
    }
}
if (Key.isDown(Key.DOWN) && (Key.isDown(Key.SPACE))) {
      if (doinghop != true && walkmode==0) {
        depth = true;
        destinationgridy = waltergridy+1;
        destinationgridx = waltergridx;
        starthop = true;
 facing=4;
        walkmode = 9;
    }
}
```

We now need to add some code to make Walter actually do the hopping animation. All we need to do for this action is to remove the current movie clip (called **walter**) and replace it with the appropriate hop animation. When we have done that, we set a variable called **doinghop** to **true** to indicate that Walter has started the hopping animation. Here's the code that does this:

```
// Check if Walter is hopping...
if (starthop==true){
// Calculate grid position
 gridpos = (waltergridy-1)*gridx+(waltergridx-1);
// Calculate depth value
 depthval = gridpos+groundlevel;
// Remove old Walter
 removeMovieClip ("walter");
// Replace with hopping Walter
 duplicateMovieClip ("hop" add facing, "walter", depthval);
// Set x, y co-ordinates
 walter._x = walterx;
 walter._y = waltery;
      doinghop=true;
}
```

When Walter has completed his little hop, we need to do the exact opposite of what we've just done. We need to remove the hopping animation and replace it with a normal, walk animation. The code to do this is very similar to the above code:

```
// This is the end of the hop...
if (endhop==true){
// Calculate grid position
 gridpos = (waltergridy-1)*gridx+(waltergridx-1);
// Calculate depth value
 depthval = gridpos+groundlevel;
// Remove old Walter
 removeMovieClip ("walter");
// Replace with walking Walter
 duplicateMovieClip ("walk" add facing, "walter", depthval);
 walter.gotoAndStop(1);
// Set x, y co-ordinates
 walter._x = walterx;
 walter._y = waltery;
 endhop = false;
      doinghop=false;
      walkmode=0;
}
```

Modifying Collision-Detection Code to Accommodate Hopping

To make everything work correctly, we need to slightly modify the existing, simple, collision-detection code so that it works correctly with our new, hopping Walter. In previous sections, when Walter was unable to move to a particular grid position, we could simply set the **walkmode** variable to **0**, and that would stop Walter from walking any further in that particular direction. In addition to this, we need to stop Walter from hopping in that particular direction; so, wherever we've set **walkmode** to **0** to stop Walter, we should also add the following code:

```
    starthop=false;
    doinghop=false;
```

For example, we use the following code to check whether Walter has walked off the edge of the grid. We need to add the above code to make sure that the routine also works when Walter is hopping rather than walking. The added code has been highlighted:

```
if (destinationgridx>gridx or destinationgridx<0
or destinationgridy>gridy or destinationgridy<0) {
    walkmode = 0;
    starthop=false;
    doinghop=false;
}
```

In addition to this modification, we need to modify the section of code that checks the destination square. At the moment, this code runs if the variable **destinationcheck** is set to **true**, and **walkmode** equals **facing**. We also need to run this code if the variable **starthop** equals **true**, to ensure that Walter doesn't hop onto a square that already contains an object.

Adding Code to Move Walter While He's Hopping

The final code that we need to add is the code that will move Walter as he is hopping. When Walter is walking, we add the variable **walkxspeed** to the current x-coordinate, and we add **walkyspeed** to the y-coordinate. The code is as follows:

```
if (walkmode == 1) {
 walterx += walkxspeed;
 waltery += walkyspeed;
}
```

This piece of code runs in every frame of the walk animation, and the walk animation for Walter is four frames long. To move from one square to another, Walter has to walk 24 pixels. Therefore, the **walkspeed** needs to be 24 pixels divided by 4 frames (or a speed of 6 pixels per frame). The hopping animation for Walter is slightly longer than the walking animation (which is six frames long), so we cannot simply use the same **walkspeed** variable; otherwise, when Walter hops, he would move more than one grid square at a time, and that would completely ruin the calculations in our game. To make Walter move the correct distance when he hops, we use the **walkspeed** variable, but we multiply it by **(4/6)**. So, the code for moving Walter as he hops will look like the following:

```
if (walkmode == 6) {
 walterx += walkxspeed*(4/6);
 waltery += walkyspeed*(4/6);
}
```

We must repeat that code for each direction:

```
if (walkmode == 7) {
 walterx -= walkxspeed*(4/6);
 waltery -= walkyspeed*(4/6);
}
if (walkmode == 8) {
 walterx += walkxspeed*(4/6);
 waltery -= walkyspeed*(4/6);
}
if (walkmode == 9) {
 walterx -= walkxspeed*(4/6);
 waltery += walkyspeed*(4/6);
}
```

That's all the code we need. To see Walter hopping, try the demonstration on the CD-ROM called *hopping*.

Adding Bonus Objects to Find

As we said at the beginning of this section, the real reason to give Walter the ability to hop was to enable him to jump on (and crush) the crates in the game to collect the bonus objects hidden inside. You can see Walter in action as he hops onto a crate in Figure 10.9.

In this section, we'll add code that allows us to check for the presence of crates and open them, and then we'll add code that exposes the objects that were beneath the crates. We'll also add a new layer and grid to the game.

Checking for Crates and Opening Them

In our simple collision detection, we already check the destination square that Walter is walking or hopping onto. At the moment, we just check so see whether the item in that destination square is empty; we can modify this code to specifically check for a crate. The variable **item** contains the item number of the object in the destination square—if **item** equals **3**, and the variable **doinghop** equals **true**, Walter is hopping onto a crate. If this is the case, we simply need to play the crate-explosion animation, and set the destination square in the **groundobjects** array to **0** (to indicate that the square is now empty). Here's the code that does this.

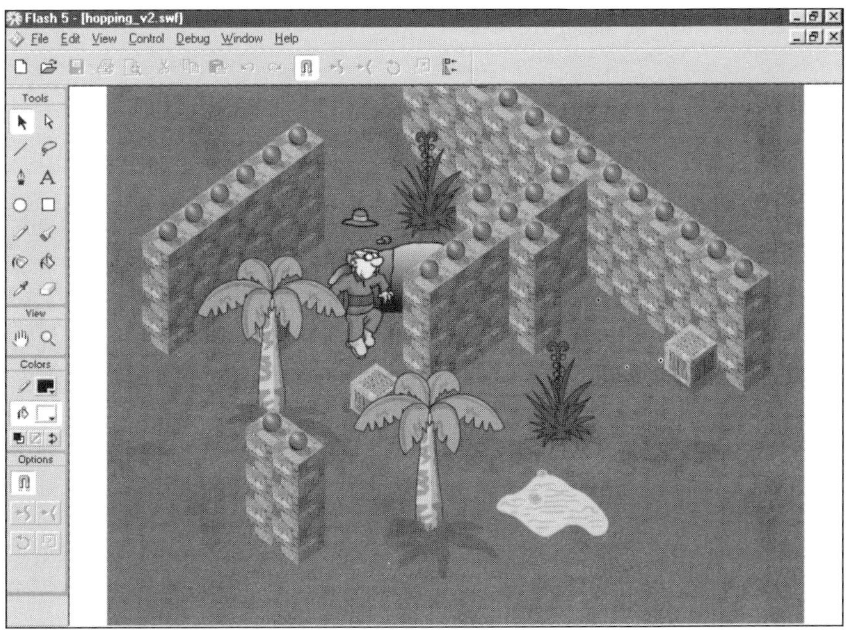

Figure 10.9
Walter in action, collecting bonus objects.

```
// If we're hopping, we can land on a crate
if (item==3 && doinghop==true)
{
// Explode the crate
 _root["object" add gridpos].gotoAndPlay (2);

// Remember old position
    jumpx=waltergridx;
    jumpy=waltergridy;
    jumpmode=walkmode;
    bonusx=destinationgridx;
    bonusy=destinationgridy;
    bonusgrid=gridpos;
    hopback = true;
// Set new Walter position
       waltergridx = destinationgridx;
       waltergridy = destinationgridy;

// Clear crate from object grid
       groundobjects[gridpos]=0;


} else {

        walkmode = 0;
      doinghop=false;
       }
```

In the preceding code, a small section remembers both the old grid position that Walter hopped from, and the position of the crate. We've added this code, because in each crate, we want to have a special bonus object, and after the crate has been smashed open, Walter needs to hop back to his original square so we can see this bonus object. So, we need to know the square that Walter came from (so we can make him hop back to the same square), and we need to know the square the crate was stored on, because we need to replace it with the bonus object.

In this section, we also set a variable called **hopback** to **true**. This variable triggers the ActionScript that makes Walter hop back to the original location when the current hop animation has finished. If the variable **doinghop** is **false**, and **hopback** is **true**, we can make Walter hop back to his original square by setting the destination grid square to the variables **jumpx** and **jumpy** that we defined in the code above. In addition to this, we need to make Walter hop in the opposite direction—so, if he originally hopped right, we need to make him hop left, and if he originally hopped down, we need to make him hop up, and so on. The following code does this:

```
// Hopback if Walter jumps on a crate
if (doinghop==false && hopback==true) {
 bonus=true;
        depth = true;
// Set destination
        destinationgridy = jumpy;
        destinationgridx = jumpx;
// Start hop…
        starthop = true;
// Make Walter face the opposite direction
if (jumpmode==6) {
walkmode=7;
}
if (jumpmode==7) {
walkmode=6;
}
if (jumpmode==8) {
walkmode=9;
}
if (jumpmode==9) {
walkmode=8;
}
// Set hopback to false because we've finished.
        hopback=false;
}
```

Exposing the Bonus Objects and Adding a New Layer

After Walter has hopped back to his original square, we want to make the bonus object appear in place of the crate. To do this, we need to add support for these bonus objects. At the moment, when we set up our game, we can define the position of objects such as crates, bricks, palm trees, and so on, but we have no way of defining an object that is placed *inside* one of these objects.

We can do this in numerous ways, but we've decided to continue with our existing grid system and add another layer, called **bonusobjects**, to our grid. These bonus objects will not be drawn on screen at the beginning of the game like the rest of the grid layers are, but they will be referred to when Walter has smashed open a crate. As with our other grid layers, we will initially define the new layer as a string of numbers, and then we will convert it to an array to make the programming side easier.

In our current demo, we have placed three crates on the screen. The items in our bonus grid should match the position of these crates—therefore, if a crate is at position 12 across and 3 down (or, at grid position 37), your bonus grid should have a bonus item defined at that same position. Our adventure game will have 10 bonus items (numbers 0 to 9), and they are as follows:

- 0=Anti-poison
- 1=bomb
- 2=canteen
- 3=heart
- 4=key
- 5=map1
- 6=map2
- 7=map3
- 8=map4
- 9=trophy

We will use these numbers to define the bonus items in our grid. So, if you wanted the crate at grid position 37 to contain a key, you should place a 4 in the bonus grid layer at grid position 37. Here's an example of a bonus grid:

```
0000000000000
0000000000000
0000000000030
0000000000000
0000000000000
0000000000000
0000000000000
0000000000000
0000000000000
0050009000000
0000000000000
0000000000000
0000000000000
0000000000000
0000000000000
```

In ActionScript, the code will look like this:

```
Tempbonus = "0000000000000000000000000000000000000300000000
0000000000000000000000000000000000000000000000000000000000
0000000000000000500090000000000000000000000000000000000000
0000000000000000000000000000000000";
```

As before, we need to convert this long string into an array. Below is the code that does this, and we've highlighted the code that has been added to include the new bonus grid:

```
// Convert to array
groundobjects = new Array();
baseobjects = new Array();
skyobjects = new Array();
bonusobjects = new Array();
for (i=0; i<gridsize; i++) {
 groundobjects[i] = tempobjects.substr(i, 1);
 baseobjects[i] = tempbaseobjects.substr(i, 1);
 skyobjects[i] = tempskyobjects.substr(i, 1);
 bonusobjects[i] = tempbonus.substr(i, 1);
}
```

Now, that we've defined the bonus objects, we can use them in the game. We've created a long movie clip that contains all our bonus-object animations; these will be exported from our library as **itemb**. In this movie clip, object 0 is stored in Frame 2, object 1 is stored in Frame 12, object 2 is stored in Frame 22, and so on. To display the bonus object, we need to place our **itemb** animation in place of the crate, and move the animation to the correct frame. As soon as Walter has finished hopping, we need to make the bonus object appear where the crate used to be. To do this, we use the following code:

```
if (bonus==true) {
// Replace crate with bonus object in the groundobjects array
 groundobjects[bonusgrid]="b";
// Set x,y co-ordinates to the position of the original crate
 x=bonusx;
 y=bonusy;
// Calculate the plot position
 plotx = plotxoffset+(x*plotxsize)-(y*plotxsize);
 ploty = (x*plotysize)+(y*plotysize);
 depthval = bonusgrid;
// Take itemb from the library, which contains
// all of our bonus objects
 attachMovie("itemb", "object" add depthval, depthval+groundlevel);
// Position the bonus object to the plotx, ploty co-ordinates
 _root["object" add depthval]._x = plotx;
 _root["object" add depthval]._y = ploty;
// Read the bonus grid to find out which item we need to display
 bonusitem=bonusobjects[bonusgrid];
```

```
// Go to the correct frame in the animation to display the bonus
 object
 _root["object" add depthval].gotoAndPlay ( (bonusitem*10)+2 );
bonus=false;
}
```

That's it. You can try out a demonstration of this in the file on the CD-ROM called *hopping_v2*.

Picking Up Objects

In the previous section, we introduced bonus objects that Walter could find by smashing open the crates, which are strewn around each layer. The next stage of game development is for Walter to be able to interact with these objects and pick them up.

In the final game, he'll be able to pick up bonus items such as extra lives, canteens, keys, map pieces, and so on. To keep track of these objects, we are going to have a scoreboard displayed at the top of the screen, which will show the current score, and how many of each object Walter has managed to collect. The scoreboard will contain some dynamic text fields so that we can update the scores using ActionScript. The names of these dynamic text fields are **score, lives, keys, bombs, antipoison**, and **map**. The scoreboard has been set to export from the library with the identifier of **scoreboard.** You can see the scoreboard and how it's been set to export from the library in Figure 10.10. We can position our scoreboard on the screen by using the following code:

```
attachMovie("scoreboard", "score", 9999);
score._x=320;
score._y=20;
```

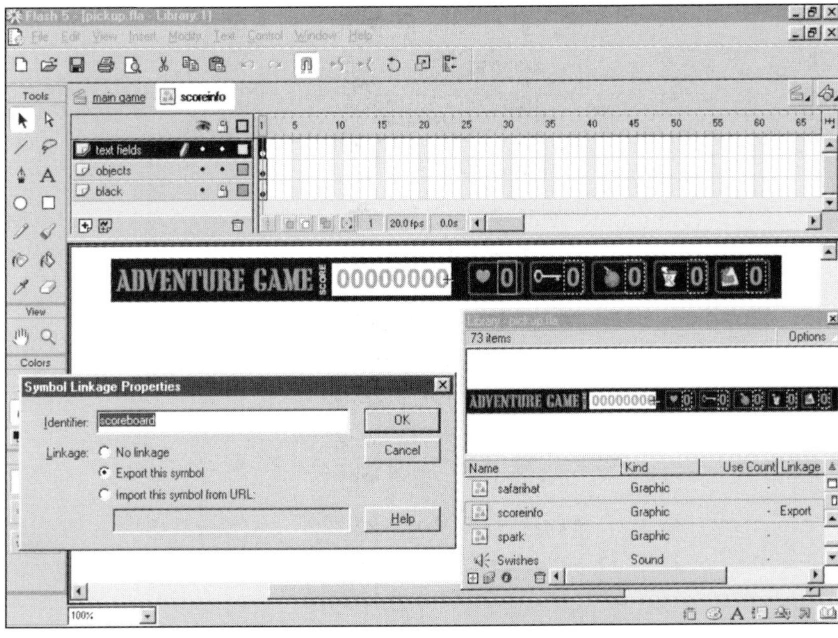

Figure 10.10
The scoreboard and its linkage to data.

Notice that we've given the scoreboard a high depth value of **9999** to ensure that it always remains on top of any in-game graphics.

Because the scoreboard has been displayed on screen, we can now add the code required to pick up our bonus objects. As with many of the previous features, we will add this code to our simple collision-detection section that checks Walter's destination square. Normally, we just check whether the destination square contains a 0 (that is, to see whether it is empty), but we can modify this action to specifically check for our bonus objects. If the destination square contains a "b" character, the square contains a bonus object. We then consult the bonus grid array to see which type of bonus object it is—this array will give a value from 0 to 9, depending upon the object located at that particular grid position. As a quick reminder, the available bonus objects are numbered as follows:

- 0=Anti-poison
- 1=bomb
- 2=canteen
- 3=heart
- 4=key
- 5=map1
- 6=map2
- 7=map3
- 8=map4
- 9=trophy

In most cases, when we try to pick up one of these objects, the result will be that we increment the value shown on the scoreboard. When you are incrementing dynamic text fields, using the **number** command, which will convert a string value to a numerical value, is advisable. By default, values in dynamic text fields are string values. If your dynamic text field called **lives** contains **1**, and you use ActionScript to increment this value, all that will happen is that the **lives** field will become **11**—that is, it has added a string value of **1** to the field. When we increment these text fields, we want a value of **1** to be changed to a value of **2**, and we do this by using the **number** command to convert the string to a number. The correct ActionScript to do this is shown below:

```
lives=number(lives)+1;
```

In our game, the dynamic text fields are stored in a movie clip called **score**, so we have to prefix our variable names with this movie-clip name. When we've updated the scoreboard, we then have to remove the object from the **groundobjects** array to indicate that we've picked up the object, and it's no longer available. We then must remove the movie clip from the screen so it is no longer visible. Finally, we set the variable **item** to **0** so that our collision-detection routine knows that the square is now empty, and Walter can move onto that grid position. Here's the code to handle this process:

```
// Did we get a bonus object?
if (item == "b") {
// Which type of bonus object?
bonusitem=bonusobjects[gridpos];

if ( bonusitem == 0 ){
 // Antipoison
 score.antipoison=number(score.antipoison)+1;
}

if ( bonusitem == 1 ){
 // Bomb
 score.bombs=number(score.bombs)+1;
}

if ( bonusitem == 2 ){
 // Canteen
 score.score=number(score.score)+canteenval;
}

if ( bonusitem == 3 ){
 // Heart
 score.lives=number(score.lives)+1;
}

if ( bonusitem == 4 ){
 // Key
 score.keys=number(score.keys)+1;
}

if ( bonusitem >= 5 && bonusitem<=8 ){
 // One of the map parts
 score.map=number(score.map)+1;;
}

// Now we've picked the object up, let's
// clear that grid position in our array
groundobjects[gridpos]="0";
// now delete the object from the screen
removeMovieClip ("object" add gridpos);

// Set item=0 so that Walter can move onto this square
item=0;
}
```

The code above simply updates the scoreboard to show that we have collected a bonus object. But these bonus objects do have a purpose in the game, so we

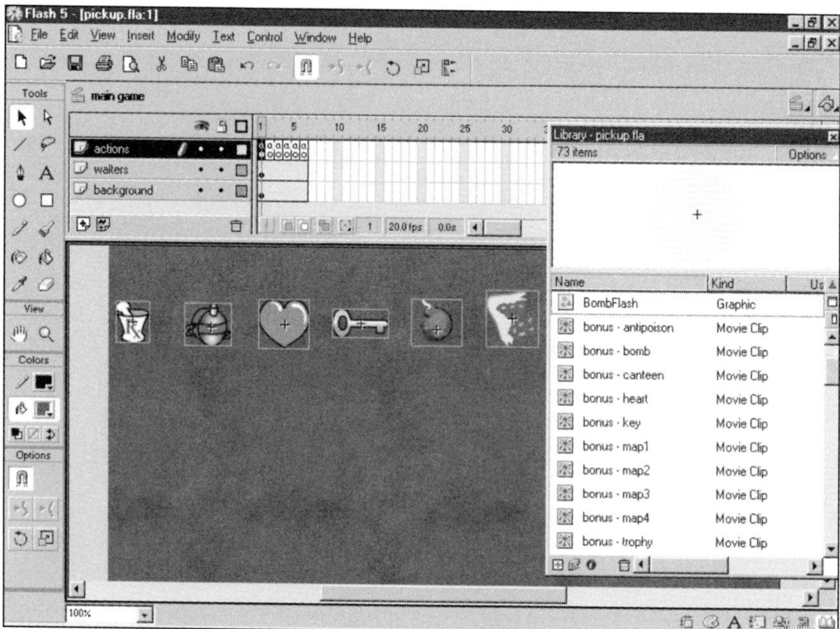

Figure 10.11
The bonus objects.

need to write some additional code to make use of them. You can see all of the bonus objects in Figure 10.11.

Let's take a close look at each object, in turn, to see what purpose each has in the game.

The Anti-Poison Object—Protection from the Bush

The anti-poison item protects Walter from the poisonous berries on our dangerous bush. If Walter touches the bush and doesn't have the anti-poison item, he will die...but if he does have it, he will be safe, but he'll use up one of the anti-poison objects every time he touches the bush.

Earlier in this chapter, when we discussed simple collision detection, we added the following code to detect when Walter touches the dangerous bush:

```
// Did we hit the bush??
if (item == 2) {
 dangerbush = true;
} else {
 dangerbush = false;
}
```

We just need to add an additional check to see whether the variable **score.antipoison** is greater than **0**. If it is, then Walter has the anti-poison object, and the bush will not kill him. We then have to reduce the **score.antipoison** variable by one, to indicate that he's used up one of his bonus objects, and we then set the **dangerbush** variable to **false**. Here's the code:

```
// Did we hit the bush??
if (item == 2) {
 if (Number(score.antipoison)>0) {
 score.antipoison = Number(score.antipoison)-1;
 dangerbush = false;
} else {
 dangerbush = true;
}
} else {
dangerbush = false;
}
```

The Canteen Object—Walter's Energy Supply

The canteen object gives Walter some valuable water, and replenishes some of his lost energy. The score in the game is linked to Walter's energy rating, and as the game progresses, this value will be constantly decreasing. When this energy value reaches **0**, Walter loses a life, and when he loses all of his extra lives, the game's over.

In the code shown earlier, when the canteen was picked up, we added the variable **canteenval** to the current score. This variable is set at the beginning of the game (we've used a value of **1,000**), and it can be varied to suit your own needs. A higher value will make the game easier, and a lower value will make the game harder. We've already added the code that increases the score when Walter picks up a canteen; we now need to add the code that sets the initial score value, and the code that decreases that value during the game. To set the initial value, we simply add the following code at the beginning of our game:

```
startscore=10000;
score.score=startscore;
```

We've set the value to **10,000**, but again, you can change this to suit your own needs. As before, a higher value will make the game easier, and a lower value will make the game harder. In addition, we want to set a variable that dictates how quickly Walter's energy decreases as you are playing the game. This variable will be called **energyspeed**, and we will be using it in the main program loop of our game by simply decreasing the current score by this variable. For now, we will use an **energyspeed** of **5**, meaning that, in every program loop, the score will be reduced by five points. After we've decreased the score, we need to do a check to see whether the score is less than or equal to **0**. If it is, Walter has died. Here's the code:

```
// Decrease the score...
score.score=number(score.score)-energyspeed;
if (number(score.score)<=0) {
dead=true;
}
```

You must place this code *before* the complex collision code, which detects whether or not Walter has died. If you don't do this, the correct "dead" animation will not be shown.

The Heart Object—An Extra Life

The heart object will give Walter an extra life. An extra life simply means that you'll be able to continue playing the game after Walter has died. In this adventure game, we'll be including *lots* of extra lives, because the game is full of traps that try to kill our friend Walter. Already, we've introduced four ways that Walter can be killed (dangerous bush, bottomless pit, quicksand, and running out of energy), and before the game is completed, we'll have several other ways, too.

When the game starts, we want to give Walter some extra lives—otherwise, if he makes one single mistake, the game will be over, and we don't think that's very fair. We've decided to give Walter three lives, and you can change this number if you want to. Again, this value is easy to implement, and it works in the same way as the score we mentioned in the previous section. At the beginning of the game, just add the following code:

```
score.lives=3;
```

When Walter dies, we'll obviously need to decrease this number and, if Walter doesn't have any extra lives remaining, the result is the end of the game. At the end of our movie, we already have a section of code that runs when Walter dies (Frame 6 in our *demonstration* file), so we just have to add our code to this section. Here it is:

```
lives=number(score.lives);
if (lives>0) {
 score.lives=number(lives)-1
} else {
 gameover=true;
}
score.score=startscore;
```

When Walter dies, we also reset the score (or energy rating) to its initial value. Now, when Walter dies, the game will just go back to Frame 1 and restart. In the final version, we'll check to see whether the **gameover** variable is **true**; if it is, we'll show a game-ending sequence.

At this stage, we need to introduce the idea of different scenes in your game. In previous sections, our demonstration has used only one scene, but from this point onward, we are going to use two scenes. In **scene1** (which we have called **setup**), we will initialize the game variables, such as number of lives, the score, and so on, and in **scene2** (called **main game**), we'll have all the other code, which runs the game. When Walter dies, we can restart the game by going back to Frame 1 in the current scene, without resetting all the scores, lives, etc., that are now defined in the previous scene.

The Key Object—Opening Locked Doors

We will use the key object to open the locked doors in the game. We implement this action in the same way that we've implemented things such as picking up the bonus objects and detecting the dangerous bush. In our simple collision-detection section, we'll add a specific check for the locked door. In this section, the value of the variable **item** contains the item number of the object in the destination square. The locked door has a value of 4, so we need to check whether **item** equals **4**. If it does, we need to check whether we are carrying any keys. If we're not, nothing happens.

If you are carrying a key, we simply tell the door object to **gotoAndPlay** Frame 2, which will show an animation of the door opening. In addition, we need to remove the door from our **groundobjects** array. Otherwise, our collision detection will still believe that a door is in the way and won't allow Walter to walk to that grid location. We remove the door object by setting the current grid position in the **groundobjects** array to **0**. If you remember, our door graphic is larger than one grid square, so we also must clear the squares to the left and right of this grid position. Here's the code that does all of this:

```
// Is it a locked door?
if (item == 4) {
// Check to see if we have a key
 if (number(score.keys)>0) {
// Show the opening door animation
  _root["object" add gridpos].gotoAndPlay(2);
// Take away one of our keys
 score.keys=number(score.keys)-1;
// Clear the ground objects array to remove the door
 groundobjects[gridpos]=0;
 groundobjects[gridpos+1]=0;
 groundobjects[gridpos-1]=0;
}
}
```

The Bomb Object—A Tool to Destroy the Dangerous Bush

The bomb is one of the most interesting bonus objects in the game. When you've collected a bomb, you can place it at any empty position on the screen, and detonate it—but don't stand too close, or you'll blow Walter up. We are going to program the game so that the bomb can explode a dangerous bush (or bushes) if it is placed next to them. This change will add an important element to the game, because it will let us hide items behind a bush, and the player will need to find a bomb and detonate it in the correct place to destroy the bush.

Assign Easy-to-Remember Keyboard Controls

When you're adding keyboard controls to a game, consider how easy the controls will be for players to use and remember. Don't overcomplicate the game by adding lots of keyboard controls.

To place and detonate the bomb, we are going to add another keyboard control. We think that the "b" key is ideal for this because it is near the spacebar, which we're already using, and it's easy to remember (b for bomb).

So, the first piece of code we need to add to the game is the keyboard control that we've just spoken about. Flash uses keycodes to detect keypresses, and you can find a list of these keycodes in Appendix 2 of the Flash user manual. We will use the "b" key, which has a keycode of 66. When the player presses the "b" key, the first thing we need the program to do is to check whether Walter is carrying any bombs—if he isn't, nothing happens. When a bomb is placed, it will be placed immediately in front of Walter, so the code will need to check which way he is facing when the bomb key is pressed. By checking which way Walter is facing, we can calculate the destination grid position of the bomb.

Our game is based on a grid that is 13 squares wide and 15 squares high, and the next thing we need to check is that the bomb will be placed inside this grid. If Walter is standing at the very top of the grid and facing the top of the screen, he will not be allowed to place a bomb, because that bomb would be located outside of our grid.

After we've checked that the destination square for the bomb lies within our grid, we need to check whether an object already exists at that position. If an object is already there, Walter cannot place his bomb in that position. If that square is empty, he can place the bomb. We position the bomb on screen, reduce the **bombs** variable on the scoreboard, and store the bomb position in the variables **bombx**, **bomby**, and **bombgrid**. We need to store these positions because we'll need them later on in the program when the bomb has exploded, and we're checking whether Walter is near enough to the explosion to be killed.

Here's the code that does all of the above:

```
if (Key.isDown(66)) {
// B key pressed so let's place a bomb
 bombs = Number(score.bombs);
// Do we have any bombs?
if (bombs>0) {
// Calculate destination grid position for bomb
 if (facing == 1) {
 destinationgridx = waltergridx+1;
 destinationgridy = waltergridy;
}
if (facing == 2) {
 destinationgridx = waltergridx-1;
 destinationgridy = waltergridy;
}
if (facing == 3) {
 destinationgridx = waltergridx;
 destinationgridy = waltergridy-1;
}
if (facing == 4) {
```

```
 destinationgridx = waltergridx;
 destinationgridy = waltergridy+1;
}
// This is the gridpos
 gridpos = (destinationgridy-1)*gridx+(destinationgridx-1);
// Check if it's a valid grid position
 if (destinationgridx<=gridx && destinationgridx>=0
&& destinationgridy<=gridy && destinationgridy>=0) {
// Check if there's already an item at this position
 item = groundobjects[gridpos];
if (item == 0) {
// All the checks are finished. Let's place the bomb
 x = destinationgridx;
 y = destinationgridy;
 plotx = plotxoffset+(x*plotxsize)-(y*plotxsize);
 ploty = (x*plotysize)+(y*plotysize);
 depthval = gridpos;
 attachMovie("bomb", "object" add depthval, depthval+groundlevel);
 _root["object" add depthval]._x = plotx;
 _root["object" add depthval]._y = ploty;
 _root["object" add depthval].gotoAndPlay(2);
// Reduce bombs value on scoreboard
 score.bombs = Number(bombs)-1;
// Remember the bomb location
 bombx = x;
 bomby = y;
 bombgrid = gridpos;
}
}
}
}
```

The above ActionScript will place a bomb on the screen and detonate it. Now, we need to add some code to check whether Walter, or a bush was near enough to the explosion to be killed. First, in the bomb animation, we set a variable called **boom** to **true** when the explosion occurs. When the variable **boom** equals **true**, we know that the bomb has just exploded, so we check to see whether the variables **bombx** and **bomby** are within one square of Walter's current position (which is stored in variables **waltergridx** and **waltergridy**). If Walter is within one square of the bomb explosion, he will be killed. The code looks like this:

```
if (waltergridx == bombx || waltergridx == bombx-1
|| waltergridx == bombx+1) {
if (waltergridy == bomby || waltergridy == bomby-1
|| waltergridy == bomby+1) {
// Walter is killed!
 dead = true;
 normaldie = true;
}
}
```

The variables **dead** and **normaldie** are set to **true** to indicate that Walter has been killed, and that we need to display the normal dying animation.

When the bomb explodes, we also want to check whether a dangerous bush is immediately above, below, to the left, or to the right of the explosion (effectively, we are checking the four directions N, S, E, and W). If a bush is NE, SE, SW, or NW from the bomb explosion, it will *not* be destroyed. To check this, all we have to do is check to see whether the grid positions around the bomb explosion contain the dangerous bush (**item** value of **2**). If it does, we simply remove that particular movie clip, and set that grid position in the **groundobjects** array to **0**. Here's the code that checks the grid position immediately above the bomb explosion:

```
// Check for surrounding dangerous bushes
  item = groundobjects[bombgrid-gridx];
if (item == 2) {
// Found one. Let's destroy it!
// Clear grid
  groundobjects[bombgrid-gridx] = 0;
// Remove bush
  removeMovieClip ("object" add (bombgrid-gridx));
}
```

We'll repeat this code for each direction. At the end of this section, remember to set the variable **boom** to **false**; otherwise, the game will constantly be checking for an explosion.

The Map Objects—Collect Them to Win

Collecting the map objects is the main purpose of the game. The final game will contain four levels, and each level will contain one part of the map. To complete the game, Walter must collect all the map parts and then make his way to the end of the level. All we need to do is check to see whether Walter has all four-map pieces. If he does, he's completed the game. We won't implement this action right at the moment, because we haven't built all of the levels yet, but we will return to this later in the chapter.

Locations, Locations, Locations

Our game is nearly fully functional—Walter can walk, hop, smash crates, and collect objects. The next thing we need to do is to create extra locations or rooms for Walter to explore. Currently, we define all the objects and their locations at the beginning of our movie in a series of string variables called **tempskyobjects, tempobjects, tempbaseobjects**, and **tempbonus**. To add more rooms for our game, we need to define this set of variables for *each* room in our game. So, if we had two rooms, we would use the variables **tempskyobjects1**, **tempobjects1**, **tempbaseobjects1**, and **tempbonus1** to define the objects for

room 1; and for **room 2** we would have the variables **tempskyobjects2**, **tempobjects2**, **tempbaseobjects2**, and **tempbonus2**. We then use an additional variable called **room** to define the room that Walter is *currently* located in. Here's a quick example:

```
// Set up room 1
tempobjects1 = "0000000000000011111111111100000010000 3000
20001000000000000110000000000001000000100000111z4z11000001
0000001000000000000103000300000010000000000000100050000050
000000000000000000000000000000000000110000";
tempbaseobjects1 = "0000000000000000000000000000000000000000
0000000000000000000000000000006000000000000000000000000000
0000000000000000000000700000000000000000000000000000009000
009000000000000000000000000000000000000000000";
tempskyobjects1 = "00000000000000000000000000000000000000000
0000000000000000000000000000000000000000000000000000000000
000000000000000000000000000000000000000000000000000a0000
0a000000000000000000000000000000000000000000";
tempbonus1 =    "00000000000000000000000000000000000000000
0000000000000000000000000000000000000000000000000000000000
0000000000000000000000001000400000000000000000000000000000
000000000000000000000000000000000000000000";

// Set up room 2
tempskyobjects2 = "000000000000000000000000000a0000000000
0000000000a00000000000000000000000000000000000000000000000
0000000000000000000000000000000000000000000a0000a00000
00000000000000000000000000000000000000000000";
tempobjects2 = "1111110001111000000000000000500000000000000
0000000500000000000000000000000000000300000000000000000
0000000000000000000000000000000000000000005000050000000000
00000000000000000000000000022222200002222";
tempbaseobjects2 = "000000000000000000000000000009000000000
0000000000090000000000000000000000000000000000000000000000
000d00060000000000000000700000000000000000000000090000900000
0000000000000000000000000000000000000000000000";
tempbonus2 = "0000000000000000000000000000000000000000000
0000000000000000000000000000000000000000050000000000000000
0000000000000000000000000000000000000000000000000000000000
0000000000000000000000000000000000000000";

// Define the current room
room=2;

// Set up current room
tempobjects = eval("tempobjects" add room);
tempbaseobjects = eval("tempbaseobjects" add room);
tempskyobjects = eval("tempskyobjects" add room);
tempbonus= eval("tempbonus" add room);
```

We've used a new command here called **eval**, which evaluates an expression to define the variable name of a string. This routine sounds complicated, but it's really quite easy. Let's look at the following command:

```
tempbaseobjects = eval("tempbaseobjects" add room);
```

This command is saying that the variable **tempbaseobjects** should equal the **evaluation of "tempbaseobjects"**, plus the variable called **room.** All this means is that, if **room** equals **1**, the **tempbaseobjects** will equal **tempbaseobjects1**—if **room** equals **2**, the **tempbaseobjects** will equal **tempbaseobjects2**, and so on. So, all the code is doing is adding the value of the variable **room** to our variable name of **tempbaseobjects**. You can try this new code in the demo called *locations_v1* on the CD-ROM, and you'll notice that if you change the **room** variable, Walter will be placed in a new location.

Moving between Locations

What we did above should work fine, but Walter is still "trapped" in a room, and we want him to be able to walk from one room to another. To enable this movement, we need to define the exits in each room. Each room in our game will have four exits (north, east, south, and west), and in each case, we need to define which room Walter will go to if he uses one of these exits. We will use the variables **exitn**, **exite**, **exitw**, and **exits** to define these four exits. So, if we are in Room 1 and we want Walter to move to Room 2 when he walks off the left side (or the west side) of the screen, we simply set variable **exitw1** to equal **2**. When we're in Room 2, if we want the east exit to take us back to Room 1, we set the variable **exite2** equal to **1**. If you don't want Walter to be able to exit from a particular direction, simply set the appropriate exit variable to **0**.

In our game, we already check to see whether Walter has attempted to walk off the edge of our game screen—if he does, we simply stop him from walking. We now need to modify this code, so that the game changes the current room to the new room defined in our exit variable. In addition to this, when Walter walks from one room to another, we will need to modify his position on the screen. For example, if he walks off the left side of the screen, he should appear on the *right* side of the screen when the new location is shown—as if he's just arrived at that location. Here's the code you need to check whether Walter has walked to the left (or west) side of the screen:

```
// Check destination - This check already exists
if (destinationgridx>gridx or destinationgridx<=0
or destinationgridy>gridy or destinationgridy<=0) {
// New code to calculate the new room
if (destinationgridx==0) {
// Walter has walked off the left (or west) side.
```

```
// In the new room, we want Walter to appear from the east side
  (as if
// he has just walked in). So we set tempx to the gridx variable.
tempx = gridx;
tempy=waltergridy;
// Newroom equals our exit west variable
newroom=exitw;
// Set changeroom variable to true
changeroom=true;
}
if (newroom==0) {
// Check to see if the exit variable is 0. If it is, then
// we don't change to a new room.
changeroom=false;
}
else {
// We're changing rooms, so set Walter to the new position and
change
// the current room number.
waltergridx=tempx;
waltergridy=tempy;
oldroom=room;
room=newroom;
}
 walkmode = 0;
 starthop = false;
 doinghop = false;
}
```

The above code works for when Walter walks off the west side of the screen; we will also need to add code to deal with the other three directions. Once we've done this, we need to make our game go back to the first frame of the movie (if the **changeroom** variable equals **true**). Frame 3 of our game is set to keep looping if Walter is still alive, so we can add a small change to this code. Here it is:

```
if (dead != true) {
if (changeroom == true) {
 gotoAndPlay (1);
} else {
 gotoAndPlay ("gameloop");
}
}
```

As you start using new locations in your game, you'll soon come across another problem. When Walter dies, the game restarts with Walter in a set location. But, if this set location contains an object such as a bottomless pit or quicksand, Walter will instantly die again. So, for each new room that we define, we must define a restart position for when Walter dies. This restart position needs to be somewhere that is safe, and a place that will not instantly kill him. We'll be using the variables **restartx** and **restarty** to store this restart position. As an example, if Walter is in Room 19, and you would like the restart position to be grid position 12,1, you would use the following code:

```
restartx19=12;
restarty19=1;
```

Saving a Player's Changes, Including Room States

One important aspect of an adventure game is to save any changes that the player makes during the game. For example, imagine that you've created a room that contains a crate holding a bonus, extra life. If Walter smashes open that crate and collects the bonus object, the game needs to remember that the crate has been smashed open, and the object has been collected. Otherwise, if Walter leaves the room and returns later in the game, he'll be able to collect that bonus object again (and again, and again).

If you remember, when we set up each room in our game, we created a string variable that defines the location of each object in the room. During the game, this string variable is copied into an array and, when items are moved, collected, and so on, the changes are made to this new array. To save the state of each room in our game when Walter moves from one room to another, we need to copy this array back into our original string variable. Here's the code:

```
if (dead != true) {
if (changeroom == true) {
// Save room positions
 temp = "";
for (i=0; i<gridsize; i++) {
 temp = temp add groundobjects[i];
}
 _root["tempobjects" add oldroom] = temp;
 gotoAndPlay (1);
} else {
 gotoAndPlay ("gameloop");
}
}
```

Defining New Locations

Using our string variables, we can manually create the locations, but doing so is a bit tricky, and it's time consuming. To make life a lot easier for you, we have created a Level Editor that you can use to create your own locations for the Walter adventure game. We'll quickly describe how the Level Editor works, and then you can get on with creating your own playable locations.

When you first run the Level Editor program, you'll be presented with a 13×15 grid, and a series of icons down the left side of the page; you can see these in Figure 10.12. This first screen represents the **groundobjects** layer in your

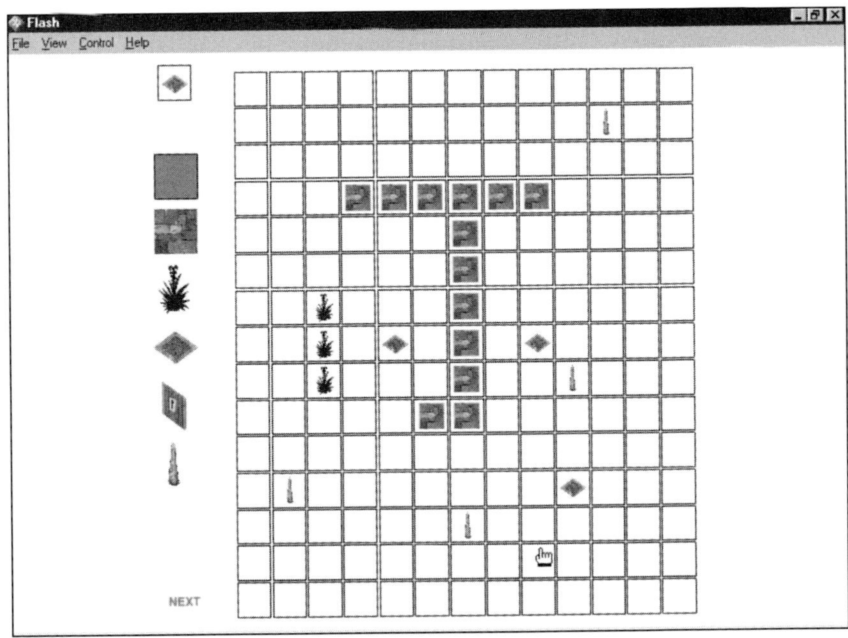

Figure 10.12
The Level Editor.

game. You can select one of the objects (grass, wall, bush, crate, door, or palm tree) by simply clicking on one of the icons down the left side of the screen. When an object is selected, it will appear in the selection box in the top-left corner. Once an object has been selected, you can then click on the grid squares to place the object at your chosen location. To remove an object, simply choose the grass icon (the green square), and click on the object you wish to remove from the grid. Using this grid system, you can quickly define an object's location for the game.

When you're happy with the placement of all your objects, click the Next button at the bottom of the screen. You'll then be presented with two text boxes that contain the exact code required to define the **skyobjects** and **groundobjects** layers in your game. Simply highlight the text in each box, copy the text, and paste it into your game.

When you have done this, click the Next button again, and you'll see your grid system reappear, but this time, you can place the base objects (such as quicksand, bottomless pits, and rivers) into your grid. The process works in exactly the same way as it did on the previous screen. Simply select the icon on the left-hand side, and then click on the grid to place the object. When you place the quicksand or bottomless pit, the icon will cover several grid squares to give you an indication of how large the object will be in your final game—this is only an indicator, and it is not 100 percent accurate. When you've finished placing your objects, click on the Next button again, and you'll see the code for the **baseobjects** layer. Again, simply highlight, copy, and paste the code directly into your game.

When you've done this, click Next again, and you'll be able to place your bonus objects. If you placed any crates in your original screen layout, these crate positions will be visible on the grid—you should *replace* these crates with your bonus objects. Placing bonus objects in other grid positions will have no effect. When you've placed your bonus objects, use the Next button again, and you'll be given the necessary code for the **bonusobjects** layer. Simply copy and paste this code into your game.

When you're creating your own locations, don't go mad and place hundreds of objects in them, because doing so will have a negative effect on the speed of the game. Also, when you're placing objects such as dangerous bushes, quicksand, and bottomless pits (all items that kill Walter), be aware that placing them right at the edge of the grid might mean that Walter will be instantly killed when he enters a new location—because he will walk straight into one of these killer objects without knowing it's there. If you're creating a game with a high difficulty level, you might like that idea. If you want to create a harder game, remember that you can hide objects behind the brick walls or palm trees.

Adding River and Bridge Objects

In the Level Editor, you'll notice that you have the capability to add rivers to the game. We've added this option to give the locations in our game a sort of boundary, to keep Walter within our map area. To implement the use of rivers in our game, we need to add more collision detection. The river object works in exactly the same way as our bottomless pits and quicksand, so it's stored on our **baseobjects** grid layer. Immediately below the river graphic, we have a **riverbase** object, which we use for collision detection. In later levels of the game, we'll include a bridge object that Walter can use to cross the river, so we'll also explain how to implement that item. The bridge will initially be invisible, and will appear only when Walter stands in the correct position.

First, in the same section in which we calculate collisions with the bottomless pit, and with quicksand, we need to add the following code to detect a collision with the bridge and the river:

```
river = _root["base" add i].riverbase.hitTest(walterx, waltery,
  true);
bridge = _root["base" add i].bridgebase.hitTest(walterx, waltery,
  true);
```

After this code, the variables **river** and **bridge** will be set to **true** if Walter is standing on one of them. If Walter is standing on the bridge, we need the code to detect whether the bridge is currently visible or invisible (if he's standing on the bridge and it's not visible, we need to make the bridge appear). The bridge object is a movie clip, and if it is not currently visible, this movie clip will be on Frame 1. Therefore, we can simply check the current frame of the bridge movie clip to detect whether or not it's visible. If the bridge is not visible, we tell the movie clip to start playing from Frame 2, and the bridge will then appear on the screen. Here's the code:

```
if (bridge==true) {
// Check to see if bridge has been opened
test=_root["base" add i]._currentframe;
if (test==1) {
// The bridge is currently closed so let's open it
_root["base" add i].gotoAndPlay (2);
}
}
```

If the variable **river** is set to **true**, we know that Walter is currently touching the river object. But it's also possible that he's currently standing on the bridge, so, if the **river** variable is true, we need to do a collision check with all the other objects on the **baseobjects** grid layer to see whether Walter is *also* standing on the bridge object. Obviously, if he's currently standing on the bridge, he is allowed to be standing over the river, too. Later in the code, we'll check to see whether **river** equals **true**—if it does, Walter will be killed by the fast-flowing water. So, if this section of code detects that Walter is currently standing on the bridge object, we set the **river** variable to **false**. Here's the code that does this:

```
if (river==true) {
for (ii=1; ii<=baseitems; ii++) {
 bridge = _root["base" add ii].bridgebase
.hitTest(walterx, waltery, true);
if (bridge==true) {
river=false;
}
}
}
```

Defining the Game's Difficulty Levels

Using the Level Editor, we've created a simple level that contains 16 locations. This level will be Level 1 of our final game. You can find this level on the CD-ROM in the file called *game_level1*. We have defined all the locations for this level as variables and have stored them in the main movie. This method is fine for our demonstration, but ultimately, if the game is going to have several levels, storing the data for each level as a separate file that we load into the main game, as we need it, is better. Storing the data this way is simple to do; we just have to put all the text variables that relate to our different locations into a single, ASCII text file. As we've already discussed in Chapter 8, the variables, are separated by the "&" character. Here's a small example, which defines the exit locations and restart variables for Room 18:

```
exitn18=16&exite18=0&exits18=19&exitw18=17&restartx18=12&
 restarty18=1
```

When you're loading variables in this way, you don't need to use quotation marks to represent string variables, and you need to ensure that you remove all unnecessary spaces. For example, the following would *not* work:

```
Test = "Thiswillnotwork"
```

The correct way to format this code is as follows:

```
Test=Thiswillwork
```

To load these variables into your movie, you can use the following command:

```
loadVariablesNum ( "level.txt", 0 );
```

When you are loading variables in this way, you must remember that Flash will treat all the variables as text variables. This situation is much like working with dynamic text variables; therefore, it's a good idea to start using the **number()** command on variables that you *know* should be treated as numerical values. For example, when Walter is killed, and we need to reset his position equal to the variables **restartx** and **restarty**, you should use the following code:

```
waltergridx = number(restartx);
waltergridy = number(restarty);
```

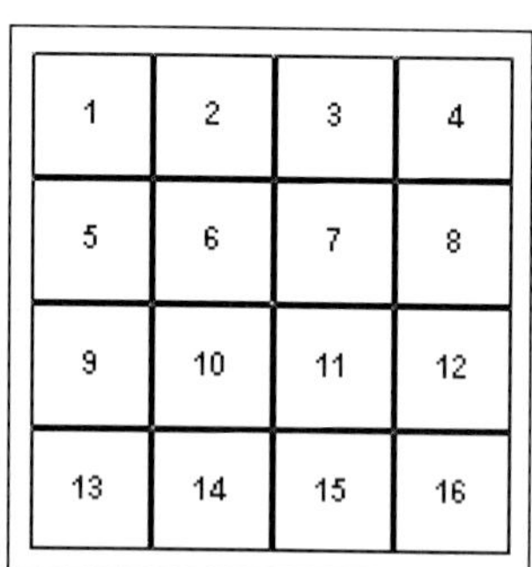

Figure 10.13
Laying out the first level's areas.

Tricks Used in Difficulty Level 2

In Figure 10.13, you can see that our first difficulty level consists of 16 locations in a simple 4×4 grid. Making your first level quite simple (but not too simple), is always a good idea, because doing so will encourage players to keep playing the game. However, in later levels, you'll want to make the game harder, and you'll probably want to avoid the square map area that we've used for the first level.

See Figure 10.14 for an overview of Level 2 of our game. Using this nonsymmetrical layout for our locations makes it harder for the player to remember where each room is, and therefore, makes the game more difficult (which is good).

In addition to the nonsymmetrical layout, we've used other techniques to increase the game's difficulty at this level. We've added an anti-mapping technique; we've hidden dangerous objects; we've added a bridge that wasn't present in the first level (the bridge will help the players, but only if they realize that it's there); and we've added a hidden room. Let's look at these, one at a time.

When you start making levels with a nonsymmetrical layout, you'll find that game players will start drawing maps of each location so that, the next time they play the game, they will know where to go. To make life harder for these people, we've added a simple anti-mapping technique. If you refer to Figure

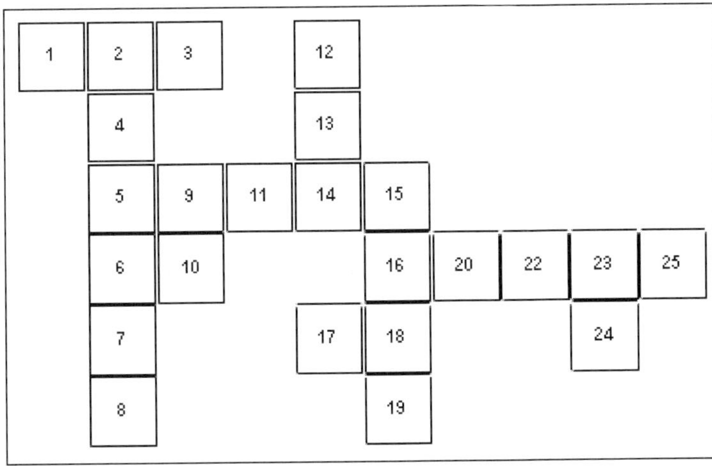

Figure 10.14

A nonsymmetrical layout for our locations will make it harder for the player to remember where each room is.

10.14, and look at Room 15, you won't be surprised to learn that moving west from this location will take you to Room 14 and, if you go north from Room 14, you'll go to Room 13, and so on. However, what happens if you go west from Room 16? According to our diagram, no location exists to the west of Room 16, so you would assume that going west of this room goes nowhere. Well, we've programmed the routine so that, if you go west from Room 16, you'll end up in Room 25, and if you go east from Room 25, you go back to Room 16. We've used this anti-mapping technique in several places (Rooms 16, 6, and 1), and it's something that will undoubtedly confuse people who are trying to make a map of your level.

Another trick we've employed to make the level harder is that we've hidden dangerous objects such as bushes, bottomless pits, and quicksand behind brick walls. The players will occasionally get caught by one of these traps, so they'll have to play the game several times to learn the correct route around the level.

Also, in this level, players can cross the river by using a bridge—however, because a bridge object didn't exist in the first level of the game, the player might take quite awhile to realize he or she can cross the river in this way. We have done this deliberately, and we recommend that you do a similar thing when creating your own game—always save some new features/objects for the later levels.

One final element we've added to this level is a hidden room. Refer to Figure 10.14 again and find Room 24; this is our hidden room. When you know this room exists, you'll be able to find it quite easily, but without the aid of our map, this room is quite difficult to find. Rooms 20, 22, 23, and 25 have a river crossing the south side of them, and it's not immediately obvious that it's possible to walk on the other side of this river. No bridge exists for crossing the river, but you can enter Room 20 on the south side of the river when you're moving east from Room 16.

We've probably added too many difficult elements to this level, but the whole purpose of doing so is to give you some ideas about how to increase the difficulty level in your own games. Try the level for yourself, and see what you think. It's on the CD-ROM, and it's called *game_level2*.

Putting the Levels Together

We've completed the first two levels of our game, and we're now very near to completing the whole game. Currently, each level is played separately, but, now, we want to put all the levels together into one movie, so that when you complete Level 1, you automatically move on to Level 2. We also need to add some programming to handle the end of each level, and the end of the game.

Loading Levels

First, let's look at how we can load each level of the game as it's required. In the previous section, we loaded the level data by using the **loadvariablesNum** command in the first frame of our movie. We need to remove this command and replace it with the following code, which defines the current level (it starts at Level 1), and sets a variable called **endoflevel** to **false**. This variable will be used later in the game to indicate when we've completed any level.

```
level=1;
endoflevel=false;
```

The second frame of our movie will be labeled **loadlevel**, and we will play this part of the movie when we want to load a new level. If we want to use this game on the Internet, loading each level of our game might take several seconds, so the first thing we want to do in this frame is to remove all the current, on-screen objects. If we don't do this, you'll be able to see the last location you visited while the new level is loading. That doesn't really matter, but the game looks better if we remove these old graphics. The code to do so looks like this:

```
// Remove old objects
for (i=0; i<gridsize; i++) {
removeMovieClip ( "base" add i );
removeMovieClip ( "object" add i );
removeMovieClip ( "sky" add i );
}
```

Each level in our game will start in a different room. On Level 1, our start room is Room 7; on Level 2, our start room is Room 15; and on Level 3, our start room is Room 2. Our code needs to define the start locations when we load a new level:

```
// Setup the start room for each level
if (level==1) {
room = 7;
}
```

```
if (level==2) {
room = 15;
}
if (level==3) {
room = 2;
}
```

Resetting Bonus Objects and Walter's Position

Our adventure game will have lots of bonus objects to collect, and we want to make sure that the player cannot take bonus objects from one level to the next. Allowing the player to do so would affect the design of our levels. For example, if your level is set up so that the player must have Walter find two bombs, which he uses to get a key, which, in turn, he uses to open a door and get the map to the next level, what happens if Walter already has a key, which he collected from the previous level? He would be able to bypass most of the level and open the door straight away. So, when the player moves from one level to the next, we want to reset the bombs, keys, and anti-poison bonus objects. Here's the code to do this:

```
// Reset the bonus objects
score.bombs=0;
score.keys=0;
score.antipoison=0;
```

Finally, we need to reset Walter's position and load the next level. Our default position for Walter is grid position 12,12, and we set that by using the following code:

```
waltergridx = 12;
waltergridy = 12;
```

To load our level data, we first set a variable named **loaded** to **false**, and then we use the **loadVariablesNum** command to load the current level:

```
// Load level data...
loaded = false;
loadVariablesNum ("level" add level add ".txt", 0);
```

In each of our level text files, we specify the necessary variables that define all locations and objects in our level. The final variable that we define in each of these level files is **loaded=true**. By having a small program loop that checks the value of the **loaded** variable, we determine when the complete text file has been loaded. If **loaded=false**, the data file has not loaded yet; otherwise, it has been completely loaded, and we can start playing the game. Here's the code that does all of this:

```
if (loaded==false) {
gotoAndPlay (3);
}
```

Level Completed

Now, that we've worked out how to load our levels, we need to modify the original game slightly so that we know when the level has been completed. Each level of our game will end when Walter manages to find one of the map parts. Earlier in this chapter, we added some code that updated the scoreboard whenever Walter collected part of the map, and we can make a small modification to this code to indicate that the level has been completed. Here's the original code, with our addition highlighted:

```
if (bonusitem>=5 && bonusitem<=8) {
// One the map parts
 score.map = Number(score.map)+1;
// Collecting a map means you've completed the level
 endoflevel=true;
}
```

So, all we need to do at this stage is set the **endoflevel** variable to **true**. In Frame 3 of the main game scene, we need to check whether this variable is **true** or **false**, and take the appropriate action. At the moment, our code in Frame 3 looks like this:

```
if (dead != true) {
 if (changeroom == true) {
// Save room positions
 temp = "";
for (i=0; i<gridsize; i++) {
 temp = temp add groundobjects[i];
}
 _root["tempobjects" add oldroom] = temp;
 gotoAndPlay (1);
} else {
 gotoAndPlay ("gameloop");
}
}
```

The part we need to modify is in the **else** part of the **if** statement. At the moment, the routine simply goes back and plays the "**gameloop**" frame. We need to add a check to see whether the level has been completed; if it has, we need to go to a different frame in the movie. Here's the code showing the new **else** part of the statement:

```
else {
        if (endoflevel == false) {
            gotoAndPlay ("gameloop");
        } else {
            gotoAndPlay ("endoflevel");
        }
    }
```

This new code will go to and play a frame called **endoflevel**, so we need to define this frame. We've defined the frame in Frame 10 of the main game scene. All we need to do in this frame is display a "Congratulations" message, and pause the game until the player clicks on the Next Level button. We've created a "Congratulations" message, and set it to export from our library with the name of **levelend**. So, in Frame 10 of our movie, we simply need to display this message in the middle of the screen, and stop the game from playing. Here's the code to do this:

```
attachMovie( "levelend", "endtext", 10001 )
endtext._x=320;
endtext._y=240;
stop ();
```

Notice that we've used a depth value of **10,001** on our attached movie clip. This value is to ensure that the clip appears on top of all the other objects on the screen. This movie clip contains a button that the player clicks on to begin loading the next level. The button has the command**_root.play** (); attached to it, which tells the main Timeline to start playing again.

In the next frame (Frame 11), we have some code that increases the current level number, removes the "Congratulations" movie clip, removes the Walter movie clip, and then goes to the **loadlevel** frame we discussed earlier, which loads the next level of the game. When we increase the level number, we have a small check to see whether the level numbers more than **3**—if it is, we set the level number back to **1**. We've done this, because currently, our game has only three levels. At the end of this chapter, we'll ask you to create your own level, which will be the fourth and final level of our game. When you do create this level, you'll have to modify this part of the code; otherwise, you'll never get to see the fourth level. Here's the code:

```
// Increment level
level += 1;
if (level>3) {
 level = 1;
}
endoflevel = false;
removeMovieClip ( "endtext" );
removeMovieClip ( "walter" );
gotoAndPlay ("setup", "loadlevel");
```

Game Over

The next part of the game, and the code we need to deal with, is what happens when Walter dies, and he doesn't have any extra lives. Currently, the game just continues, but, obviously, we need to change this. We already have most of the code in place for Walter's death, and in Frame 6 of the main game scene, we do check to see whether Walter has any remaining lives. If he hasn't, we set the variable **gameover** equal to **true**. We now need to add some code to make the game display a "Game Over" message if this variable is true. So, at the end of Frame 6, we currently have the following command, which makes the game repeat if Walter dies:

```
gotoAndPlay (1);
```

We need to add to this code, and check to see whether the **gameover** variable is **true**. If it is **true**, we want to go to a different frame, which displays our "Game Over" message.

```
if (gameover==true) {
gotoAndPlay ( "gameover" );
} else {
gotoAndPlay (1);
}
```

This new code will go to and play a frame called **gameover**, so, as we did with our "Level Completed" section, we need to define this frame. We've defined it in Frame 15 of the main game scene. Now, in this frame, we will display a "Game Over" message, and pause the game, until the player clicks on the New Game button. We've created a "Game Over" message and set it to export from our library with the name of **gameover**. This action uses the same code as the "Level Completed" section. Here it is:

```
attachMovie( "gameover", "endtext", 10001 )
endtext._x=320;
endtext._y=240;
stop ();
```

Again, as before, notice that we've used a depth value of **10001** on our attached movie clip to ensure that it appears on top of all the other objects on the screen. This movie clip contains a button that the player clicks on to restart the game. The button has the command **_root.play** (); attached to it, which tells the main Timeline to start playing again. In the next frame (Frame 16), we have some code that removes the "Game Over" message and then restarts our movie from Frame 1. Here's the code:

```
removeMovieClip ( "endtext" );
gotoAndPlay ("setup", 1);
```

The **gameover=false** statement should be in Frame 16 of the main movie. The entire code for Frame 16 should now look like this:

```
gameover=false;
removeMovieClip ("endtext");
gotoAndPlay ("setup", 1);
```

Tidying Up

At this point, our game is 99 percent complete, and we're now at the stage of development where it's a good idea to just sit down and play the game over, and over again, to see whether you can spot any problems. One problem that we've noticed with the game is that, when Walter dies, the room he is in resets itself to its initial state. Now, most of the time, this is not a problem. But, imagine what happens if you're near the end of a level, and Walter's managed to find the key he needs to open the door at the end of the level. But, just as he opens the door, he runs out of energy, and he dies. The room is then reset to its initial state, and the door is now locked again, but Walter lost the key when he used it to open the door. This is a disaster—he now can't finish the level. At the moment, we save the state of the room objects only when Walter moves to a new room. We need to make sure that we do this when Walter dies, as well. In Frame 6 of our main game scene, we reset the variables when Walter has been killed, so we can add the "save room" code to the start of this frame. The code looks like this:

```
// Save room positions
temp = "";
for (i=0; i<gridsize; i++) {
    temp = temp add groundobjects[i];
}
_root["tempobjects" add room] = temp;
```

And that's it. We've now completed our game. You can find the final version, now with three levels of difficulty, on the CD-ROM. The file is called *finalgame*, and we hope that you enjoy playing it. In Figure 10.15, you can see Walter in the final location in Level 3—but how will he get to that final crate?

Figure 10.15
The final objective.

PROJECT Creating Your Own Isometric 3D Environment

For this chapter's project, we would like you to use the supplied Level Editor to create your own level for our adventure game. This will be the fourth, and final level of the game, in which Walter finds the fourth piece of the map, which in turn, will lead him to find the Golden Chalice (the only item that we haven't used in our game so far). How large or small this final level is will be up to you—it's your game. You can finish it in any way you like.

When you've done this, the next stage is to try to modify the game to possibly include some new objects. Maybe including some extra scenery—such as rocks, boulders, and so on—would be good; or, perhaps, you want to add more bonus objects for Walter to find. Also, you can change all the graphics, and make the game appear to be based indoors, rather than outdoors. Replace the grass with a carpet, the trees with desks, and so on; then, you can completely alter the style of the game. When you are 100 percent happy with modifying our game, it's time to put the new techniques you've learned into practice, and start building your own 3D adventure game. We wish you the best of luck. Have fun!

Chapter 11

Collaboration Across the Internet

Interactive games require design, graphics, animations, programming, bug testing, and more bug testing. A person with expertise in all of these areas would be a rare find, indeed. At some point, you'll have to work with at least one other person (and probably several people) to create that top-selling, world-famous game that you've been dreaming about.

By James Robertson and Bill Turner

The Virtual Office

When a game (or, indeed, any kind of product) is being designed in Flash, several people often need to work together on the project. A group of people, rather than an individual, have created most of the top Flash productions you see on the Internet. And, on most occasions, these people work together at the same company, in the same office, and maybe even at the same desk. But that arrangement's obvious, right? You have to do it that way, don't you? Well, the short answer is "No, you don't."

James Robertson (of EDesign, in the U.K.) and I, Bill Turner (of Turnertoons, in the U.S.), have worked together on several Flash projects (including this book you're reading right now), and yet we don't work for the same company. We don't live in the same city, or the same country, or even on the same continent, and we have never even met each other in person. In addition, we not only work in different time zones, but we also use different computer systems—one company is PC-based, and the other is Mac-based. Yet, despite all of these differences, we are able to work together on Macromedia Flash projects. We are a good example of how companies can work in a virtual office. The Internet has become our boardroom, where we share ideas, discuss projects, and plan our next business ideas. To work together in this way, however, we have had to adopt slightly different working practices, which we'll discuss in this chapter.

Communication Is Key

When you're sitting in an office (the brick and mortar kind), communicating ideas can be as simple as leaning over to your fellow Flash designer and saying, "Hey, what do you think about this?" Communication is often easier in person, simply because of the convenience. If you want to bounce an idea off someone, you can just go to the designer or programmer at the next desk.

Communication that's strictly oral has one drawback, though: the potential for miscommunication. We all know that, in the traditional office setting, communication among participants—particularly oral communication—can become confused and muddled, just as in the game in which you start with a statement and pass that statement along by whispering it to your neighbor. After it has gone through a few people, the original statement has changed, sometimes dramatically. If the statement's written down, it's far less likely to change.

Working over the Internet provides the advantage of requiring written communication. In the virtual office, where you're working with associates via email messages and FTP file transfers, you inherently have a communication trail. This trail can be very helpful when you have a question about a past discussion. We are always amazed when other people, even though they're very Internet savvy, wonder how anyone can work this way. The Internet was invented as a communications tool, not a shopping catalog, as it's popularly perceived. So, using the Internet as we do shouldn't be surprising.

Email and file-transfer applications are the basic tools you need for collaborating over the Internet, but other tools are available as well. Another communications device that's emerging with broadband Internet is video conferencing. With the right setup, such as CuSeeMe (**www.cuseeme.com**) or ClearPhone (**www.clearphone.com**), you can set up a video Internet meeting with associates, no matter where they are on the Big Blue Marble. Some applications even allow you to share documents in a whiteboard type of setup. These applications are cross-platform, which is important when you're dealing in Flash game and cartoon creation—an area that includes a great number of both Mac and PC users. The only drawback to video conferencing, especially if you work from home, is that you have to brush your hair more often.

Even with the wonders of digital communications at hand, sometimes you simply can't beat POTS (plain old telephone service). The telephone is an established hit—everyone has one, and you don't have to worry about software conflicts or compatibility issues. Immediate feedback, which is difficult by email, is no problem by phone (although that method might be tough on your budget). If you make many overseas calls, you'll find the wisdom in a package deal for the country you call that can let you make those $150 calls for $6. You'll also be wise to use either your computer or a PDA (Personal Digital Assistant) that can do the dialing for you and keep track of the time you've spent on the phone. This approach will help keep you from talking away all your profits on a project. The big drawback to phone use is that you have no paper or digital trail of what you've discussed—unless you're really good at taking notes while you're talking. Of course, you can always record the conversation, but recorded conversations can make some people uncomfortable.

It really takes a mixture of all these communication technologies to get the job done. Email is certainly better for informal text communication (though snail mail, FedEx etc., is necessary for signed contracts, etc.). FTP is best for exchanging files because some email systems frown (or fail entirely) on large, multi-megabyte files. The good old phone is important for that instant feedback you sometimes need and, as the technology matures, video conferencing will probably replace the need for phone (except when you're away from a computer, but how often is that?). It should go without saying the fastest Internet connection you can afford is probably the single biggest value.

Coming Up with a Plan

When you're designing something as complicated as a game, you need a plan. We discussed this point in Chapter 8. Here, we want to discuss how we go about coming up with that plan that works from a distance.

At Turnertoons and EDesign, we've been PlayStation and computer game players for years. Some people would see this obsessive game playing as a colossal waste of time. We see it quite differently: For us, it's research. Although we don't play *every* game created, we do play all the popular ones. (Why investigate the boring games, when we hardly have time to play the great ones fully?) Furthermore, and more importantly, we are aware of which genre we like and agree upon. This awareness gives us a common understanding of the games we like and the games we'd like to create. So the next time your spouse, girlfriend, boyfriend, or parents complain that you're spending way too much time on these frivolous games, tell them you're conducting in-depth research in a multibillion-dollar industry. Certainly, the tough part is to know when to stop playing—and start creating.

Collaborative discussions generally consist of subjects such as theme, strategy, graphics, and what's possible and probable. The theme part generally comes first. As we discussed in Chapter 8, this is a conversation about genre. Shall we make a shooter, puzzle, or adventure game? Then, how will we make the game playable? What will the player need to do? Here, we might talk about things such as, "You know how Crash Bandicoot needs to find fruit in boxes, and then the puzzle becomes how to get to those boxes? How about making secret boxes in our game, and setting up a series of distractions and dangers to thwart the player's mission?" Then—the fun part—how will we confound the players and make them pull their hair out trying to figure out how to win? Then, there's the player's point of view, which will dictate the graphics we need. We don't really follow a "1 through 10" list verbatim, in chronological order, because doing so would certainly stifle creativity; but we do follow a rough outline of thought.

In our method, we usually go back and forth about what we envision as a great game, and then we apply our vision to what we can realistically achieve. Sometimes, we might be on a certain path, and then we change direction slightly as a result of aspects that reveal themselves during production. For example, "While animating the walk cycle, I thought it'd be cool if he stumbled a bit here and there." And then James might chime in, "Yeah, he stumbles when he's walking on the rocks, and that takes away points unless he's acquired the rock-climbing shoes hidden in a box." Going beyond what you think can be done with every project is always good practice. When you're thinking this way, you tend to find solutions that further your ability to create. We always try to push each other into doing what we previously thought was impossible. You should do the same if you want the resulting project to be the best it can be.

Graphics Concerns

If your part in the creation of games in the virtual office is graphics and animation, you should think about a few specific points.

Choosing Fonts and Font Types

The Number 1 problem when you're collaborating at a distance is fonts. You must make absolutely sure that all places (computers) to which the game project goes have *exactly* the same font sets. Nothing's worse than having spent lots of time perfecting just the right text layouts with exact kerning, leading (line spacing), and font choices, only to have the layouts totally banished when the file is opened on a machine that lacks the font sets you've used.

Before you go through this frustration, synchronizing font schemes is a good idea. Make sure that all machines that the project (the FLA authoring file) will pass through have all fonts you plan to use. Flash uses a few simple, standard device fonts internally, but these fonts are unlikely to win any design awards. They're there mostly for standard text input when you're creating forms for use in browsers (where, presumably, millions of Web page visitors may not have the same fonts installed).

Even though Apple created the TrueType font definition that's standard on PCs, Macs rarely use these fonts. Mac users lean more toward the Adobe Type 1 format, and the broadly accepted ATM (Adobe Type Manager) application, which Figure 11.1 shows. PCs can also use ATM and Type 1 Postscript fonts, so this set of technologies is the best way to go. With ATM Deluxe, you can use Type 1 fonts, and you can also organize them into sets you use on individual projects—a very helpful function, indeed.

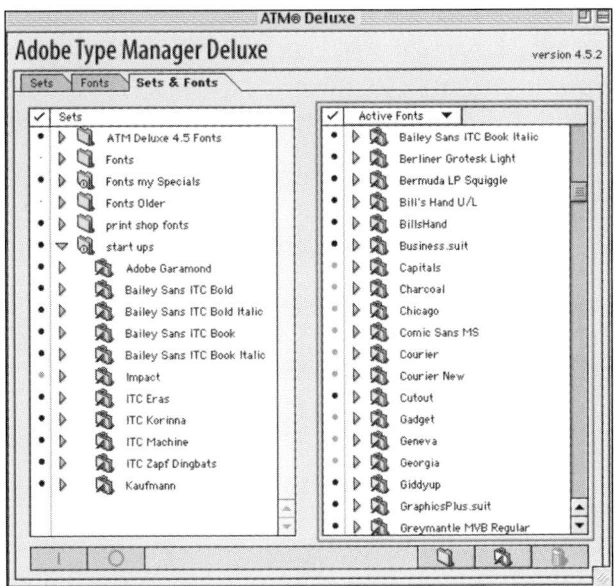

Figure 11.1
Adobe Type Manager Deluxe is a good way to organize fonts on both the Mac and PC platforms.

So, standardizing all project collaborators on the same font sets and font type is essential. That's easy enough to do. Unfortunately, that standardization in itself is not enough, because even the same font, of the same font type, can look different on the PC and on the Mac. Because of varying standards across platforms, you'll want to ensure compatibility by doing a test run of the various fonts you'd like to use on both platforms. Look for things such as consistency in kerning, kerning pairs (for example, how the A falls next to a V, as in Figure 11.2), tracking (the general spacing between all letters), and leading (line spacing). Even when you're using exactly the same font on both platforms, their metrics might have differences, however slight, that can cause big problems when you're trying to fit type into tight spaces—a situation that happens frequently in game design.

Figure 11.2
Look for kerning differences in fonts used on different platforms (exaggerated here for visual effect).

Note: Over the years, the TrueType fonts on PCs and Macs have become somewhat incompatible with each other, a situation that requires you to convert the fonts from one platform to the other in an application such as Fontographer from Macromedia.

A way exists to avoid font inconsistencies across platforms at the expense of file size. Once the text's designed, simply break it all apart (select the text block and choose **Modify|Break Apart**). Doing this turns the font into a graphic, so the text font no longer requires the font to be installed on other authoring machines. A real drawback to this approach, however, is that the type will no longer be editable as text. Also, when the file is exported as a SWF file for Web delivery, having a lot of broken-apart text can add significantly to the file's size. But, if your game has only a few words in it, breaking the text apart, as Figure 11.3 shows, could be an acceptable technique. Breaking text apart turns it into a graphic and eliminates ties to the font that created it, but makes the file size larger.

Naming Symbols for Programming Ease

When you're creating the animation parts for a game, you're not wise to simply give the programmer a big timeline of linear animation. You should use symbols in nearly all instances—specifically, the movie clip variety of symbols—because they can be programmed more efficiently.

Create a naming convention that all people involved can understand. If the programmer has determined beforehand the naming conventions being used

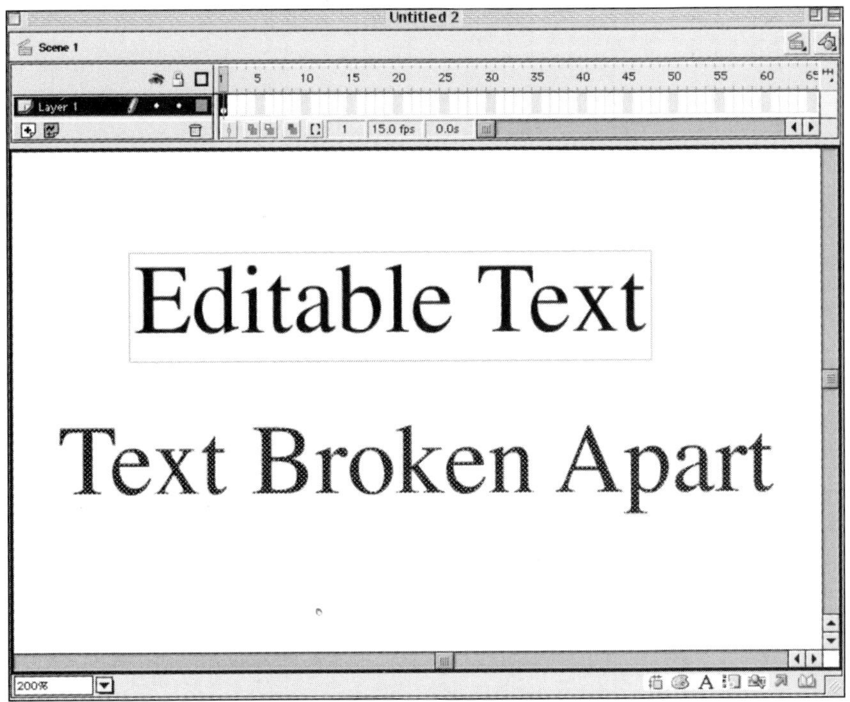

Figure 11.3
Here, we have editable text (which relies on the font being installed) and the same font, broken apart.

in the script, artists must follow those conventions *exactly*. As the artist, though, you most likely will be the person creating the initial elements. Do not name these elements indiscriminately. Make the names clear, understandable, and short. For example, if you have a character named Joseph in a sequence in which he jumps forward, name the sequence "joejumpfore", not "Joseph jumping forward". If you have another sequence in which the character jumps backward, naming this sequence "joejumpback" makes sense. This convention forces the movie-clip symbols together alphabetically in the library window and keeps the programmer from having to type excessive text in the code. In Figure 11.4, you can see how we handled naming elements in the adventure game from Chapter 10.

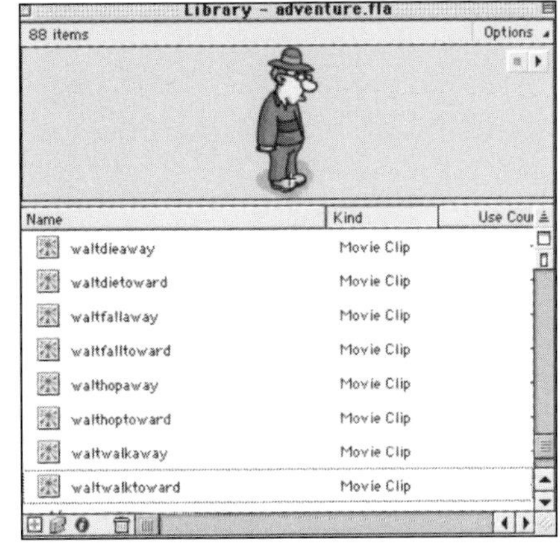

Figure 11.4
The Flash library window, showing some of the named symbols used in a game project collaboration.

Check the Number of Frames Available

Be sure of how many frames a certain animation in the game can have. If the game is running at 20 frames per second, and the programmer has a script that should execute in half a second, you cannot have a sequence that takes 25 frames. Such a sequence could destroy the timing the programmer wants the game to have.

These are some of the most common issues the artist should think about when collaborating with a programmer across the Internet. As with any creative endeavor, you can never envision everything beforehand, so it's best to keep the lines of communication open at all times.

Code Concerns

If your part in the creation of games in the virtual office is writing the ActionScript codes, you should think about a couple of code-related issues. You need to code for flexibility, and you need to make sure that other participants in the project can understand your code.

Coding for Flexibility

We game programmers have become quite used to creating games without seeing the graphics; we just write the code in such a way that the size and shape of the final graphic are irrelevant. The key to doing this programming correctly is to make everything you write as configurable as possible—don't assume anything. Avoid using direct values in any of your calculations; make sure that you use variables instead, because you can amend things more easily with variables, if you need to.

In a recent project, for example, we had to provide the ActionScript for a game in which the player catches falling objects; as is often the case, we had to do this without seeing any graphics from the game. In the game, the player controls the "catcher" by using the arrow keys, and we needed to make sure that the "catcher" doesn't move off the edge of the play area. This requirement sounds quite simple, so let's look at how we might program it.

Method 1: Writing Code without Variables

As a guide, to ensure that our code works correctly, we need to create a simple red rectangle to represent the "catcher," and we give this rectangle the instance name **catcher**. The rectangle is 100 pixels wide, and we are using the default movie size of 550×400 pixels. Here's some code that would handle the movement of the "catcher":

```
// If you press the RIGHT key, then move
// the "catcher" 10 pixels to the right
if (Key.isDown(Key.RIGHT)) {
 catcher._x +=10;
}

// If you press the LEFT key, then move
// the "catcher" 10 pixels to the left
if (Key.isDown(Key.LEFT)) {
 catcher._x -=10;
}
```

```
// The catcher is 100 pixels wide, so
// if the center of the catcher is less
// than 50, we have hit the left edge
// of the screen.
if (catcher._x<50) {
 catcher._x=50;
}

// The catcher is 100 pixels wide, so if
// the center of the catcher is more
// than 500, we have hit the right edge of the screen.
if (catcher._x>500) {
 catcher._x=500;
}
```

That code all works well, so what's the problem? Well, we've assumed several things in this code. First, we've assumed that the "catcher" size will be 100 pixels. If the person who is designing the graphics makes the "catcher" larger or smaller, our code will not work. We've also assumed that the play area will be the same as the default movie size of 550 pixels. Finally, we've assumed that when the player moves left or right, the catcher should move 10 pixels.

Our code needs to be much more generic than this. We can create more generic code by replacing all of these values with variables that can be defined at the start of the movie and modified if necessary. The next section shows how the coding should be done.

Method 2: Using Variables for Flexibility

In Frame 1, we set up the variables for our game. We place the variables in the first frame so they are easy to find and easy to modify.

```
// We define the play area as a variable.
playarea=550;
// We use the width property to determine
// the exact width of the "catcher" movie clip.
catchersize=catcher._width;
// The movement speed of the "catcher" is defined here
speed=10;
```

In the main game, we have the following code:

```
if (Key.isDown(Key.RIGHT)) {
 catcher._x +=speed;
}

if (Key.isDown(Key.LEFT)) {
 catcher._x -=speed;
}
```

```
if (catcher._x<(catchersize/2)) {
 catcher._x=catchersize/2;
}

if (catcher._x>(playarea-(catchersize/2))) {
 catcher._x=playarea-(catchersize/2);
}
```

This code does exactly the same thing as the previous example did, but everything is defined as variables here and, therefore, this code is more suited to a collaborative project in which we don't have any details about the graphics that will be used in the game. In this example, the catcher can be any size, and the game will still work correctly without any modifications. The speed and the play area are defined as variables, so they can be changed quickly and easily; altogether, the perfect solution. Worth remembering is that programming in this generic style is not only useful for collaborative projects; using this programming style is also a good habit with all of your projects, because it does make it easier for you to modify the game at a later date.

Making Your Code Understandable

Another important issue when you're working remotely with somebody is to keep the ActionScript as clear as possible by using meaningful variable names, frame labels, and lots of comments in your code. Also, format your code by including each command on a new line—don't try to save space by combining commands into single lines of code. Here's an example of some code from our Walter adventure game, which we featured in Chapter 10. All we've done is change the variable names and modify the layout. Can you tell what this code is doing?

```
if (x2>0 && x2 != yt4){ yt4=x2; removeMovieClip ("wdc");
duplicateMovieClip ("bgfvg" add yt4, "wdc", 1);
wdc._x=varwx; wdc._y=ghye; x2=0;}
if (x2 == 1) { varwx +=fgh6; ghye +=tiok;}
if (x2 == 2) { varwx -= fgh6; ghye -= tiok;}
if (x2 == 3) {varwx += fgh6; ghye -= tiok;}
if (x2 == 4) {varwx -= fgh6; ghye += tiok;}
if (x2>0) {wdc._x = varwx; wdc._y = ghye;wdc.nextFrame ();}
```

Here's the same piece of code, but with some meaningful variable names, comments, and an improved layout:

```
// Make Walter face the right direction
if (walkmode>0 && walkmode != facing){
 facing=walkmode;
 removeMovieClip ("walter");
 duplicateMovieClip ("walk" add facing, "walter", 1);
 walter._x=walterx;
```

```
 walter._y=waltery;
 walkmode=0;
}

// Update the x- and y-coordinates of Walter
if (walkmode == 1) {
 walterx +=walkxspeed;
 waltery +=walkyspeed;
}
if (walkmode == 2) {
 walterx -= walkxspeed;
 waltery -= walkyspeed;
}
if (walkmode == 3) {
 walterx += walkxspeed;
 waltery -= walkyspeed;
}
if (walkmode == 4) {
 walterx -= walkxspeed;
 waltery += walkyspeed;
}

// Move the walk animation to the next frame
if (walkmode>0) {
 walter._x = walterx;
 walter._y = waltery;
 walter.nextFrame ();
}
```

Hopefully, you'll agree that this new version of the code is clearer and easier to understand than the previous example.

Once you've finished writing it, sharing the source code of your Flash movies is incredibly easy. Any movie you create in Flash automatically has cross-platform compatibility—that is, a file created on the PC can be read on the Mac, and vice versa. Graphics can be added, and scripts edited, as needed.

Testing the Game

Once you're all done with that new game, you need to make sure it works under all circumstances and on all platforms. Here's where the collaboration across the Internet becomes absolutely necessary. You'll need to have others play the game—over and over. Unless you have a significant number of people at your command (expensive), you'll need the Internet. After the people involved in making the game have played it thoroughly, it's a good idea to have others who aren't close to the project give it a go. Fresh minds on the subject can be revealing. The new players will reveal the game's strengths and weaknesses. They might reveal that something you thought was intuitive is actually a real chore. They'll also do things to the game you did not intend, such as hitting the fire button 346 times per second. They will also be the ones to complain about some function not working. Don't be angered by these comments—they are worth a great deal. They give you insight to make the game even better, and the advice usually is free.

Luckily, getting folks to play a good game is fairly easy. The novelty of games on the Internet is intriguing to many people, and most will give the game at least a go or two. Some will play the game for hours, and find every little crack and crevice in it. Give the players a way to get in touch with you, via an email link in the game, or in the page on which the game is played. Encourage feedback and bug reports whenever you can. When players take the time to write you, they care. Even if they tell you the game is terrible, answer their messages quickly. Express thanks for their time in finding the bug or problem, and let them know you want to do everything you can to make the game the best it can be. Let them know you value their opinions. Keep their email addresses, and drop them a line when you have a new version that fixes what they found wrong. Doing this makes them feel like they are part of the process—and they are. Treating your players well, even when they complain, creates the best sort of advertising you can have for your game—positive word of mouth. Before you know it, you'll have a vast number of collaborators and players across the Internet.

PROJECT Collaborative Simulation

This project is a bit different from the previous ones we've used in the book. We're going to ask you to work on a collaborative project with us. We'll give you the basic outline for a game idea, and then your job is to create either the necessary graphics or the ActionScript code for this game. Artists and programmers both have "jobs" in this project:

- *If you're an artist*—Go ahead and create some graphics and, in the *catchcode.fla* file on the CD-ROM, you'll find the necessary code to complete the game. See if you can combine your graphics with our code to make a fully working game. Figure 11.5 shows you what you will receive from the programmer.
- *If you're an ActionScript programmer*—You can start programming on the game idea. In the *catchart.fla* file on the CD-ROM, will be all the graphics you'll need to complete the game. Figure 11.6 shows you what you will receive from the artist.

Here's the idea for the game. The game will involve a "catcher" at the bottom of the screen; the player can move this catcher left or right by using the arrow keys. At the top of the screen, another character will be moving from side to side and, at random intervals, dropping an object that the player has to catch before it hits the ground. The player will have three lives. Every time the player fails to catch the falling object, he will lose one life. When the player has lost

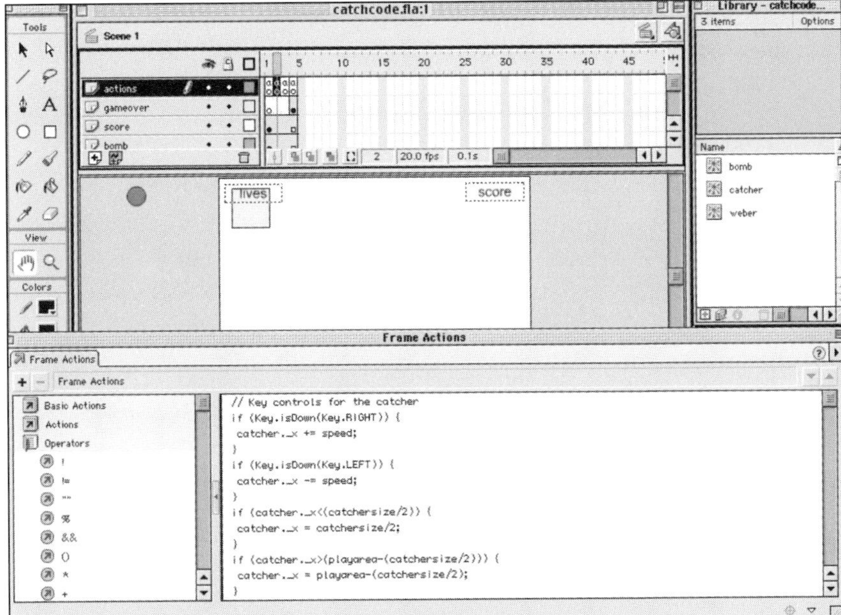

Figure 11.5

Here are the elements included in the collaboration simulation. This is what the artist receives from the programmer.

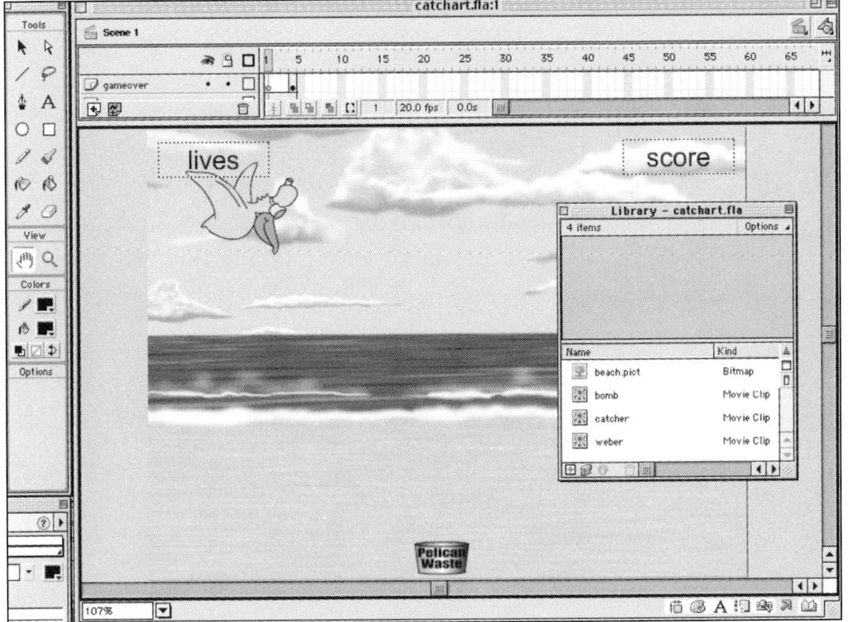

Figure 11.6

This is the same simulation as in Figure 11.5, only this is what the programmer receives from the artist.

all of his lives, the game is over. If the player catches a falling object, he scores points. As the player progresses and catches more objects, the game should move faster and faster, making it harder to continue playing.

This little collaboration project should give you a good idea of what a real situation would be like, in which you have one talent, but not the other. If you get stuck anywhere along the way, the CD-ROM also contains a finished version of the game in a file named *catchdone.fla*.

Moving On

Well, that about does it for the chapters of this book. Following are appendixes about ASP, Javalets, and Flash, and some reading about artificial intelligence in Flash. We hope you have enjoyed the information we've supplied, and that it inspires you to go out and create some killer Flash stuff that blows away anything to come before it. Anything worth doing is worth doing the best you can.

Appendix A

Using Active Server Pages (ASP) with Flash Games

Most interactive Web applications developed today will require some method of persistent storage. Whether your application is a Flash game or a database-driven shopping cart, storing information that you can readily access and update is essential.

By Corey A. Johnson

What Is ASP?

Let's say you've developed a Flash game, and you want it to store players' scores. If your game is being distributed over the Web, you can let the Web server store that data and send it out when a user requests it. Many server-side technologies available today make storing simple, text-based information easy. Some of the more popular technologies are ASP (Active Server Pages), Perl, Cold Fusion, and Server-Side Java (Servlets).

Files created with ASP have the extension .asp. An ASP file can contain any combination of HTML, scripting, and calls to components. When you change the ASP file on the server, you need only save the changes in that file; the next time the Web page is loaded, the script will automatically be run. ASP runs as a service of the Web server, and is optimized for multiple threads and multiple users. Using ASP lets you separate the design of your Web page from the programming details.

This appendix provides a brief example of using ASP to store text information on the server. We will be using the VBScript (Visual Basic Scripting Edition) language. ASP can be written in either VBScript or JScript (Microsoft's version of JavaScript). VBScript is very similar to the Visual Basic (VB) programming language, and JScript resembles both the C programming language and Java. What language you use is a matter of personal preference. Keep in mind that this appendix is not an attempt to fully explain ASP. The purpose here is to give you the necessary information so you can immediately begin taking advantage of this extremely powerful, scripting technology.

To begin, let's discuss the Web server requirements: Microsoft's IIS (Internet Information Server) is a standard component included with Windows NT/2000 that includes built-in support for ASP. Installing Chili!Soft's ASP, an add-on scripting engine, can enhance many other Web servers to support ASP. Either of these combinations will successfully execute the example script. If you are not sure whether your Web server supports ASP, contact your server administrator or Web-host technical support. Now, on to the fun stuff.

Using ASP to Store High-Score Data

The following code example demonstrates an easy way to store "high-score" data on the Web server with ASP. You must enclose all ASP in <% and %> tags. Use the apostrophe to begin single-line code comments. You can intermingle ASP within HTML, or use ASP only. I'll explain the code a line or two at a time. You can find a complete listing of the code at the end of this appendix. The script can be executed either from within a Flash movie, or from a form in an HTML document. Either method will need to **POST** the high score info to the ASP script.

First, open with the <% tag, and declare the necessary variables:

```
<%
' Declare variables
Dim fileSysObj, fileLocObj, fileObj
```

The **Dim** statement declares three variables and allocates storage for them. The **fileSysObj** variable will hold the reference to the Web server's local file system. The **fileLocObj** variable will store the absolute physical folder path to our data file. And finally, the **fileObj** variable will hold the reference to the actual file where we will store our high-score information:

```
' Determine the location of the data file
fileLocObj = Server.MapPath("./highscore.txt")
```

This statement simply stores the physical location of the highscore.txt file in the variable named **fileLocObj**. The file should be located in the same folder as the script itself. On a Windows server, this location might be something such as the following: **C:\InetPub\wwwroot\highscore.txt**.

The **Server.MapPath** method determines this location for you and allows you to locate your data file on the Web server. The next step is to create the objects. In programming, an *object* is a functional unit of methods (tools) and properties (characteristics) that lets you accomplish some predefined task. In our case, that task is accessing the Web server's file system:

```
' Create objects
Set fileSysObj = CreateObject("Scripting.FileSystemObject")
Set fileObj = fileSysObj.CreateTextFile(fileLocObj, True)
```

Creating the **FileSystemObject** variable is just as easy. The **CreateObject** method handles this task and stores a reference to the object in our variable **fileSysObject**. A call to the **FileSystemObject**'s (which we have stored in the variable **fileSysObject**) **CreateTextFile** method creates our file (the **True** parameter specifies that the file should be overwritten if it already exists) and opens our highscore.txt file for writing.

> **Note:** Writing to a file on your Web server's hard drive will require the appropriate file permissions. If you are not sure about proper file permissions, contact your server administrator or Web-host technical support.

Now, we are ready to write our high score data to the file:

```
' Write a line to the data file
fileObj.WriteLine(Request.Form("highscore"))
```

Creating a file and opening it for writing are actually two, separate method calls. If this script is being accessed via an HTML form, the **Request.Form** method retrieves the value entered in a form field. When calling the script from your Flash movie, this function retrieves the variable passed to the Flash movie's **getURL** action call. The value is then written to the file by the **WriteLine** method. Any expression that represents a string can be passed to this method. If you need to combine two strings and/or variables, use the concatenation operator &. So, you could also do this as follows:

```
'  Write a line to the data file
fileObj.WriteLine("highscore is="&Request.Form("highscore"))
```

Or, you could write the code like this:

```
' Write a line to the data file
fileObj.WriteLine(Request.Form("name")&"high score is
 "&Request.Form("highscore"))
```

Finally, we close the data file. This step is very important. The **Close** method flushes the buffer, completes any write, and closes the file.

```
fileObj.Close
%>
```

Pretty easy, right? Following is the complete code for the script, which we'll store in a file named **recordHighscore.asp**:

```
<%
' Declare variables
Dim fileSysObj, fileLocObj, fileObj

' Determine file location
fileLocObj = Server.MapPath("./highscore.txt")

' Create objects
Set fileSysObj = CreateObject("Scripting.FileSystemObject")
Set fileObj = fileSysObj.CreateTextFile(fileLocObj, True)

' Write a line terminated with a newline character.
fileObj.WriteLine(Request.Form("highscore"))
fileObj.Close
%>

Highscore Recorded Successfully.
```

If you were to use the previous script in conjunction with a very simple HTML form, your HTML would look something like the following:

```
<HTML>
<HEAD>
<TITLE>script test</TITLE>
</HEAD>
<BODY>
<FORM ACTION="recordHighscore.asp" METHOD="POST">
<INPUT TYPE="TEXT" NAME="highscore">
```

```
<INPUT TYPE="SUBMIT" NAME="SUBMITME" VALUE="Submit High Score">
</FORM>
</BODY>
</HTML>
```

And that is all there is to it. Armed with the information above, you should be able to easily write a quick ASP script to store basic information in a text file on the Web server's local file system. Again, please keep in mind that this is a basic example. You can do many more things with ASP. If you need more data-storage functionality, you might want to consider using a database of some sort. ASP makes any type of information management pretty simple. So, your imagination is the only limiting factor. Have fun.

Corey A. Johnson is President and Director of Technology for Creative Network Innovations, Inc., based in Melbourne, Florida. He can be reached at ***cjohnson@cniweb.net***.

Appendix B
Artificial Intelligence

In Chapter 9, we looked at how we can add some intelligence to our trivia quiz game. The intelligence routines we used in that chapter were simple, but, in this chapter, we want to give you some ideas about how to create some more complex artificial-intelligence routines in your own games.

By James Robertson

What Is Artificial Intelligence?

The term *artificial intelligence (AI)* often evokes an image of some kind of robot that tries to emulate human actions, and you might be wondering what relevance that has to game design. But artificial intelligence isn't reserved for robots or for supercomputers with neural networks. You might be surprised to learn that nearly all computer games contain some form of AI, and implementing a good AI system in your game can make it much more exciting to play. Artificial intelligence is simply the capability of a machine to imitate intelligent human behavior. (AI is also the branch of computer science that deals with the simulation of intelligent behavior in computers.) AI addresses many aspects of intelligence—including deductive reasoning, speech recognition, creative response, the ability to learn from experience, and the ability to make reasonable inferences from incomplete information—and some of these capabilities are used in games.

One of the first games to make use of AI was the arcade classic called Pac-Man. You may not have been aware of this, but the four ghosts in Pac-Man used different strategies to try to defeat you, and they worked together as a team. One ghost would try to follow the shortest path to you, making you directly avoid him. Another ghost would try to go to a junction that was closest to where you would have to move to avoid the first ghost. A third ghost would stay near the middle and try to cut you off from using the tunnel through the sides. And the last ghost would wander around aimlessly in an area that you hadn't visited yet, in the hope that it would get in your way.

Giving the in-game enemies some kind of intelligence, as in Pac-Man, is one of the most common uses of AI, but it's not the only use. You'll also need to use AI if you want to give people a computer-controlled opponent to play against. For example, in classic board games such as chess, checkers, and Othello, you'll need to implement some kind of AI routine for the computer player.

Many methods exist for adding intelligence to your games, and doing some research on the game you're creating would be worthwhile before you try to write your own AI routines. Artificial intelligence is a vast and complex subject that is beyond the scope of this book, but we want to introduce you to some of its basic ideas that will help you increase the playability of your games. The aim of writing an AI routine is to find a way to evaluate your game and give each aspect of the game a numerical value, so that your computer-controlled player can appear to be making intelligent decisions.

As an example of how AI systems work in a game, we will look at how you would go about creating a computer-controlled player in an Othello game. A number of well-known algorithms already exist for this game, and most of these algorithms use several methods to evaluate which move is the best one available. We will look at a single method, which may not give you the most powerful AI routine, but it is a good demonstration of how to create your own artificial intelligence.

AI in Othello

Othello (also known as Reversi) was invented in the late 19th century and, like all good strategy games, it is simple to play but difficult to master. The game is played on a board with 64 squares (8×8), with the adjacent squares colored differently—alternating between black and white (like a chess or checkers board). At the start of the game, each player has two pieces positioned at the center of the board. The start position is shown in Figure B.1.

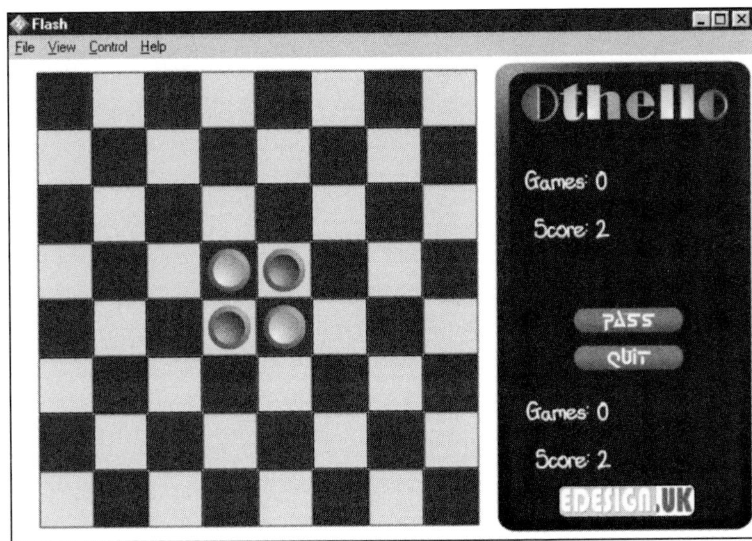

Figure B.1
The starting position in Othello.

In each turn, you place one new piece on the board and attempt to capture one or more of your opponent's pieces. To capture your opponent, you must place your piece in a square next to a square that contains an opposition piece, and your piece must trap at least one opposition piece between itself and another one of your own pieces. If you cannot capture an opponent's piece, then you must pass and allow the other player to make a move. If neither player can capture any pieces then the game has ended. After you have placed a piece on the board, any of your opponent's pieces that have been trapped are replaced with your own pieces. The winner is the player with the highest number of pieces left at the end of the game. In Figure B.2, you can see all the possible moves (marked with a red cross) that Blue's player can make on his or her first move.

So, how do we add intelligence to a game like this? What you need to do is find a way to rank each move by giving it a numerical value, and then your computer-controlled player can make the move that has been given the highest ranking. The most obvious way to rank a move in Othello is to count how many of your opponent's pieces, you manage to capture. Figure B.3 shows a game in progress. It is the Yellow player's turn, and we've marked all the possible moves with a number. Table B.1 shows how many of the Blue opponent's pieces each move will capture.

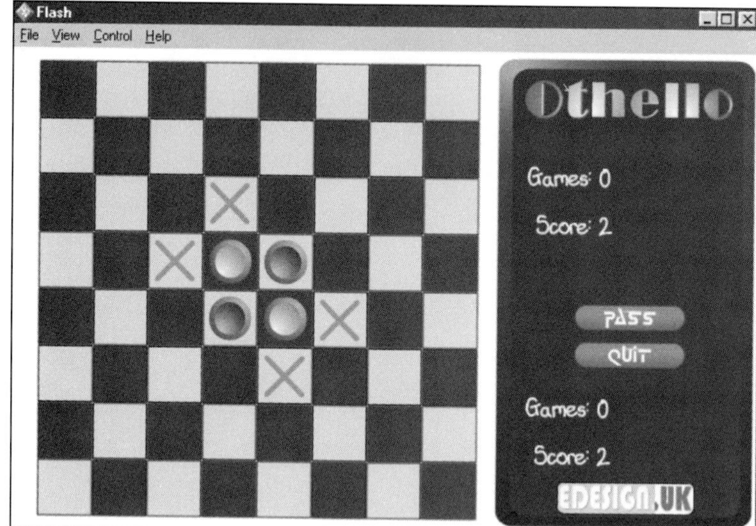

Figure B.2
All the possible moves (marked with a red cross) that Blue's player can make as a first move in Othello.

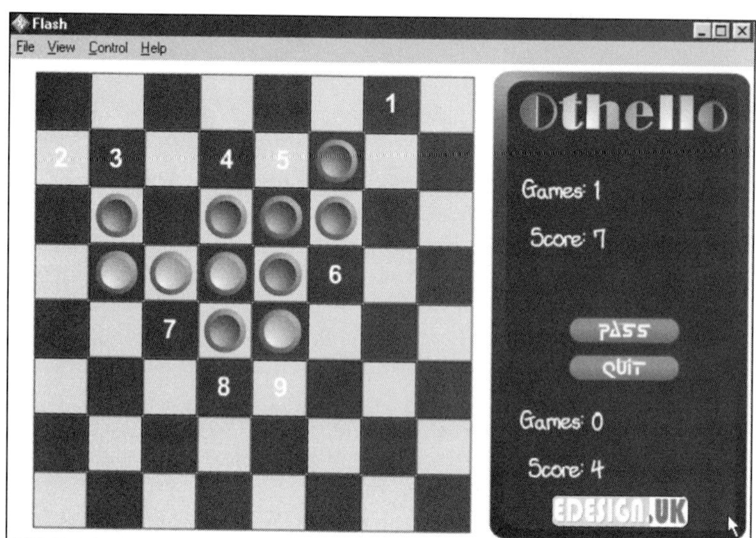

Figure B.3
A game of Othello in progress.

Table B.1 A breakdown of how many Blue pieces will be captured in each potential move by the Yellow player in Othello, from the point shown in Figure B.3.

Move	Captured Pieces
1	2
2	1
3	1
4	1
5	3
6	1
7	1
8	1
9	1

According to Table B.1, the best move would seem to be number 5, because it captures the most pieces. And, in this particular situation, move number 5 might be the best move. However, if you use this method—choosing a move based on how many of your opponent's pieces you can capture—throughout an entire game, you'll soon discover that it doesn't work particularly well.

If you play Othello, you will quickly learn that some squares on the board are more important than others. If you manage to get one of your counters on a corner square, you cannot lose that counter. Therefore, the corner squares are very important, and you should consider them to be more valuable than the other squares on the board. To a lesser degree, the side squares are also important because counters on side squares are also quite difficult to capture. To increase the intelligence of your computer player, you should take these positional advantages into account. Basically, squares near the center of the board are less valuable, and squares near the edge of the board are more valuable.

So, we need a way to assign numbers to rank the relative values of the *squares* based on their positions. To do that, we'll calculate each square's distance from the *edge* of the board. (The further from the edge a square is, the *less* valuable it is.) The two values for calculating this distance are an *x* distance and a *y* distance. The *x* distance is the number of squares from the current square to the *left or right* side of the board (whichever is closest). The *y* distance is the number of squares from the current square to the *top or bottom* of the board (again, whichever is closest). You can see an example of this in Figure B.4, which shows a piece 5 squares across the board and 4 squares down.

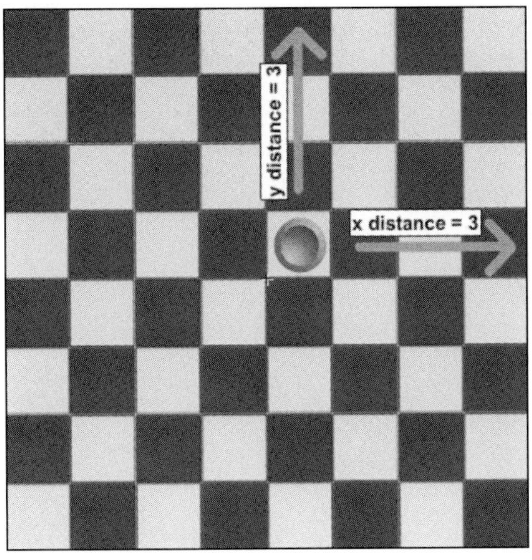

Figure B.4
Sample game board demonstrating x distance and y distance values relative to current square.

The *x* distance for this piece is 3, and the *y* distance is also 3. If we add these two values together, we get a result, which gives us a *positional ranking* for that particular square. On a board that is 8 squares by 8 squares, you can never have a square that is more than 3 squares away from the edge of the board. So, the maximum value for our positional ranking is 6 (an *x* distance of 3 squares plus a *y* distance of 3 squares). The minimum value for our positional ranking is 0 (a corner square has an *x* and *y* distance of 0 squares). Therefore, our positional ranking ranges from 0 to 6. To increase this range, we can multiply our positional ranking by a factor of maybe 2 or 3 (varying this factor to give different results). By multiplying the positional ranking by a specified factor, we are increasing the difference between a good move (near the edge of the board, thus a lower factor), and a bad move (near the center, thus a higher factor). A value with a higher factor will make the computer player more likely to choose a side or corner square (whose value will be lower). So far, our calculations give us rankings that evaluate the board position of each particular square. If, during the game, we evaluate several possible moves from a given position, we will pick the move that puts our game piece on the square with the lowest value—we'll choose the square that's closest to the edge or the corner of the board.

Now, let's add another level of complexity: If we use the designated value (determined by ranking squares by position) together with the number of captured pieces that we calculated earlier, our computer player will play a much better game. How shall we use these numbers together? Because we're aiming for the lowest value, we'll subtract the number of captured pieces from what we've called the positional value (xdistance+ydistance×3) of the square on which our game piece lands (for this example, we've arbitrarily used a factor of 3 to increase the range between the positional rank of each square). Our new formula will be this: [(xdistance+ydistance)×3]-captured pieces.

So, using our new formula, let's recalculate the possible moves shown in Figure B.3. Table B.2 shows the number of pieces captured, the positional value, and the combined evaluation of each of the nine possible moves.

Table B.2 A breakdown of the number of pieces captured, the positional value, and the final evaluation of each of the nine possible moves shown in Figure B.3.

Move	Position	Captured	Evaluation (Position-Captured)
1	3	2	1
2	3	1	2
3	6	1	5
4	12	1	11
5	12	3	9
6	15	1	14
7	15	1	14
8	15	1	14
9	15	1	14

When we use this evaluation method—in which a low evaluation number indicates a good move, and a high number indicates a bad move—the best move would appear to be Move 1 (which evaluates to 1). This method is quite effective, but it does have one serious weakness. We've already mentioned how important the corner squares are in this game; therefore, we need to ensure that our opponent does not capture these squares. If we place a counter on one of the squares that surrounds a corner square, our opponent very likely will be able to capture that particular corner. Therefore, we need to modify our AI algorithm to avoid the squares that surround the corner squares. We can do this by making two additional checks on the x and y distance variables. If xdistance and ydistance equals 1, or xdistance+ydistance equals 1, we are looking at a square next to a corner square. For these cases, we simply increase the evaluation factor by, say, 20 instead of 2 or 3.

This method is a great improvement over the original, and it should be good enough to beat the average Othello player. However, we can still make it even better in many ways. In this example, we've analyzed the game by looking at the board position and the number of captured pieces, but this is not the only way we can analyze the game. Our technique is a variation on a well-known method called disk-square tables. Another technique is mobility-based evaluation, in which we would look at how many possible moves our opponent can make—the more possible moves there are, the more likely it is that our opponent can make a good move. The idea is that we try to reduce our opponent's mobility while increasing our own. We can also look at the number of frontier disks: the empty spaces surrounding our own counters. Counters that are surrounded by several empty spaces are more open to attack, so we need to reduce our frontier disks. We could use several other methods (some of which might produce better results), but we'll let you explore those methods yourself. The ultimate AI routine would probably make use of all the available techniques.

To complete this algorithm and make the AI routine much stronger, you should look ahead to the next move, and calculate the best move that your opponent can make. After all, making a fantastic move that captures 10 pieces is no good if it means that your opponent can also make an equally good move. By looking ahead and calculating the best move your opponent can make, and adding this evaluation to the best move you can make, you will ensure that your AI routine is strong enough to beat most players. You can further increase the strength of this routine by searching ahead on even more possible moves. You have to be aware, however, that as you look further ahead, the number of possible positions grows rapidly. Looking as far as 10 moves ahead for each player results in one billion possible positions to investigate, which is far too many for your average computer system to calculate.

Write Your Own AI Routines

Now that we've given you the basic ideas behind creating AI routines, we encourage you to start programming your own AI games. The best place to start is with a simple game such as Tic-Tac-Toe (also known as Noughts and Crosses). This is a game we all know how to play (and win), so why not try to write a Flash game that uses AI to calculate the best possible move? When you've done this, why not try programming an AI routine for a game such as Four in a Row? When you've mastered both of those games, you'll be ready to tackle games such as Othello, checkers, and others. Learning to program games with superior artificial intelligence will really make your work stand out from the crowd. So, start practicing now, and you could be the author of the next game that takes the world by storm. Good luck, and happy programming.

Appendix C
Links

The following pages contain URLs for some interesting cartoon and game sites. Also included are links to Web sites containing software and hardware information that may be of interest to entertainment developers.

By Bill Turner

Cartoon Sites

Cartoons are everywhere on the Web, and while we could never track them all down, we'd like to give you a list of some of our favorites. Some sites are quite popular, while others you may have never heard of. Hopefully, all will be entertaining, and help to inspire your creation of cartoons. Please be aware that Internet cartoons may sometimes contain mature subject matter. Have fun!

www.a2zcartoons.com

At this site, you can take a peek at the award-winning and thoroughly charming *Hat Bat Louie* cartoon show.

www.bazleyfilms.com

This is Richard Bazley's site, that is devoted to his short Flash animated film, *The Journal of Edwin Carp.*

www.bulbo.com

Mishmash Media produces this great series of cartoons about Bulbo, a cool 1920's style character, as he traverses society.

www.campchaos.com

This is an ever-changing, and refreshingly funny cartoon and game site from Camp Chaos studios and others.

www.cartoovie.com

This site contains a nice assortment of cartoon styles. The short, *There's Something in My Phone*, uses some very nice hand drawn morphs, with an appealing graphic style.

www.debreuil.com

This is a Flash interactive cartoon production company.

www.ehollywood.net

Electronic Hollywood produces the award-winning cartoon series, *Cyber Slacker,* created by Jamie Levy, and animated by Joe Corrao.

www.eruptor.com

Although they may be more famous for their *Eruptor Girls*, they also carry some cool Flash cartoons.

www.icebox.com

Nothing frozen here. One of the better cartoon publishers on the Internet, *Rock 'n' Roll Dad.* Created by Peter Bagge and Dana Gould, it is a very funny look at the fathers behind some of the world's most famous rockers.

www.joecorrao.com

Joe's home page contains some really great Flash cartoon art.

www.mondomedia.com

The *Mondo Mini Shows* include cartoon productions, such as the wildly popular, *The God and Devil Show*, and *Thugs on Film*.

www.mumbleboy.com

This site contains the Mumbleboy shows, an eclectic mix of graphically appealing Flash cartoon animations.

www.pitchtv.com

Even though this site doesn't specialize in Flash, there are some very well done animations to be found here. You'll probably want to have a cable modem, DSL, or higher for this site.

www.RDAStudio.com

This Canadian animation studio takes an interesting approach to Flash cartoon animation. Take a tour through the dreamlike world of Irth.

www.shockwave.com

The content publishing sister company to Macromedia, **Shockwave.com**, is probably one of the best-known destination sites for Flash cartoons and games.

www.turnertoons.com

This is Bill Turner's studio site. The home of Weber, the snorkeled, wisecracking yellow pelican, who battles the human mess. Also the source for mind-bending Flash game productions.

www.wildbrain.com

If you're into Flash cartoons and don't know about *Wild Brain*, you should. They publish some of the coolest toons on the Internet.

www.wwbc.net

Worldwide Broadcast Network contains links to all sorts of entertainment, from Flash animations, to short films and video. It also includes an audio/video search engine.

Game Sites

Lots of the cartoon sites above also carry games. Here, we'll give you some links to the games sites you may find inspiring (though some of these sites carry cartoons too).

www.artifactinteractive.com.au

This is the site from the award-winning Flash game developer of *Flash Golf* and *Grand Prix Challenge*.

www.edesign.uk.com

This is James Robertson's game production site. Here, you'll find some of the most cutting edge and challenging Flash games available.

www.e-fantasia.co.uk

This is the home of many exciting Flash games you can play and study. Also included, is a section where the developers reveal their secrets.

www.romeodesign.com

This is a very stylish Flash games site. *Takion* is a cool Flash space shooter game. *South Pole Snowfight* will have you chucking snowballs at the elusive penguins. Very nice graphics abound in Romeo Design.

www.sarbakan.com

This is the site from the developer of the popular *Goodnight Mr. Snoozleberg* Flash game.

www.sess.net

This site is a Flash game arcade. A really good place to waste your life away with *Hextris,* and various animal arcade games.

www.sporeproductions.com

This is Spore Productions Web site; Flash, Shockwave, and Direct X games developer.

www.ultimatearcade.com

If you like Flash games, you'll want to spend some time here. The site also features a Flash Game Lab with lots of good information on creating Flash games.

Hardware and Software Sites

In case you need some new equipment or software to create that great new cartoon or game. Here, we give you some good starting points in your research.

www.adobe.com

Developers of Photoshop, After Effects, Premiere, Illustrator, Go Live, and many other Web and graphics development tools. You can download demos, search a wealth of information, and research technical support issues here.

www.bhphotovideo.com

B&H Photo-Video Pro Audio offers all sorts of equipment such as MiniDV video recording decks, cameras, and professional audio gear.

www.bias-inc.com

BIAS develops sophisticated sound editing and creations software for the Macintosh. Packages, such as Peak and Deck, are simply some of the best sound editors available for the Mac.

www.macromedia.com

This is the site of the developers of Flash, Director, Dreamweaver, Freehand, and many other Web and graphics development tools. You can download demos, search a wealth of information, and research technical support issues here.

www.media100.com

Media 100 specializes in digital video expansion cards for everything, from MiniDV Firewire boards, to high-end component video digitizer/playback hardware. They also have video conversion/compression software covered, with the award-winning Media Cleaner Pro 5.

www.smartsound.com

Sonic Desktop Software is the maker of the SmartSound family of audio software products for Macintosh and PC.

www.sonicfoundry.com

This is the Web site for developers of Sound Forge and Acid Pro, sound creation and editing tools for Windows PCs.

www.thirdwishsoftware.com

This is the site of the developers of Magpie Pro lip-synching software that works with Flash 5. They also offer Flicker, a Flash export plug-in for Newtek's Lightwave 6.0.

www.wacom.com

What could be more natural than drawing with a pencil? Certainly not a mouse. Wacom makes this possible with pressure sensitive drawing tablets for your setup.

Flash Information Sites

Here, we list some Web sites that deal mostly in teaching Flash techniques. Not necessarily cartoons and games, but very useful when you're stuck with a problem.

www.Flahoo.com

This site is a Flash directory of links, with a wide variety of categories.

www.Flash-Guru.Com

This site was founded by Jon Warren Lentz, co-author of the *Flash 4 and 5 Bible*. This site is being set up to fill the need for sustained learner-centered training on a wide range of Flash topics, from intermediate to advanced.

www.flashkit.com

Flash Kit is a Flash developer resource site.

www.flashmove.com

This is the Flash resource for everyone.

www.macromedia.com/go/12046

This site is the mother load of links useful to Flash artists and developers.

www.makemagic.com

This site provides tutorials and a really cool Yo-Yo.

www.moock.org

This site has been a great help to me more than once. Plenty of good information on solutions to Flash problems, mostly concerning ActionScripting.

www.were-here.com

At this site you'll find forums that cover nearly all the bases in the world of Flash.

Animation Information Sites

Under this heading, we list a few sites that deal in the animation business.

www.animationartist.com

This Web site is devoted to the people behind the pencils, tablets, and mice that make animation worth watching.

www.awn.com

This is Animation World Network's Web site, devoted to the art and business of animation, from Web to silver screen. The site also includes the Web versions of the magazines, *Animation World Magazine* and *Visual Magic Magazine*.

www.dv.com

This is *DV (or Digital Video) Magazine's* Web site. Lots of good information on the subject of video and computers.

www.ev.variety.com

At this site, you'll find the Web presence for the magazine EV, the sister publication of *Variety Magazine*, dedicated to digital entertainment.

www.hollywoodreporter.com

This is the Web site for the entertainment industry magazine, *The Hollywood Reporter*.

www.reuben.org

This is the National Society of Cartoonists' Web site.

www.wired.com/news/digiwood

This is *Wired Magazine's* news section devoted to digital entertainment.

General

The following are a few useful URLs that do not fit the other headings properly.

www.internic.net/alpha.html

This is a listing of Internic-accredited registrars. At this site, you can find out how to secure your own domain name.

www.lcweb.loc.gov/copyright

This is the United States Copyright office's Web site. No more guessing. If you need to know about copyrights, here's the place.

www.uspto.gov

This is the United States Patent and Trademark office's Web site. The mother ship of information in protecting your material.

Index

B

C

D

G

H

I

J

K

L

M

N

O

P

Q

R

S

T

U

V

W

Z

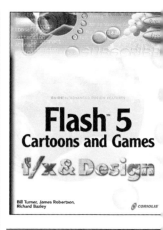

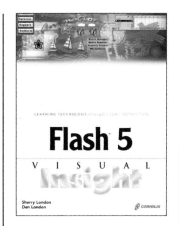